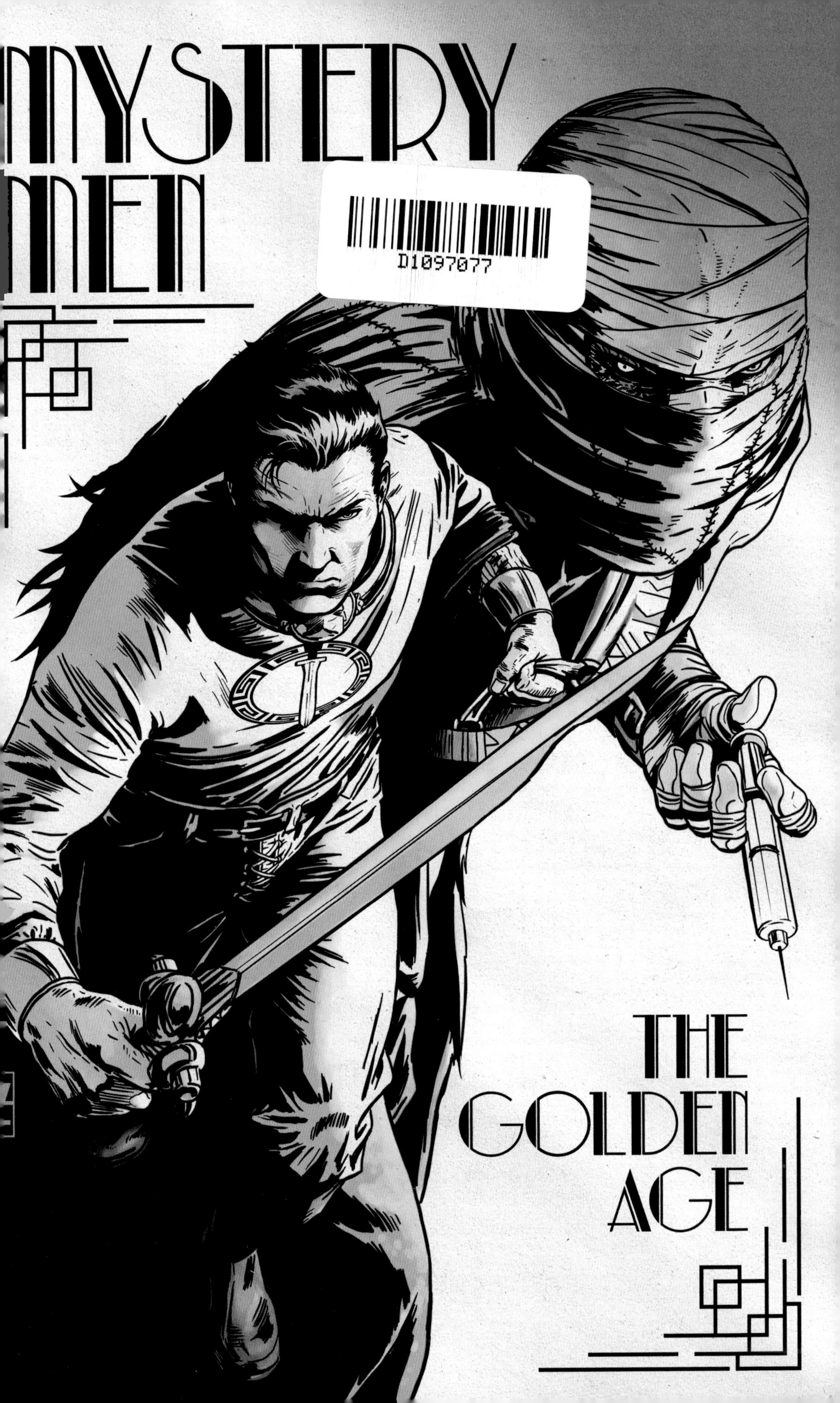
MYSTERY MEN
THE GOLDEN AGE

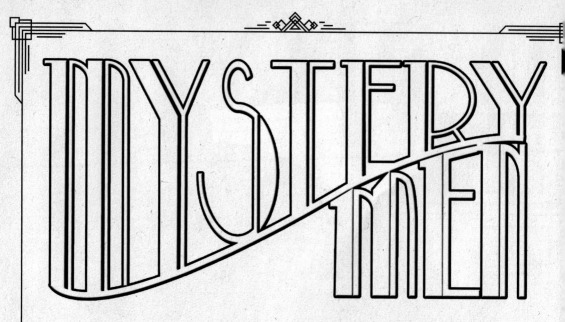

MYSTERY MEN

THE GOLDEN AGE

WRITER:
DAVID LISS

MYSTERY MEN #1–5
ARTIST:
PATCH ZIRCHER
COLORIST:
ANDY TROY
COVER ART:
PATCH ZIRCHER &
ANDY TROY

DARING MYSTERY COMICS 70TH ANNIVERSARY SPECIAL
ARTIST:
JASON ARMSTRONG
COLORIST:
VAL STAPLES
COVER ART:
CLINT LANGLEY

LETTERER:
DAVE SHARPE
ASSISTANT EDITORS:
RACHEL PINNELAS, JOHN DENNING & **MICHAEL HORWITZ**
EDITOR:
BILL ROSEMANN

COLLECTION EDITOR: **MARK D. BEAZLEY** • ASSISTANT EDITOR: **CAITLIN O'CONNELL**
ASSOCIATE MANAGING EDITOR: **KATERI WOODY** • ASSOCIATE MANAGER, DIGITAL ASSETS: **JOE HOCHSTEIN**
SENIOR EDITOR, SPECIAL PROJECTS: **JENNIFER GRÜNWALD** • VP PRODUCTION & SPECIAL PROJECTS: **JEFF YOUNGQUIST**
RESEARCH & LAYOUT: **JEPH YORK** • BOOK DESIGNER: **RODOLFO MURAGUCHI**
SVP PRINT, SALES & MARKETING: **DAVID GABRIEL**

EDITOR IN CHIEF: **C.B. CEBULSKI** • CHIEF CREATIVE OFFICER: **JOE QUESADA**
PRESIDENT: **DAN BUCKLEY** • EXECUTIVE PRODUCER: **ALAN FINE**

MYSTERY MEN: THE GOLDEN AGE. Contains material originally published in magazine form as MYSTERY MEN #1-5 and DARING MYSTERY COMICS 70TH ANNIVERSARY SPECIAL #1. First printing 2018. ISBN 9 302-91015-0. Published by MARVEL WORLDWIDE, INC., a subsidiary of MARVEL ENTERTAINMENT, LLC. OFFICE OF PUBLICATION: 135 West 50th Street, New York, NY 10020. Copyright © 2018 MARVEL No sim between any of the names, characters, persons, and/or institutions in this magazine with those of any living or dead person or institution is intended, and any such similarity which may exist is purely coincidental. **P in the U.S.A**. DAN BUCKLEY, President, Marvel Entertainment; JOE QUESADA, Chief Creative Officer; TOM BREVOORT, SVP of Publishing; DAVID BOGART, SVP of Business Affairs & Operations, Publishing & Partne DAVID GABRIEL, SVP of Sales & Marketing, Publishing; JEFF YOUNGQUIST, VP of Production & Special Projects; DAN CARR, Executive Director of Publishing Technology; ALEX MORALES, Director of Publishing Opera SUSAN CRESPI, Production Manager; STAN LEE, Chairman Emeritus. For information regarding advertising in Marvel Comics or on Marvel.com, please contact Vit DeBellis, Custom Solutions & Integrated Adve Manager, at vdebellis@marvel.com. For Marvel subscription inquiries, please call 888-511-5480. **Manufactured between 12/8/2017 and 1/8/2018 by LSC COMMUNICATIONS INC., KENDALLVILLE, IN,**
10 9 8 7 6 5 4 3 2 1

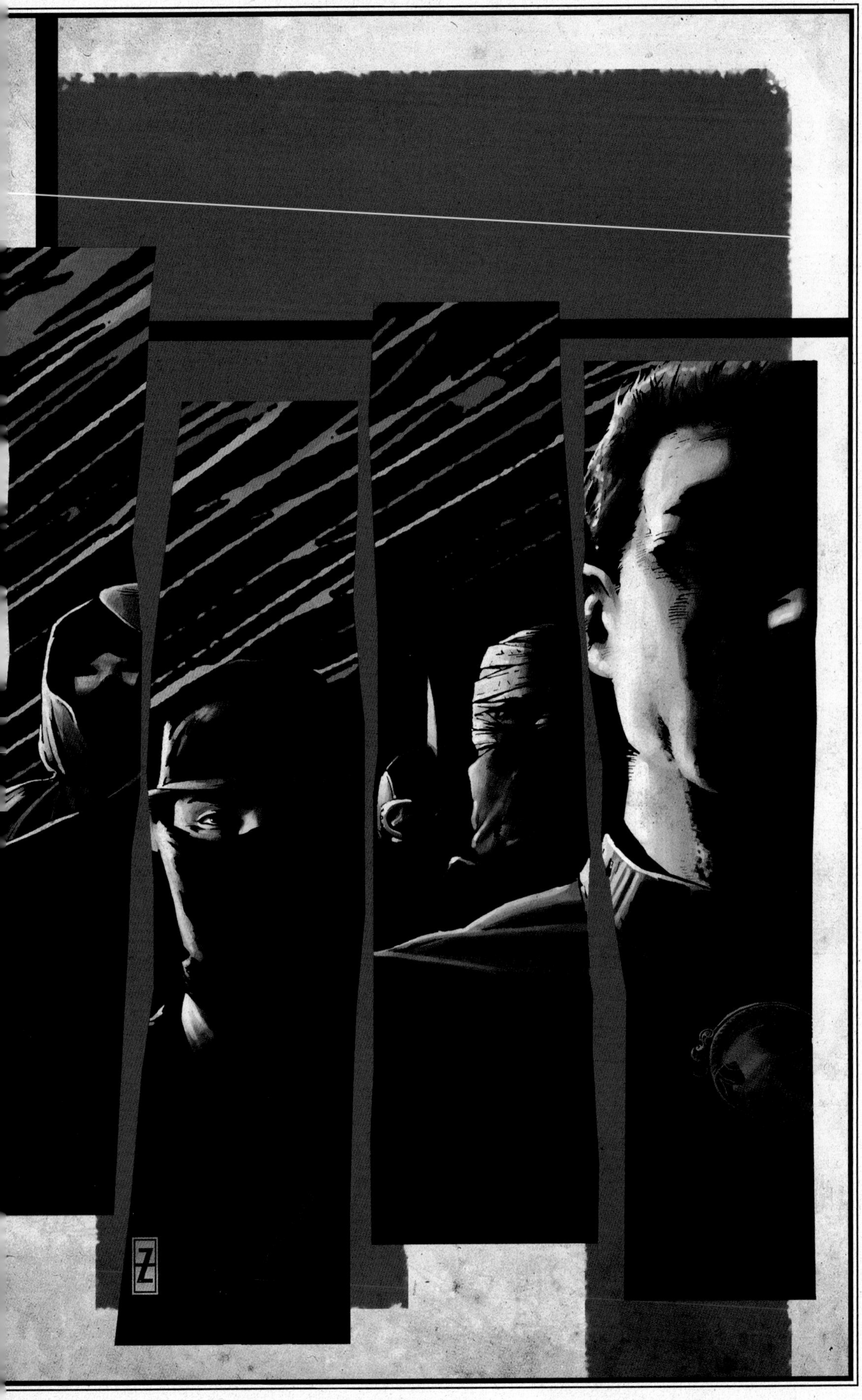

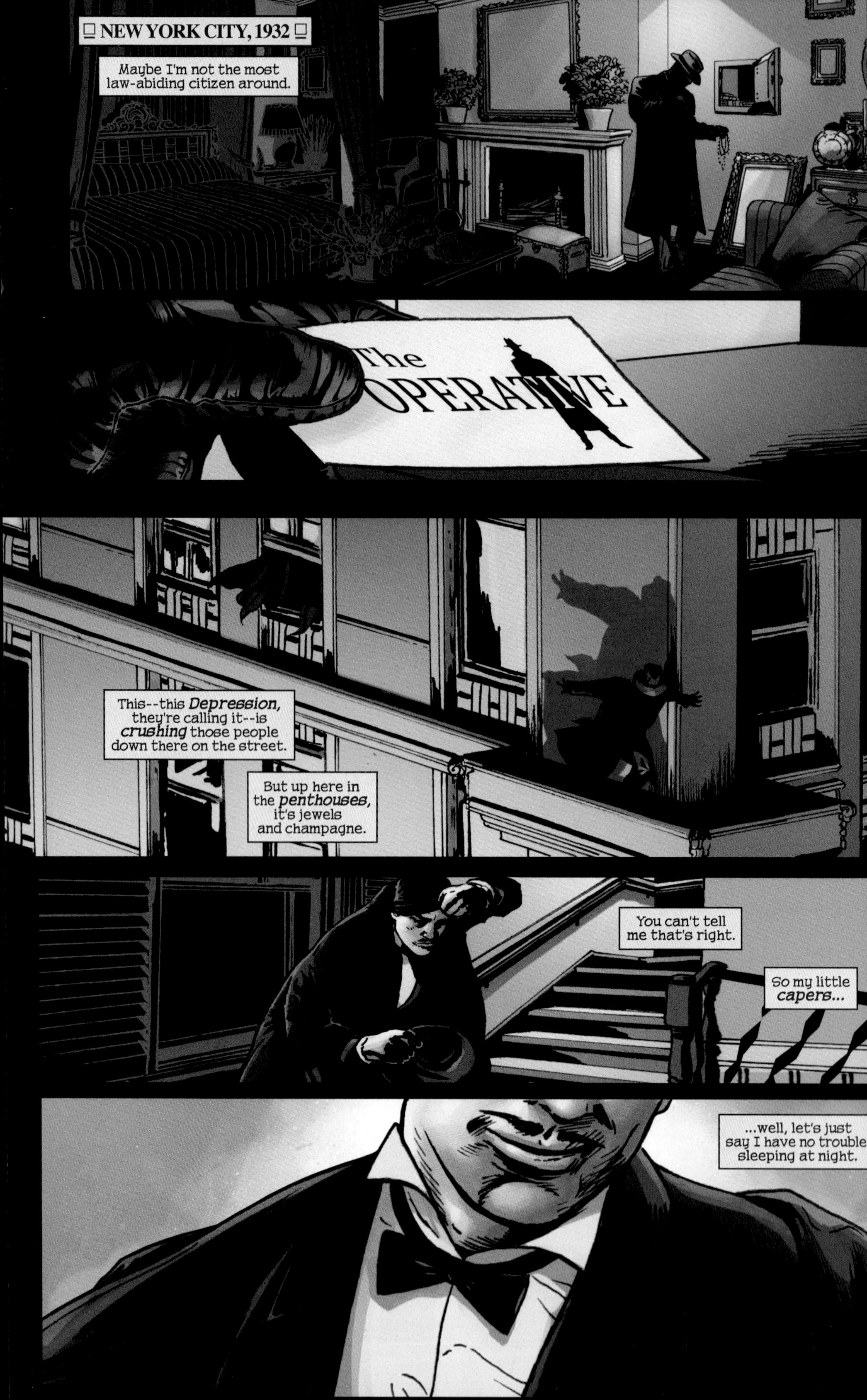
NEW YORK CITY, 1932
Maybe I'm not the most law-abiding citizen around.
The OPERATIVE
This--this *Depression,* they're calling it--is *crushing* those people down there on the street.
But up here in the *penthouses,* it's jewels and champagne.
You can't tell me that's right.
So my little *capers...*
...well, let's just say I have no trouble sleeping at night.

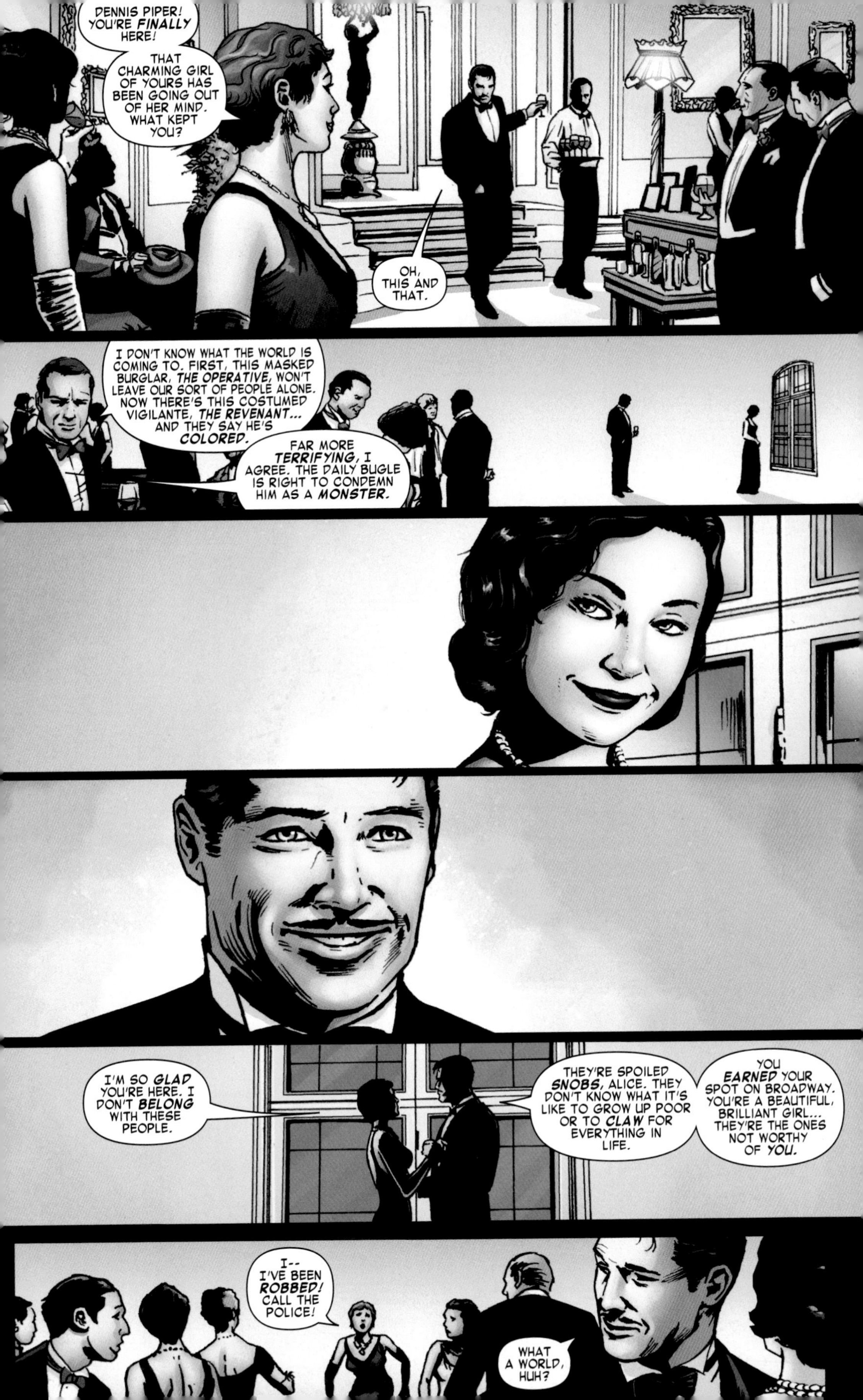
DENNIS PIPER! YOU'RE FINALLY HERE!
THAT CHARMING GIRL OF YOURS HAS BEEN GOING OUT OF HER MIND. WHAT KEPT YOU?
OH, THIS AND THAT.
I DON'T KNOW WHAT THE WORLD IS COMING TO. FIRST, THIS MASKED BURGLAR, THE OPERATIVE, WON'T LEAVE OUR SORT OF PEOPLE ALONE. NOW THERE'S THIS COSTUMED VIGILANTE, THE REVENANT... AND THEY SAY HE'S COLORED.
FAR MORE TERRIFYING, I AGREE. THE DAILY BUGLE IS RIGHT TO CONDEMN HIM AS A MONSTER.
I'M SO GLAD YOU'RE HERE. I DON'T BELONG WITH THESE PEOPLE.
THEY'RE SPOILED SNOBS, ALICE. THEY DON'T KNOW WHAT IT'S LIKE TO GROW UP POOR OR TO CLAW FOR EVERYTHING IN LIFE.
YOU EARNED YOUR SPOT ON BROADWAY. YOU'RE A BEAUTIFUL, BRILLIANT GIRL... THEY'RE THE ONES NOT WORTHY OF YOU.
I-- I'VE BEEN ROBBED! CALL THE POLICE!
WHAT A WORLD, HUH?

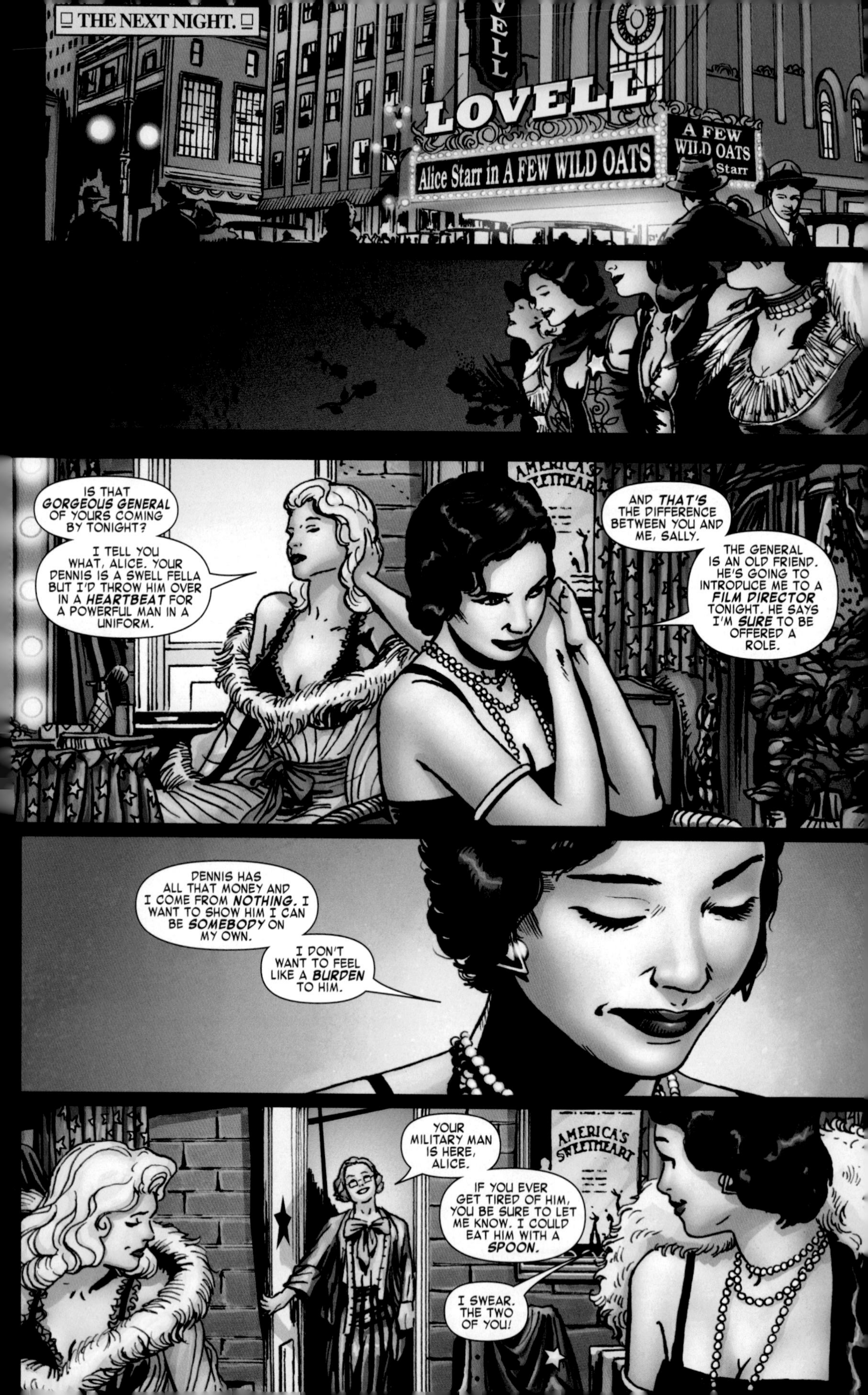
THE NEXT NIGHT.
LOVELL
Alice Starr in A FEW WILD OATS
A FEW WILD OATS Starr
AMERICA'S SWEETHEART
IS THAT GORGEOUS GENERAL OF YOURS COMING BY TONIGHT?
I TELL YOU WHAT, ALICE. YOUR DENNIS IS A SWELL FELLA BUT I'D THROW HIM OVER IN A HEARTBEAT FOR A POWERFUL MAN IN A UNIFORM.
AND THAT'S THE DIFFERENCE BETWEEN YOU AND ME, SALLY.
THE GENERAL IS AN OLD FRIEND. HE'S GOING TO INTRODUCE ME TO A FILM DIRECTOR TONIGHT. HE SAYS I'M SURE TO BE OFFERED A ROLE.
DENNIS HAS ALL THAT MONEY AND I COME FROM NOTHING. I WANT TO SHOW HIM I CAN BE SOMEBODY ON MY OWN.
I DON'T WANT TO FEEL LIKE A BURDEN TO HIM.
YOUR MILITARY MAN IS HERE, ALICE.
IF YOU EVER GET TIRED OF HIM, YOU BE SURE TO LET ME KNOW. I COULD EAT HIM WITH A SPOON.
AMERICA'S SWEETHEART
I SWEAR. THE TWO OF YOU!

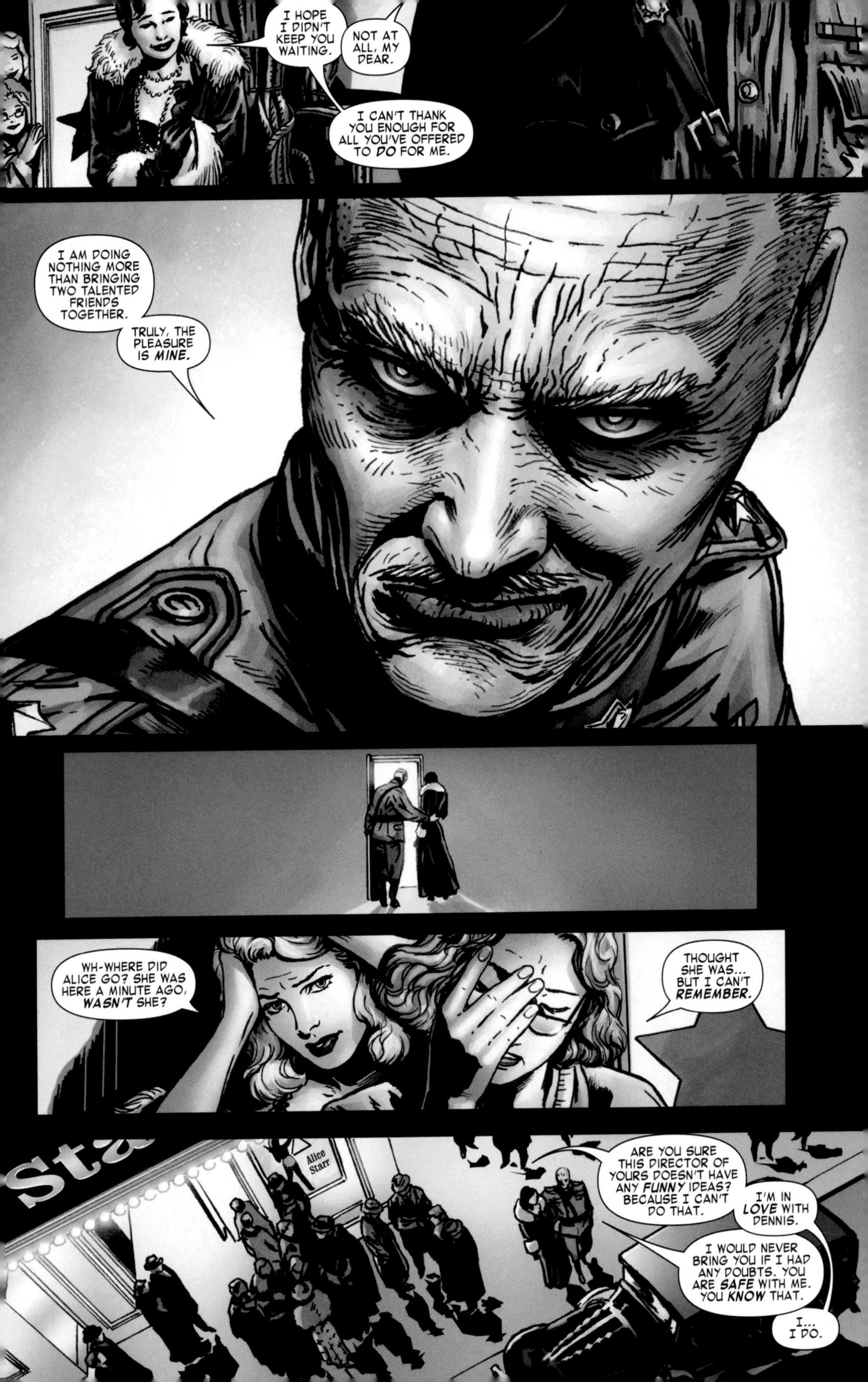
I HOPE I DIDN'T KEEP YOU WAITING.
NOT AT ALL, MY DEAR.
I CAN'T THANK YOU ENOUGH FOR ALL YOU'VE OFFERED TO *DO* FOR ME.
I AM DOING NOTHING MORE THAN BRINGING TWO TALENTED FRIENDS TOGETHER.
TRULY, THE PLEASURE IS *MINE.*
WH-WHERE DID ALICE GO? SHE WAS HERE A MINUTE AGO, *WASN'T* SHE?
THOUGHT SHE WAS... BUT I CAN'T *REMEMBER.*
Alice Starr
ARE YOU SURE THIS DIRECTOR OF YOURS DOESN'T HAVE ANY *FUNNY* IDEAS? BECAUSE I CAN'T DO THAT.
I'M IN *LOVE* WITH DENNIS.
I WOULD NEVER BRING YOU IF I HAD ANY DOUBTS. YOU ARE *SAFE* WITH ME. YOU *KNOW* THAT.
I... I DO.

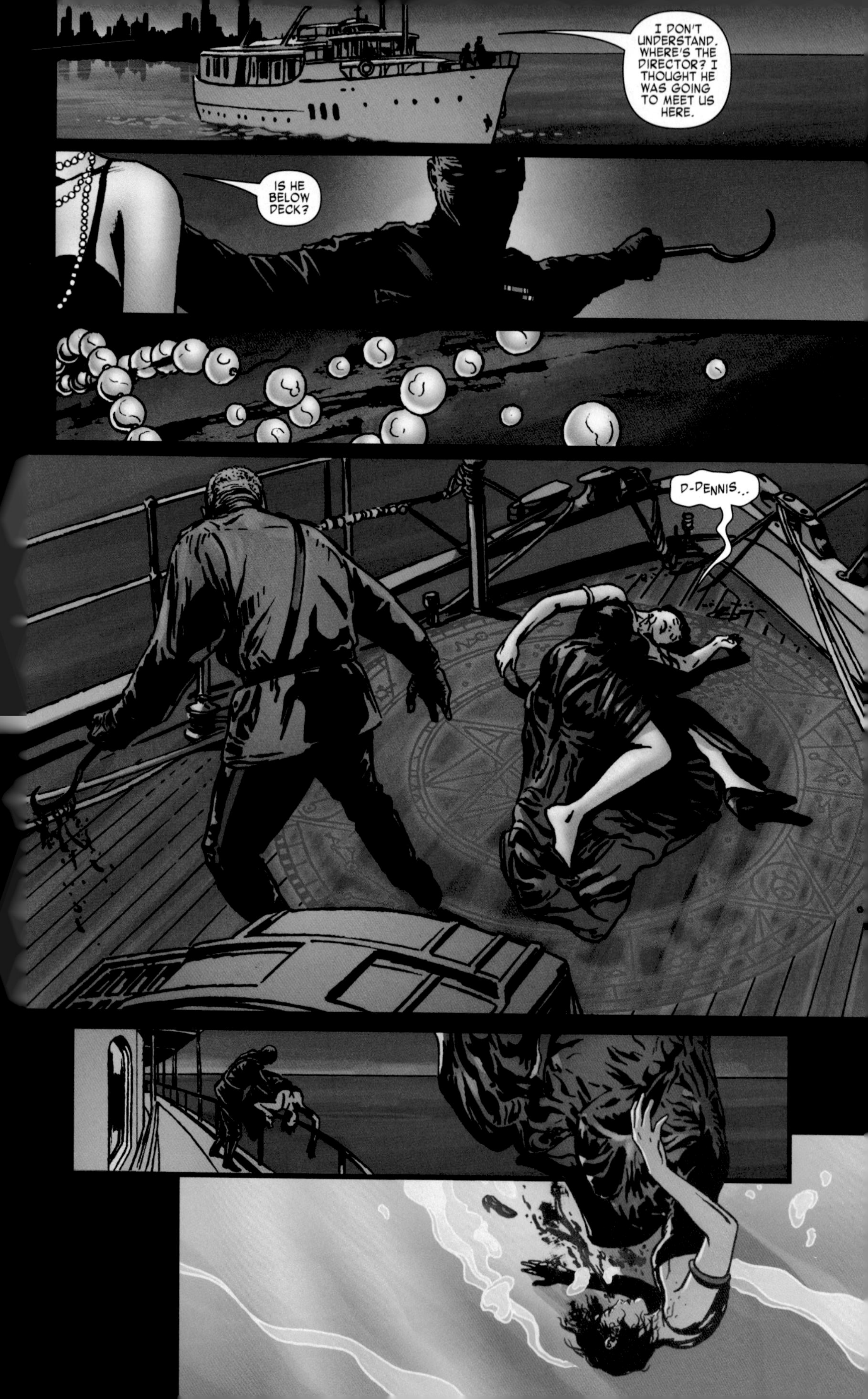
I DON'T UNDERSTAND. WHERE'S THE DIRECTOR? I THOUGHT HE WAS GOING TO MEET US HERE.
IS HE BELOW DECK?
D-DENNIS...

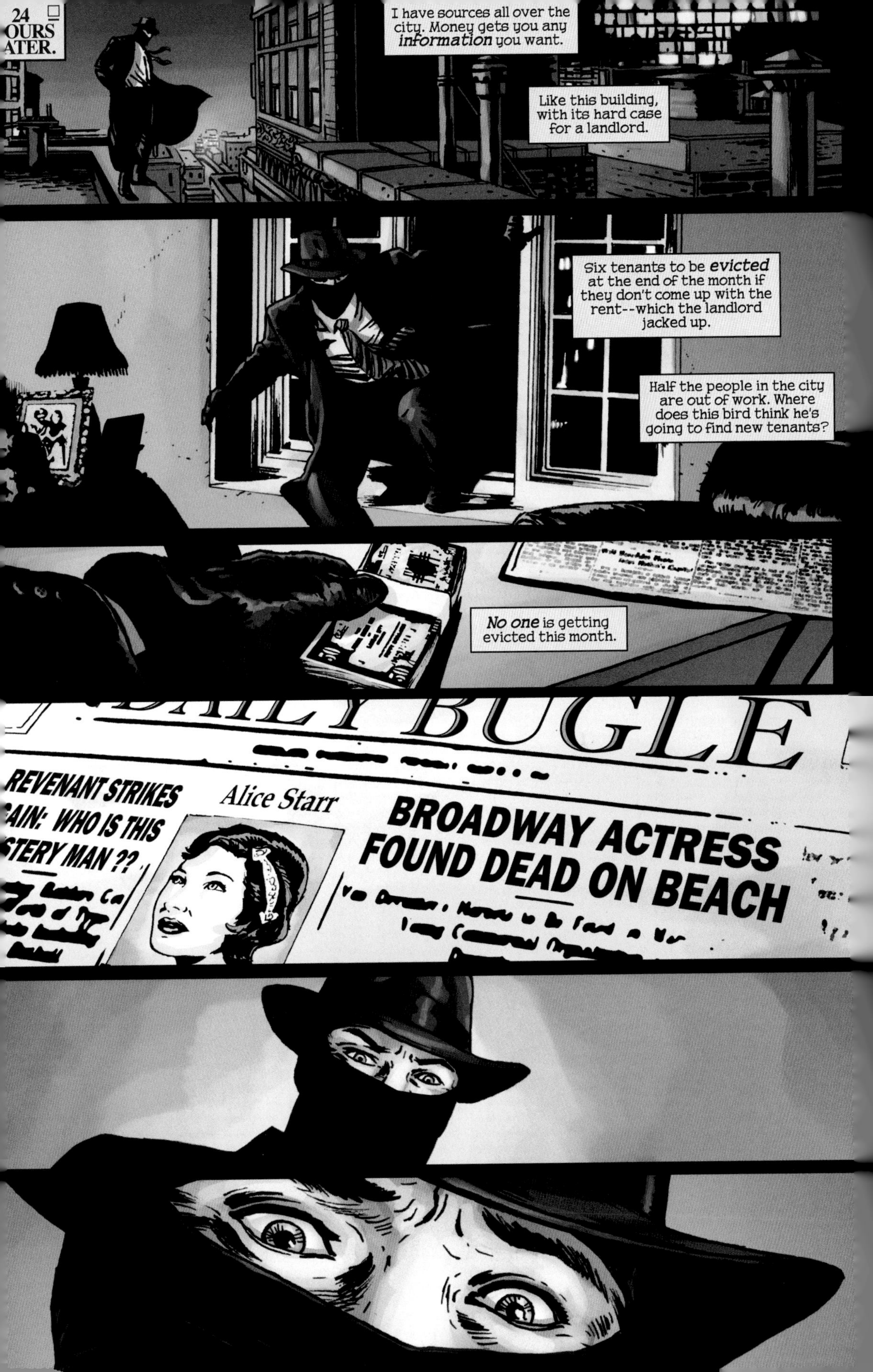
24 HOURS LATER.
I have sources all over the city. Money gets you any *information* you want.
Like this building, with its hard case for a landlord.
Six tenants to be *evicted* at the end of the month if they don't come up with the rent--which the landlord jacked up.
Half the people in the city are out of work. Where does this bird think he's going to find new tenants?
No one is getting evicted this month.
DAILY BUGLE
REVENANT STRIKES AGAIN: WHO IS THIS MYSTERY MAN??
Alice Starr
BROADWAY ACTRESS FOUND DEAD ON BEACH

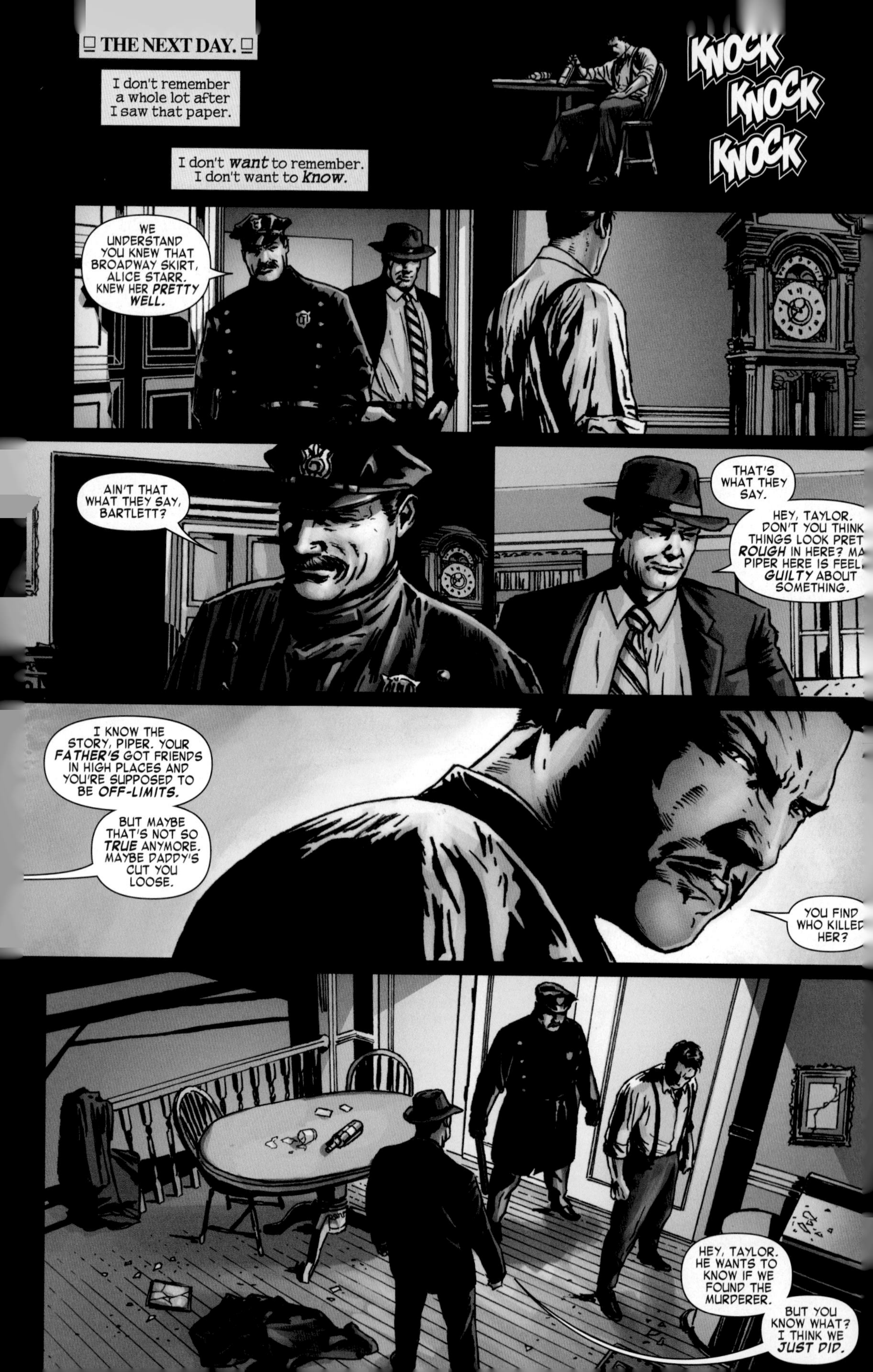
THE NEXT DAY.
I don't remember a whole lot after I saw that paper.
I don't want to remember. I don't want to know.
KNOCK KNOCK KNOCK
WE UNDERSTAND YOU KNEW THAT BROADWAY SKIRT, ALICE STARR. KNEW HER PRETTY WELL.
AIN'T THAT WHAT THEY SAY, BARTLETT?
THAT'S WHAT THEY SAY.
HEY, TAYLOR. DON'T YOU THINK THINGS LOOK PRET ROUGH IN HERE? MA PIPER HERE IS FEEL GUILTY ABOUT SOMETHING.
I KNOW THE STORY, PIPER. YOUR FATHER'S GOT FRIENDS IN HIGH PLACES AND YOU'RE SUPPOSED TO BE OFF-LIMITS.
BUT MAYBE THAT'S NOT SO TRUE ANYMORE. MAYBE DADDY'S CUT YOU LOOSE.
YOU FIND WHO KILLED HER?
HEY, TAYLOR. HE WANTS TO KNOW IF WE FOUND THE MURDERER.
BUT YOU KNOW WHAT? I THINK WE JUST DID.

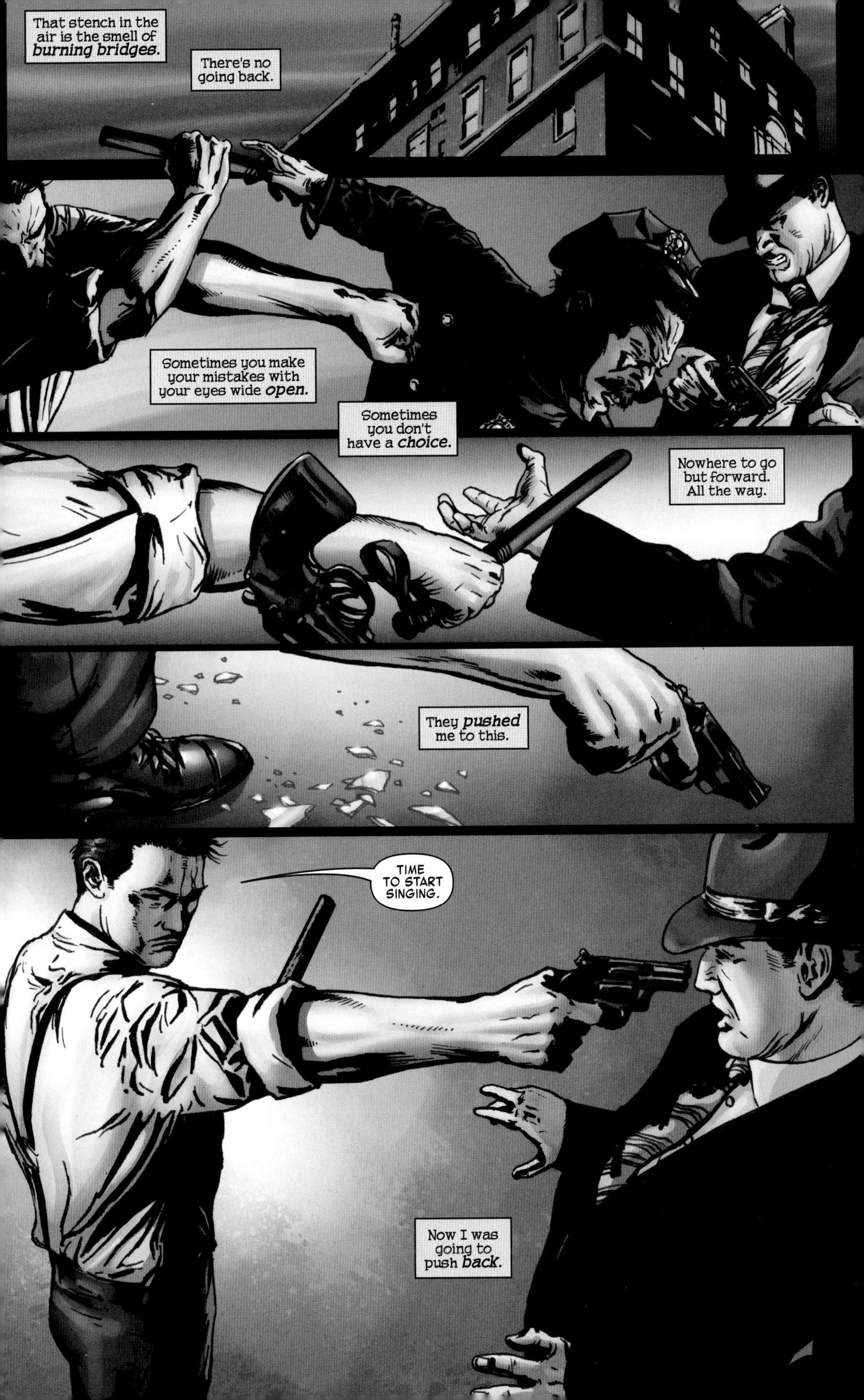
That stench in the air is the smell of *burning bridges.*
There's no going back.
Sometimes you make your mistakes with your eyes wide *open.*
Sometimes you don't have a *choice.*
Nowhere to go but forward. All the way.
They *pushed* me to this.
TIME TO START SINGING.
Now I was going to push *back.*

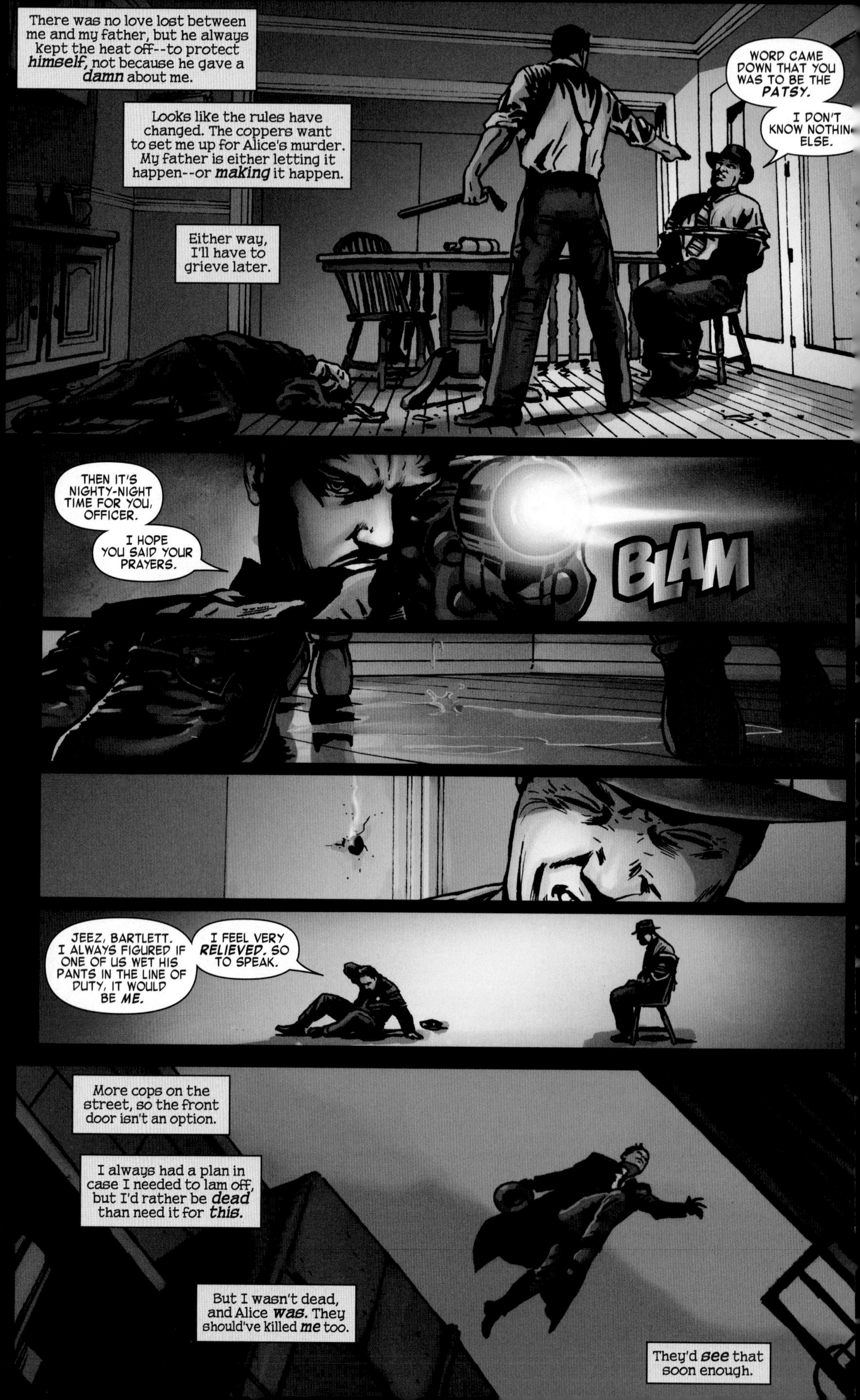
There was no love lost between me and my father, but he always kept the heat off--to protect *himself,* not because he gave a *damn* about me.
Looks like the rules have changed. The coppers want to set me up for Alice's murder. My father is either letting it happen--or *making* it happen.
Either way, I'll have to grieve later.
WORD CAME DOWN THAT YOU WAS TO BE THE *PATSY.*
I DON'T KNOW NOTHING ELSE.
THEN IT'S NIGHTY-NIGHT TIME FOR YOU, OFFICER.
I HOPE YOU SAID YOUR PRAYERS.
BLAM
JEEZ, BARTLETT. I ALWAYS FIGURED IF ONE OF US WET HIS PANTS IN THE LINE OF DUTY, IT WOULD BE *ME.*
I FEEL VERY *RELIEVED.* SO TO SPEAK.
More cops on the street, so the front door isn't an option.
I always had a plan in case I needed to lam off, but I'd rather be *dead* than need it for *this.*
But I wasn't dead, and Alice *was.* They should've killed *me* too.
They'd *see* that soon enough.

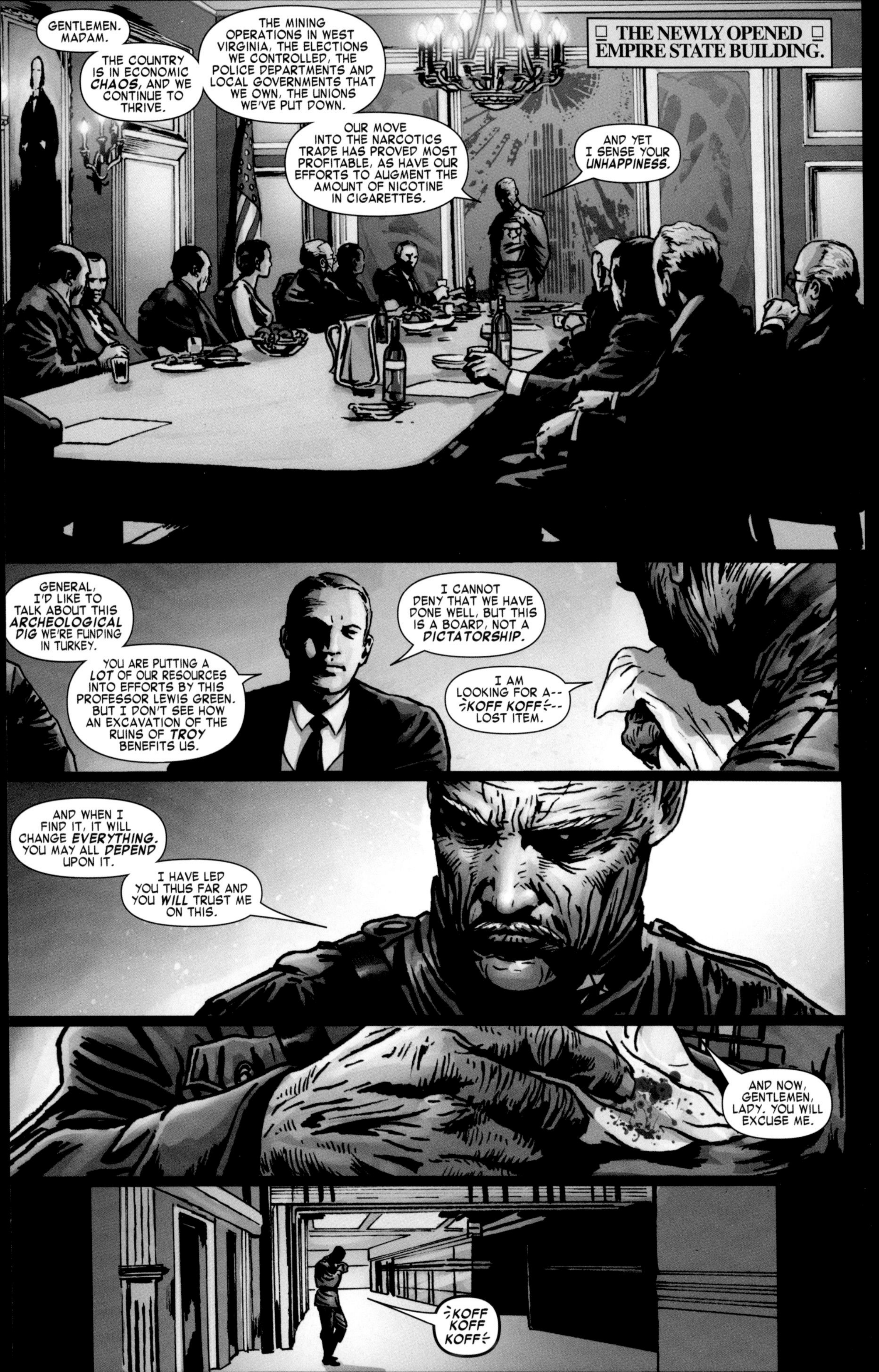
THE NEWLY OPENED EMPIRE STATE BUILDING.
GENTLEMEN. MADAM.
THE COUNTRY IS IN ECONOMIC CHAOS, AND WE CONTINUE TO THRIVE.
THE MINING OPERATIONS IN WEST VIRGINIA, THE ELECTIONS WE CONTROLLED, THE POLICE DEPARTMENTS AND LOCAL GOVERNMENTS THAT WE OWN, THE UNIONS WE'VE PUT DOWN.
OUR MOVE INTO THE NARCOTICS TRADE HAS PROVED MOST PROFITABLE, AS HAVE OUR EFFORTS TO AUGMENT THE AMOUNT OF NICOTINE IN CIGARETTES.
AND YET I SENSE YOUR UNHAPPINESS.
GENERAL, I'D LIKE TO TALK ABOUT THIS ARCHEOLOGICAL DIG WE'RE FUNDING IN TURKEY.
YOU ARE PUTTING A LOT OF OUR RESOURCES INTO EFFORTS BY THIS PROFESSOR LEWIS GREEN. BUT I DON'T SEE HOW AN EXCAVATION OF THE RUINS OF TROY BENEFITS US.
I CANNOT DENY THAT WE HAVE DONE WELL, BUT THIS IS A BOARD, NOT A DICTATORSHIP.
I AM LOOKING FOR A-- KOFF KOFF-- LOST ITEM.
AND WHEN I FIND IT, IT WILL CHANGE EVERYTHING. YOU MAY ALL DEPEND UPON IT.
I HAVE LED YOU THUS FAR AND YOU WILL TRUST ME ON THIS.
AND NOW, GENTLEMEN, LADY. YOU WILL EXCUSE ME.
KOFF KOFF KOFF

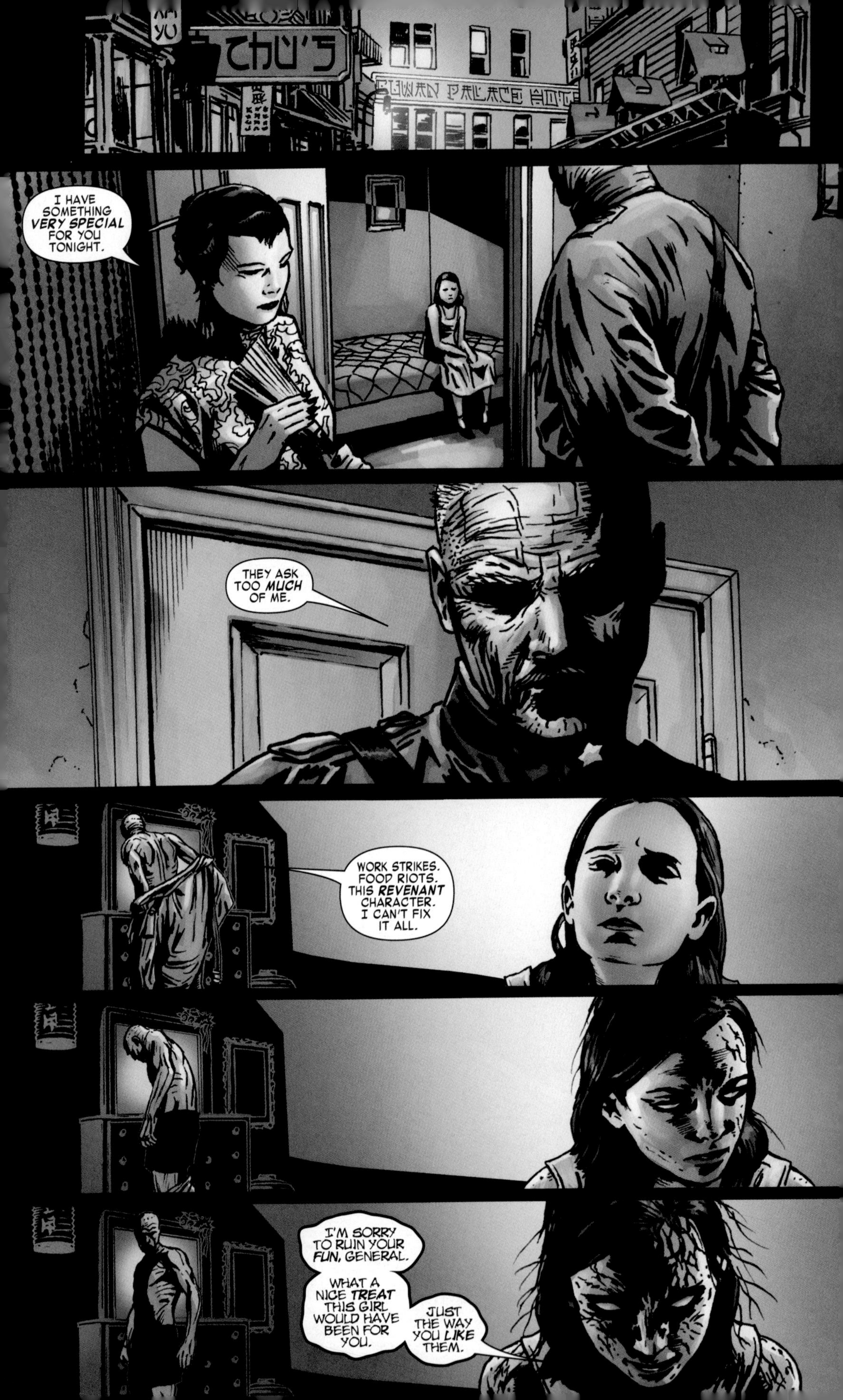

I HAVE SOMETHING VERY SPECIAL FOR YOU TONIGHT.
THEY ASK TOO MUCH OF ME.
WORK STRIKES. FOOD RIOTS. THIS REVENANT CHARACTER. I CAN'T FIX IT ALL.
I'M SORRY TO RUIN YOUR FUN, GENERAL.
WHAT A NICE TREAT THIS GIRL WOULD HAVE BEEN FOR YOU.
JUST THE WAY YOU LIKE THEM.

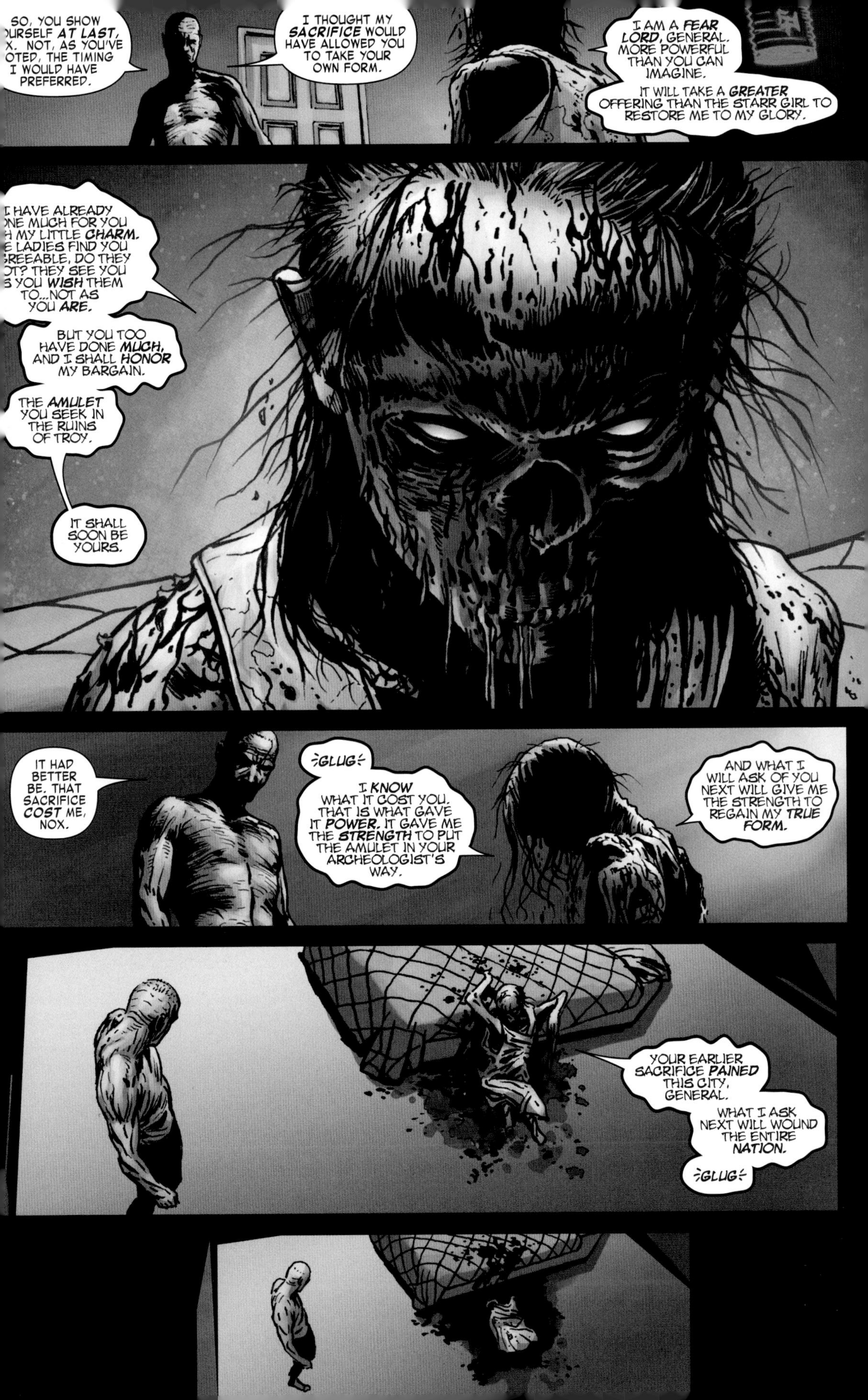
SO, YOU SHOW OURSELF AT LAST, X. NOT, AS YOU'VE OTED, THE TIMING I WOULD HAVE PREFERRED.
I THOUGHT MY SACRIFICE WOULD HAVE ALLOWED YOU TO TAKE YOUR OWN FORM.
I AM A FEAR LORD, GENERAL. MORE POWERFUL THAN YOU CAN IMAGINE.
IT WILL TAKE A GREATER OFFERING THAN THE STARR GIRL TO RESTORE ME TO MY GLORY.
I HAVE ALREADY ONE MUCH FOR YOU H MY LITTLE CHARM. E LADIES FIND YOU GREEABLE, DO THEY OT? THEY SEE YOU S YOU WISH THEM TO...NOT AS YOU ARE.
BUT YOU TOO HAVE DONE MUCH, AND I SHALL HONOR MY BARGAIN.
THE AMULET YOU SEEK IN THE RUINS OF TROY.
IT SHALL SOON BE YOURS.
IT HAD BETTER BE. THAT SACRIFICE COST ME, NOX.
GLUG
I KNOW WHAT IT COST YOU. THAT IS WHAT GAVE IT POWER. IT GAVE ME THE STRENGTH TO PUT THE AMULET IN YOUR ARCHEOLOGIST'S WAY.
AND WHAT I WILL ASK OF YOU NEXT WILL GIVE ME THE STRENGTH TO REGAIN MY TRUE FORM.
YOUR EARLIER SACRIFICE PAINED THIS CITY, GENERAL.
WHAT I ASK NEXT WILL WOUND THE ENTIRE NATION.
GLUG

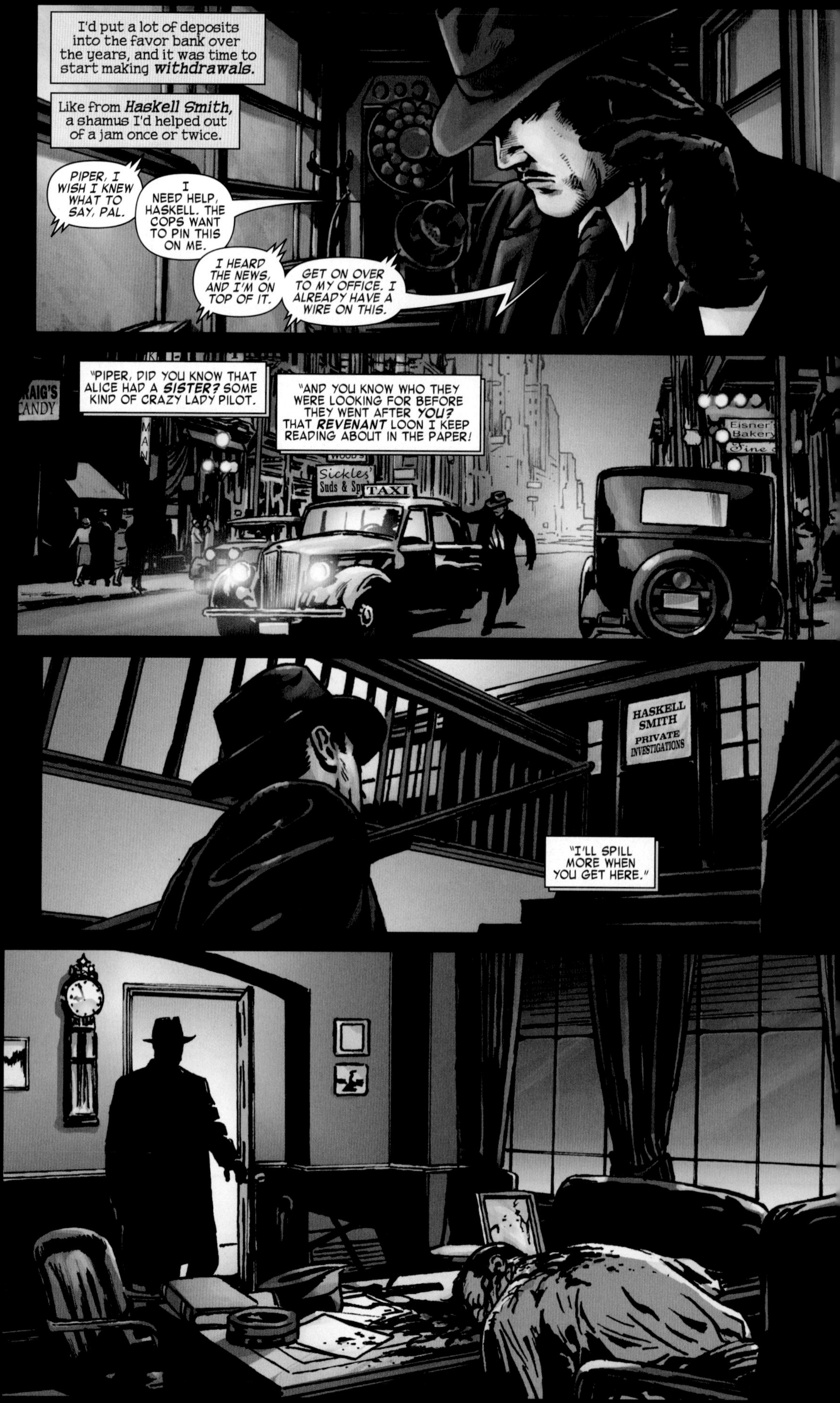

I'd put a lot of deposits into the favor bank over the years, and it was time to start making withdrawals.
Like from Haskell Smith, a shamus I'd helped out of a jam once or twice.
PIPER, I WISH I KNEW WHAT TO SAY, PAL.
I NEED HELP, HASKELL. THE COPS WANT TO PIN THIS ON ME.
I HEARD THE NEWS, AND I'M ON TOP OF IT.
GET ON OVER TO MY OFFICE. I ALREADY HAVE A WIRE ON THIS.
"PIPER, DID YOU KNOW THAT ALICE HAD A SISTER? SOME KIND OF CRAZY LADY PILOT.
"AND YOU KNOW WHO THEY WERE LOOKING FOR BEFORE THEY WENT AFTER YOU? THAT REVENANT LOON I KEEP READING ABOUT IN THE PAPER!
CRAIG'S CANDY
Sickles' Suds & Sp
TAXI
Eisner's Bakery
HASKELL SMITH PRIVATE INVESTIGATIONS
"I'LL SPILL MORE WHEN YOU GET HERE."

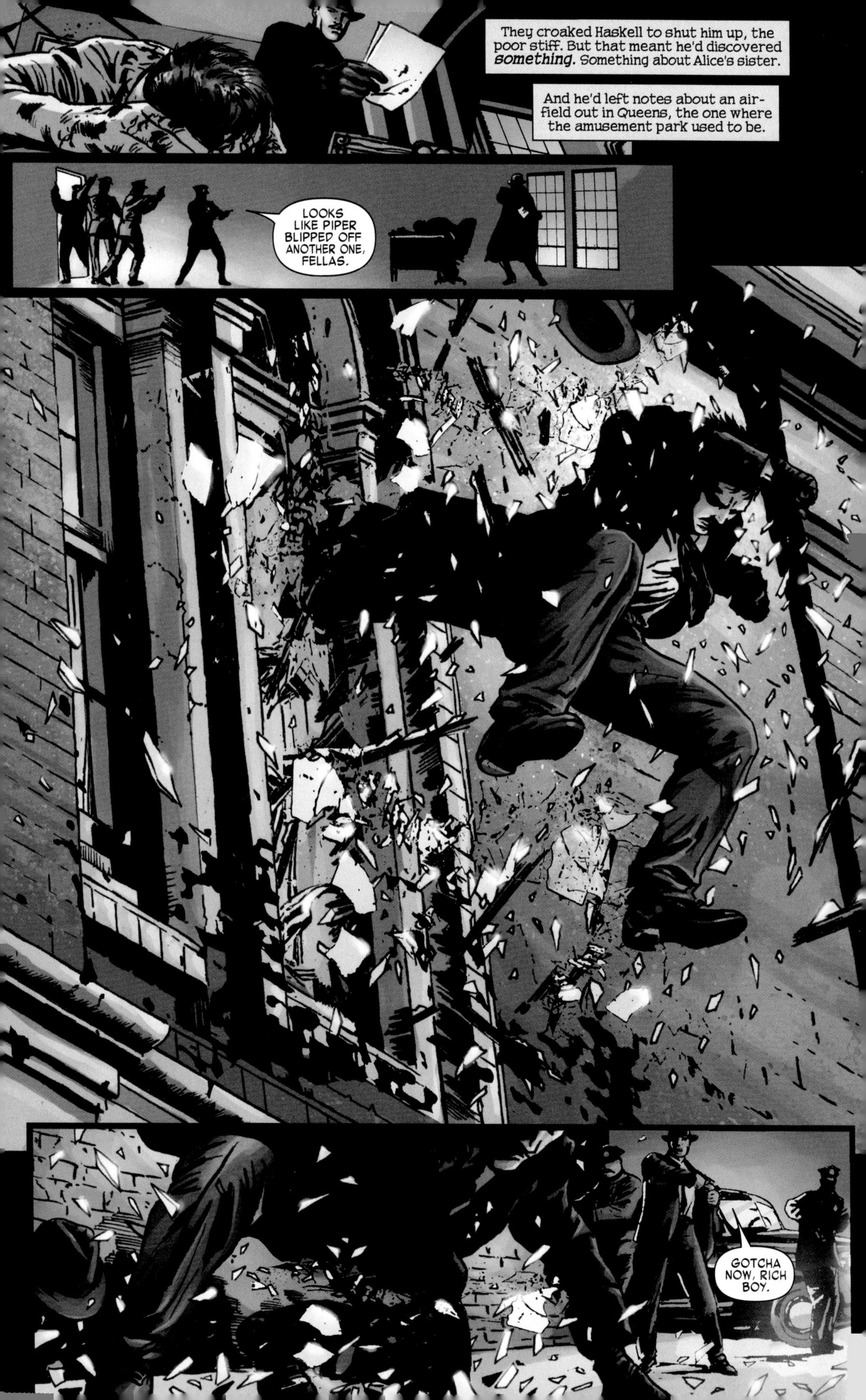
They croaked Haskell to shut him up, the poor stiff. But that meant he'd discovered *something*. Something about Alice's sister.
And he'd left notes about an air-field out in Queens, the one where the amusement park used to be.
LOOKS LIKE PIPER BLIPPED OFF ANOTHER ONE, FELLAS.
GOTCHA NOW, RICH BOY.

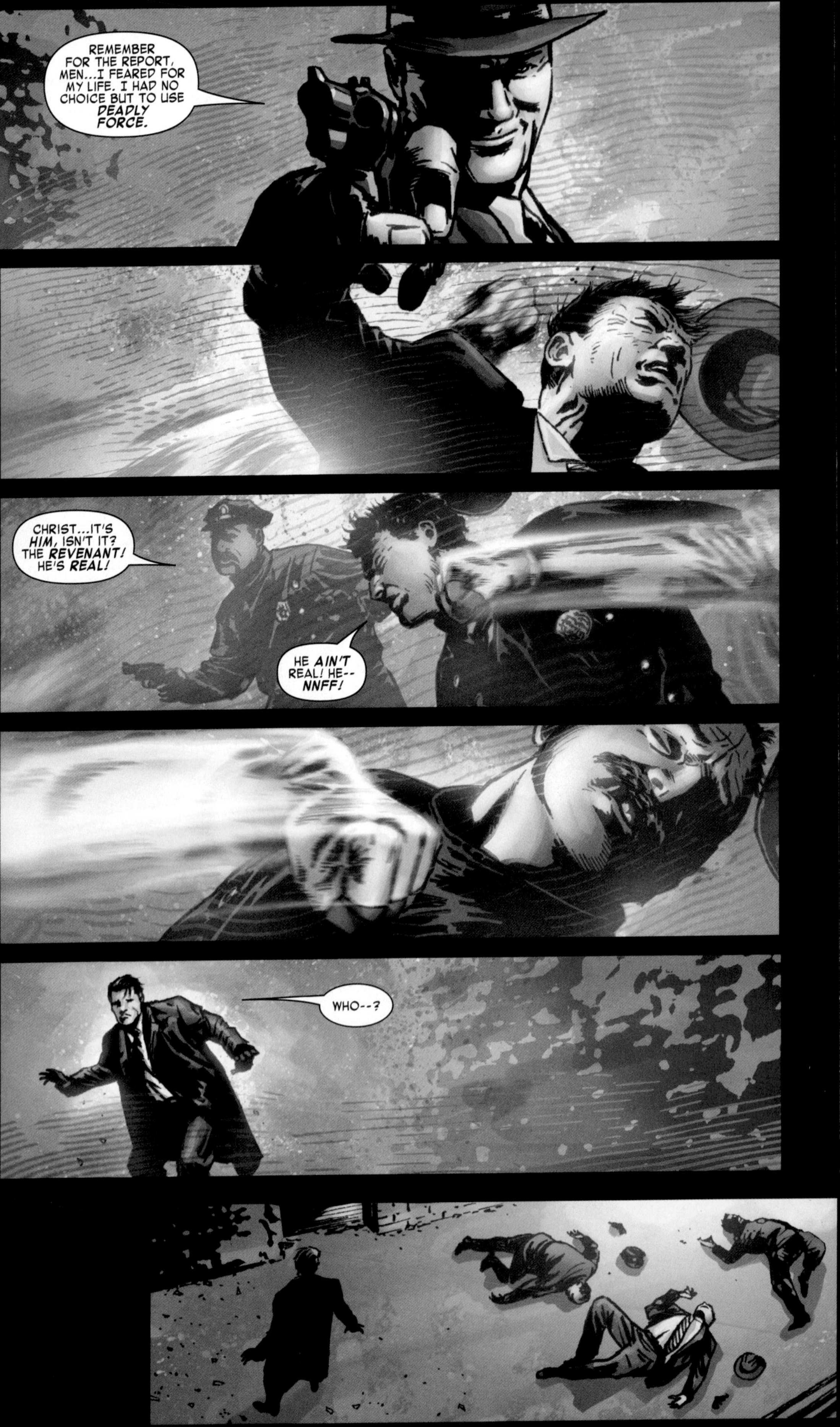
REMEMBER FOR THE REPORT, MEN...I FEARED FOR MY LIFE. I HAD NO CHOICE BUT TO USE DEADLY FORCE.
CHRIST...IT'S HIM, ISN'T IT? THE REVENANT! HE'S REAL!
HE AIN'T REAL! HE-- NNFF!
WHO--?

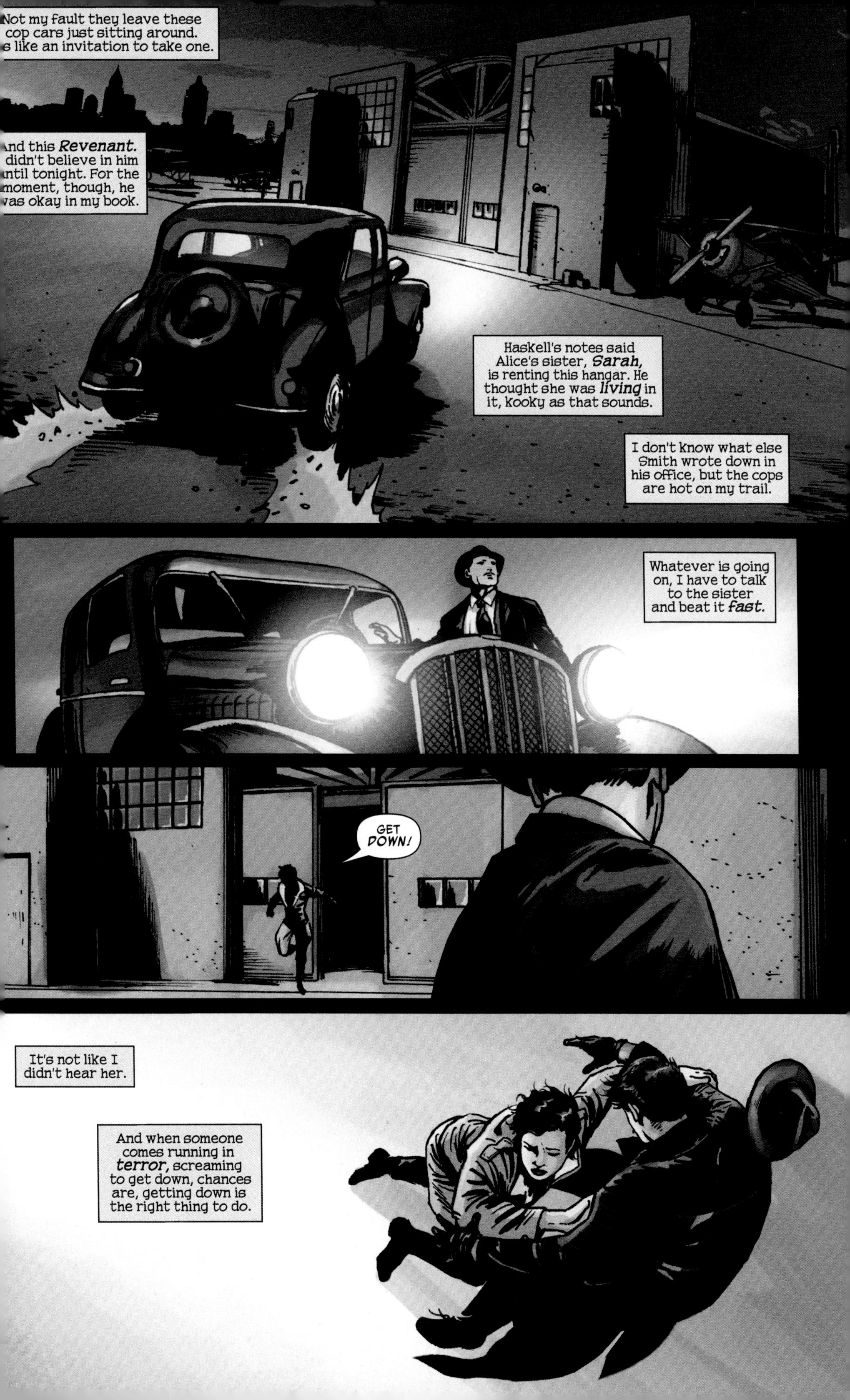
Not my fault they leave these cop cars just sitting around. s like an invitation to take one.
nd this Revenant. didn't believe in him ntil tonight. For the moment, though, he vas okay in my book.
Haskell's notes said Alice's sister, Sarah, is renting this hangar. He thought she was living in it, kooky as that sounds.
I don't know what else Smith wrote down in his office, but the cops are hot on my trail.
Whatever is going on, I have to talk to the sister and beat it fast.
GET DOWN!
It's not like I didn't hear her.
And when someone comes running in terror, screaming to get down, chances are, getting down is the right thing to do.

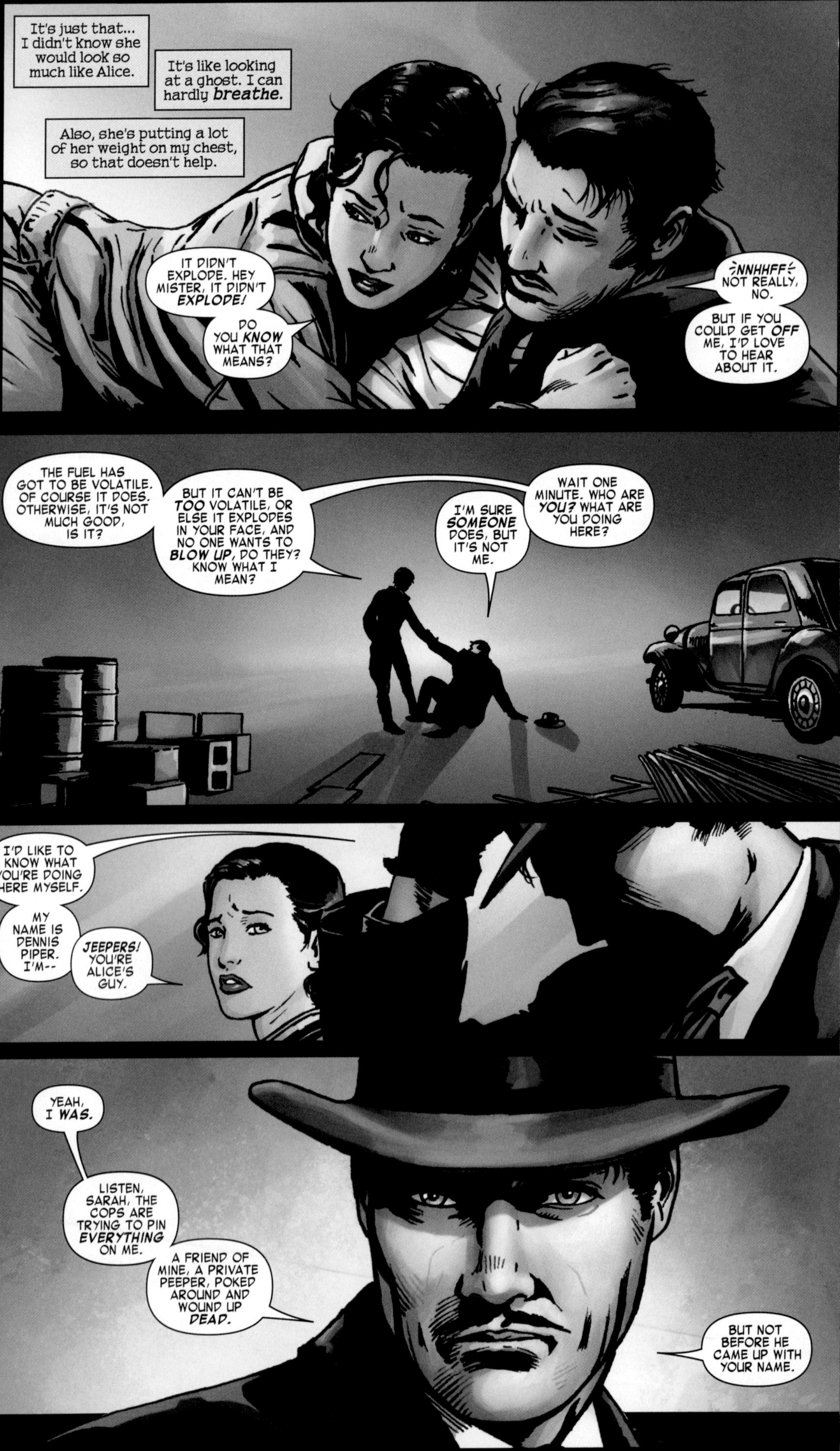
It's just that... I didn't know she would look so much like Alice.
It's like looking at a ghost. I can hardly breathe.
Also, she's putting a lot of her weight on my chest, so that doesn't help.
IT DIDN'T EXPLODE. HEY MISTER, IT DIDN'T EXPLODE!
DO YOU KNOW WHAT THAT MEANS?
NNHHFF NOT REALLY, NO.
BUT IF YOU COULD GET OFF ME, I'D LOVE TO HEAR ABOUT IT.
THE FUEL HAS GOT TO BE VOLATILE. OF COURSE IT DOES. OTHERWISE, IT'S NOT MUCH GOOD, IS IT?
BUT IT CAN'T BE TOO VOLATILE, OR ELSE IT EXPLODES IN YOUR FACE, AND NO ONE WANTS TO BLOW UP, DO THEY? KNOW WHAT I MEAN?
I'M SURE SOMEONE DOES, BUT IT'S NOT ME.
WAIT ONE MINUTE. WHO ARE YOU? WHAT ARE YOU DOING HERE?
I'D LIKE TO KNOW WHAT YOU'RE DOING HERE MYSELF.
MY NAME IS DENNIS PIPER. I'M--
JEEPERS! YOU'RE ALICE'S GUY.
YEAH, I WAS.
LISTEN, SARAH, THE COPS ARE TRYING TO PIN EVERYTHING ON ME.
A FRIEND OF MINE, A PRIVATE PEEPER, POKED AROUND AND WOUND UP DEAD.
BUT NOT BEFORE HE CAME UP WITH YOUR NAME.

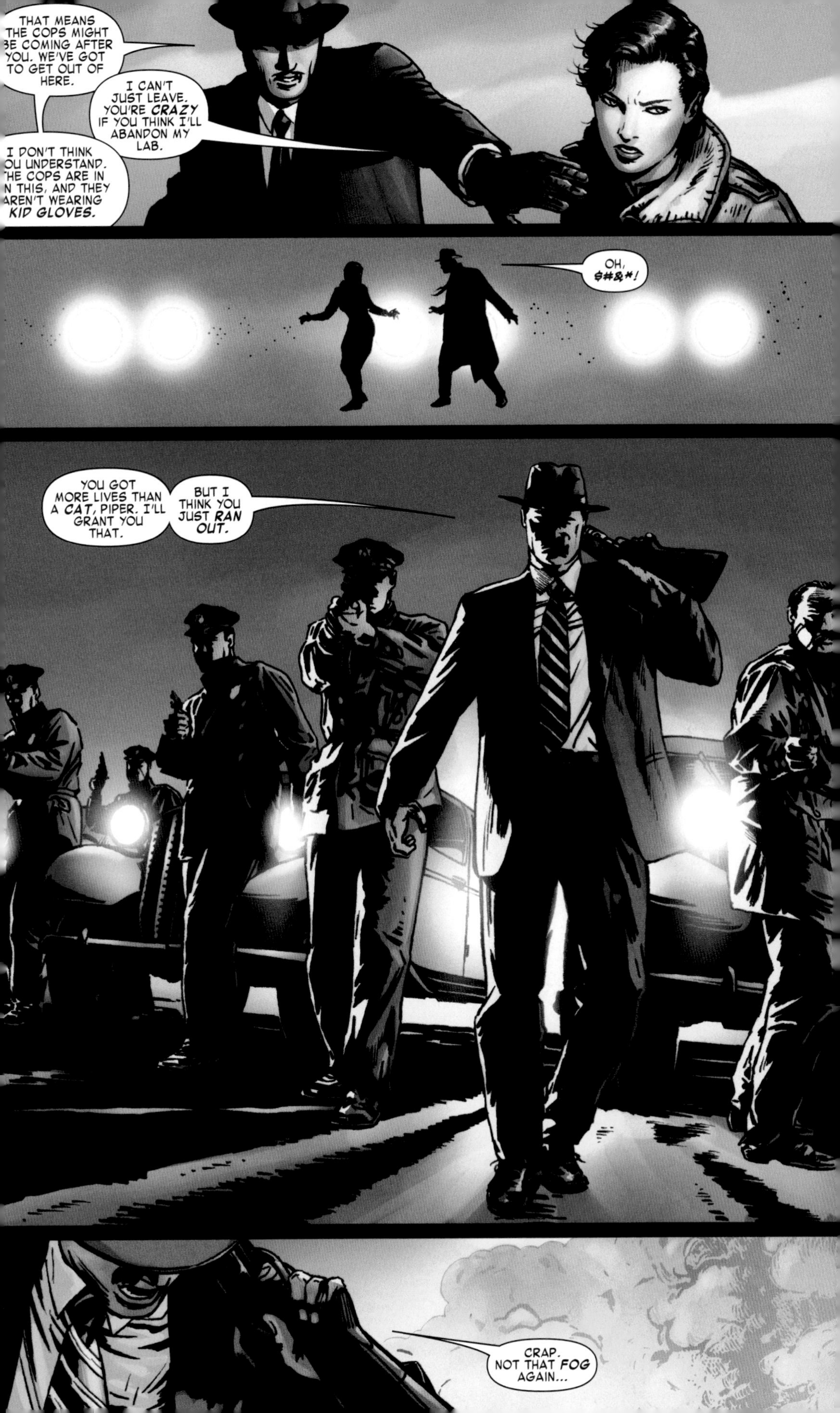
THAT MEANS THE COPS MIGHT BE COMING AFTER YOU. WE'VE GOT TO GET OUT OF HERE.
I CAN'T JUST LEAVE. YOU'RE *CRAZY* IF YOU THINK I'LL ABANDON MY LAB.
I DON'T THINK OU UNDERSTAND. HE COPS ARE IN N THIS, AND THEY AREN'T WEARING ***KID GLOVES.***
OH, $#&*!
YOU GOT MORE LIVES THAN A *CAT*, PIPER. I'LL GRANT YOU THAT.
BUT I THINK YOU JUST *RAN OUT.*
CRAP. NOT THAT *FOG* AGAIN...

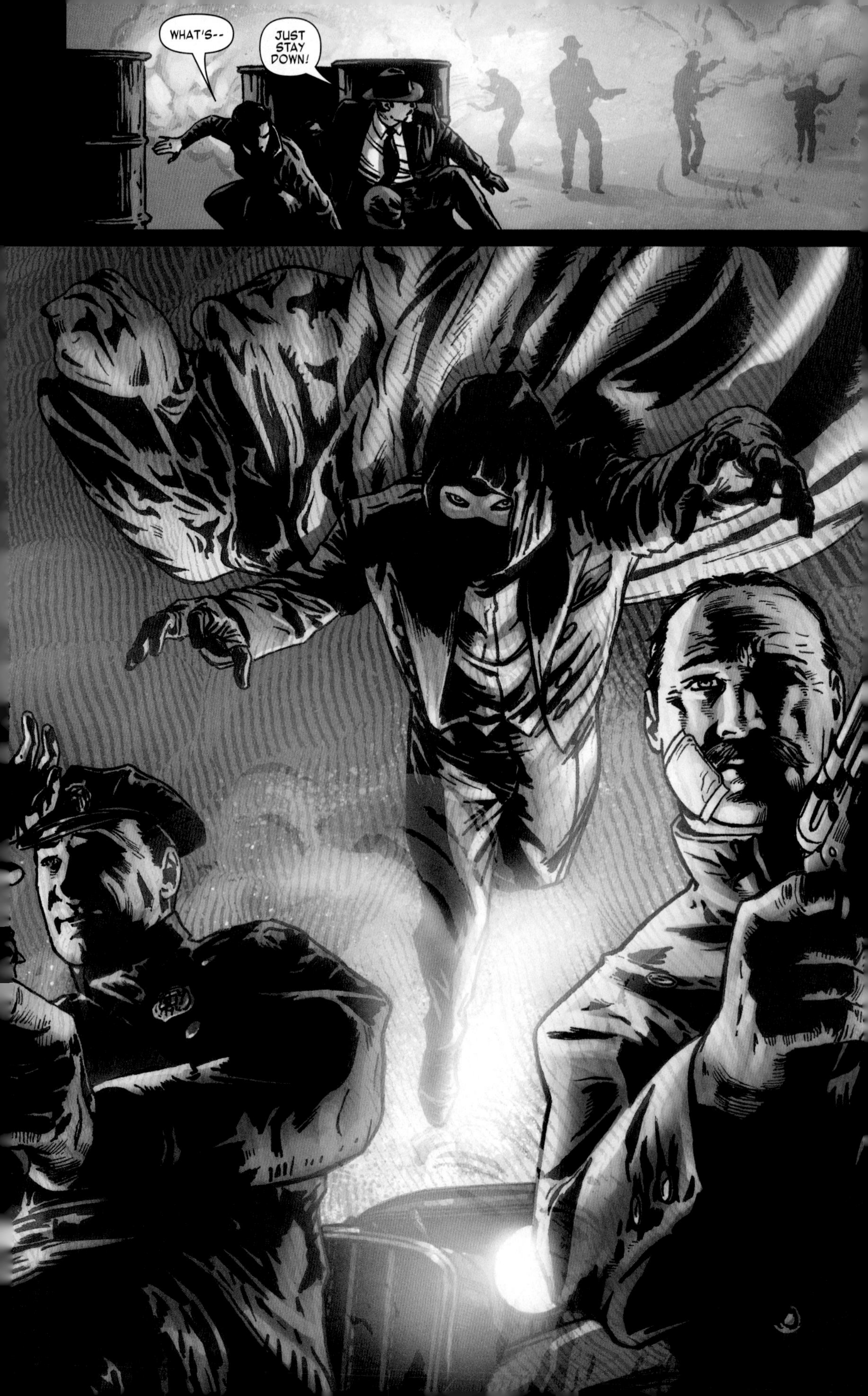
WHAT'S--
JUST STAY DOWN!

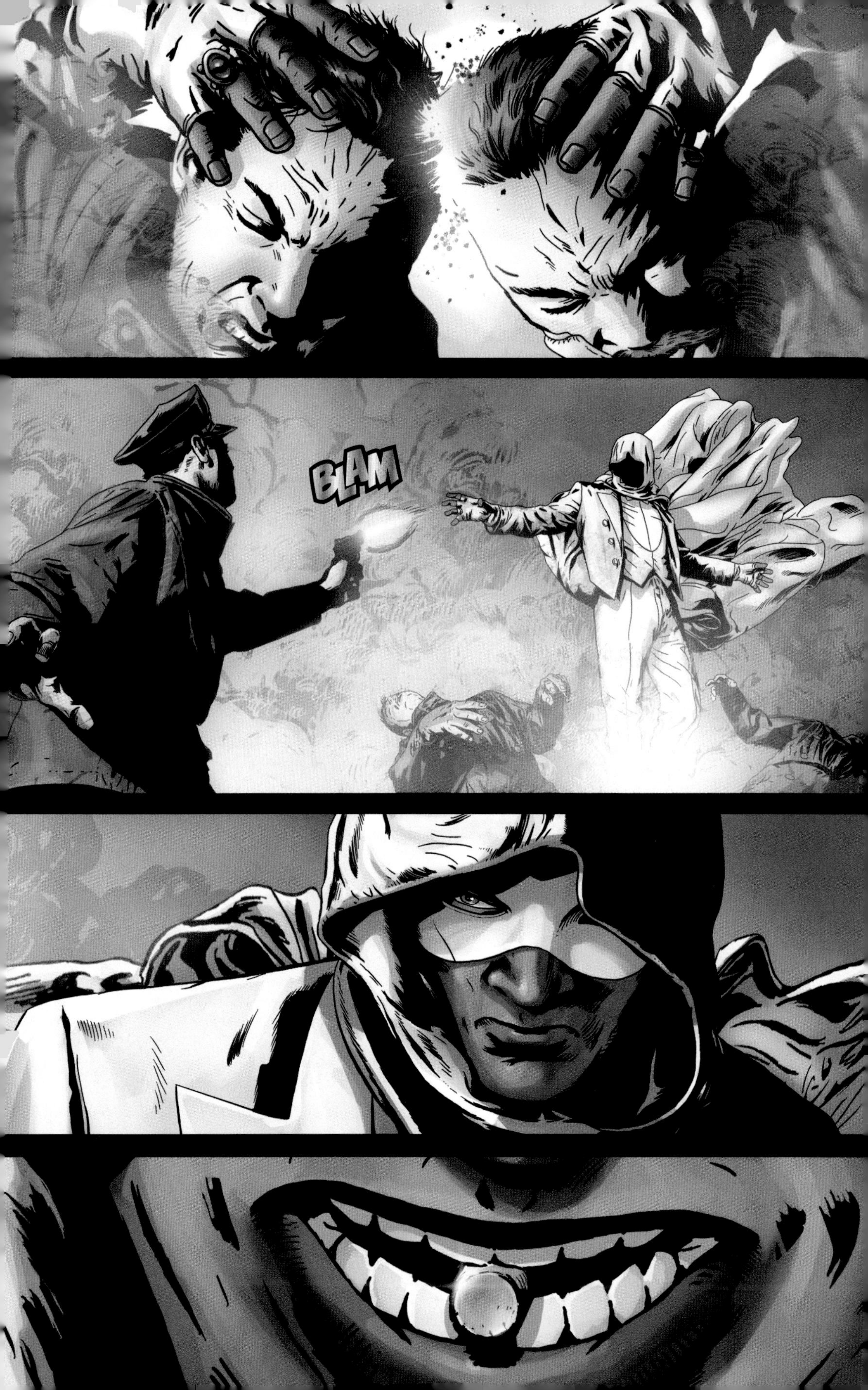
BLAM

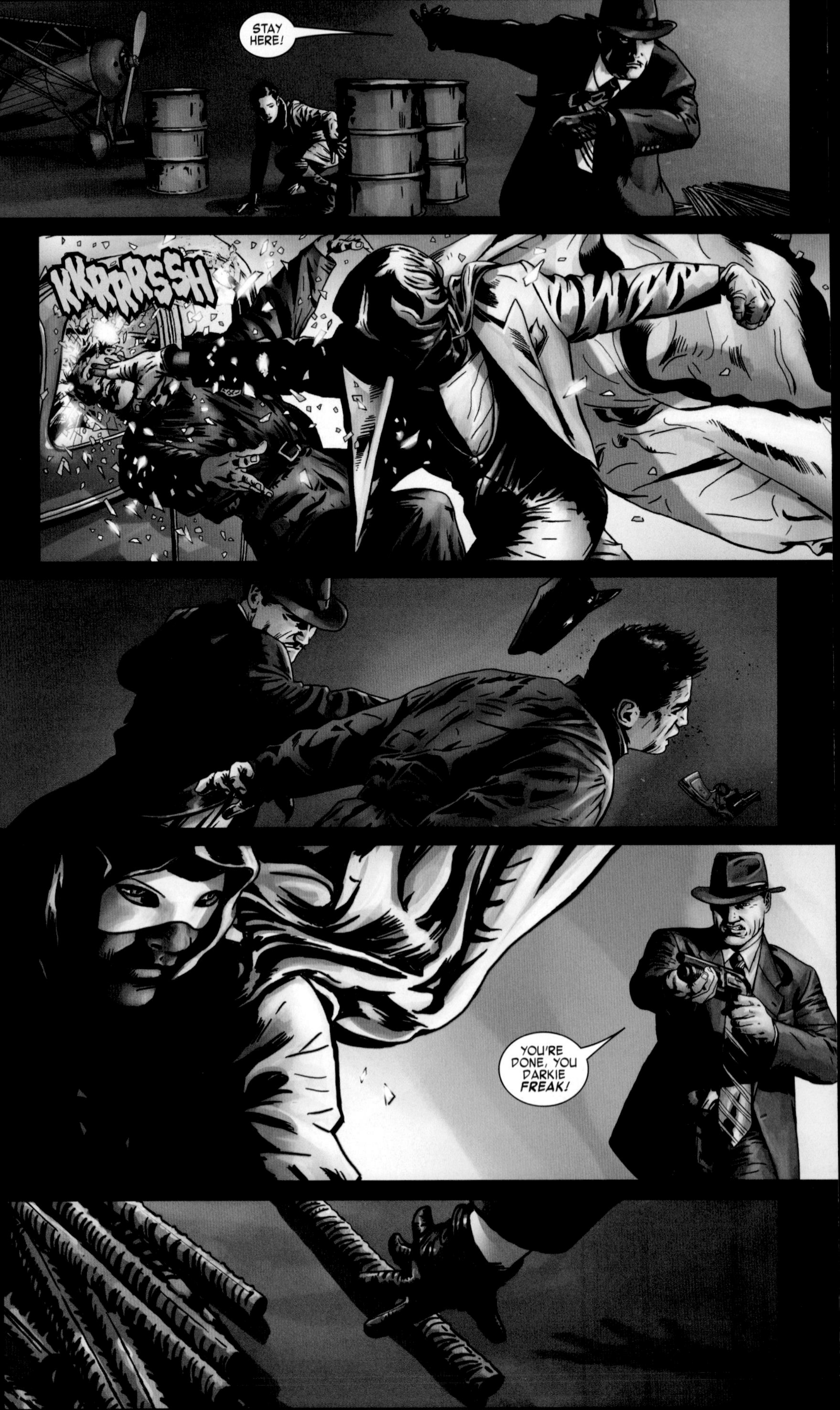
STAY HERE!
KKRRRSSH
YOU'RE DONE, YOU DARKIE FREAK!

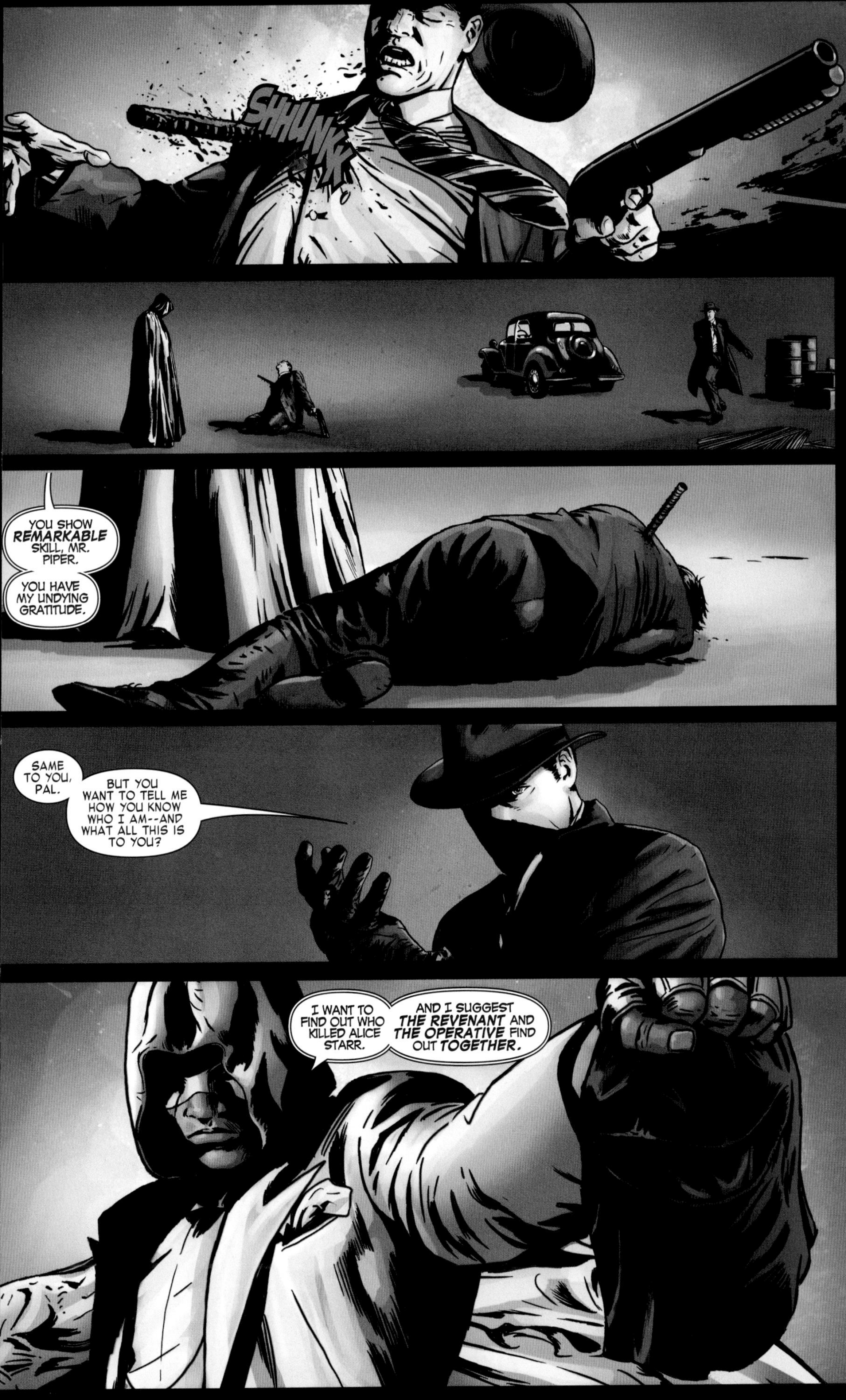
SHHUNKK
YOU SHOW REMARKABLE SKILL, MR. PIPER.
YOU HAVE MY UNDYING GRATITUDE.
SAME TO YOU, PAL.
BUT YOU WANT TO TELL ME HOW YOU KNOW WHO I AM--AND WHAT ALL THIS IS TO YOU?
I WANT TO FIND OUT WHO KILLED ALICE STARR.
AND I SUGGEST THE REVENANT AND THE OPERATIVE FIND OUT TOGETHER.

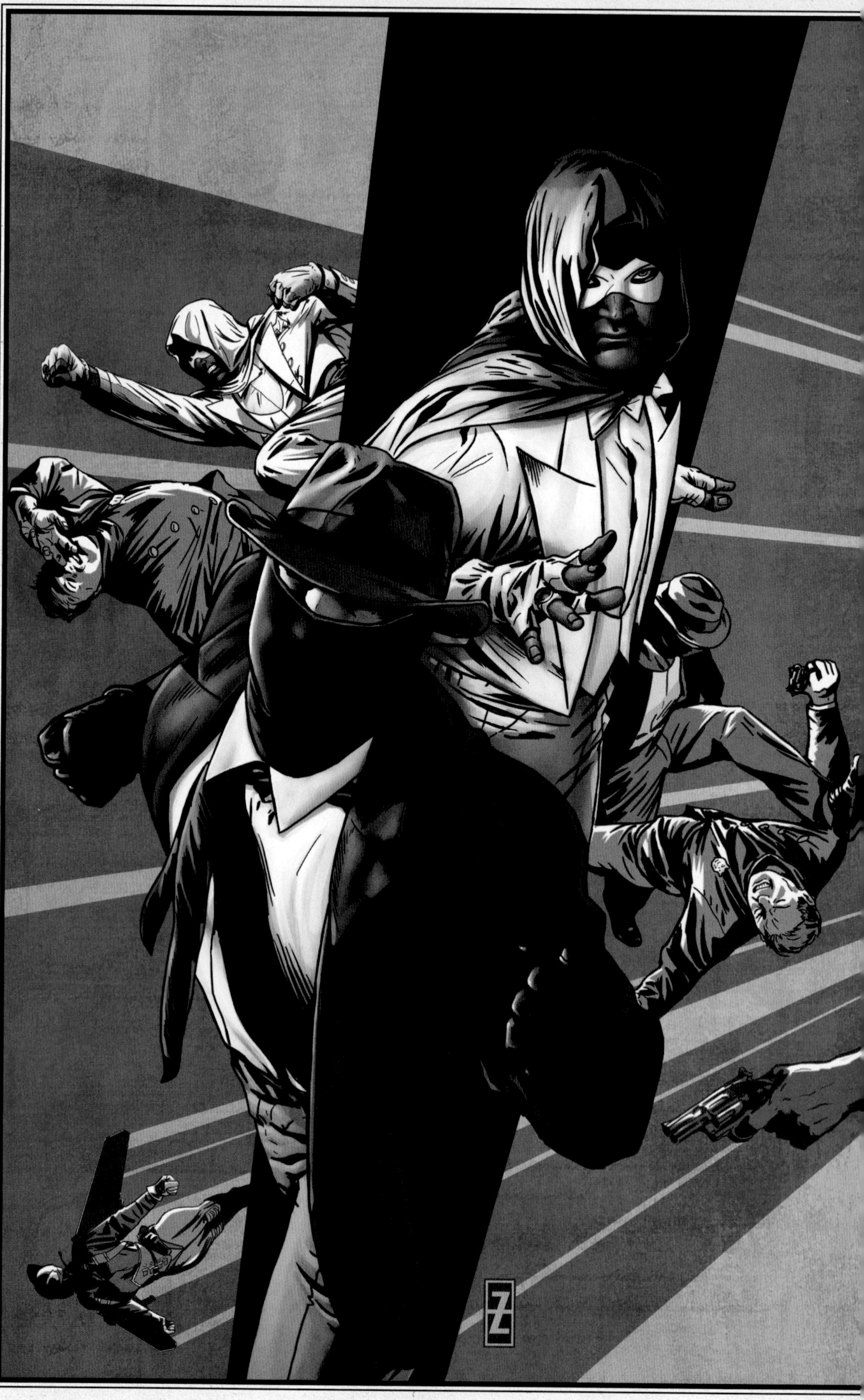

MYSTERY MEN #2

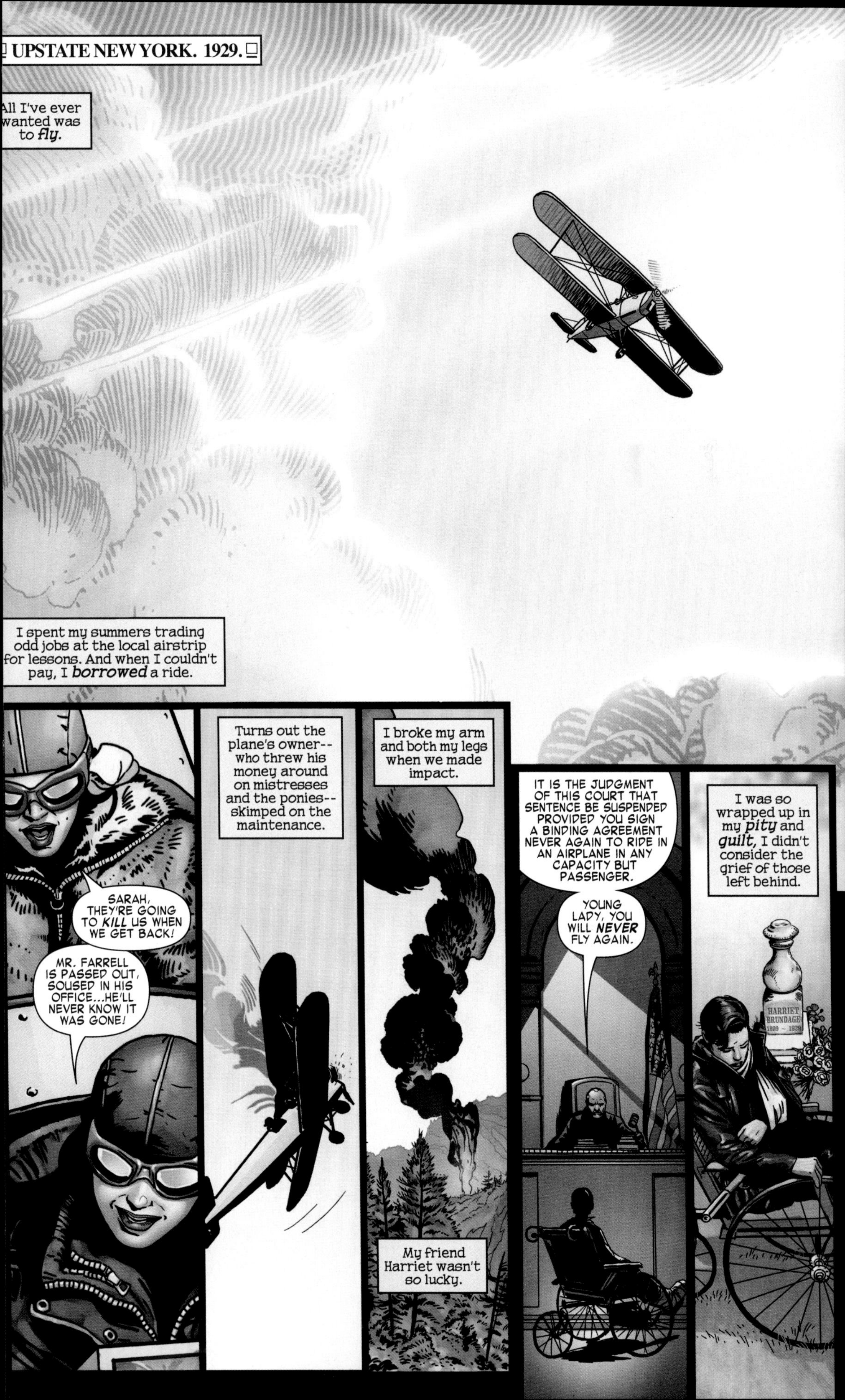
UPSTATE NEW YORK. 1929.
All I've ever wanted was to *fly*.
I spent my summers trading odd jobs at the local airstrip for lessons. And when I couldn't pay, I *borrowed* a ride.
SARAH, THEY'RE GOING TO *KILL* US WHEN WE GET BACK!
MR. FARRELL IS PASSED OUT, SOUSED IN HIS OFFICE...HE'LL NEVER KNOW IT WAS GONE!
Turns out the plane's owner--who threw his money around on mistresses and the ponies--skimped on the maintenance.
I broke my arm and both my legs when we made impact.
My friend Harriet wasn't so lucky.
IT IS THE JUDGMENT OF THIS COURT THAT SENTENCE BE SUSPENDED PROVIDED YOU SIGN A BINDING AGREEMENT NEVER AGAIN TO RIDE IN AN AIRPLANE IN ANY CAPACITY BUT PASSENGER.
YOUNG LADY, YOU WILL *NEVER* FLY AGAIN.
I was so wrapped up in my *pity* and *guilt*, I didn't consider the grief of those left behind.
HARRIET BRUNDAGE 1909 ~ 1929

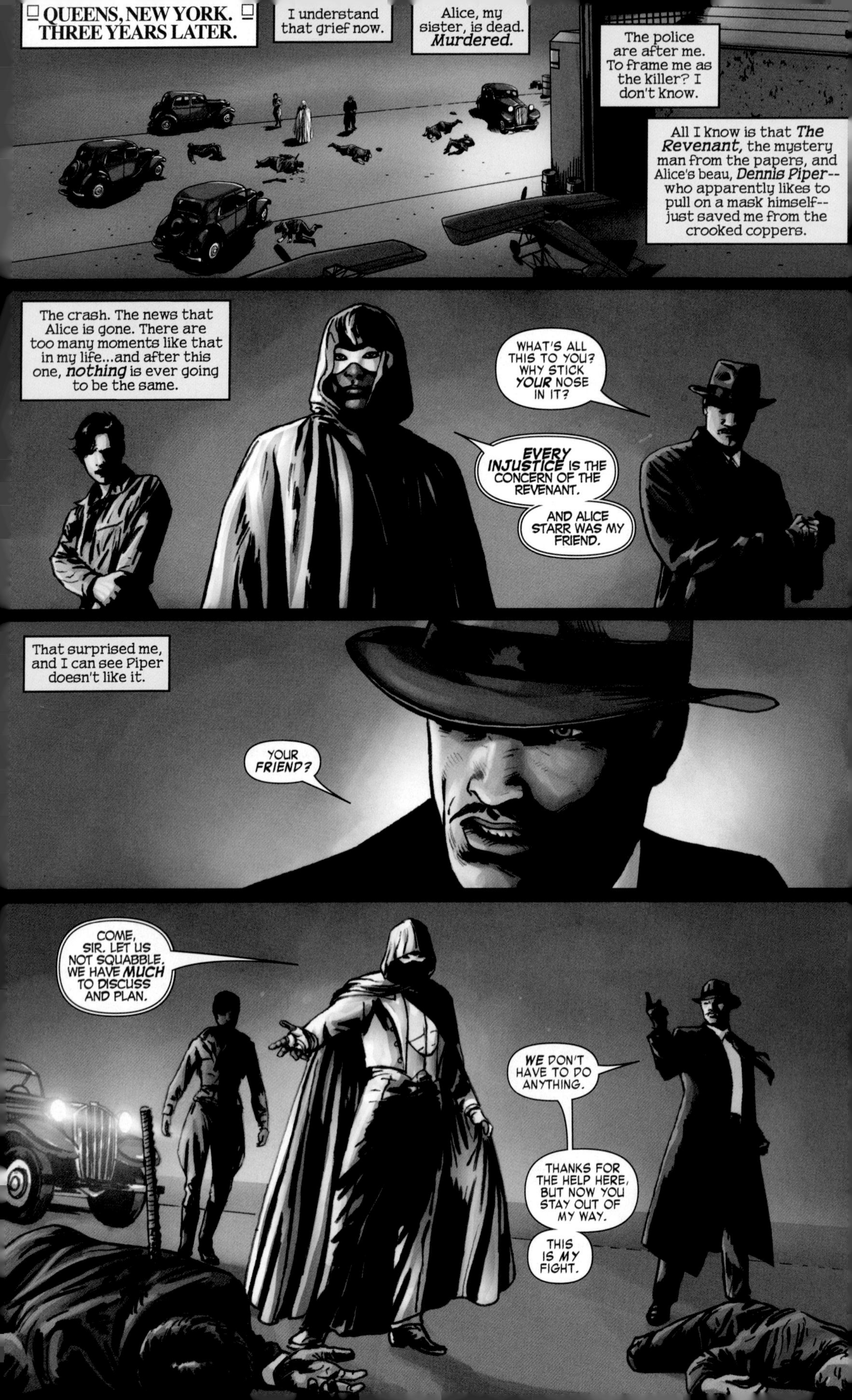
QUEENS, NEW YORK. THREE YEARS LATER.
I understand that grief now.
Alice, my sister, is dead. Murdered.
The police are after me. To frame me as the killer? I don't know.
All I know is that The Revenant, the mystery man from the papers, and Alice's beau, Dennis Piper-- who apparently likes to pull on a mask himself-- just saved me from the crooked coppers.
The crash. The news that Alice is gone. There are too many moments like that in my life...and after this one, nothing is ever going to be the same.
WHAT'S ALL THIS TO YOU? WHY STICK YOUR NOSE IN IT?
EVERY INJUSTICE IS THE CONCERN OF THE REVENANT.
AND ALICE STARR WAS MY FRIEND.
That surprised me, and I can see Piper doesn't like it.
YOUR FRIEND?
COME, SIR. LET US NOT SQUABBLE. WE HAVE MUCH TO DISCUSS AND PLAN.
WE DON'T HAVE TO DO ANYTHING.
THANKS FOR THE HELP HERE, BUT NOW YOU STAY OUT OF MY WAY.
THIS IS MY FIGHT.

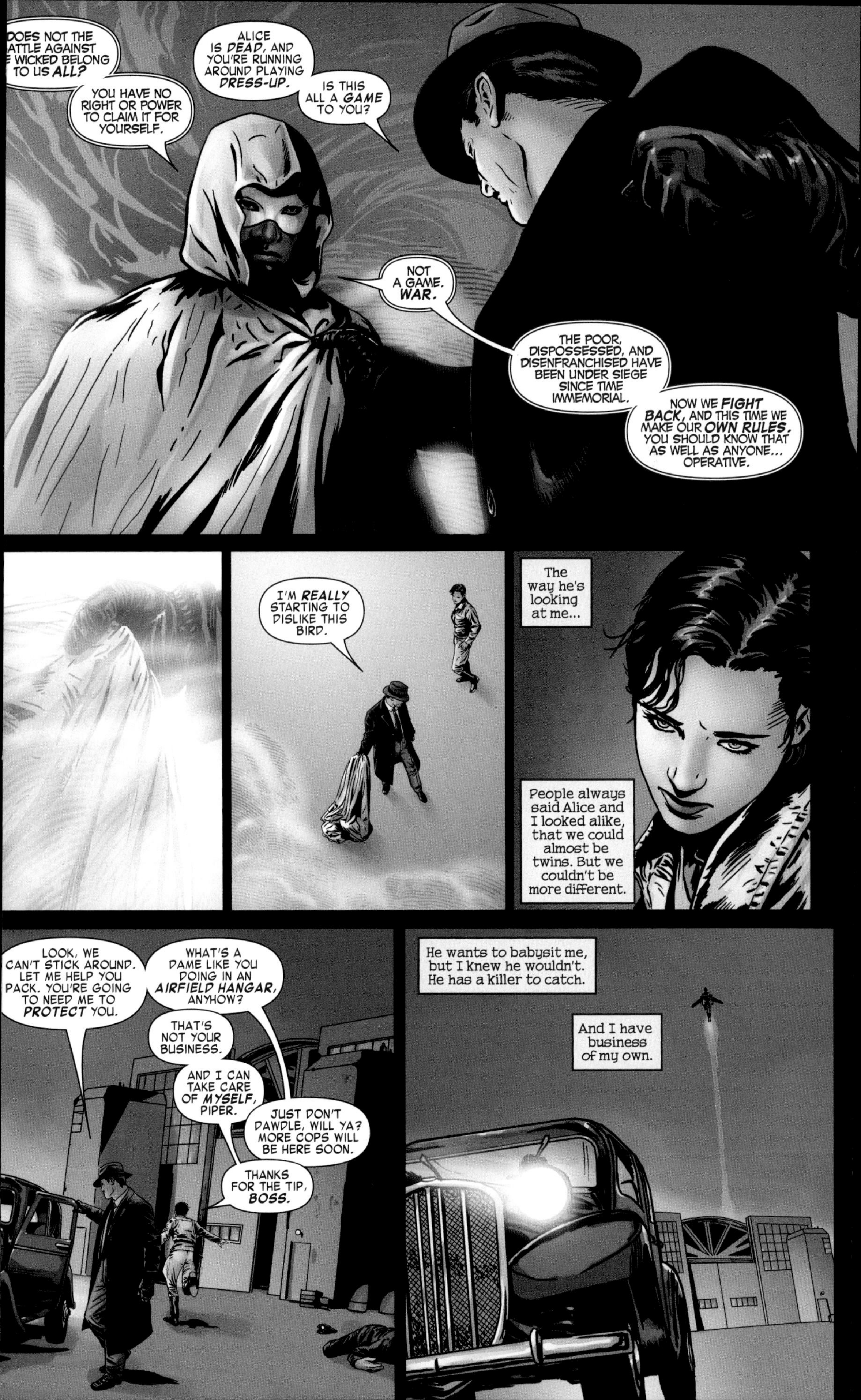

DOES NOT THE BATTLE AGAINST THE WICKED BELONG TO US ALL?
YOU HAVE NO RIGHT OR POWER TO CLAIM IT FOR YOURSELF.
ALICE IS DEAD, AND YOU'RE RUNNING AROUND PLAYING DRESS-UP.
IS THIS ALL A GAME TO YOU?
NOT A GAME. WAR.
THE POOR, DISPOSSESSED, AND DISENFRANCHISED HAVE BEEN UNDER SIEGE SINCE TIME IMMEMORIAL.
NOW WE FIGHT BACK, AND THIS TIME WE MAKE OUR OWN RULES. YOU SHOULD KNOW THAT AS WELL AS ANYONE... OPERATIVE.
I'M REALLY STARTING TO DISLIKE THIS BIRD.
The way he's looking at me...
People always said Alice and I looked alike, that we could almost be twins. But we couldn't be more different.
LOOK, WE CAN'T STICK AROUND. LET ME HELP YOU PACK. YOU'RE GOING TO NEED ME TO PROTECT YOU.
WHAT'S A DAME LIKE YOU DOING IN AN AIRFIELD HANGAR, ANYHOW?
THAT'S NOT YOUR BUSINESS.
AND I CAN TAKE CARE OF MYSELF, PIPER.
JUST DON'T DAWDLE, WILL YA? MORE COPS WILL BE HERE SOON.
THANKS FOR THE TIP, BOSS.
He wants to babysit me, but I knew he wouldn't. He has a killer to catch.
And I have business of my own.

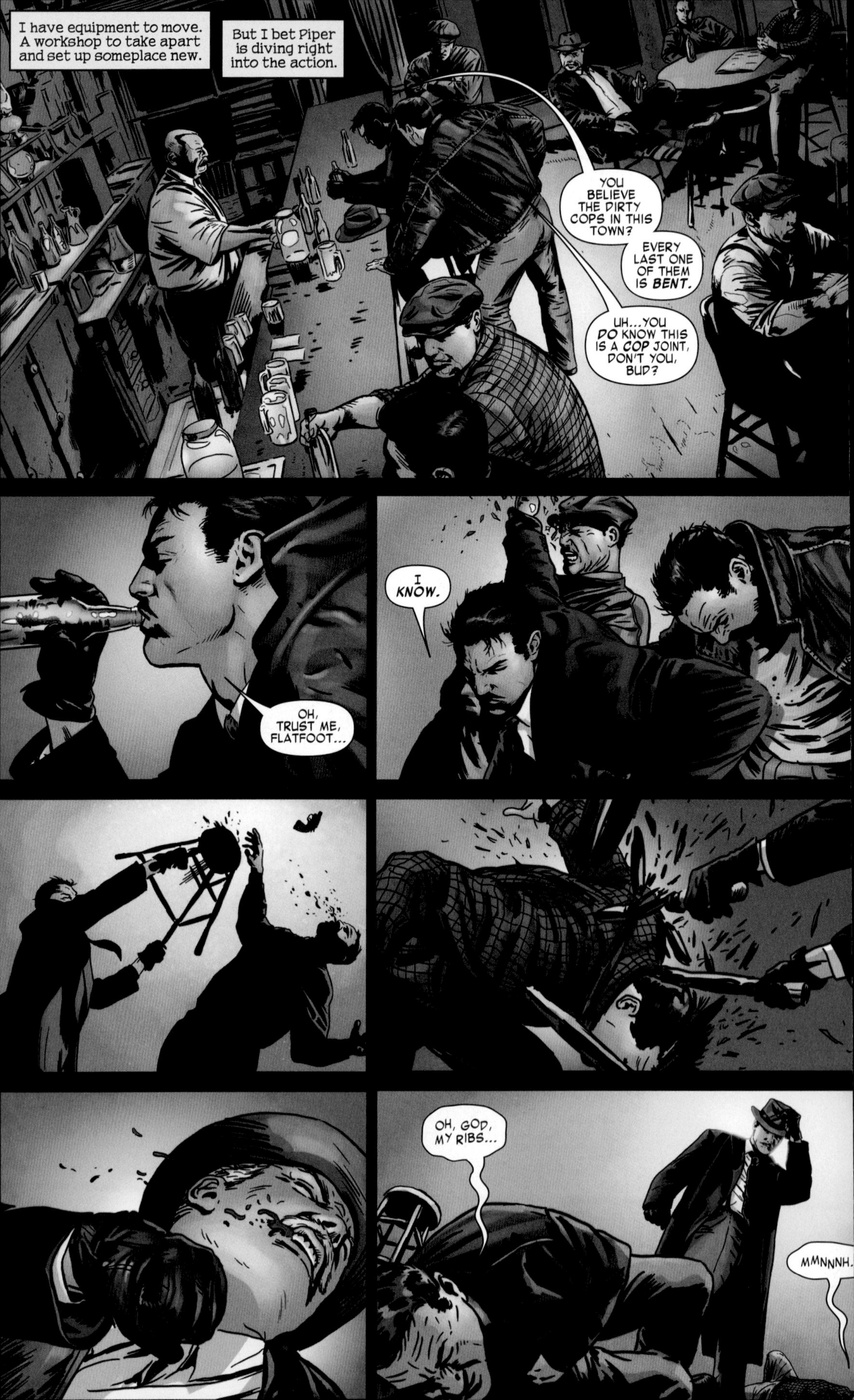
I have equipment to move. A workshop to take apart and set up someplace new.
But I bet Piper is diving right into the action.
YOU BELIEVE THE DIRTY COPS IN THIS TOWN?
EVERY LAST ONE OF THEM IS BENT.
UH...YOU DO KNOW THIS IS A COP JOINT, DON'T YOU, BUD?
OH, TRUST ME, FLATFOOT...
I KNOW.
OH, GOD, MY RIBS...
MMNNNH.

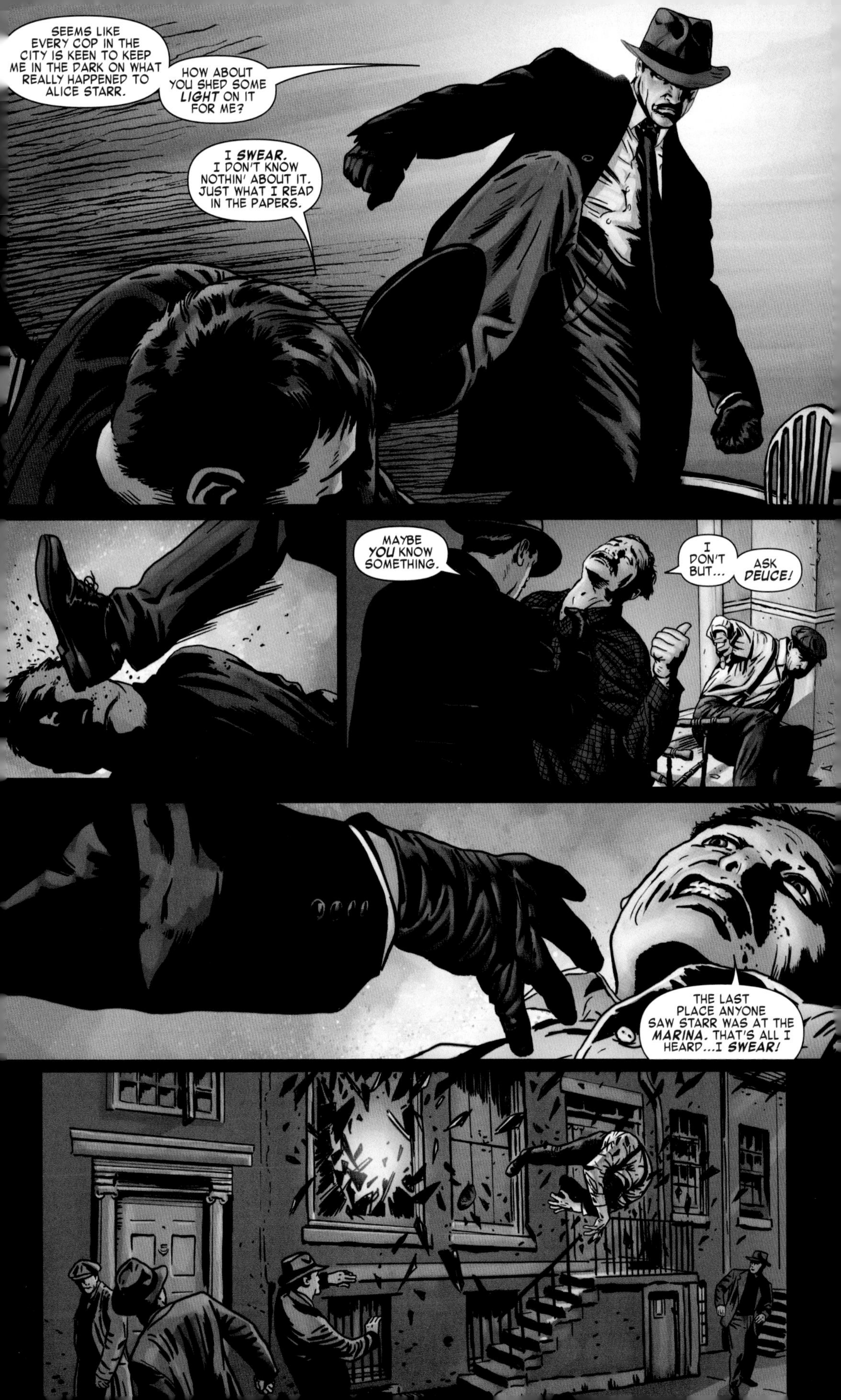
SEEMS LIKE EVERY COP IN THE CITY IS KEEN TO KEEP ME IN THE DARK ON WHAT REALLY HAPPENED TO ALICE STARR.
HOW ABOUT YOU SHED SOME *LIGHT* ON IT FOR ME?
I *SWEAR.* I DON'T KNOW NOTHIN' ABOUT IT. JUST WHAT I READ IN THE PAPERS.
MAYBE *YOU* KNOW SOMETHING.
I DON'T BUT...
ASK *DEUCE!*
THE LAST PLACE ANYONE SAW STARR WAS AT THE *MARINA.* THAT'S ALL I HEARD...I *SWEAR!*

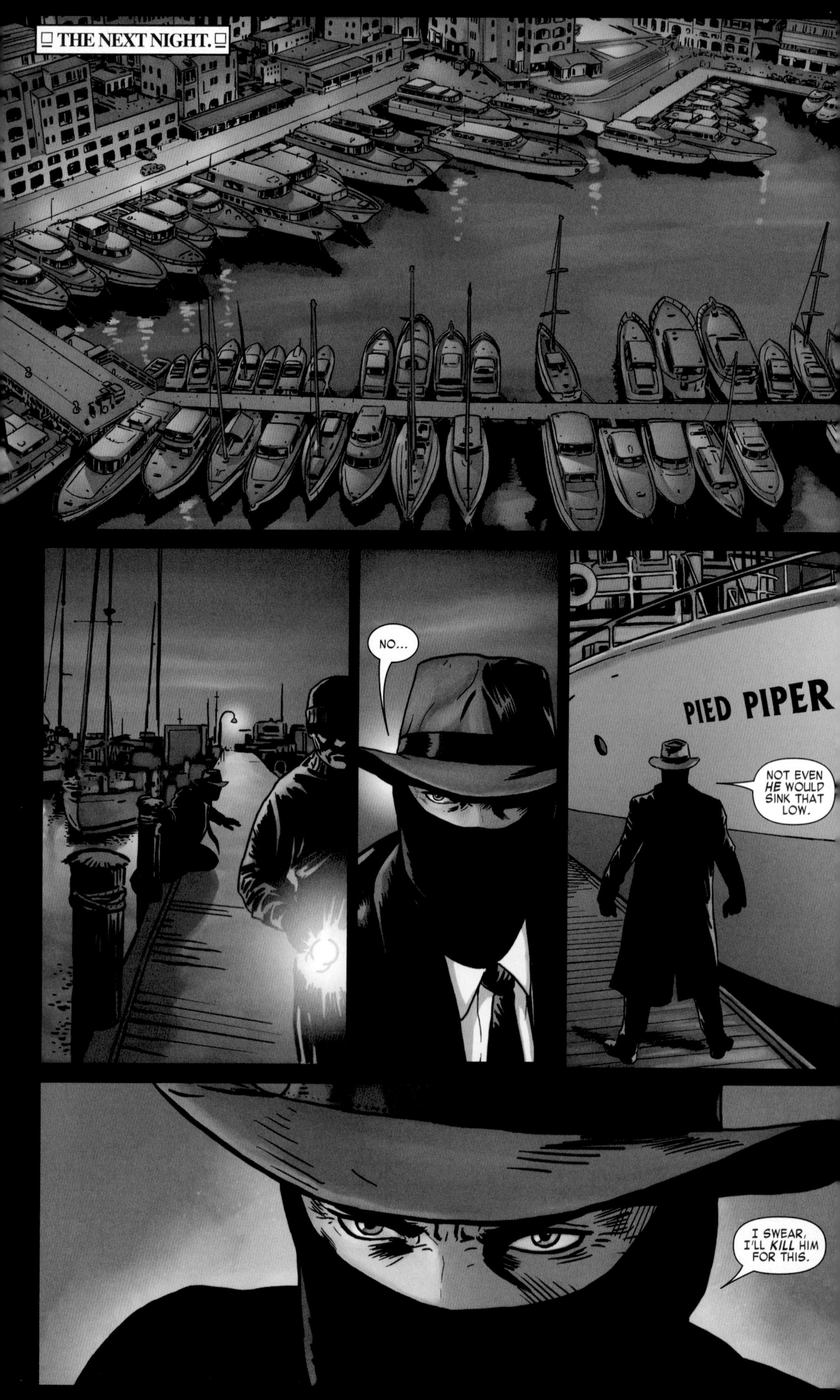
THE NEXT NIGHT.
NO...
PIED PIPER
NOT EVEN HE WOULD SINK THAT LOW.
I SWEAR, I'LL KILL HIM FOR THIS.

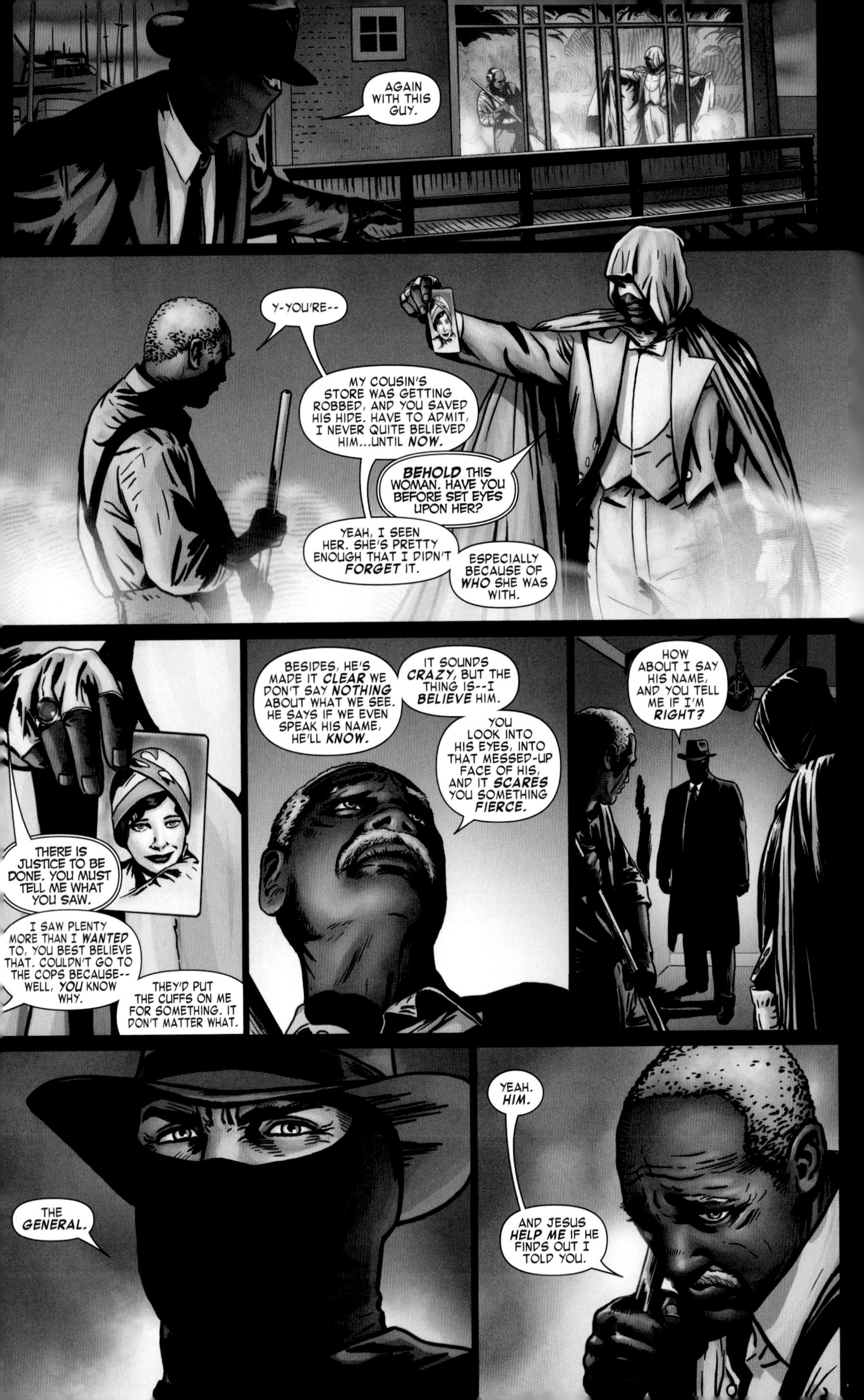
AGAIN WITH THIS GUY.
Y-YOU'RE--
MY COUSIN'S STORE WAS GETTING ROBBED, AND YOU SAVED HIS HIDE. HAVE TO ADMIT, I NEVER QUITE BELIEVED HIM...UNTIL NOW.
BEHOLD THIS WOMAN. HAVE YOU BEFORE SET EYES UPON HER?
YEAH, I SEEN HER. SHE'S PRETTY ENOUGH THAT I DIDN'T FORGET IT.
ESPECIALLY BECAUSE OF WHO SHE WAS WITH.
THERE IS JUSTICE TO BE DONE. YOU MUST TELL ME WHAT YOU SAW.
I SAW PLENTY MORE THAN I WANTED TO, YOU BEST BELIEVE THAT. COULDN'T GO TO THE COPS BECAUSE-- WELL, YOU KNOW WHY.
THEY'D PUT THE CUFFS ON ME FOR SOMETHING. IT DON'T MATTER WHAT.
BESIDES, HE'S MADE IT CLEAR WE DON'T SAY NOTHING ABOUT WHAT WE SEE. HE SAYS IF WE EVEN SPEAK HIS NAME, HE'LL KNOW.
IT SOUNDS CRAZY, BUT THE THING IS--I BELIEVE HIM.
YOU LOOK INTO HIS EYES, INTO THAT MESSED-UP FACE OF HIS, AND IT SCARES YOU SOMETHING FIERCE.
HOW ABOUT I SAY HIS NAME, AND YOU TELL ME IF I'M RIGHT?
THE GENERAL.
YEAH. HIM.
AND JESUS HELP ME IF HE FINDS OUT I TOLD YOU.

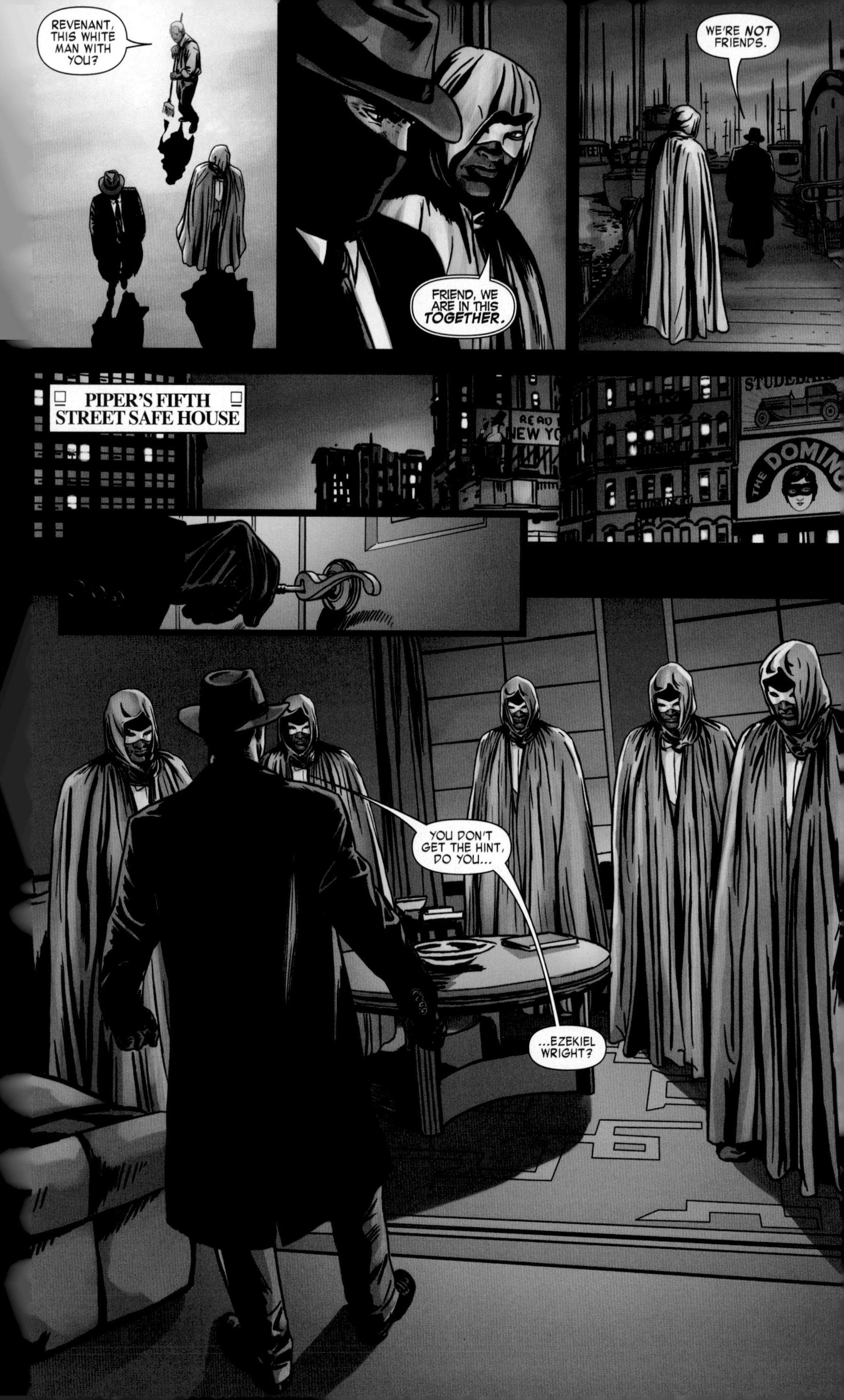
REVENANT, THIS WHITE MAN WITH YOU?
FRIEND, WE ARE IN THIS TOGETHER.
WE'RE NOT FRIENDS.
PIPER'S FIFTH STREET SAFE HOUSE
YOU DON'T GET THE HINT, DO YOU...
...EZEKIEL WRIGHT?

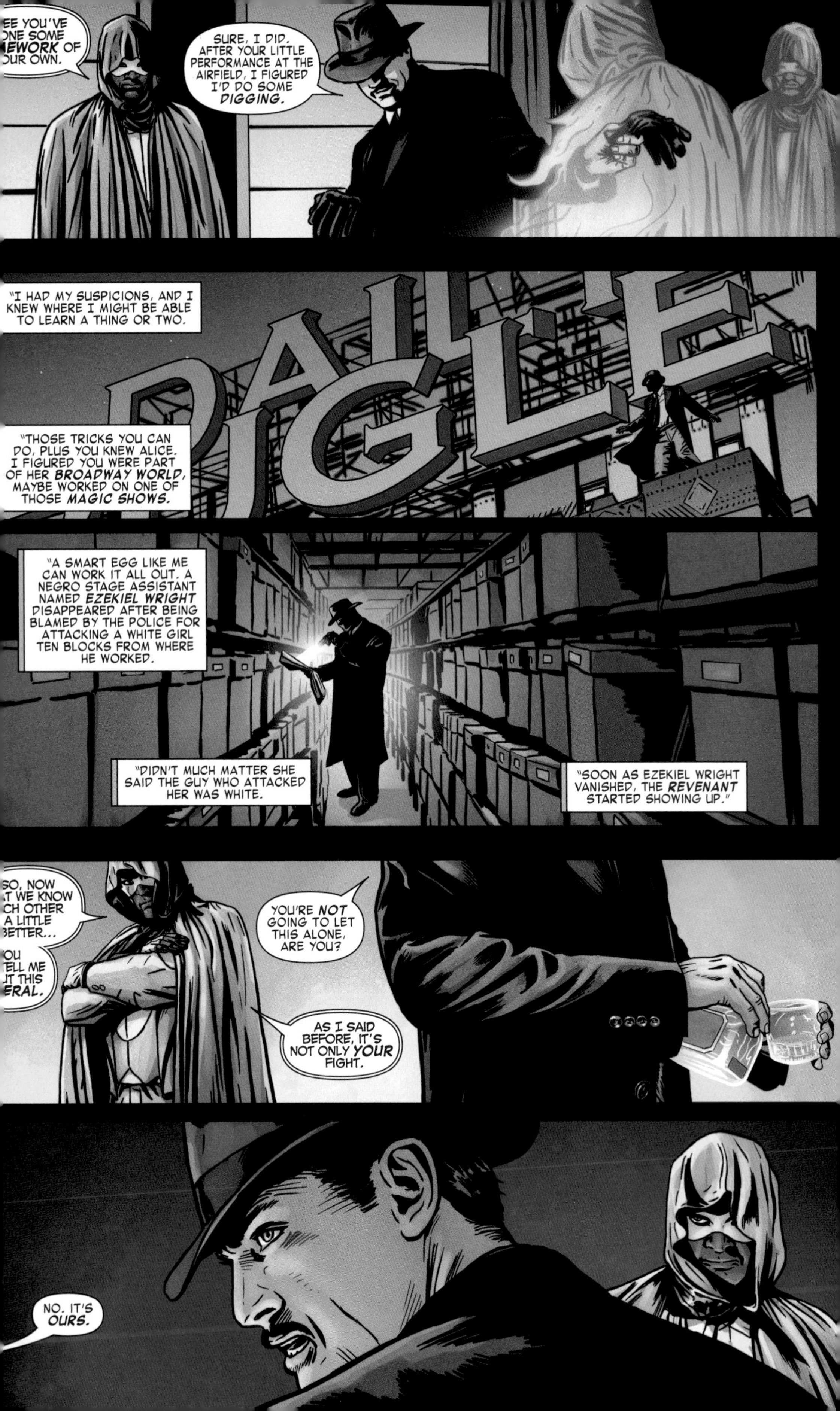
EE YOU'VE
ONE SOME
EWORK OF
OUR OWN.
SURE, I DID. AFTER YOUR LITTLE PERFORMANCE AT THE AIRFIELD, I FIGURED I'D DO SOME DIGGING.
"I HAD MY SUSPICIONS, AND I KNEW WHERE I MIGHT BE ABLE TO LEARN A THING OR TWO.
"THOSE TRICKS YOU CAN DO, PLUS YOU KNEW ALICE. I FIGURED YOU WERE PART OF HER BROADWAY WORLD, MAYBE WORKED ON ONE OF THOSE MAGIC SHOWS.
"A SMART EGG LIKE ME CAN WORK IT ALL OUT. A NEGRO STAGE ASSISTANT NAMED EZEKIEL WRIGHT DISAPPEARED AFTER BEING BLAMED BY THE POLICE FOR ATTACKING A WHITE GIRL TEN BLOCKS FROM WHERE HE WORKED.
"DIDN'T MUCH MATTER SHE SAID THE GUY WHO ATTACKED HER WAS WHITE.
"SOON AS EZEKIEL WRIGHT VANISHED, THE REVENANT STARTED SHOWING UP."
SO, NOW
T WE KNOW
CH OTHER
A LITTLE
BETTER...
OU
ELL ME
T THIS
ERAL.
YOU'RE NOT GOING TO LET THIS ALONE, ARE YOU?
AS I SAID BEFORE, IT'S NOT ONLY YOUR FIGHT.
NO. IT'S OURS.

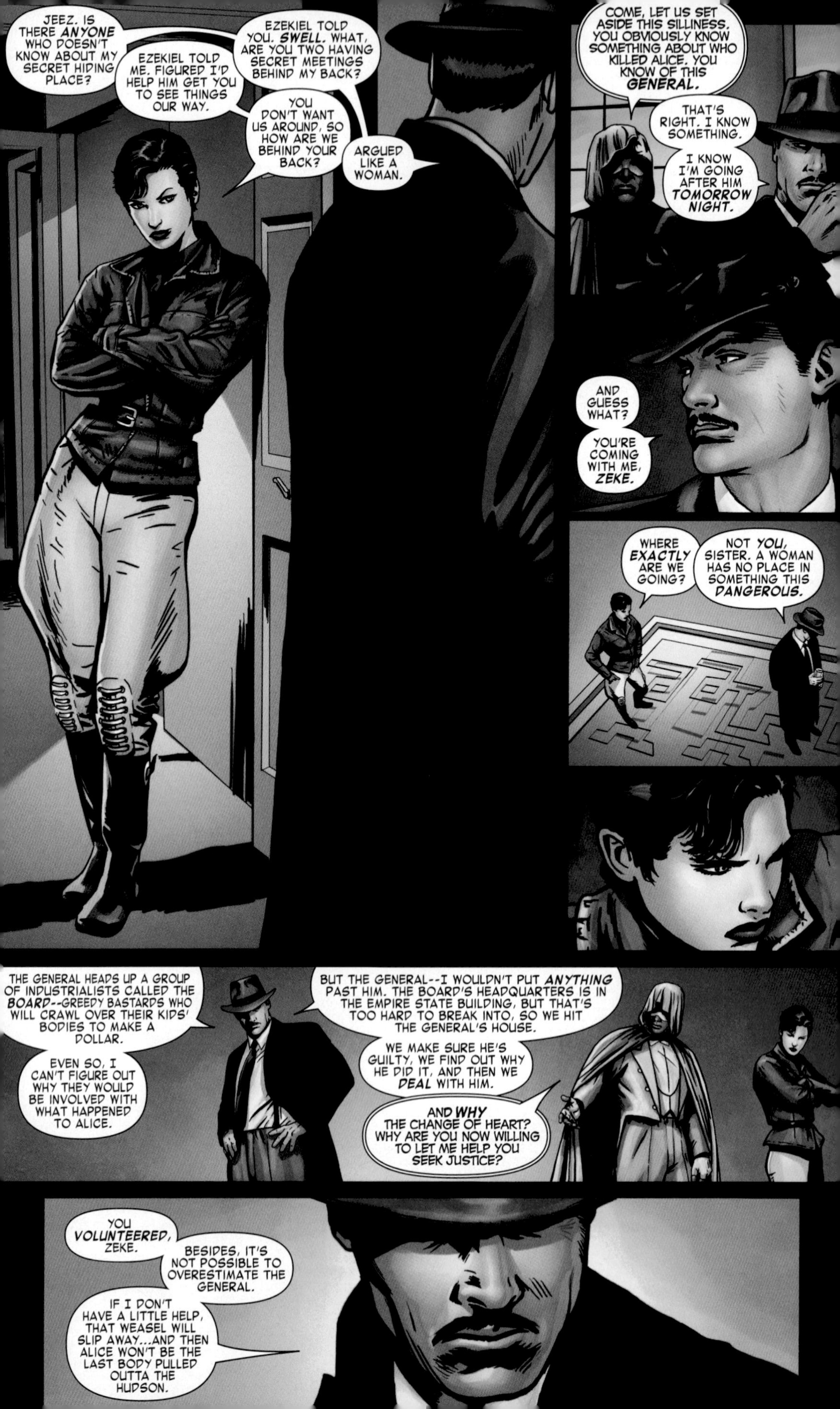

JEEZ. IS THERE ANYONE WHO DOESN'T KNOW ABOUT MY SECRET HIDING PLACE?
EZEKIEL TOLD ME. FIGURED I'D HELP HIM GET YOU TO SEE THINGS OUR WAY.
EZEKIEL TOLD YOU. SWELL. WHAT, ARE YOU TWO HAVING SECRET MEETINGS BEHIND MY BACK?
YOU DON'T WANT US AROUND, SO HOW ARE WE BEHIND YOUR BACK?
ARGUED LIKE A WOMAN.
COME, LET US SET ASIDE THIS SILLINESS. YOU OBVIOUSLY KNOW SOMETHING ABOUT WHO KILLED ALICE. YOU KNOW OF THIS GENERAL.
THAT'S RIGHT. I KNOW SOMETHING.
I KNOW I'M GOING AFTER HIM TOMORROW NIGHT.
AND GUESS WHAT?
YOU'RE COMING WITH ME, ZEKE.
WHERE EXACTLY ARE WE GOING?
NOT YOU, SISTER. A WOMAN HAS NO PLACE IN SOMETHING THIS DANGEROUS.
THE GENERAL HEADS UP A GROUP OF INDUSTRIALISTS CALLED THE BOARD--GREEDY BASTARDS WHO WILL CRAWL OVER THEIR KIDS' BODIES TO MAKE A DOLLAR.
EVEN SO, I CAN'T FIGURE OUT WHY THEY WOULD BE INVOLVED WITH WHAT HAPPENED TO ALICE.
BUT THE GENERAL--I WOULDN'T PUT ANYTHING PAST HIM. THE BOARD'S HEADQUARTERS IS IN THE EMPIRE STATE BUILDING, BUT THAT'S TOO HARD TO BREAK INTO, SO WE HIT THE GENERAL'S HOUSE.
WE MAKE SURE HE'S GUILTY, WE FIND OUT WHY HE DID IT, AND THEN WE DEAL WITH HIM.
AND WHY THE CHANGE OF HEART? WHY ARE YOU NOW WILLING TO LET ME HELP YOU SEEK JUSTICE?
YOU VOLUNTEERED, ZEKE.
BESIDES, IT'S NOT POSSIBLE TO OVERESTIMATE THE GENERAL.
IF I DON'T HAVE A LITTLE HELP, THAT WEASEL WILL SLIP AWAY...AND THEN ALICE WON'T BE THE LAST BODY PULLED OUTTA THE HUDSON.

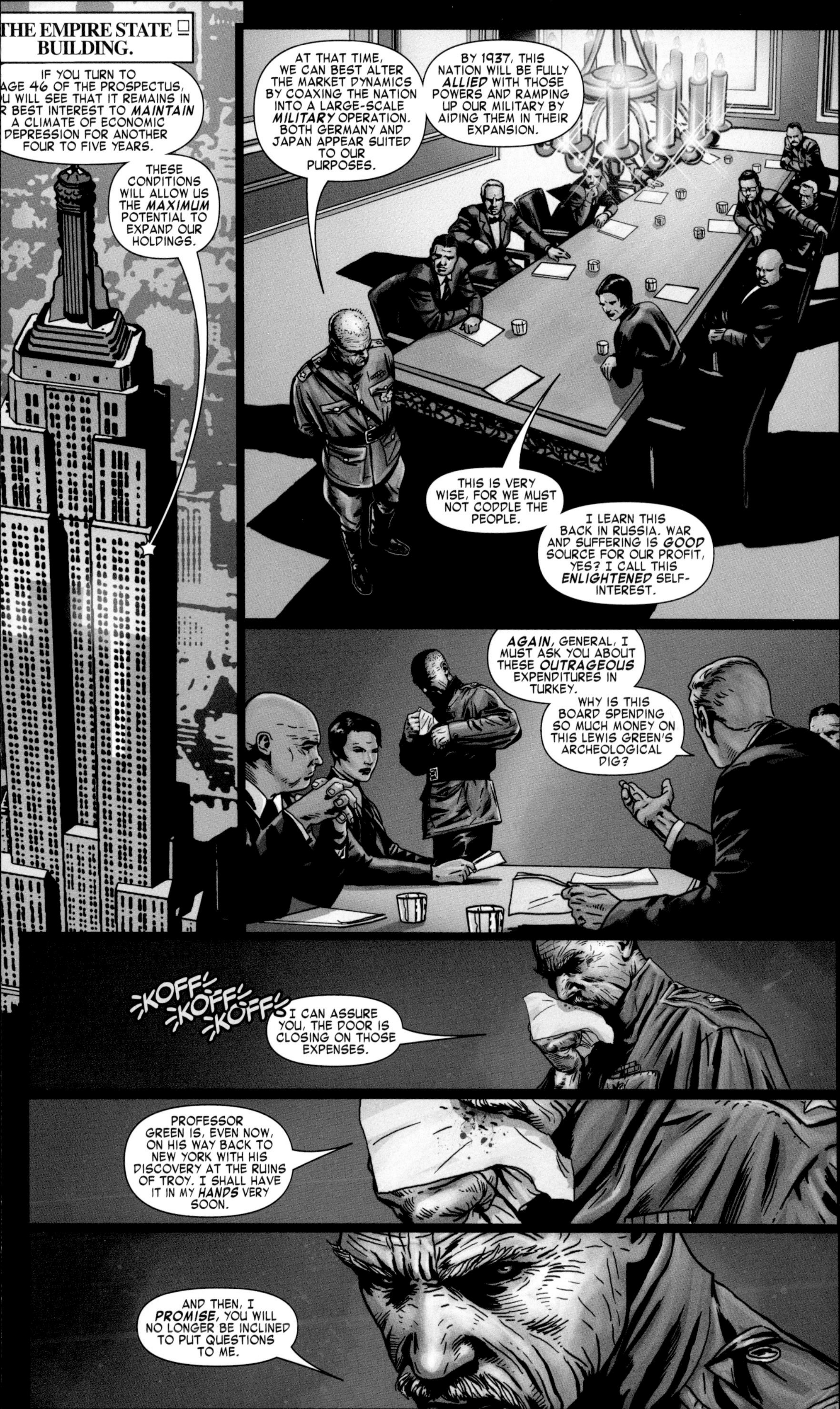

THE EMPIRE STATE BUILDING.
IF YOU TURN TO AGE 46 OF THE PROSPECTUS, U WILL SEE THAT IT REMAINS IN R BEST INTEREST TO MAINTAIN A CLIMATE OF ECONOMIC DEPRESSION FOR ANOTHER FOUR TO FIVE YEARS.
THESE CONDITIONS WILL ALLOW US THE MAXIMUM POTENTIAL TO EXPAND OUR HOLDINGS.
AT THAT TIME, WE CAN BEST ALTER THE MARKET DYNAMICS BY COAXING THE NATION INTO A LARGE-SCALE MILITARY OPERATION. BOTH GERMANY AND JAPAN APPEAR SUITED TO OUR PURPOSES.
BY 1937, THIS NATION WILL BE FULLY ALLIED WITH THOSE POWERS AND RAMPING UP OUR MILITARY BY AIDING THEM IN THEIR EXPANSION.
THIS IS VERY WISE, FOR WE MUST NOT CODDLE THE PEOPLE.
I LEARN THIS BACK IN RUSSIA. WAR AND SUFFERING IS GOOD SOURCE FOR OUR PROFIT, YES? I CALL THIS ENLIGHTENED SELF-INTEREST.
AGAIN, GENERAL, I MUST ASK YOU ABOUT THESE OUTRAGEOUS EXPENDITURES IN TURKEY.
WHY IS THIS BOARD SPENDING SO MUCH MONEY ON THIS LEWIS GREEN'S ARCHEOLOGICAL DIG?
KOFF KOFF KOFF
I CAN ASSURE YOU, THE DOOR IS CLOSING ON THOSE EXPENSES.
PROFESSOR GREEN IS, EVEN NOW, ON HIS WAY BACK TO NEW YORK WITH HIS DISCOVERY AT THE RUINS OF TROY. I SHALL HAVE IT IN MY HANDS VERY SOON.
AND THEN, I PROMISE, YOU WILL NO LONGER BE INCLINED TO PUT QUESTIONS TO ME.

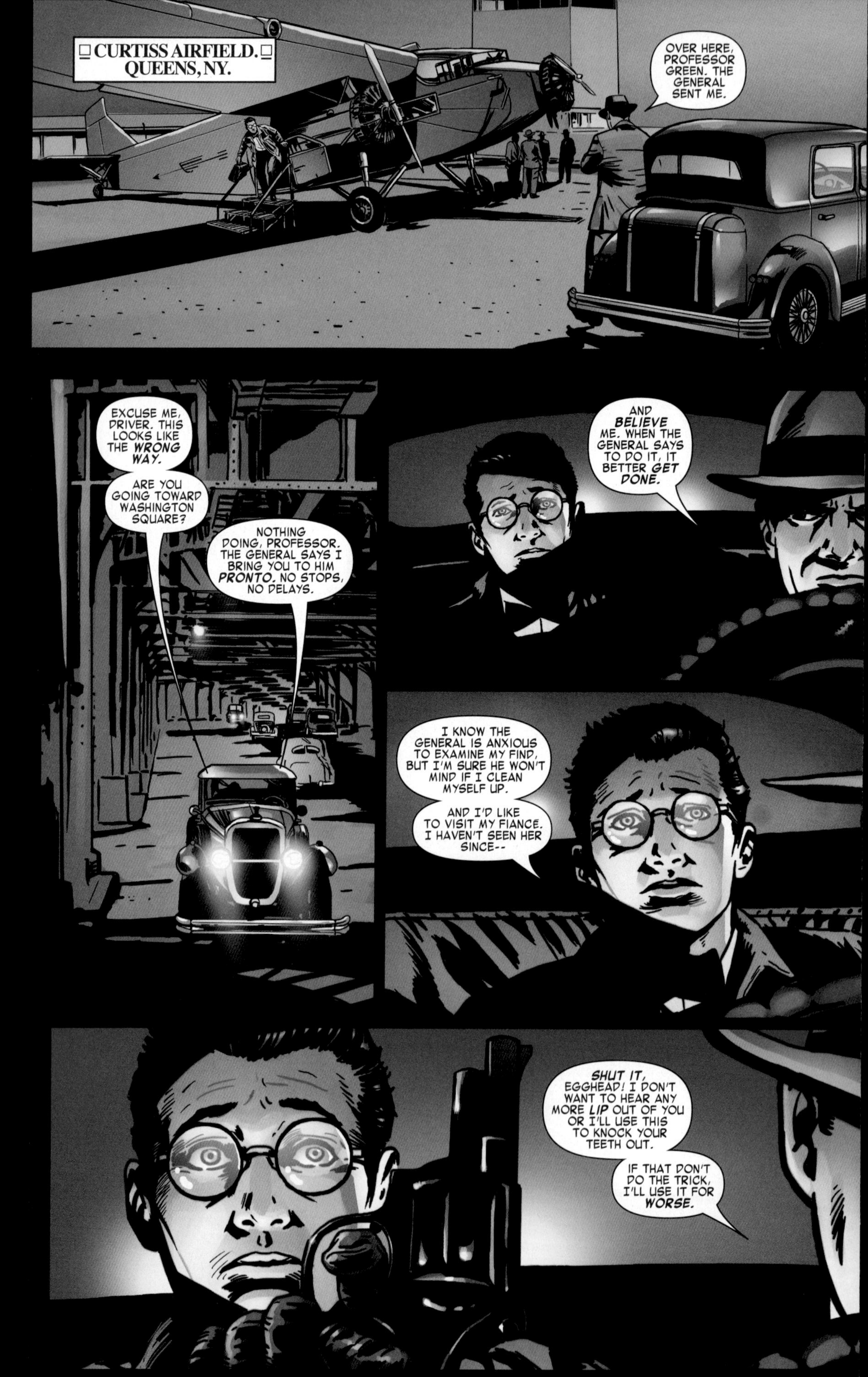
CURTISS AIRFIELD. QUEENS, NY.
OVER HERE, PROFESSOR GREEN. THE GENERAL SENT ME.
EXCUSE ME, DRIVER. THIS LOOKS LIKE THE WRONG WAY.
ARE YOU GOING TOWARD WASHINGTON SQUARE?
NOTHING DOING, PROFESSOR. THE GENERAL SAYS I BRING YOU TO HIM PRONTO. NO STOPS, NO DELAYS.
AND BELIEVE ME. WHEN THE GENERAL SAYS TO DO IT, IT BETTER GET DONE.
I KNOW THE GENERAL IS ANXIOUS TO EXAMINE MY FIND, BUT I'M SURE HE WON'T MIND IF I CLEAN MYSELF UP.
AND I'D LIKE TO VISIT MY FIANCE. I HAVEN'T SEEN HER SINCE--
SHUT IT, EGGHEAD! I DON'T WANT TO HEAR ANY MORE LIP OUT OF YOU OR I'LL USE THIS TO KNOCK YOUR TEETH OUT.
IF THAT DON'T DO THE TRICK, I'LL USE IT FOR WORSE.

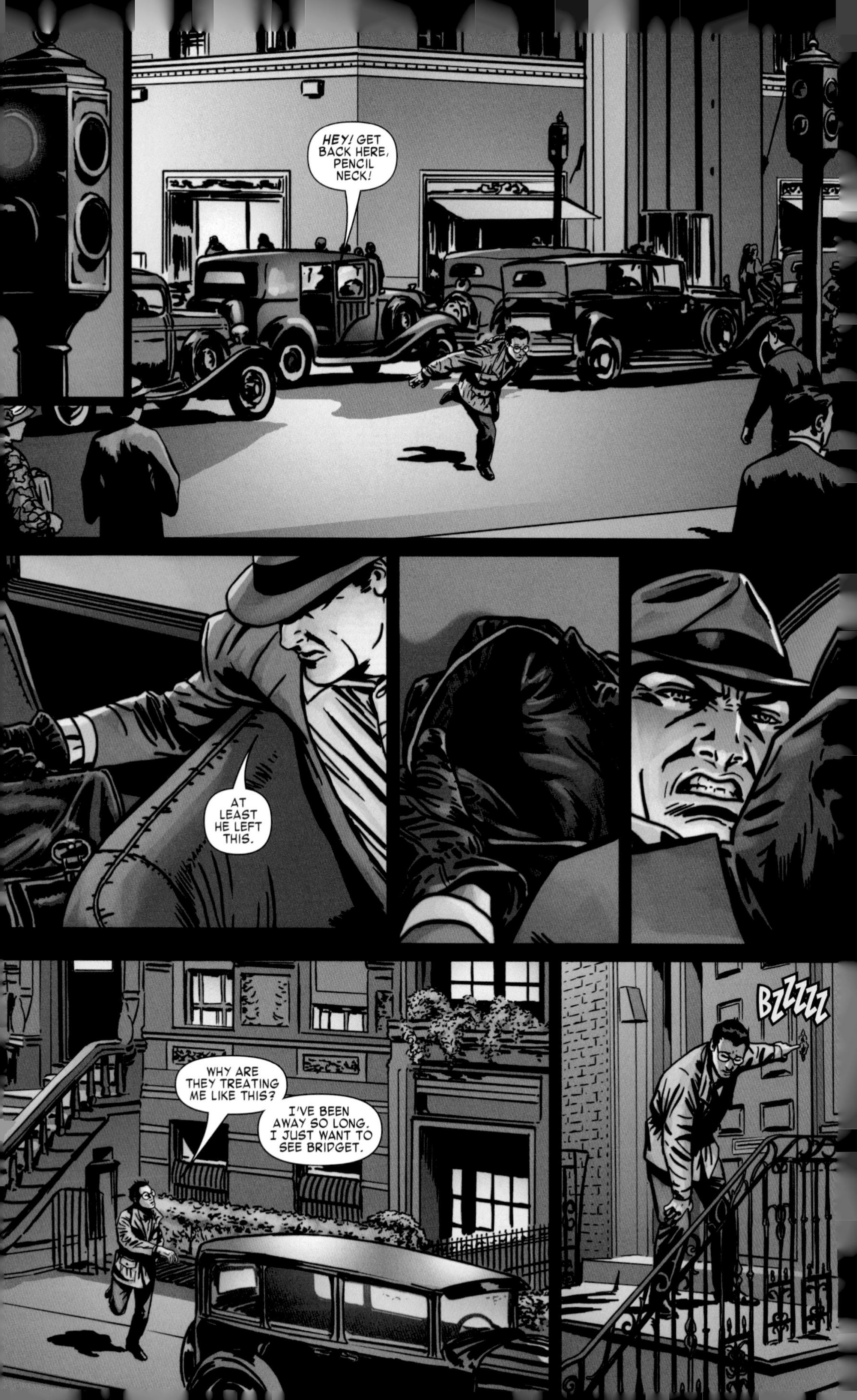
HEY! GET BACK HERE, PENCIL NECK!
AT LEAST HE LEFT THIS.
WHY ARE THEY TREATING ME LIKE THIS?
I'VE BEEN AWAY SO LONG. I JUST WANT TO SEE BRIDGET.
BZZZZZ

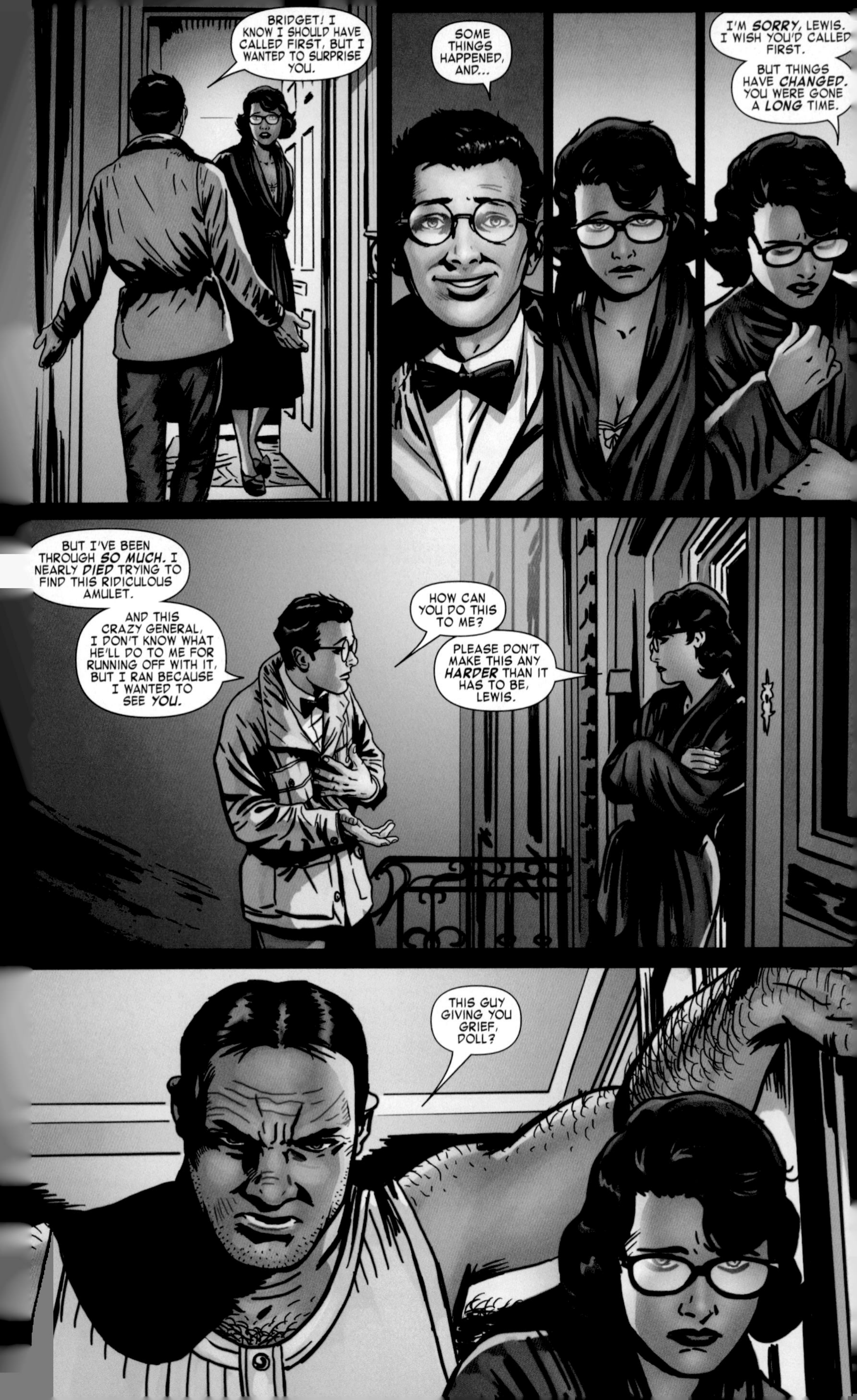
BRIDGET! I KNOW I SHOULD HAVE CALLED FIRST, BUT I WANTED TO SURPRISE YOU.
SOME THINGS HAPPENED, AND...
I'M SORRY, LEWIS. I WISH YOU'D CALLED FIRST.
BUT THINGS HAVE CHANGED. YOU WERE GONE A LONG TIME.
BUT I'VE BEEN THROUGH SO MUCH. I NEARLY DIED TRYING TO FIND THIS RIDICULOUS AMULET.
AND THIS CRAZY GENERAL, I DON'T KNOW WHAT HE'LL DO TO ME FOR RUNNING OFF WITH IT, BUT I RAN BECAUSE I WANTED TO SEE YOU.
HOW CAN YOU DO THIS TO ME?
PLEASE DON'T MAKE THIS ANY HARDER THAN IT HAS TO BE, LEWIS.
THIS GUY GIVING YOU GRIEF, DOLL?

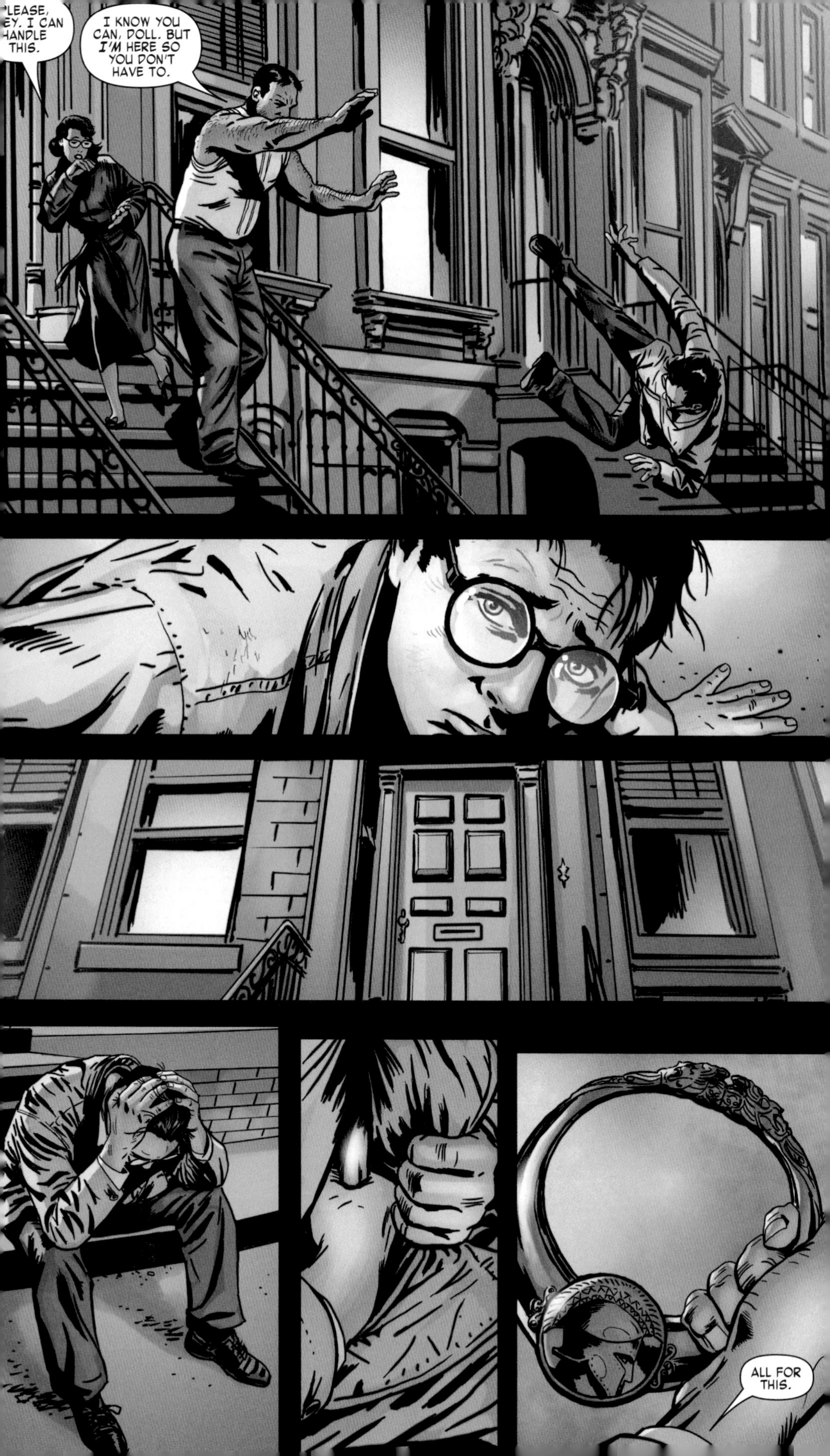

PLEASE,
EY. I CAN
HANDLE
THIS.
I KNOW YOU CAN, DOLL. BUT I'M HERE SO YOU DON'T HAVE TO.
ALL FOR THIS.

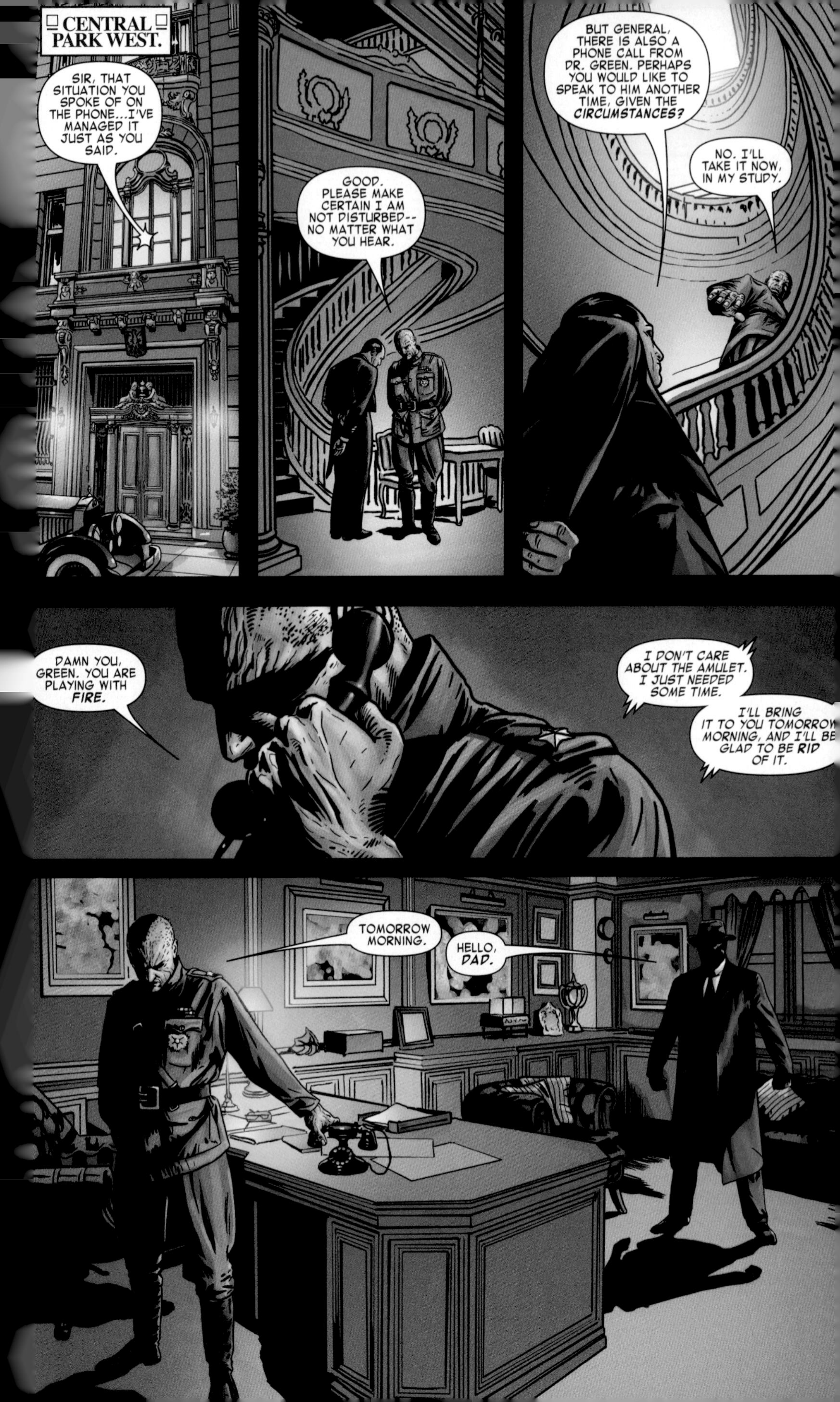
CENTRAL PARK WEST.
SIR, THAT SITUATION YOU SPOKE OF ON THE PHONE...I'VE MANAGED IT JUST AS YOU SAID.
GOOD. PLEASE MAKE CERTAIN I AM NOT DISTURBED-- NO MATTER WHAT YOU HEAR.
BUT GENERAL, THERE IS ALSO A PHONE CALL FROM DR. GREEN. PERHAPS YOU WOULD LIKE TO SPEAK TO HIM ANOTHER TIME, GIVEN THE CIRCUMSTANCES?
NO. I'LL TAKE IT NOW, IN MY STUDY.
DAMN YOU, GREEN. YOU ARE PLAYING WITH FIRE.
I DON'T CARE ABOUT THE AMULET. I JUST NEEDED SOME TIME.
I'LL BRING IT TO YOU TOMORROW MORNING, AND I'LL BE GLAD TO BE RID OF IT.
TOMORROW MORNING.
HELLO, DAD.

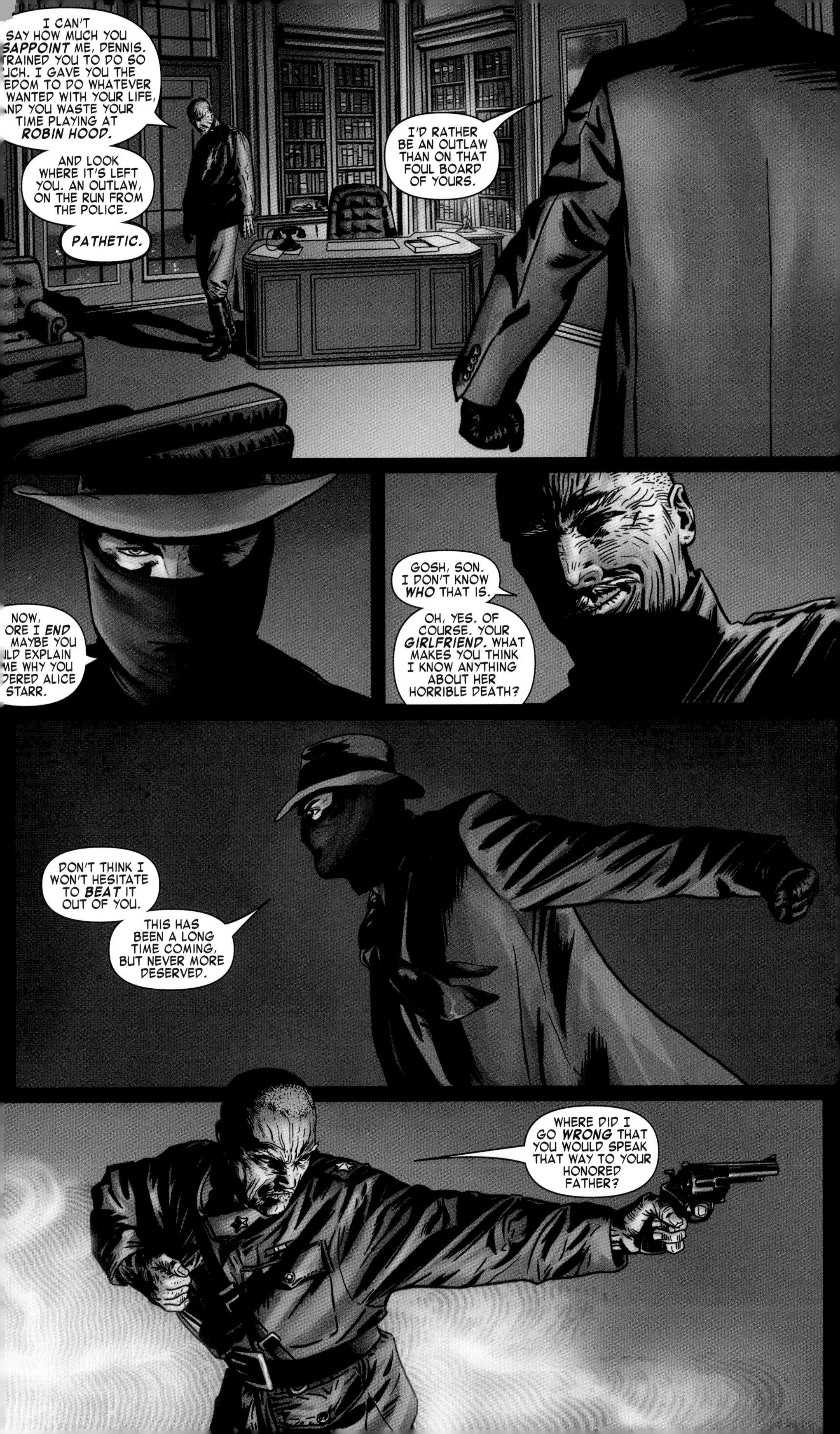
I CAN'T SAY HOW MUCH YOU SAPPOINT ME, DENNIS. TRAINED YOU TO DO SO UCH. I GAVE YOU THE EDOM TO DO WHATEVER WANTED WITH YOUR LIFE, ND YOU WASTE YOUR TIME PLAYING AT ROBIN HOOD.
AND LOOK WHERE IT'S LEFT YOU. AN OUTLAW, ON THE RUN FROM THE POLICE.
PATHETIC.
I'D RATHER BE AN OUTLAW THAN ON THAT FOUL BOARD OF YOURS.
NOW, ORE I END MAYBE YOU LD EXPLAIN ME WHY YOU DERED ALICE STARR.
GOSH, SON. I DON'T KNOW WHO THAT IS.
OH, YES. OF COURSE. YOUR GIRLFRIEND. WHAT MAKES YOU THINK I KNOW ANYTHING ABOUT HER HORRIBLE DEATH?
DON'T THINK I WON'T HESITATE TO BEAT IT OUT OF YOU.
THIS HAS BEEN A LONG TIME COMING, BUT NEVER MORE DESERVED.
WHERE DID I GO WRONG THAT YOU WOULD SPEAK THAT WAY TO YOUR HONORED FATHER?

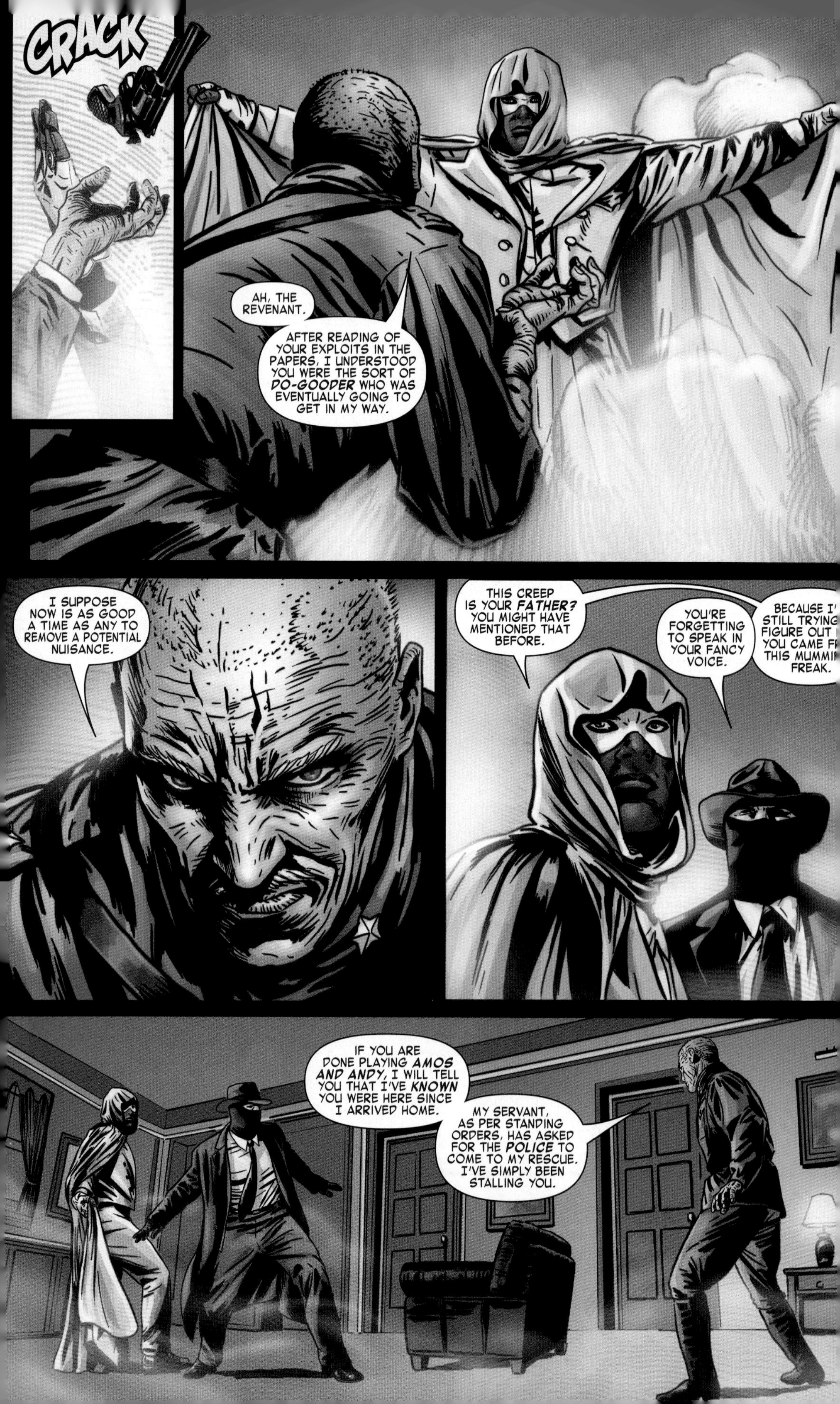
CRACK
AH, THE REVENANT.
AFTER READING OF YOUR EXPLOITS IN THE PAPERS, I UNDERSTOOD YOU WERE THE SORT OF DO-GOODER WHO WAS EVENTUALLY GOING TO GET IN MY WAY.
I SUPPOSE NOW IS AS GOOD A TIME AS ANY TO REMOVE A POTENTIAL NUISANCE.
THIS CREEP IS YOUR FATHER? YOU MIGHT HAVE MENTIONED THAT BEFORE.
YOU'RE FORGETTING TO SPEAK IN YOUR FANCY VOICE.
BECAUSE I' STILL TRYING FIGURE OUT YOU CAME F THIS MUMMI FREAK.
IF YOU ARE DONE PLAYING AMOS AND ANDY, I WILL TELL YOU THAT I'VE KNOWN YOU WERE HERE SINCE I ARRIVED HOME.
MY SERVANT, AS PER STANDING ORDERS, HAS ASKED FOR THE POLICE TO COME TO MY RESCUE. I'VE SIMPLY BEEN STALLING YOU.

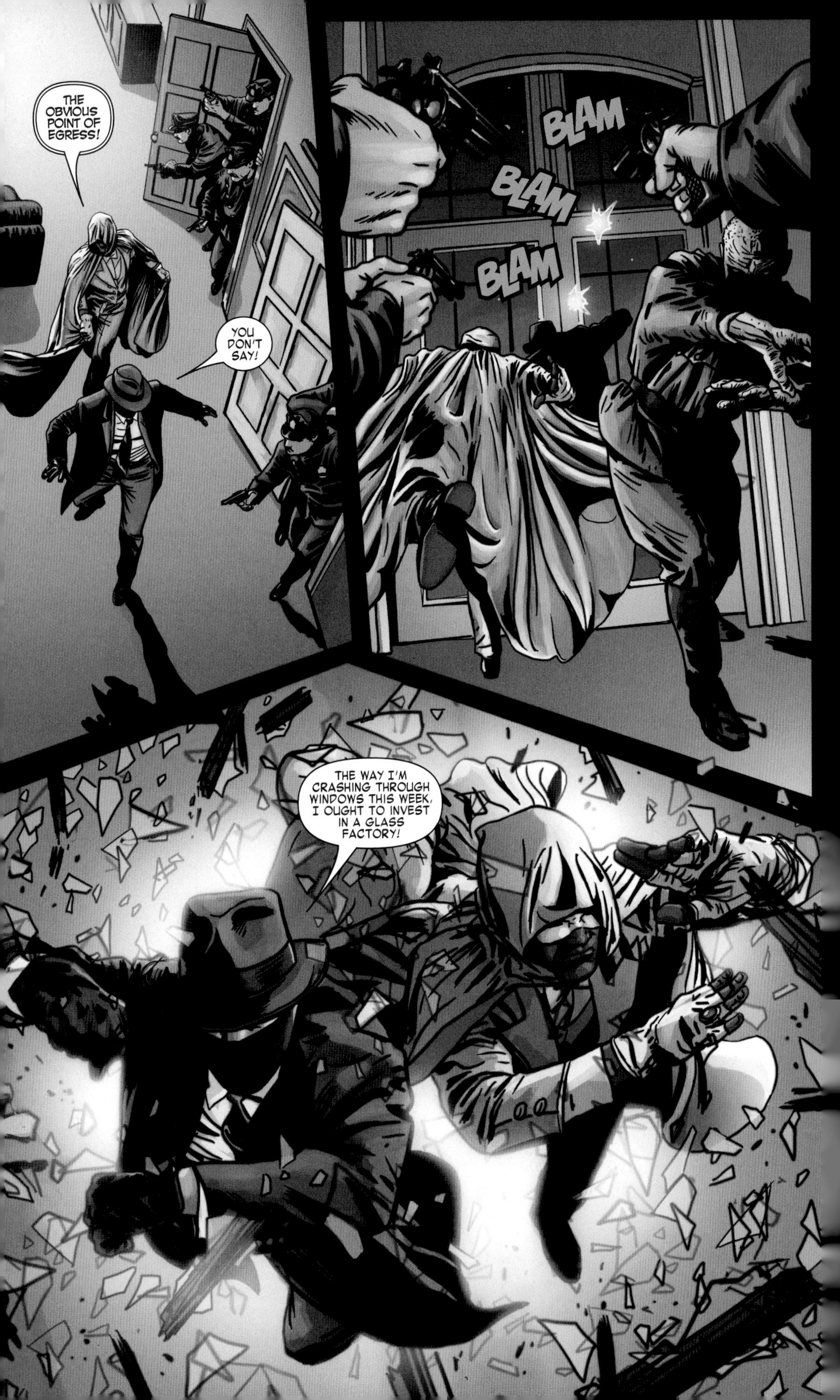
THE OBVIOUS POINT OF EGRESS!
YOU DON'T SAY!
BLAM
BLAM
BLAM
THE WAY I'M CRASHING THROUGH WINDOWS THIS WEEK, I OUGHT TO INVEST IN A GLASS FACTORY!

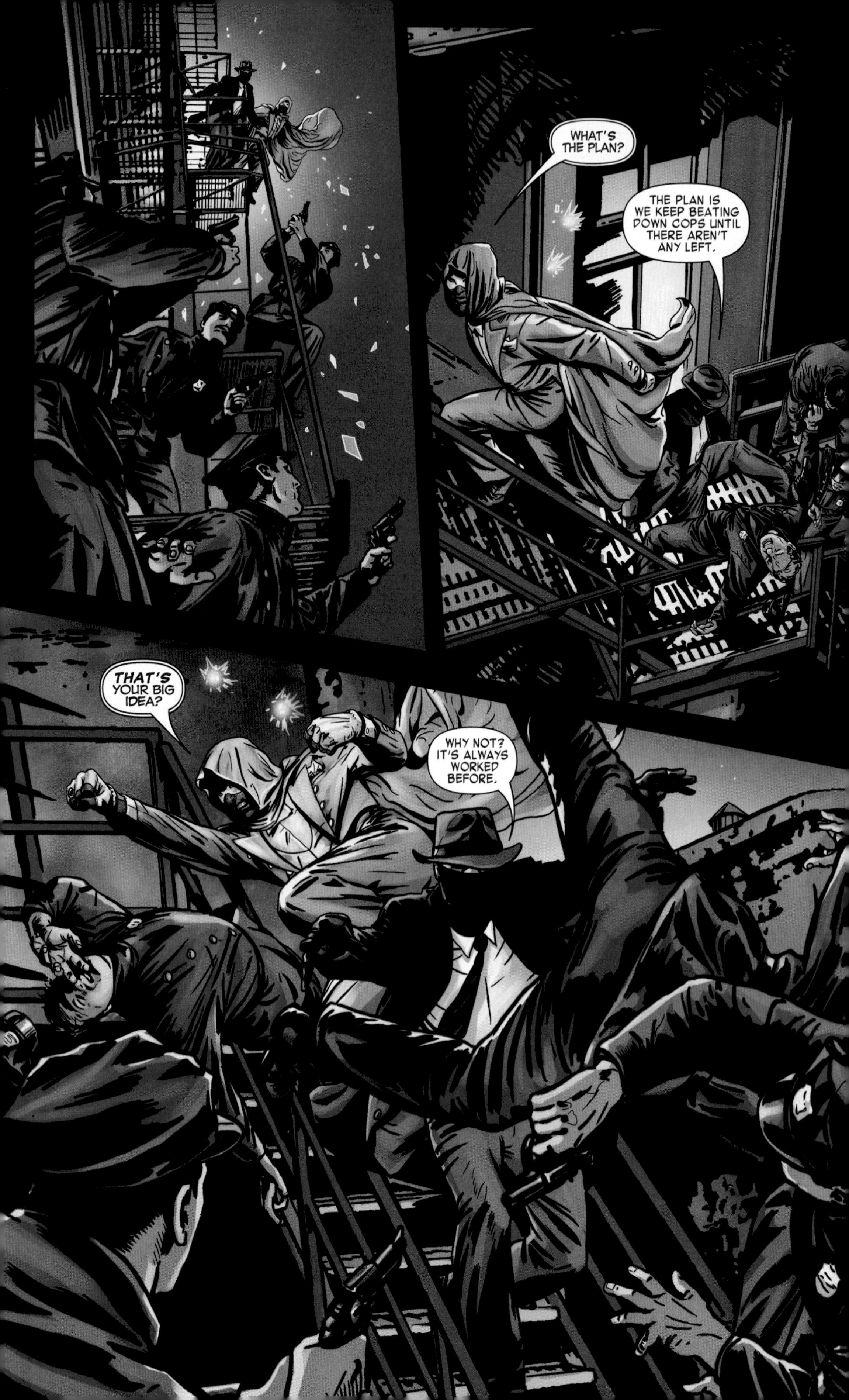

WHAT'S THE PLAN?
THE PLAN IS WE KEEP BEATING DOWN COPS UNTIL THERE AREN'T ANY LEFT.
THAT'S YOUR BIG IDEA?
WHY NOT? IT'S ALWAYS WORKED BEFORE.

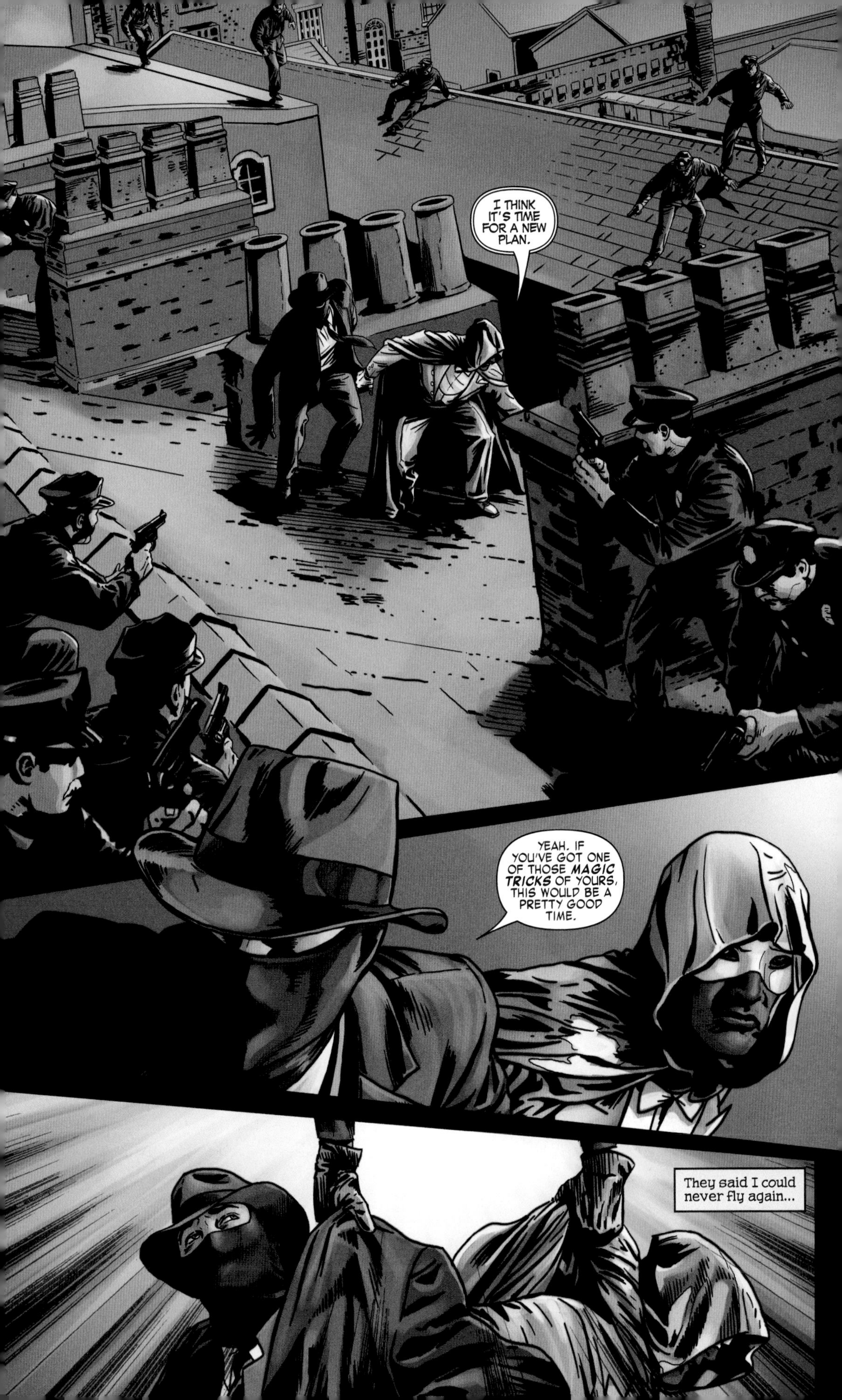

I THINK IT'S TIME FOR A NEW PLAN.
YEAH. IF YOU'VE GOT ONE OF THOSE MAGIC TRICKS OF YOURS, THIS WOULD BE A PRETTY GOOD TIME.
They said I could never fly again...

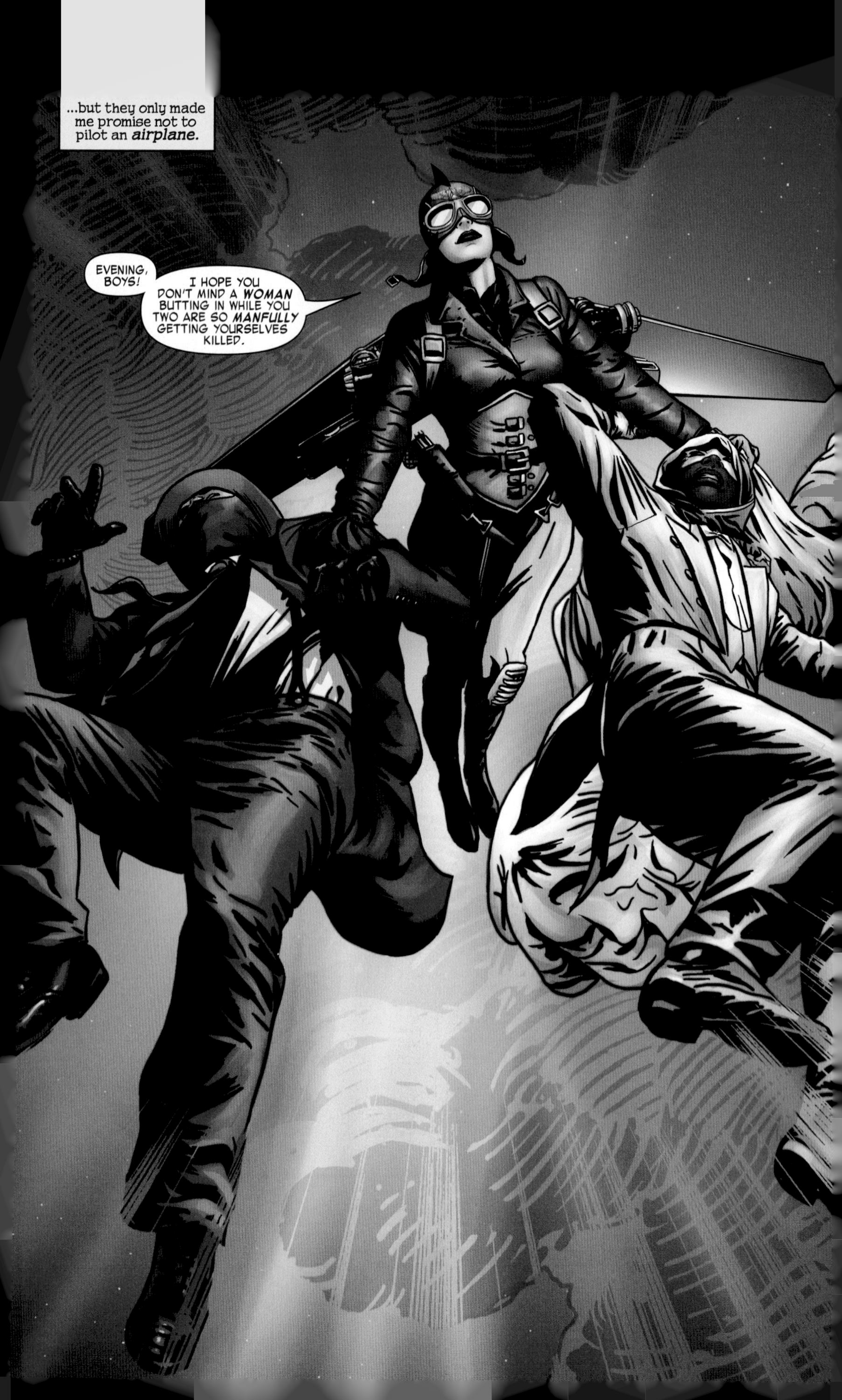

...but they only made me promise not to pilot an *airplane.*
EVENING, BOYS!
I HOPE YOU DON'T MIND A *WOMAN* BUTTING IN WHILE YOU TWO ARE SO *MANFULLY* GETTING YOURSELVES KILLED.

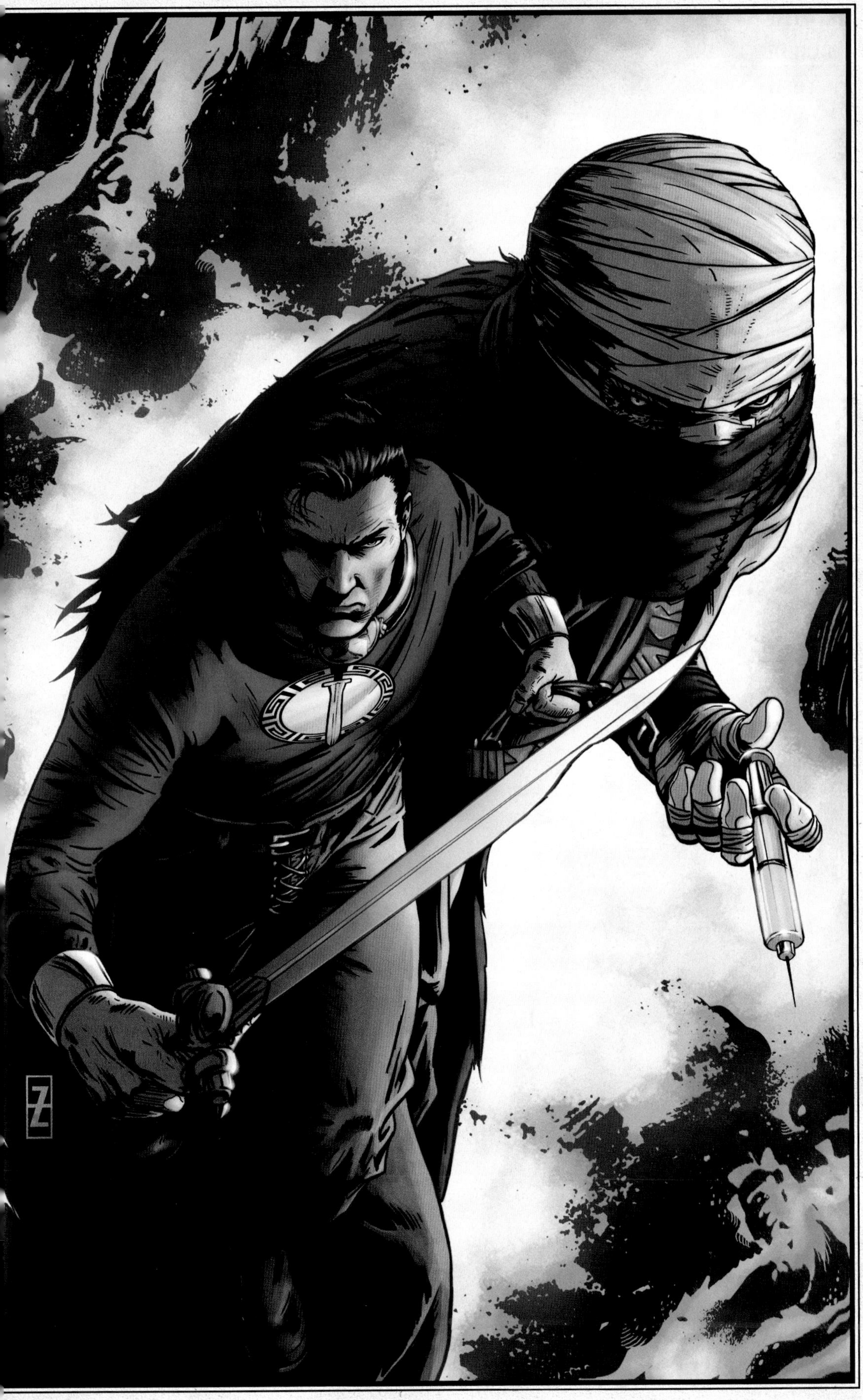

MYSTERY MEN #3

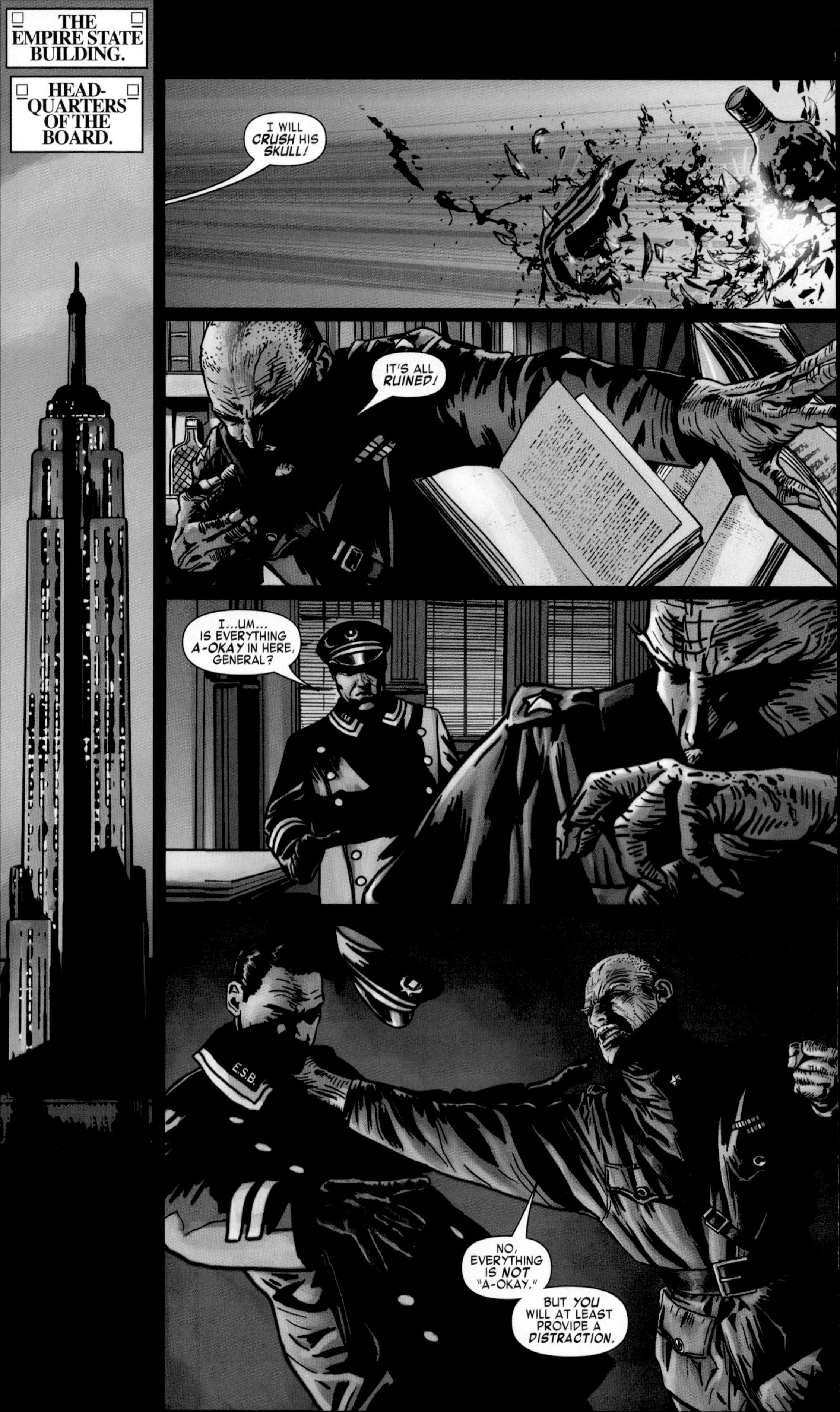
THE EMPIRE STATE BUILDING.
HEAD-QUARTERS OF THE BOARD.
I WILL CRUSH HIS SKULL!
IT'S ALL RUINED!
I...UM... IS EVERYTHING A-OKAY IN HERE, GENERAL?
NO, EVERYTHING IS NOT "A-OKAY."
BUT YOU WILL AT LEAST PROVIDE A DISTRACTION.

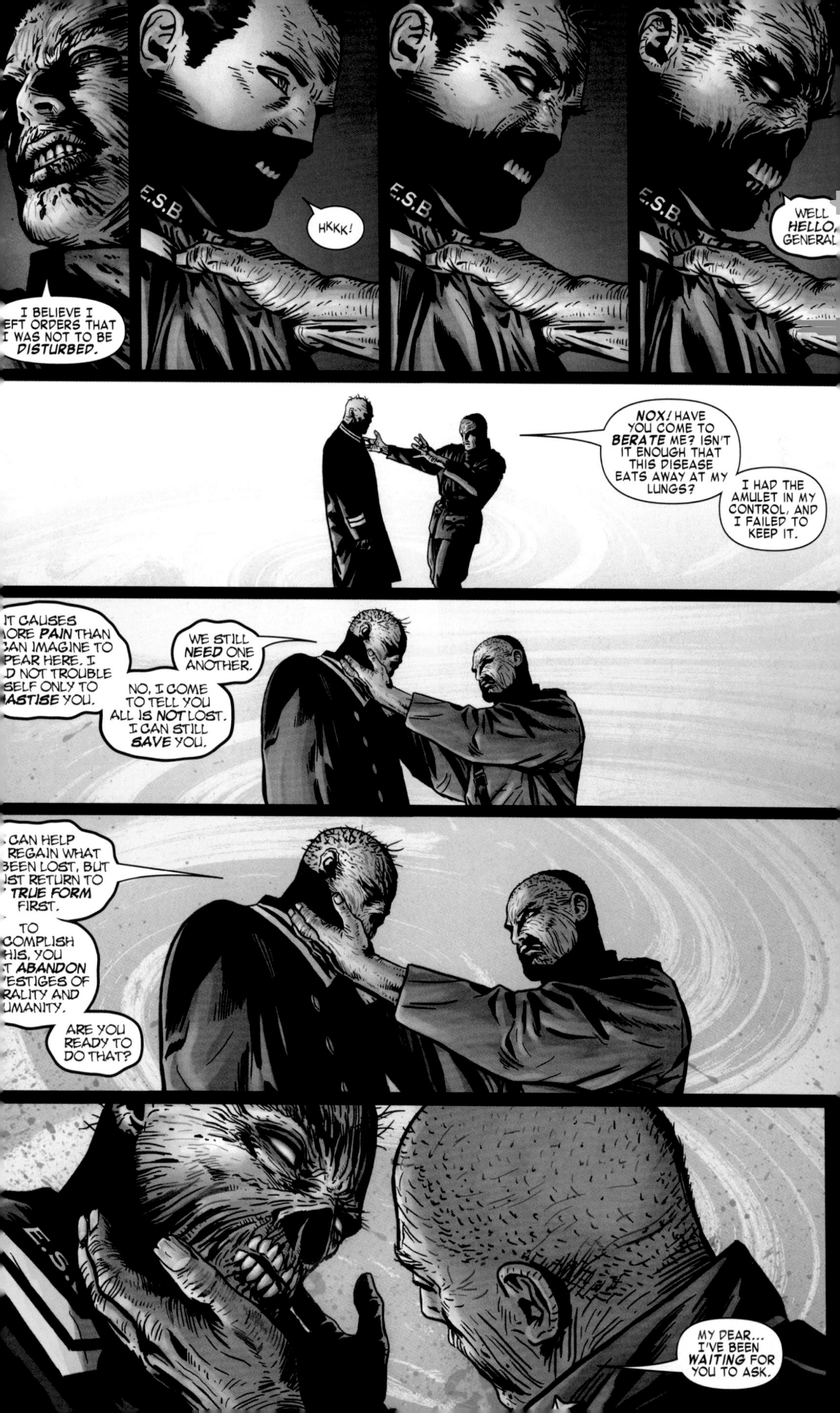
I BELIEVE I
EFT ORDERS THAT
I WAS NOT TO BE
DISTURBED.
HKKK!
WELL
HELLO,
GENERAL
NOX! HAVE
YOU COME TO
BERATE ME? ISN'T
IT ENOUGH THAT
THIS DISEASE
EATS AWAY AT MY
LUNGS?
I HAD THE
AMULET IN MY
CONTROL, AND
I FAILED TO
KEEP IT.
IT CAUSES
ORE PAIN THAN
CAN IMAGINE TO
PEAR HERE. I
D NOT TROUBLE
SELF ONLY TO
ASTISE YOU.
WE STILL
NEED ONE
ANOTHER.
NO, I COME
TO TELL YOU
ALL IS NOT LOST.
I CAN STILL
SAVE YOU.
CAN HELP
REGAIN WHAT
BEEN LOST, BUT
ST RETURN TO
TRUE FORM
FIRST.
TO
COMPLISH
HIS, YOU
T ABANDON
VESTIGES OF
RALITY AND
UMANITY.
ARE YOU
READY TO
DO THAT?
MY DEAR...
I'VE BEEN
WAITING FOR
YOU TO ASK.

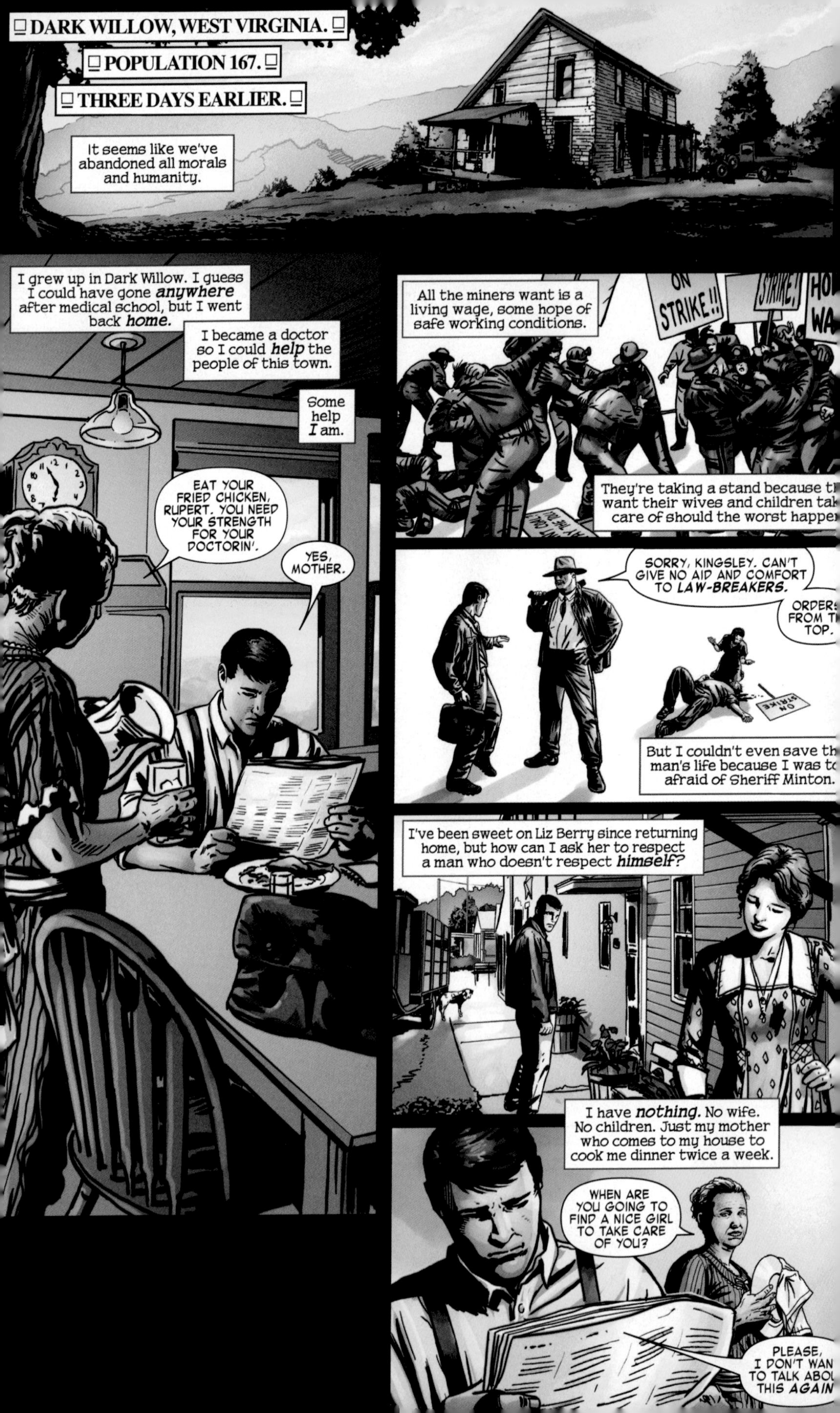
DARK WILLOW, WEST VIRGINIA.
POPULATION 167.
THREE DAYS EARLIER.
It seems like we've abandoned all morals and humanity.
I grew up in Dark Willow. I guess I could have gone *anywhere* after medical school, but I went back *home.*
I became a doctor so I could *help* the people of this town.
Some help *I* am.
EAT YOUR FRIED CHICKEN, RUPERT. YOU NEED YOUR STRENGTH FOR YOUR DOCTORIN'.
YES, MOTHER.
All the miners want is a living wage, some hope of safe working conditions.
ON STRIKE!!
STRIKE!
They're taking a stand because th
want their wives and children tak
care of should the worst happe
SORRY, KINGSLEY. CAN'T GIVE NO AID AND COMFORT TO *LAW-BREAKERS.*
ORDERS FROM T TOP.
ON STRIKE
But I couldn't even save th man's life because I was to afraid of Sheriff Minton.
I've been sweet on Liz Berry since returning home, but how can I ask her to respect a man who doesn't respect *himself?*
I have *nothing.* No wife. No children. Just my mother who comes to my house to cook me dinner twice a week.
WHEN ARE YOU GOING TO FIND A NICE GIRL TO TAKE CARE OF YOU?
PLEASE, I DON'T WAN TO TALK ABO THIS *AGAIN*

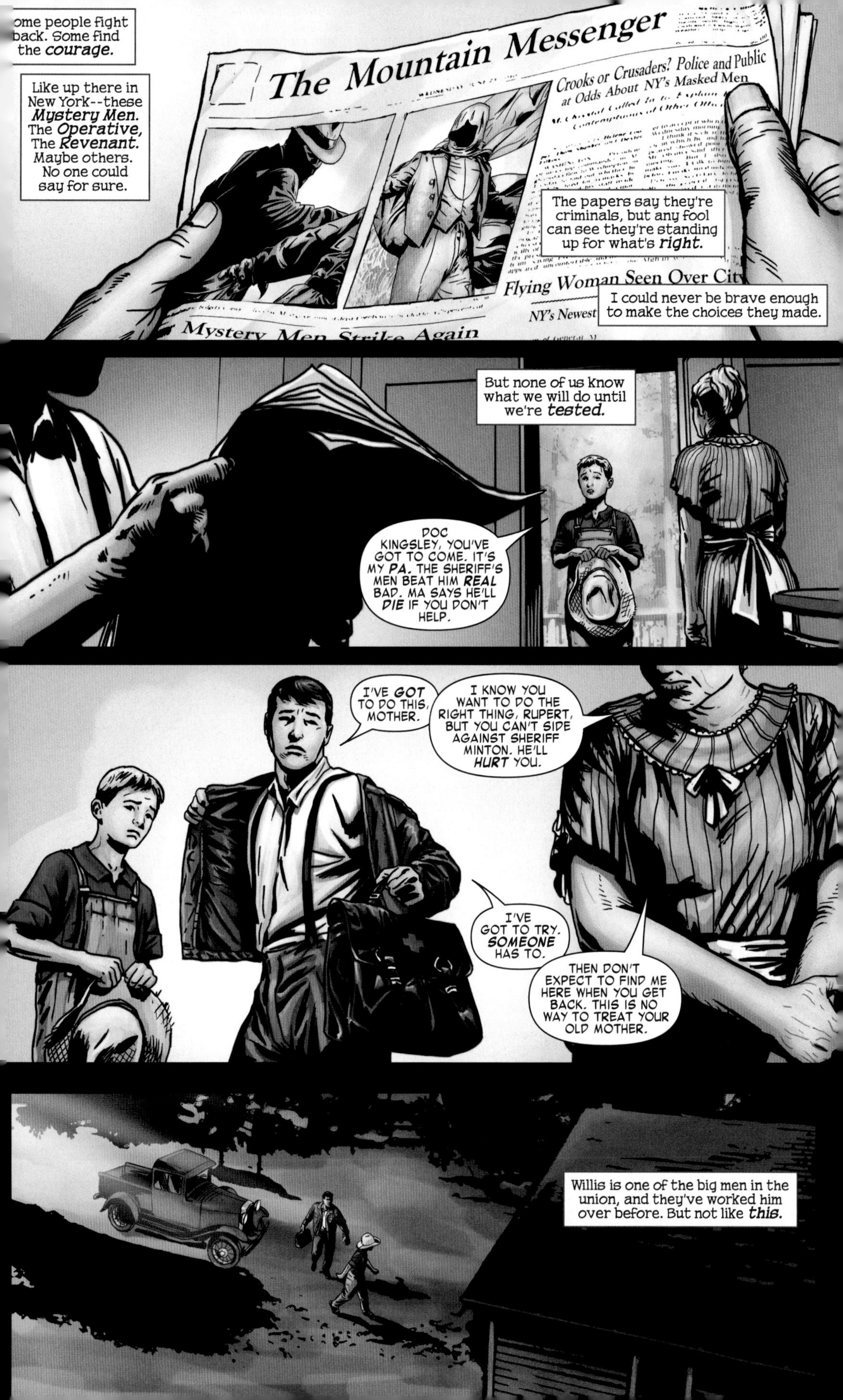

ome people fight back. Some find the courage.
Like up there in New York--these Mystery Men. The Operative, The Revenant. Maybe others. No one could say for sure.
The Mountain Messenger
Crooks or Crusaders? Police and Public at Odds About NY's Masked Men
The papers say they're criminals, but any fool can see they're standing up for what's right.
Flying Woman Seen Over City
I could never be brave enough to make the choices they made.
Mystery Men Strike Again
But none of us know what we will do until we're tested.
DOC KINGSLEY, YOU'VE GOT TO COME. IT'S MY PA. THE SHERIFF'S MEN BEAT HIM REAL BAD. MA SAYS HE'LL DIE IF YOU DON'T HELP.
I'VE GOT TO DO THIS, MOTHER.
I KNOW YOU WANT TO DO THE RIGHT THING, RUPERT, BUT YOU CAN'T SIDE AGAINST SHERIFF MINTON. HE'LL HURT YOU.
I'VE GOT TO TRY. SOMEONE HAS TO.
THEN DON'T EXPECT TO FIND ME HERE WHEN YOU GET BACK. THIS IS NO WAY TO TREAT YOUR OLD MOTHER.
Willis is one of the big men in the union, and they've worked him over before. But not like this.

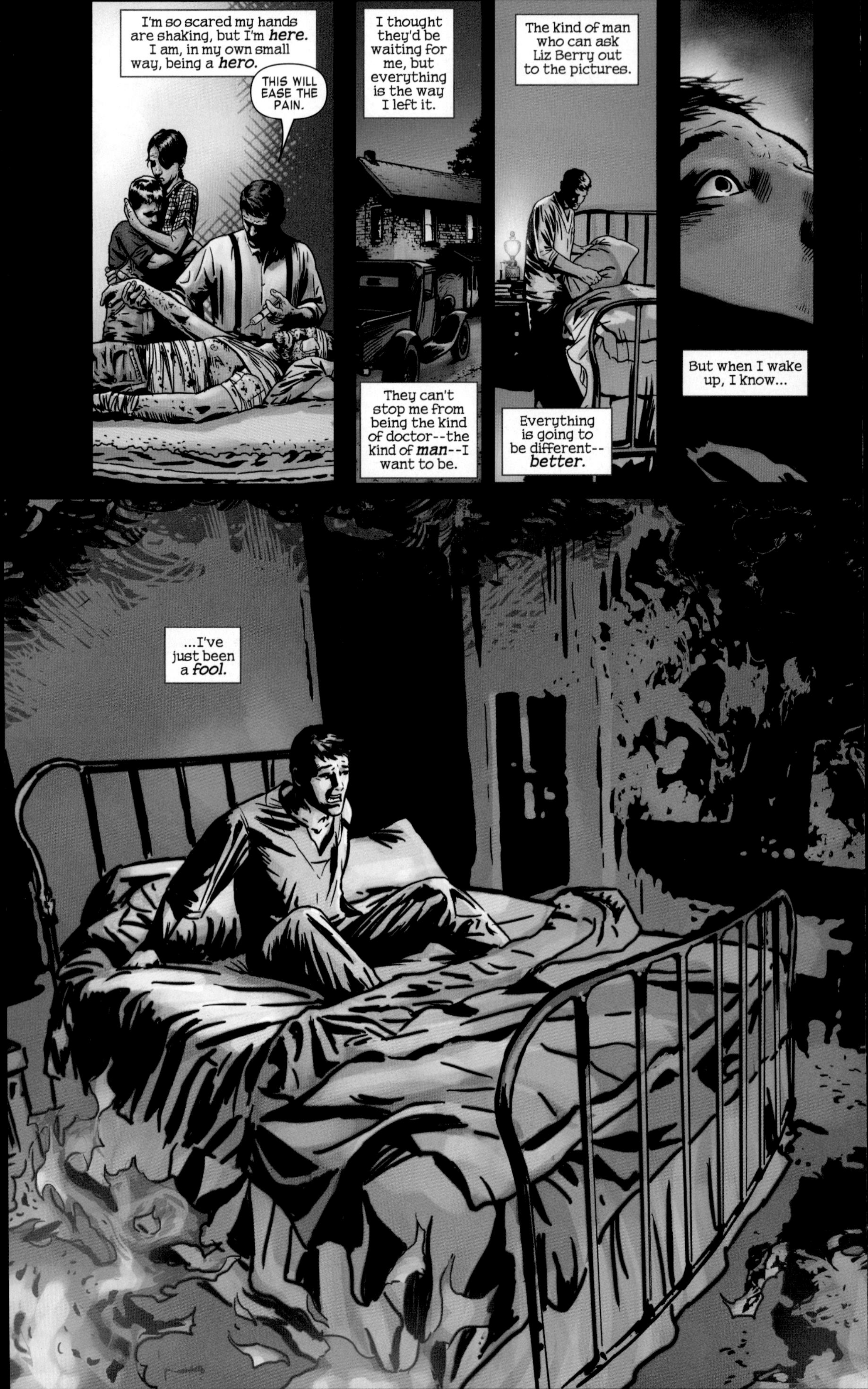
I'm so scared my hands are shaking, but I'm *here*. I am, in my own small way, being a *hero*.
THIS WILL EASE THE PAIN.
I thought they'd be waiting for me, but everything is the way I left it.
They can't stop me from being the kind of doctor--the kind of *man*--I want to be.
The kind of man who can ask Liz Berry out to the pictures.
Everything is going to be different--*better*.
But when I wake up, I know...
...I've just been a *fool*.

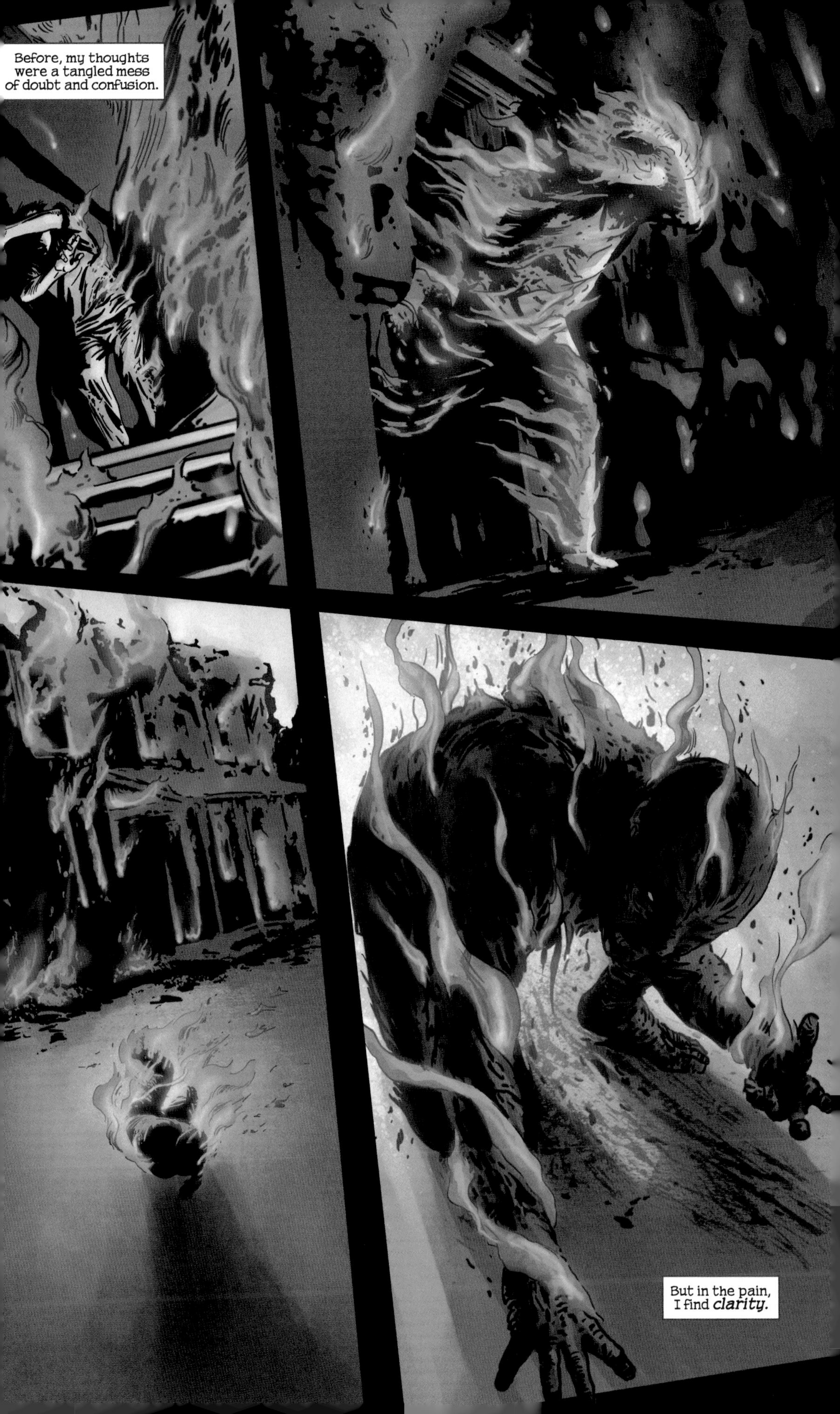
Before, my thoughts were a tangled mess of doubt and confusion.
But in the pain, I find *clarity*.

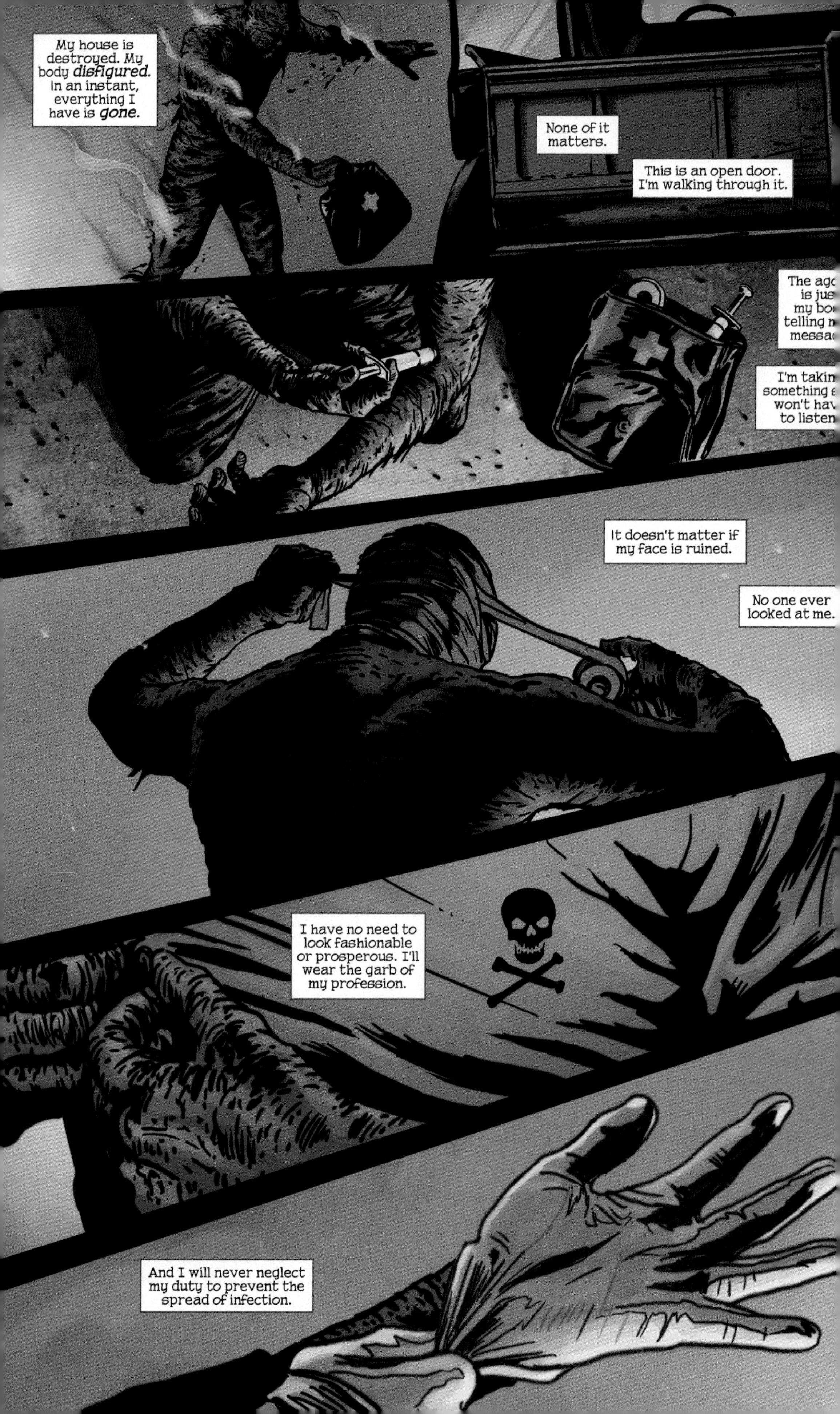
My house is destroyed. My body *disfigured.* In an instant, everything I have is *gone.*
None of it matters.
This is an open door. I'm walking through it.
The ag is jus my bo telling n messa
I'm takin something e won't hav to listen
It doesn't matter if my face is ruined.
No one ever looked at me.
I have no need to look fashionable or prosperous. I'll wear the garb of my profession.
And I will never neglect my duty to prevent the spread of infection.

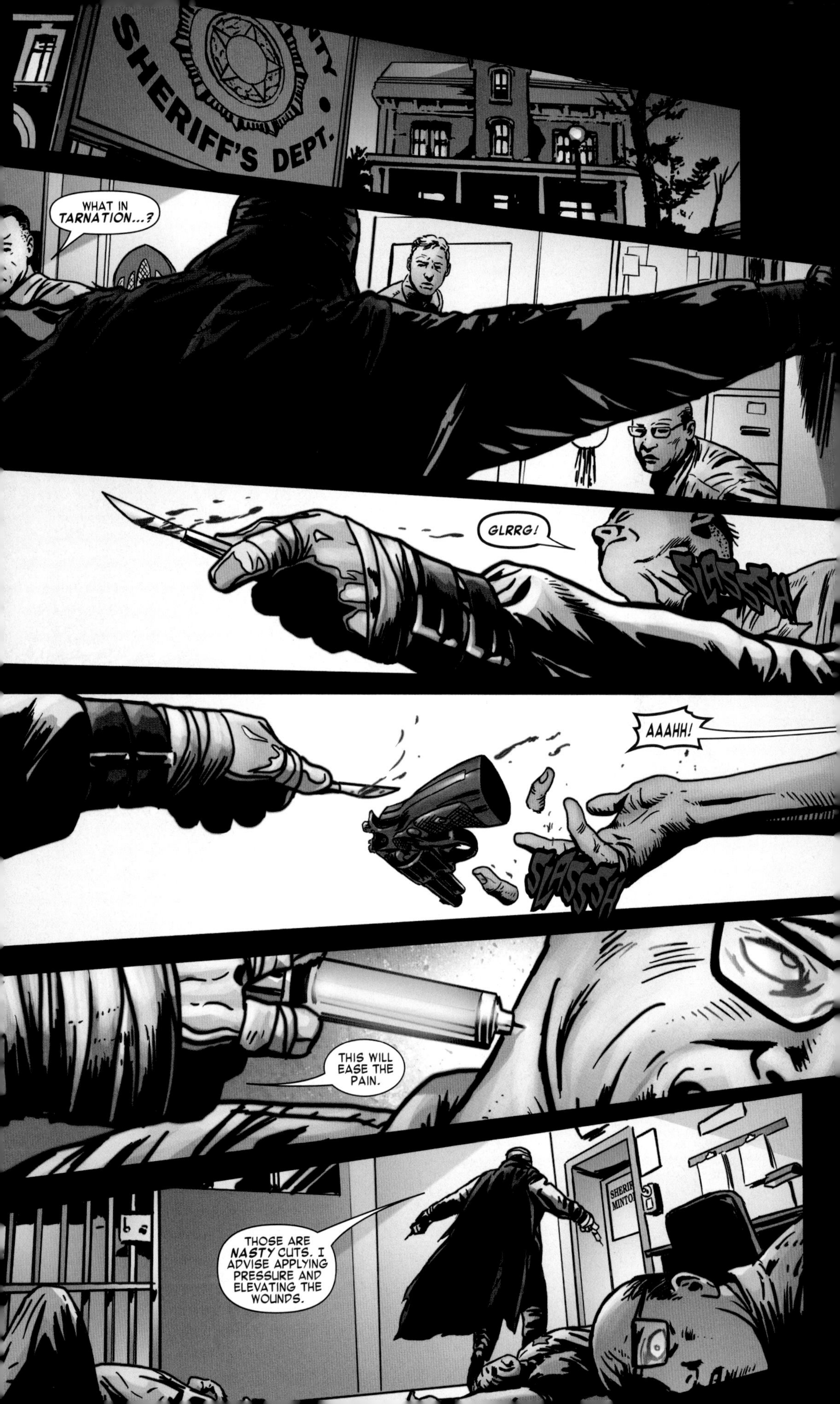
SHERIFF'S DEPT.
WHAT IN TARNATION...?
GLRRG!
SLASSSH
AAAHH!
SLASSSH
THIS WILL EASE THE PAIN.
THOSE ARE NASTY CUTS. I ADVISE APPLYING PRESSURE AND ELEVATING THE WOUNDS.
SHERIFF MINTON

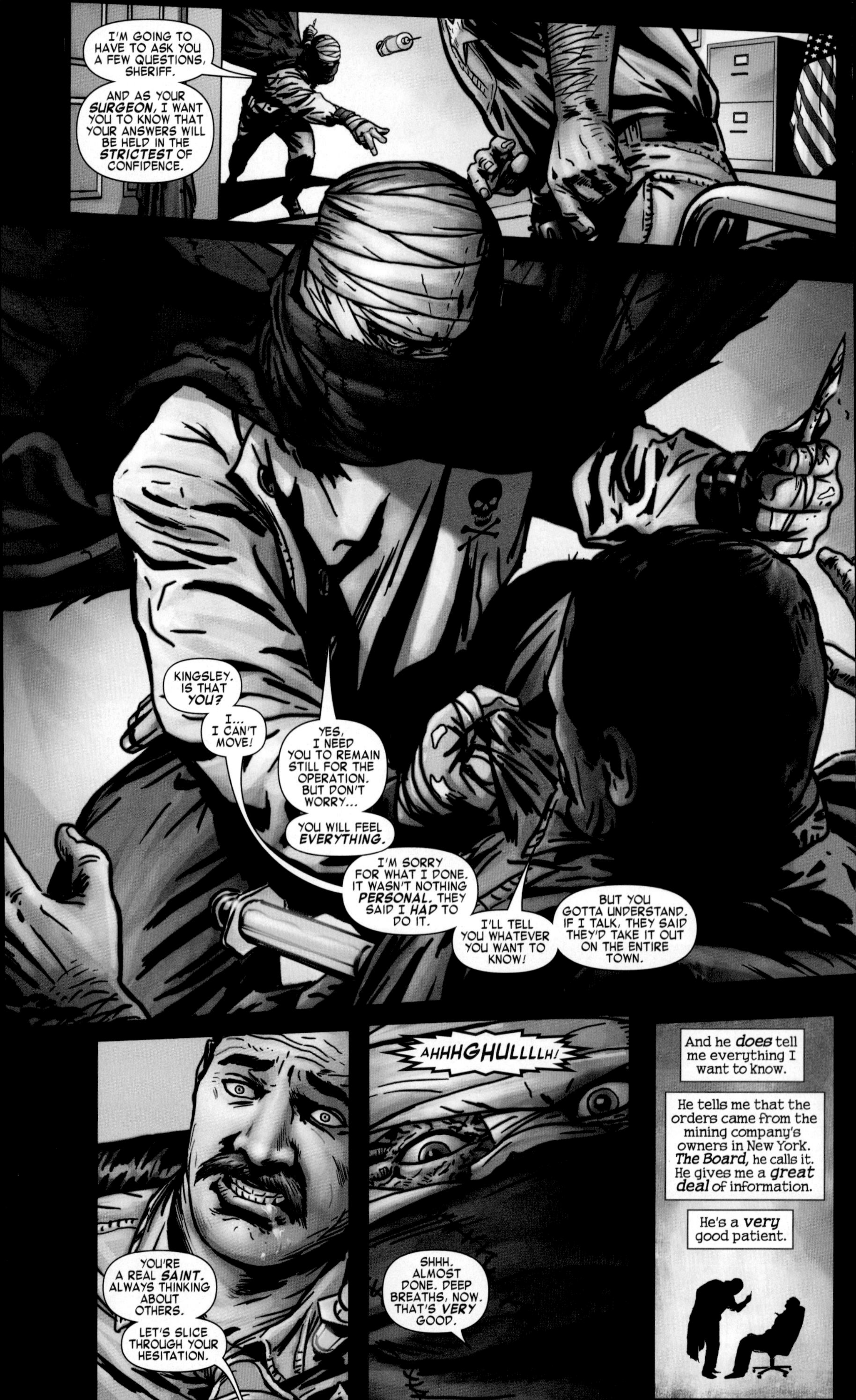

I'M GOING TO HAVE TO ASK YOU A FEW QUESTIONS, SHERIFF.
AND AS YOUR SURGEON, I WANT YOU TO KNOW THAT YOUR ANSWERS WILL BE HELD IN THE STRICTEST OF CONFIDENCE.
KINGSLEY. IS THAT YOU?
I... I CAN'T MOVE!
YES, I NEED YOU TO REMAIN STILL FOR THE OPERATION. BUT DON'T WORRY...
YOU WILL FEEL EVERYTHING.
I'M SORRY FOR WHAT I DONE. IT WASN'T NOTHING PERSONAL. THEY SAID I HAD TO DO IT.
I'LL TELL YOU WHATEVER YOU WANT TO KNOW!
BUT YOU GOTTA UNDERSTAND. IF I TALK, THEY SAID THEY'D TAKE IT OUT ON THE ENTIRE TOWN.
YOU'RE A REAL SAINT. ALWAYS THINKING ABOUT OTHERS.
LET'S SLICE THROUGH YOUR HESITATION.
AHHHGHULLLLLH!
SHHH. ALMOST DONE. DEEP BREATHS, NOW. THAT'S VERY GOOD.
And he does tell me everything I want to know.
He tells me that the orders came from the mining company's owners in New York. The Board, he calls it. He gives me a great deal of information.
He's a very good patient.

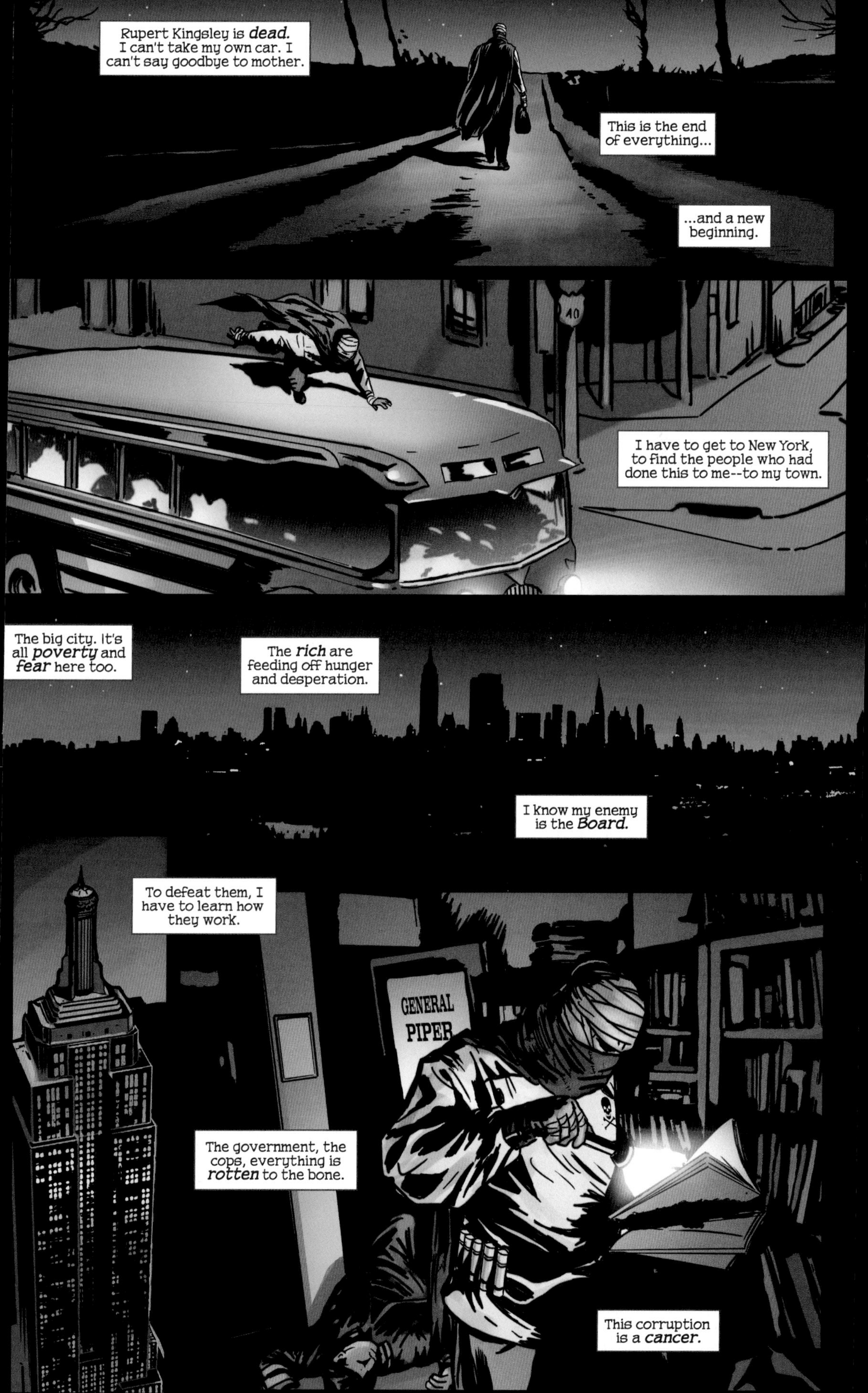
Rupert Kingsley is *dead.* I can't take my own car. I can't say goodbye to mother.
This is the end of everything...
...and a new beginning.
40
I have to get to New York, to find the people who had done this to me--to my town.
The big city. It's all *poverty* and *fear* here too.
The *rich* are feeding off hunger and desperation.
I know my enemy is the *Board.*
To defeat them, I have to learn how they work.
GENERAL PIPER
The government, the cops, everything is *rotten* to the bone.
This corruption is a *cancer.*

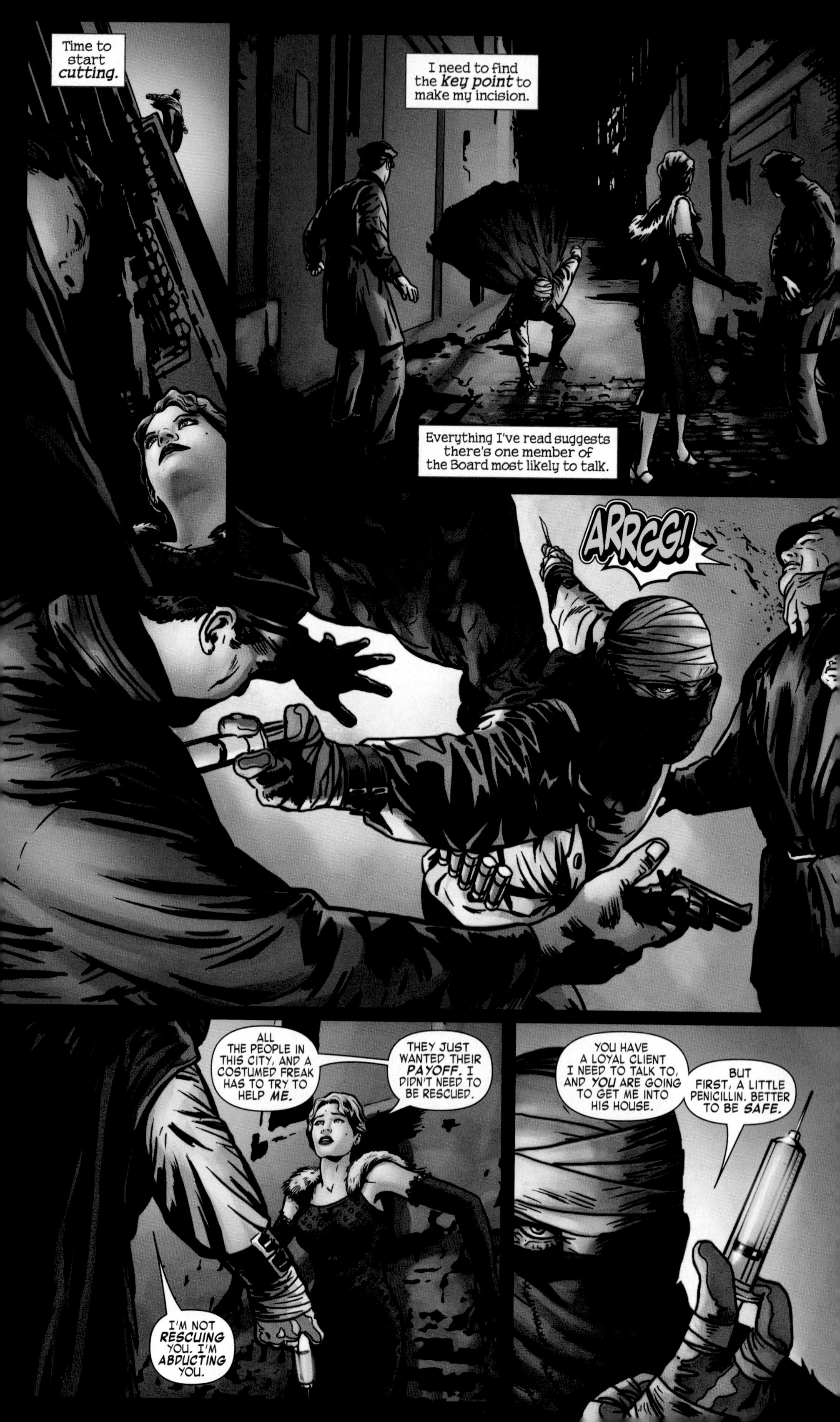
Time to start *cutting.*
I need to find the *key point* to make my incision.
Everything I've read suggests there's one member of the Board most likely to talk.
ARRGG!
ALL THE PEOPLE IN THIS CITY, AND A COSTUMED FREAK HAS TO TRY TO HELP *ME.*
THEY JUST WANTED THEIR *PAYOFF.* I DIDN'T NEED TO BE RESCUED.
I'M NOT *RESCUING* YOU. I'M *ABDUCTING* YOU.
YOU HAVE A LOYAL CLIENT I NEED TO TALK TO, AND *YOU* ARE GOING TO GET ME INTO HIS HOUSE.
BUT FIRST, A LITTLE PENICILLIN. BETTER TO BE *SAFE.*

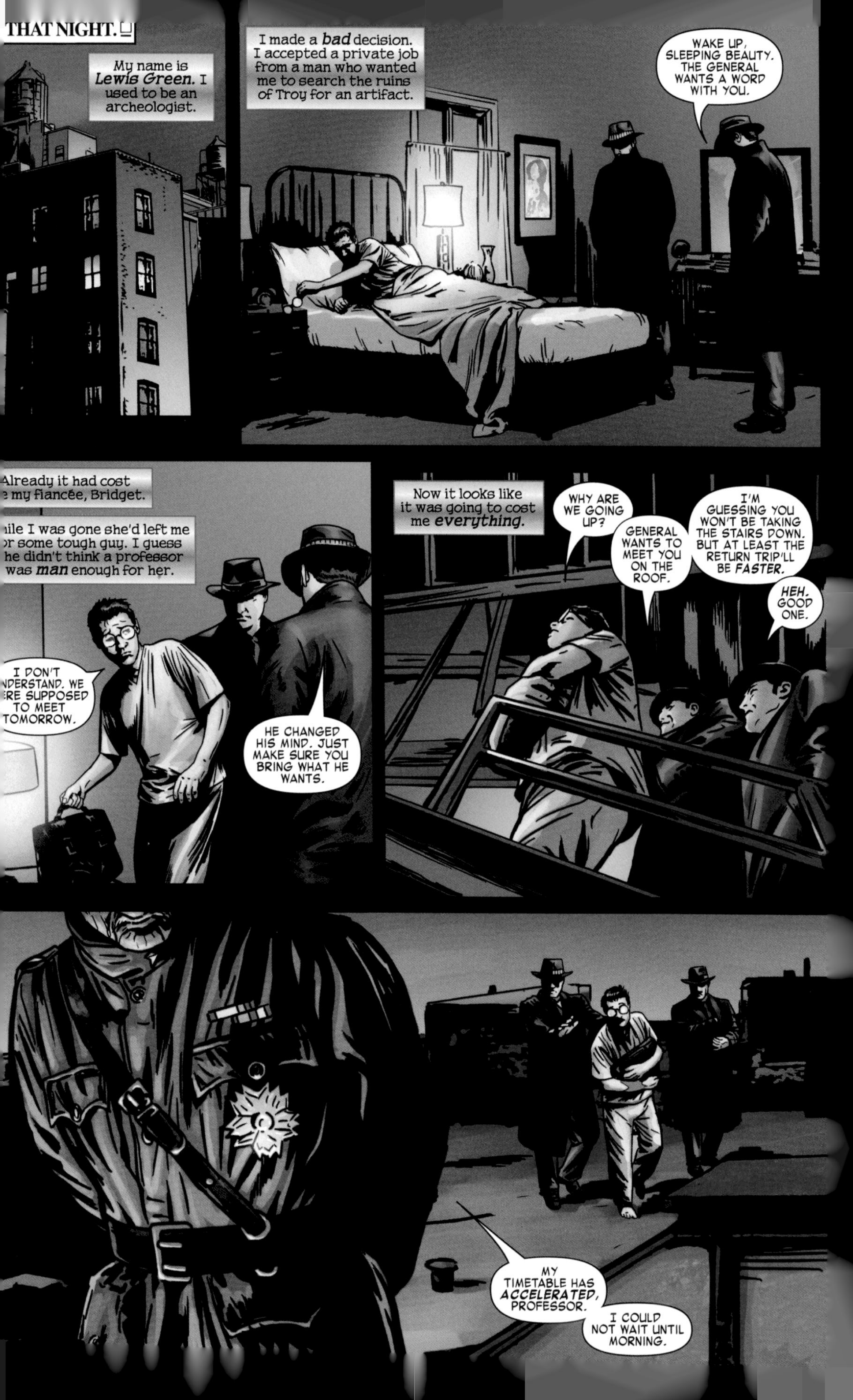
THAT NIGHT.
My name is *Lewis Green.* I used to be an archeologist.
I made a **bad** decision. I accepted a private job from a man who wanted me to search the ruins of Troy for an artifact.
WAKE UP, SLEEPING BEAUTY. THE GENERAL WANTS A WORD WITH YOU.
Already it had cost
e my fiancée, Bridget.
hile I was gone she'd left me
or some tough guy. I guess
he didn't think a professor
was *man* enough for her.
I DON'T
NDERSTAND. WE
ERE SUPPOSED
TO MEET
TOMORROW.
HE CHANGED HIS MIND. JUST MAKE SURE YOU BRING WHAT HE WANTS.
Now it looks like it was going to cost me *everything.*
WHY ARE WE GOING UP?
GENERAL WANTS TO MEET YOU ON THE ROOF.
I'M GUESSING YOU WON'T BE TAKING THE STAIRS DOWN. BUT AT LEAST THE RETURN TRIP'LL BE *FASTER.*
HEH. GOOD ONE.
MY TIMETABLE HAS *ACCELERATED,* PROFESSOR.
I COULD NOT WAIT UNTIL MORNING.

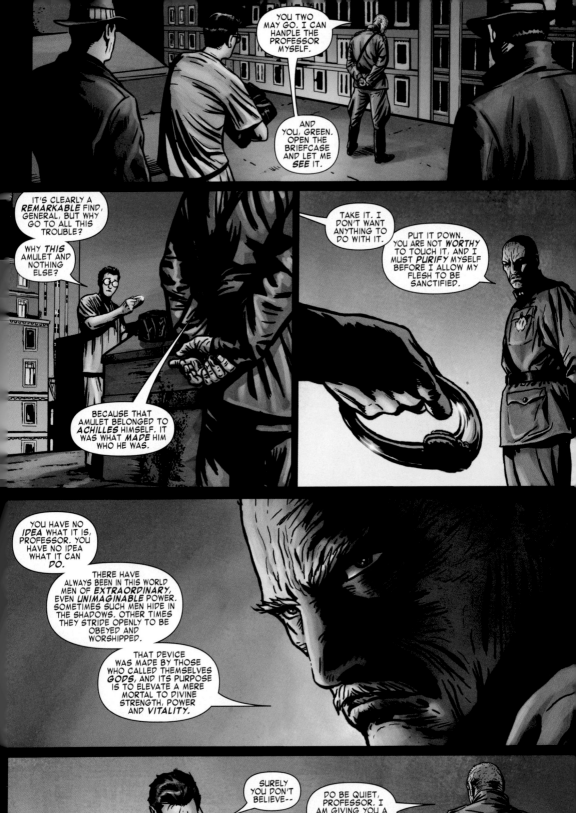

YOU TWO MAY GO. I CAN HANDLE THE PROFESSOR MYSELF.

AND YOU, GREEN. OPEN THE BRIEFCASE AND LET ME *SEE* IT.

IT'S CLEARLY A *REMARKABLE* FIND, GENERAL, BUT WHY GO TO ALL THIS TROUBLE?

WHY *THIS* AMULET AND NOTHING ELSE?

BECAUSE THAT AMULET BELONGED TO *ACHILLES* HIMSELF. IT WAS WHAT *MADE* HIM WHO HE WAS.

TAKE IT. I DON'T WANT ANYTHING TO DO WITH IT.

PUT IT DOWN. YOU ARE NOT *WORTHY* TO TOUCH IT, AND I MUST *PURIFY* MYSELF BEFORE I ALLOW MY FLESH TO BE SANCTIFIED.

YOU HAVE NO *IDEA* WHAT IT IS, PROFESSOR. YOU HAVE NO IDEA WHAT IT CAN *DO*.

THERE HAVE ALWAYS BEEN IN THIS WORLD MEN OF *EXTRAORDINARY*, EVEN *UNIMAGINABLE* POWER. SOMETIMES SUCH MEN HIDE IN THE SHADOWS. OTHER TIMES THEY STRIDE OPENLY TO BE OBEYED AND WORSHIPPED.

THAT DEVICE WAS MADE BY THOSE WHO CALLED THEMSELVES *GODS*, AND ITS PURPOSE IS TO ELEVATE A MERE MORTAL TO DIVINE STRENGTH, POWER AND *VITALITY*.

SURELY YOU DON'T BELIEVE--

DO BE QUIET, PROFESSOR. I AM GIVING YOU A PARTING GIFT OF *KNOWLEDGE*.

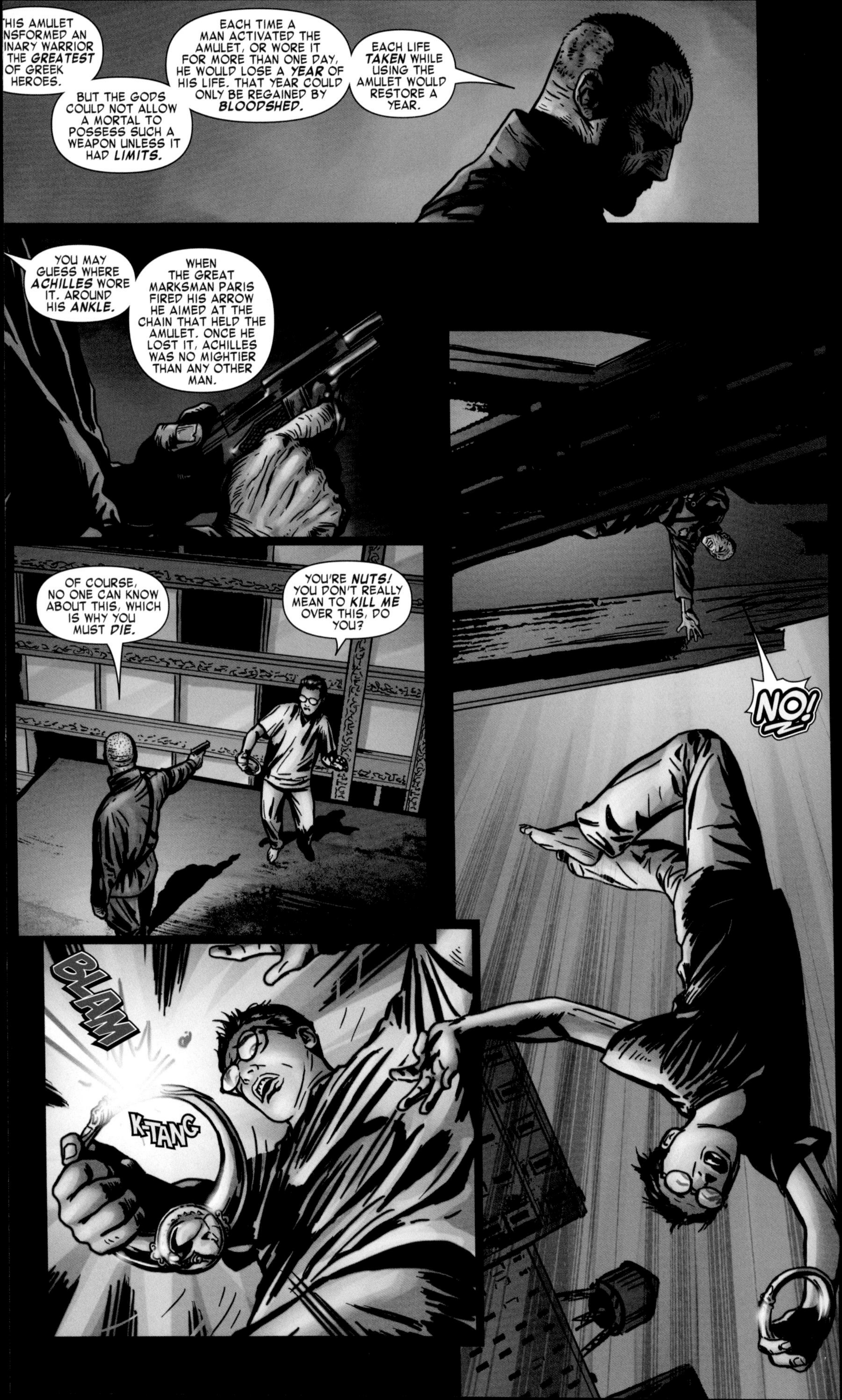

THIS AMULET
NSFORMED AN
INARY WARRIOR
THE GREATEST
OF GREEK
HEROES.
BUT THE GODS COULD NOT ALLOW A MORTAL TO POSSESS SUCH A WEAPON UNLESS IT HAD LIMITS.
EACH TIME A MAN ACTIVATED THE AMULET, OR WORE IT FOR MORE THAN ONE DAY, HE WOULD LOSE A YEAR OF HIS LIFE. THAT YEAR COULD ONLY BE REGAINED BY BLOODSHED.
EACH LIFE TAKEN WHILE USING THE AMULET WOULD RESTORE A YEAR.
YOU MAY GUESS WHERE ACHILLES WORE IT. AROUND HIS ANKLE.
WHEN THE GREAT MARKSMAN PARIS FIRED HIS ARROW HE AIMED AT THE CHAIN THAT HELD THE AMULET. ONCE HE LOST IT, ACHILLES WAS NO MIGHTIER THAN ANY OTHER MAN.
OF COURSE, NO ONE CAN KNOW ABOUT THIS, WHICH IS WHY YOU MUST DIE.
YOU'RE NUTS! YOU DON'T REALLY MEAN TO KILL ME OVER THIS, DO YOU?
NO!
BLAM
K-TANG

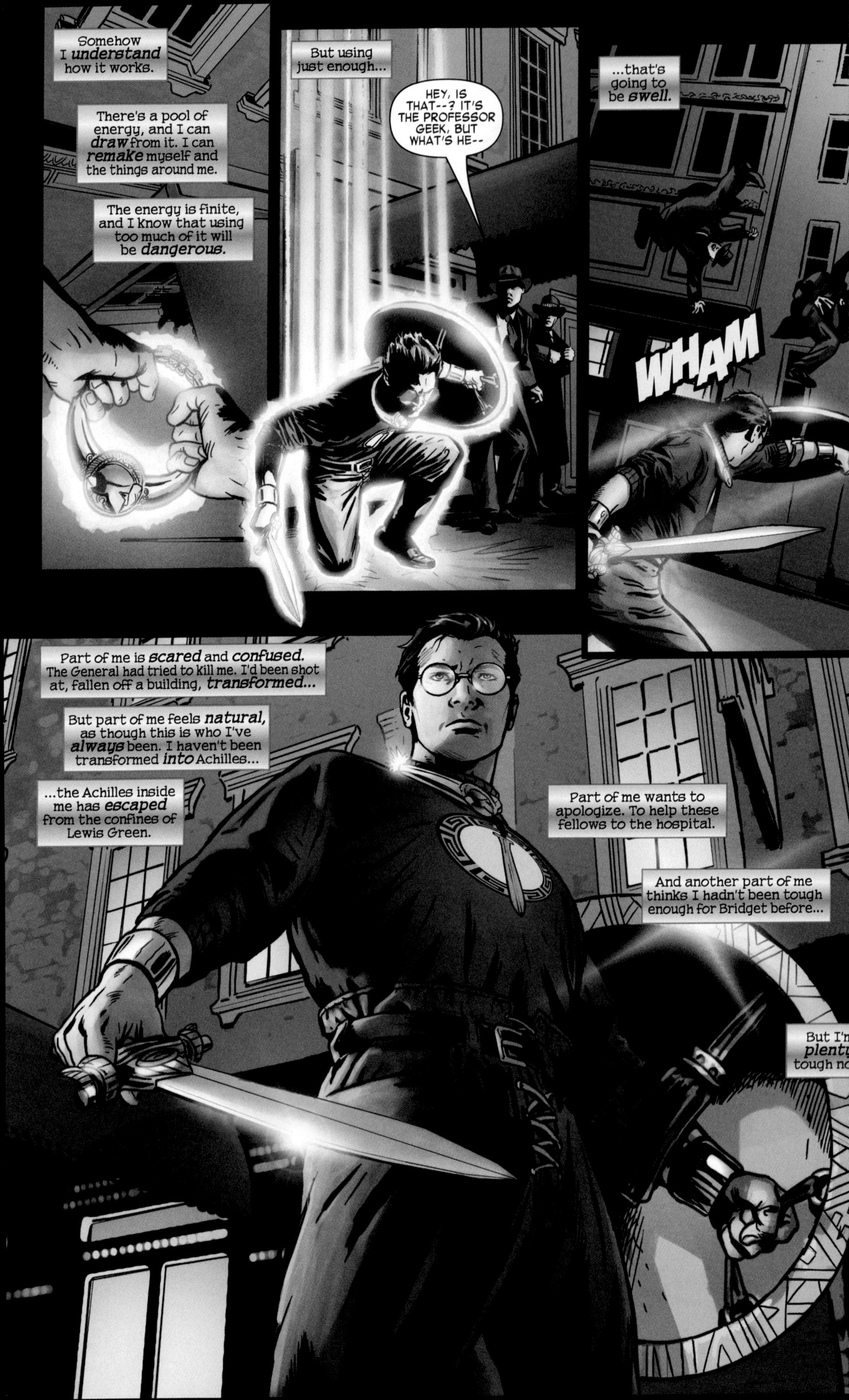
Somehow I *understand* how it works.
There's a pool of energy, and I can *draw* from it. I can *remake* myself and the things around me.
The energy is finite, and I know that using too much of it will be *dangerous.*
But using just enough...
HEY, IS THAT--? IT'S THE PROFESSOR GEEK, BUT WHAT'S HE--
...that's going to be *swell.*
WHAM
Part of me is *scared* and *confused.* The General had tried to kill me. I'd been shot at, fallen off a building, *transformed...*
But part of me feels *natural,* as though this is who I've *always* been. I haven't been transformed *into* Achilles...
...the Achilles inside me has *escaped* from the confines of Lewis Green.
Part of me wants to apologize. To help these fellows to the hospital.
And another part of me thinks I hadn't been tough enough for Bridget before...

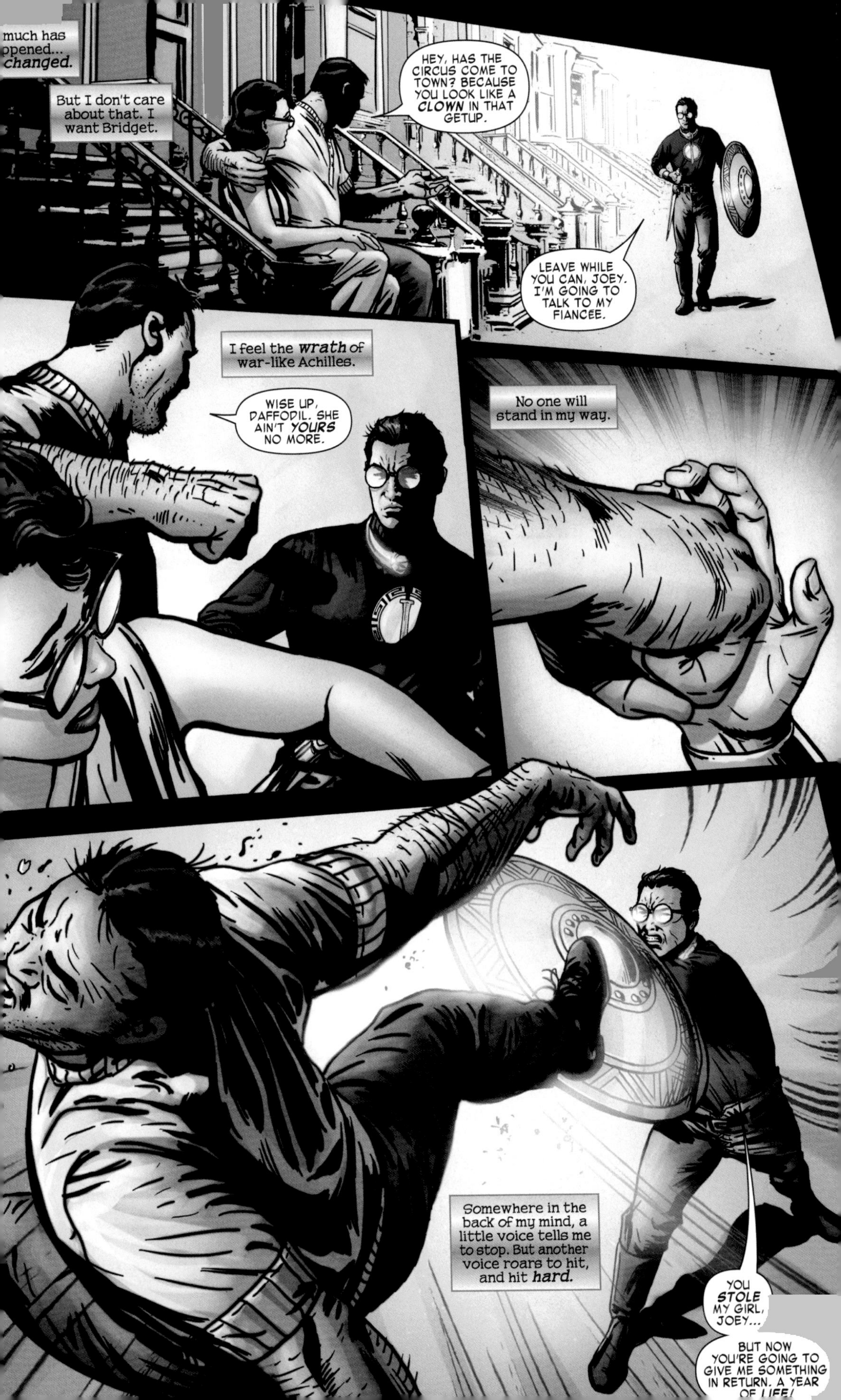

much has
ppened...
changed.
But I don't care about that. I want Bridget.
HEY, HAS THE CIRCUS COME TO TOWN? BECAUSE YOU LOOK LIKE A ***CLOWN*** IN THAT GETUP.
LEAVE WHILE YOU CAN, JOEY. I'M GOING TO TALK TO MY FIANCEE.
I feel the ***wrath*** of war-like Achilles.
WISE UP, DAFFODIL. SHE AIN'T ***YOURS*** NO MORE.
No one will stand in my way.
Somewhere in the back of my mind, a little voice tells me to stop. But another voice roars to hit, and hit ***hard.***
YOU ***STOLE*** MY GIRL, JOEY...
BUT NOW YOU'RE GOING TO GIVE ME SOMETHING IN RETURN. A YEAR OF ***LIFE!***

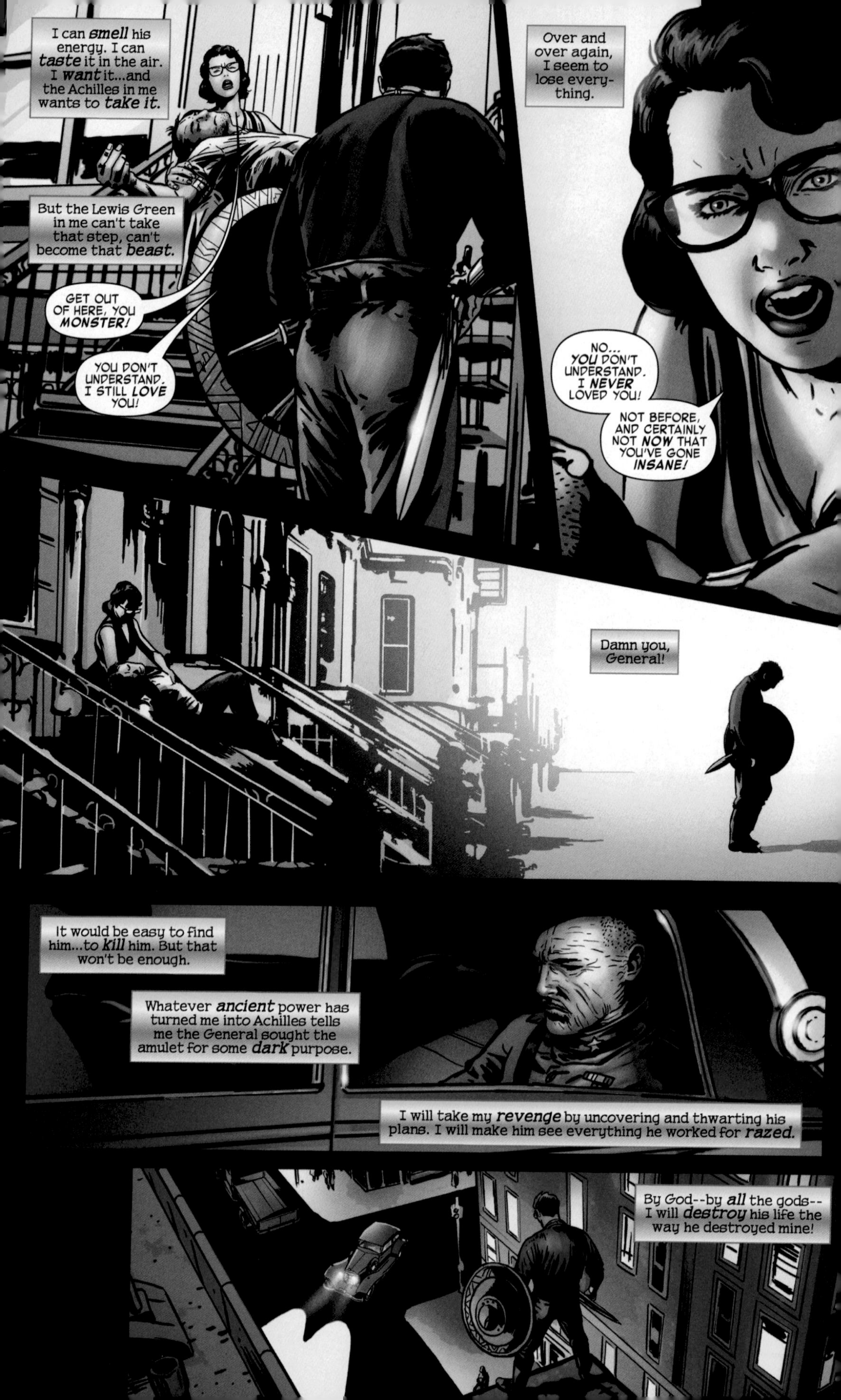
I can *smell* his energy. I can *taste* it in the air. I *want* it...and the Achilles in me wants to *take it*.
But the Lewis Green in me can't take that step, can't become that *beast*.
GET OUT OF HERE, YOU **MONSTER!**
YOU DON'T UNDERSTAND. I STILL **LOVE** YOU!
Over and over again, I seem to lose everything.
NO... **YOU** DON'T UNDERSTAND. I **NEVER** LOVED YOU!
NOT BEFORE, AND CERTAINLY NOT **NOW** THAT YOU'VE GONE **INSANE!**
Damn you, General!
It would be easy to find him...to *kill* him. But that won't be enough.
Whatever *ancient* power has turned me into Achilles tells me the General sought the amulet for some *dark* purpose.
I will take my *revenge* by uncovering and thwarting his plans. I will make him see everything he worked for *razed*.
By God--by *all* the gods--I will *destroy* his life the way he destroyed mine!

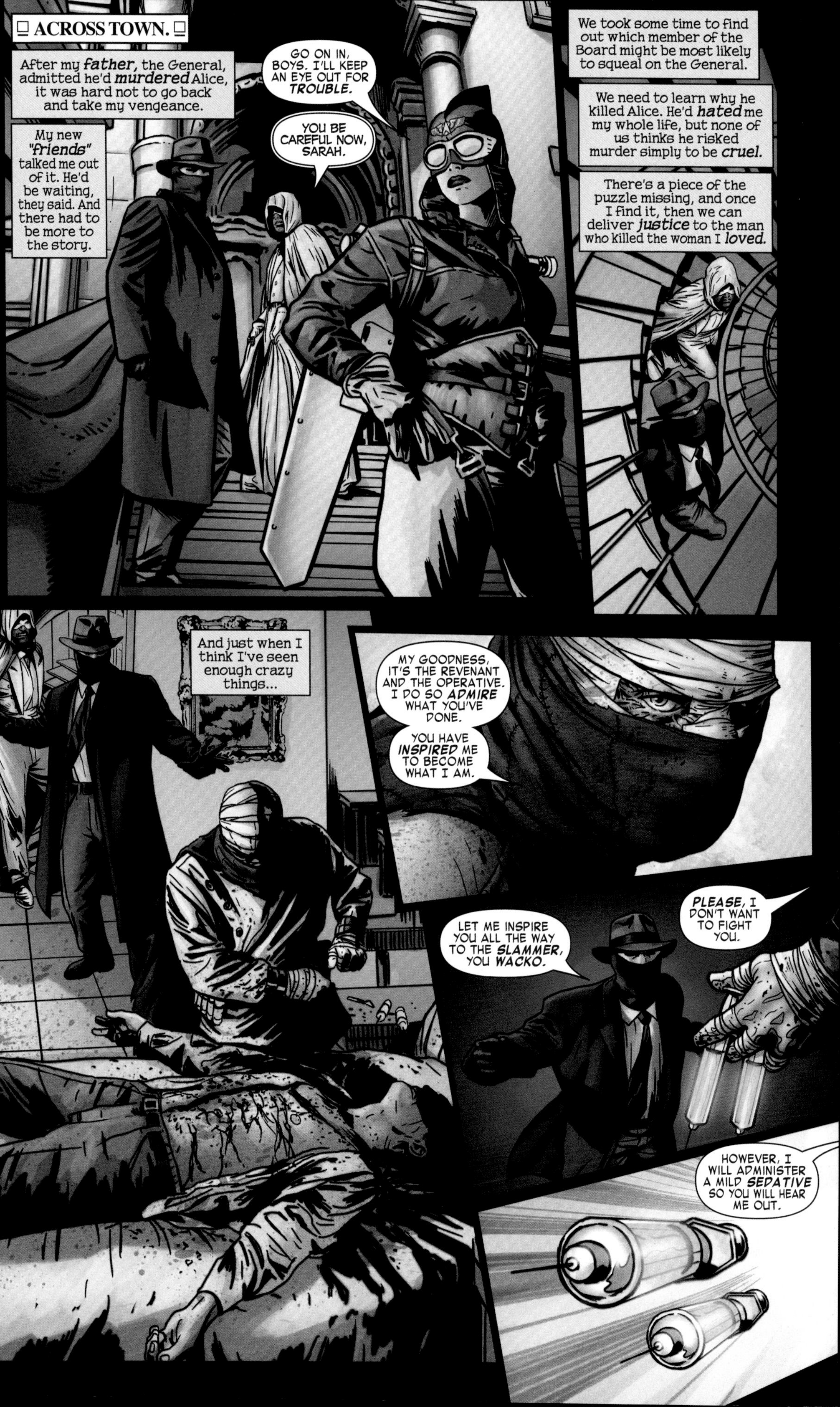
ACROSS TOWN.
After my father, the General, admitted he'd murdered Alice, it was hard not to go back and take my vengeance.
My new "friends" talked me out of it. He'd be waiting, they said. And there had to be more to the story.
GO ON IN, BOYS. I'LL KEEP AN EYE OUT FOR TROUBLE.
YOU BE CAREFUL NOW, SARAH.
We took some time to find out which member of the Board might be most likely to squeal on the General.
We need to learn why he killed Alice. He'd hated me my whole life, but none of us thinks he risked murder simply to be cruel.
There's a piece of the puzzle missing, and once I find it, then we can deliver justice to the man who killed the woman I loved.
And just when I think I've seen enough crazy things...
MY GOODNESS, IT'S THE REVENANT AND THE OPERATIVE. I DO SO ADMIRE WHAT YOU'VE DONE.
YOU HAVE INSPIRED ME TO BECOME WHAT I AM.
LET ME INSPIRE YOU ALL THE WAY TO THE SLAMMER, YOU WACKO.
PLEASE, I DON'T WANT TO FIGHT YOU.
HOWEVER, I WILL ADMINISTER A MILD SEDATIVE SO YOU WILL HEAR ME OUT.

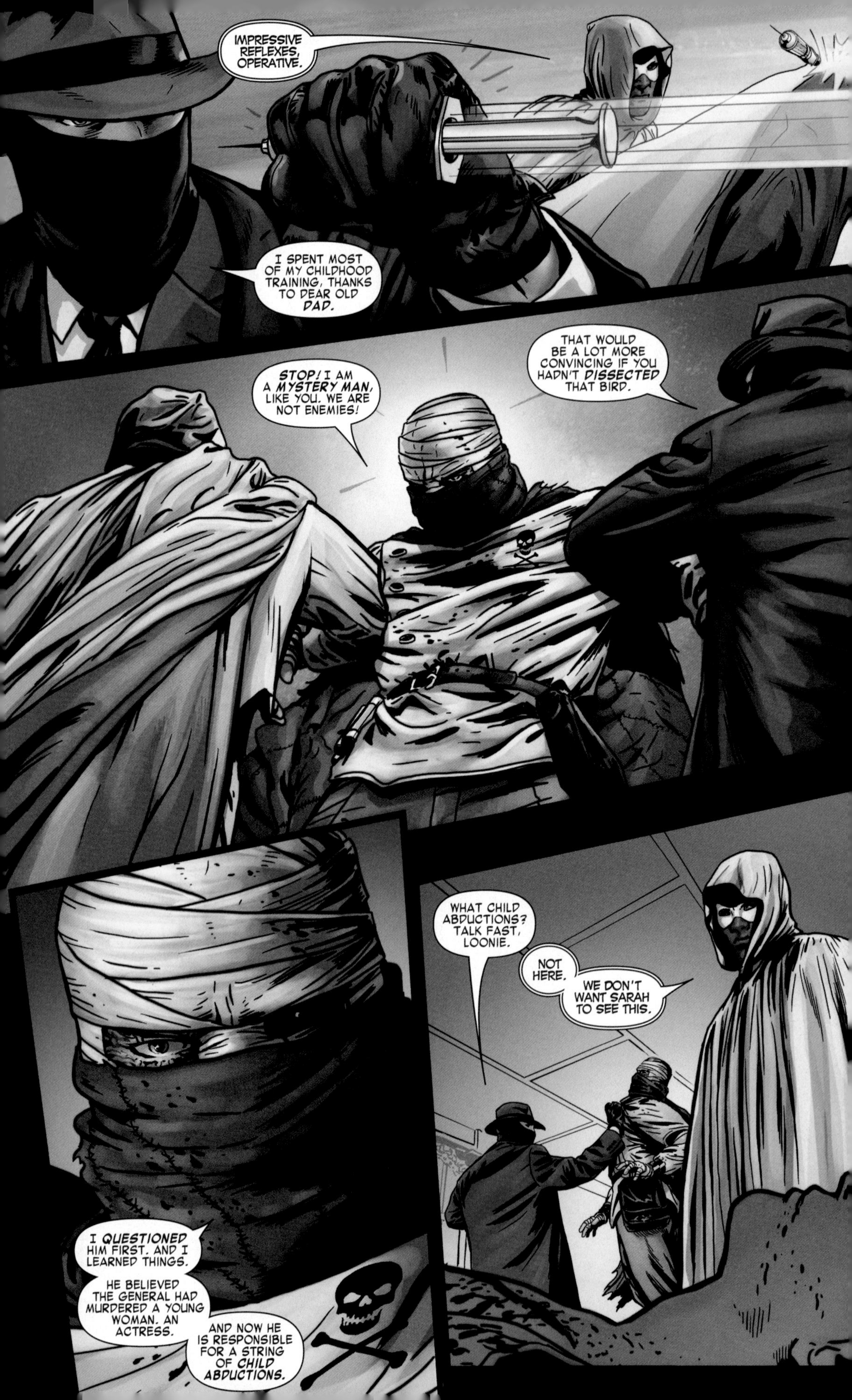
IMPRESSIVE REFLEXES, OPERATIVE.
I SPENT MOST OF MY CHILDHOOD TRAINING, THANKS TO DEAR OLD DAD.
STOP! I AM A MYSTERY MAN, LIKE YOU. WE ARE NOT ENEMIES!
THAT WOULD BE A LOT MORE CONVINCING IF YOU HADN'T DISSECTED THAT BIRD.
I QUESTIONED HIM FIRST. AND I LEARNED THINGS.
HE BELIEVED THE GENERAL HAD MURDERED A YOUNG WOMAN. AN ACTRESS.
AND NOW HE IS RESPONSIBLE FOR A STRING OF CHILD ABDUCTIONS.
WHAT CHILD ABDUCTIONS? TALK FAST, LOONIE.
NOT HERE.
WE DON'T WANT SARAH TO SEE THIS.

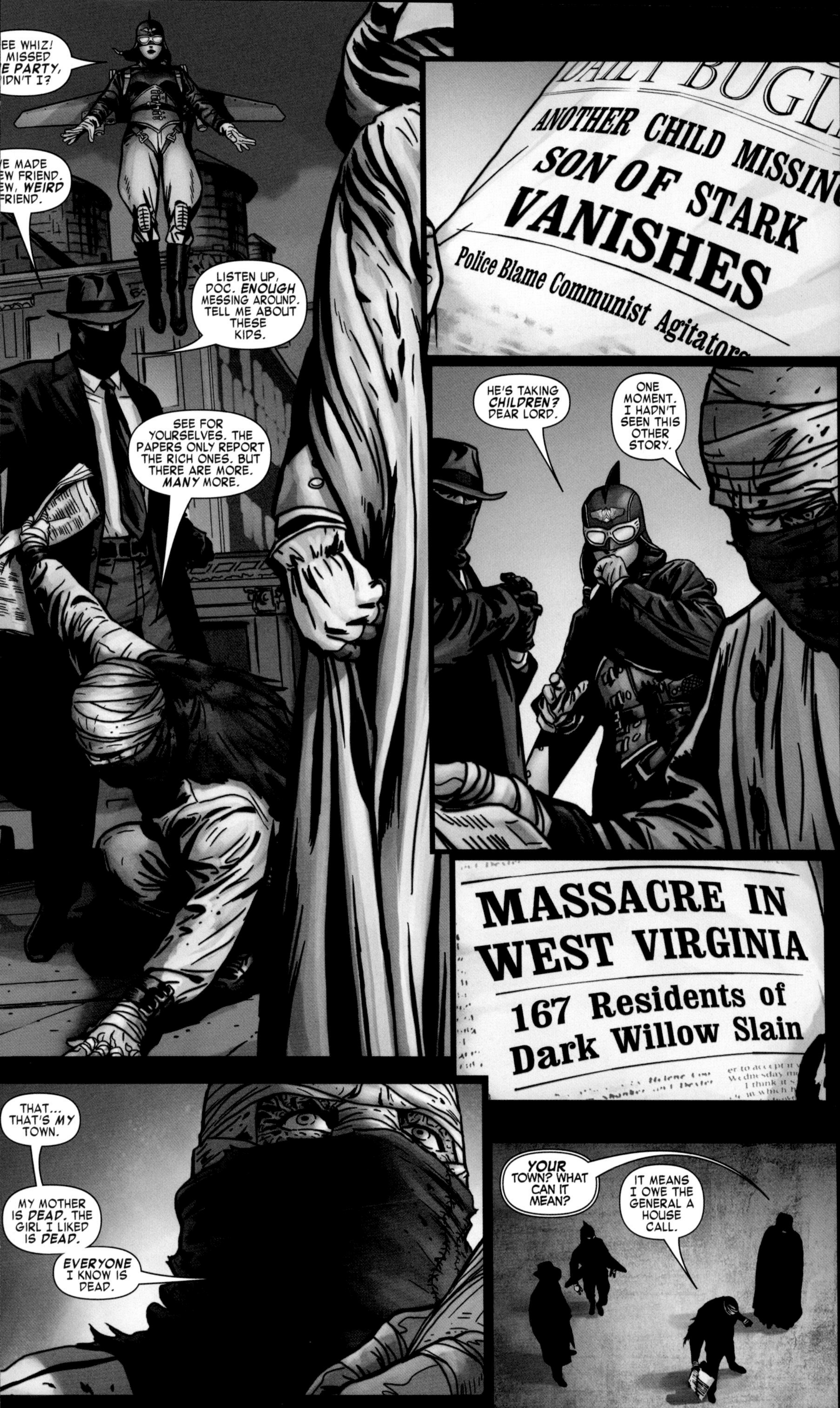

EE WHIZ! MISSED E PARTY, IDN'T I?
E MADE EW FRIEND. EW, WEIRD FRIEND.
LISTEN UP, DOC. ENOUGH MESSING AROUND. TELL ME ABOUT THESE KIDS.
SEE FOR YOURSELVES. THE PAPERS ONLY REPORT THE RICH ONES. BUT THERE ARE MORE. MANY MORE.
DAILY BUGL
ANOTHER CHILD MISSING
SON OF STARK VANISHES
Police Blame Communist Agitators
HE'S TAKING CHILDREN? DEAR LORD.
ONE MOMENT. I HADN'T SEEN THIS OTHER STORY.
MASSACRE IN WEST VIRGINIA
167 Residents of Dark Willow Slain
THAT... THAT'S MY TOWN.
MY MOTHER IS DEAD. THE GIRL I LIKED IS DEAD.
EVERYONE I KNOW IS DEAD.
YOUR TOWN? WHAT CAN IT MEAN?
IT MEANS I OWE THE GENERAL A HOUSE CALL.

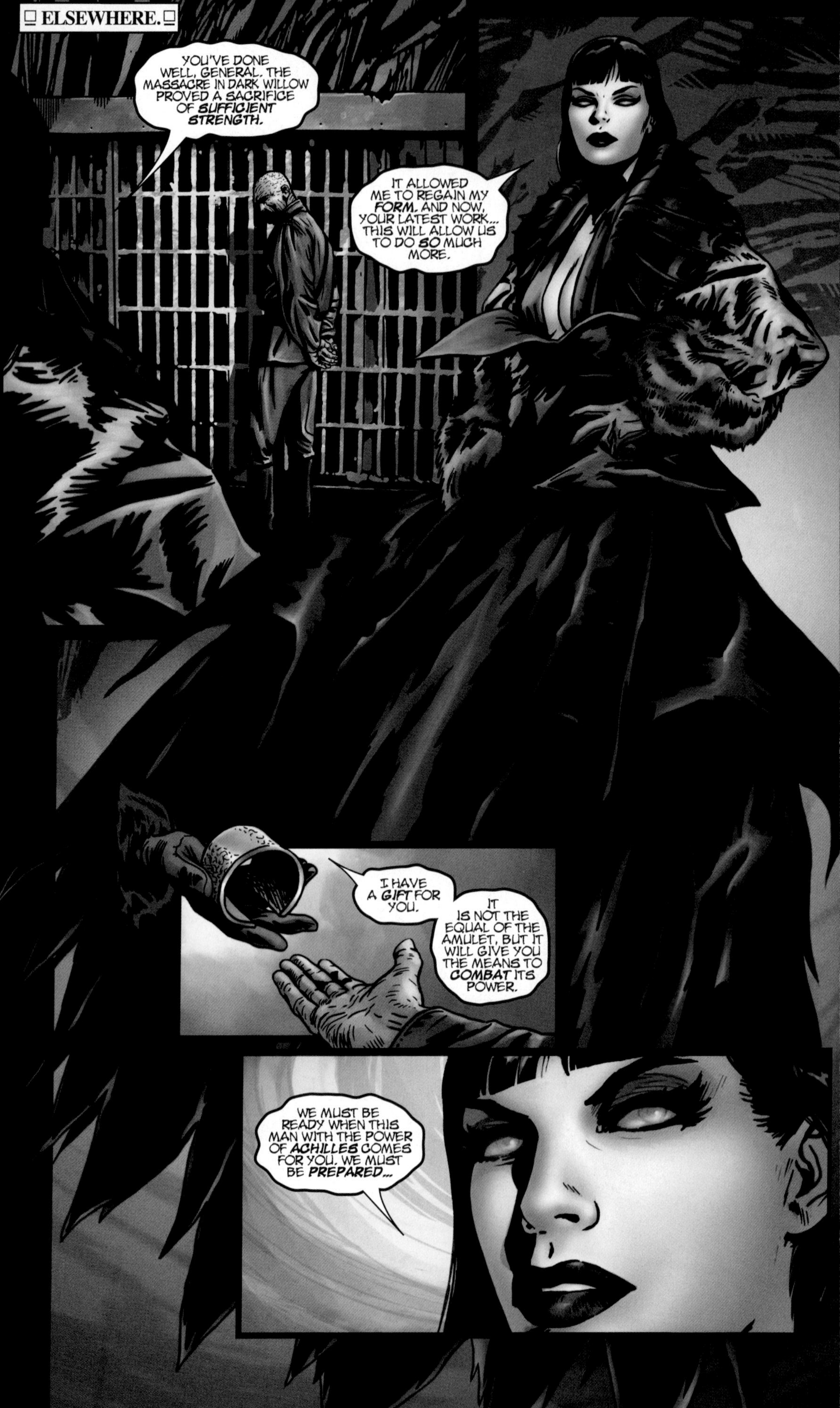
ELSEWHERE.
YOU'VE DONE WELL, GENERAL. THE MASSACRE IN DARK WILLOW PROVED A SACRIFICE OF SUFFICIENT STRENGTH.
IT ALLOWED ME TO REGAIN MY FORM. AND NOW, YOUR LATEST WORK... THIS WILL ALLOW US TO DO SO MUCH MORE.
I HAVE A GIFT FOR YOU.
IT IS NOT THE EQUAL OF THE AMULET, BUT IT WILL GIVE YOU THE MEANS TO COMBAT ITS POWER.
WE MUST BE READY WHEN THIS MAN WITH THE POWER OF ACHILLES COMES FOR YOU. WE MUST BE PREPARED...

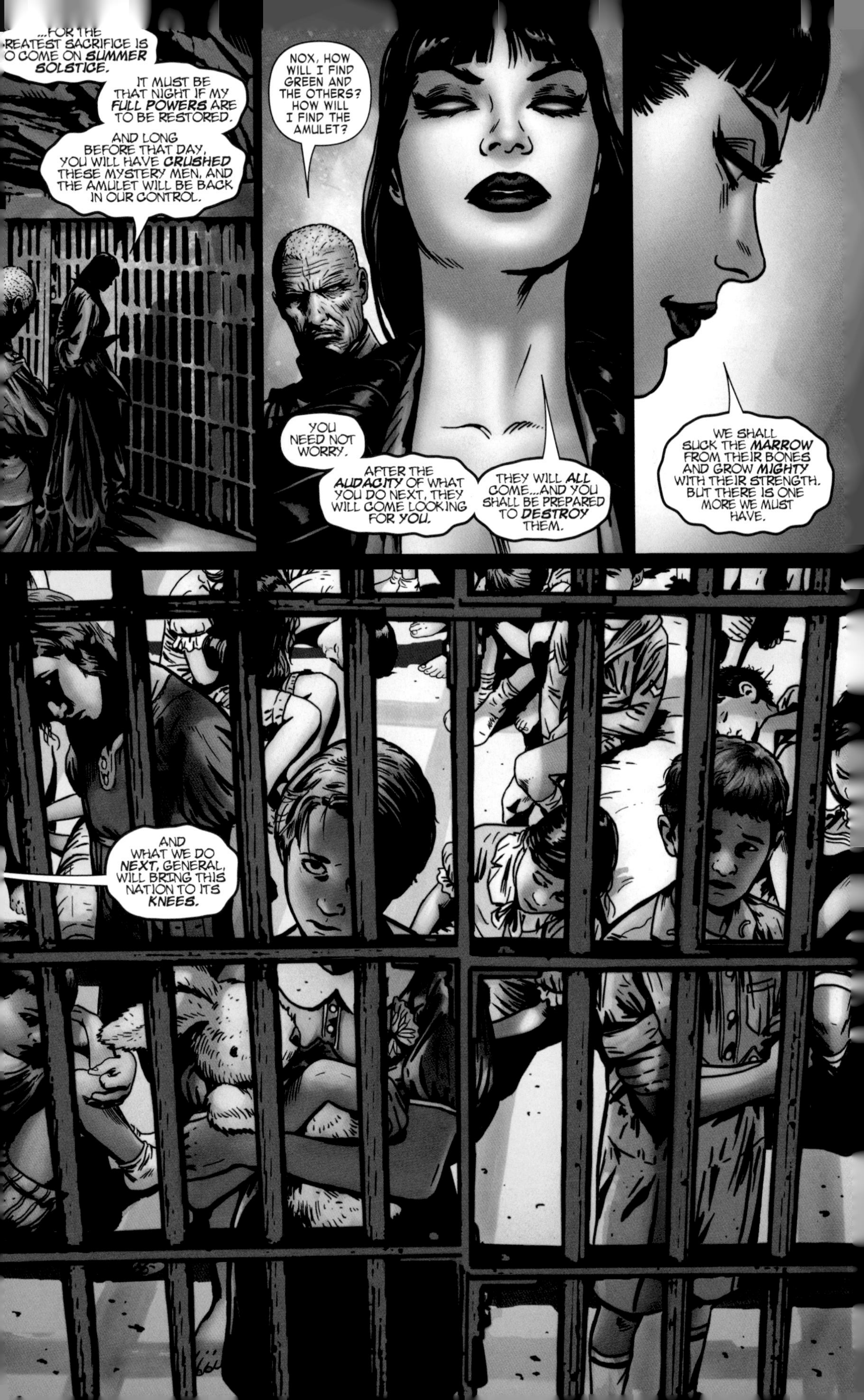
...FOR THE
REATEST SACRIFICE IS
O COME ON SUMMER SOLSTICE.
IT MUST BE THAT NIGHT IF MY FULL POWERS ARE TO BE RESTORED.
AND LONG BEFORE THAT DAY, YOU WILL HAVE CRUSHED THESE MYSTERY MEN, AND THE AMULET WILL BE BACK IN OUR CONTROL.
NOX, HOW WILL I FIND GREEN AND THE OTHERS? HOW WILL I FIND THE AMULET?
YOU NEED NOT WORRY.
AFTER THE AUDACITY OF WHAT YOU DO NEXT, THEY WILL COME LOOKING FOR YOU.
THEY WILL ALL COME...AND YOU SHALL BE PREPARED TO DESTROY THEM.
WE SHALL SUCK THE MARROW FROM THEIR BONES AND GROW MIGHTY WITH THEIR STRENGTH. BUT THERE IS ONE MORE WE MUST HAVE.
AND WHAT WE DO NEXT, GENERAL, WILL BRING THIS NATION TO ITS KNEES.

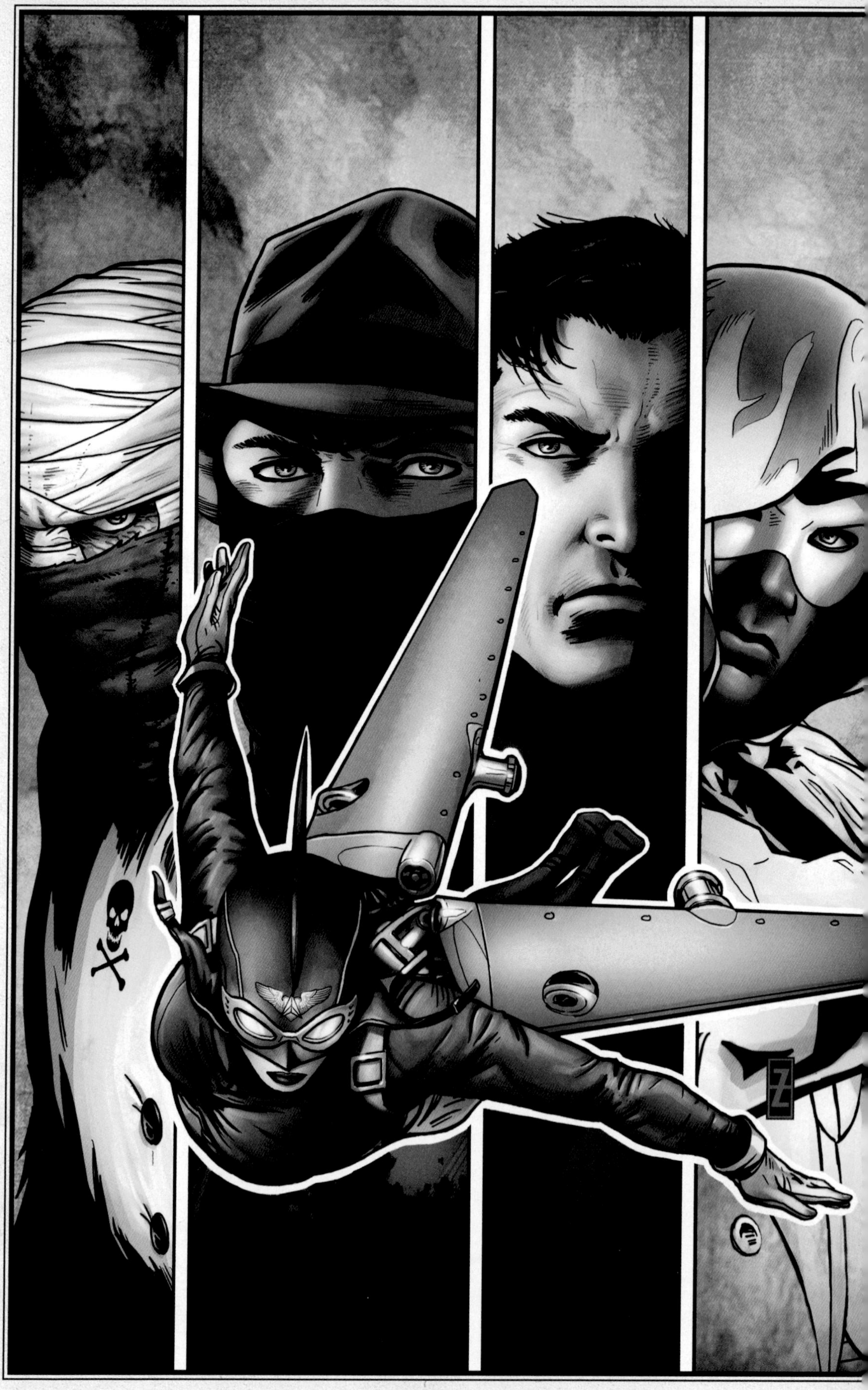

MYSTERY MEN #4

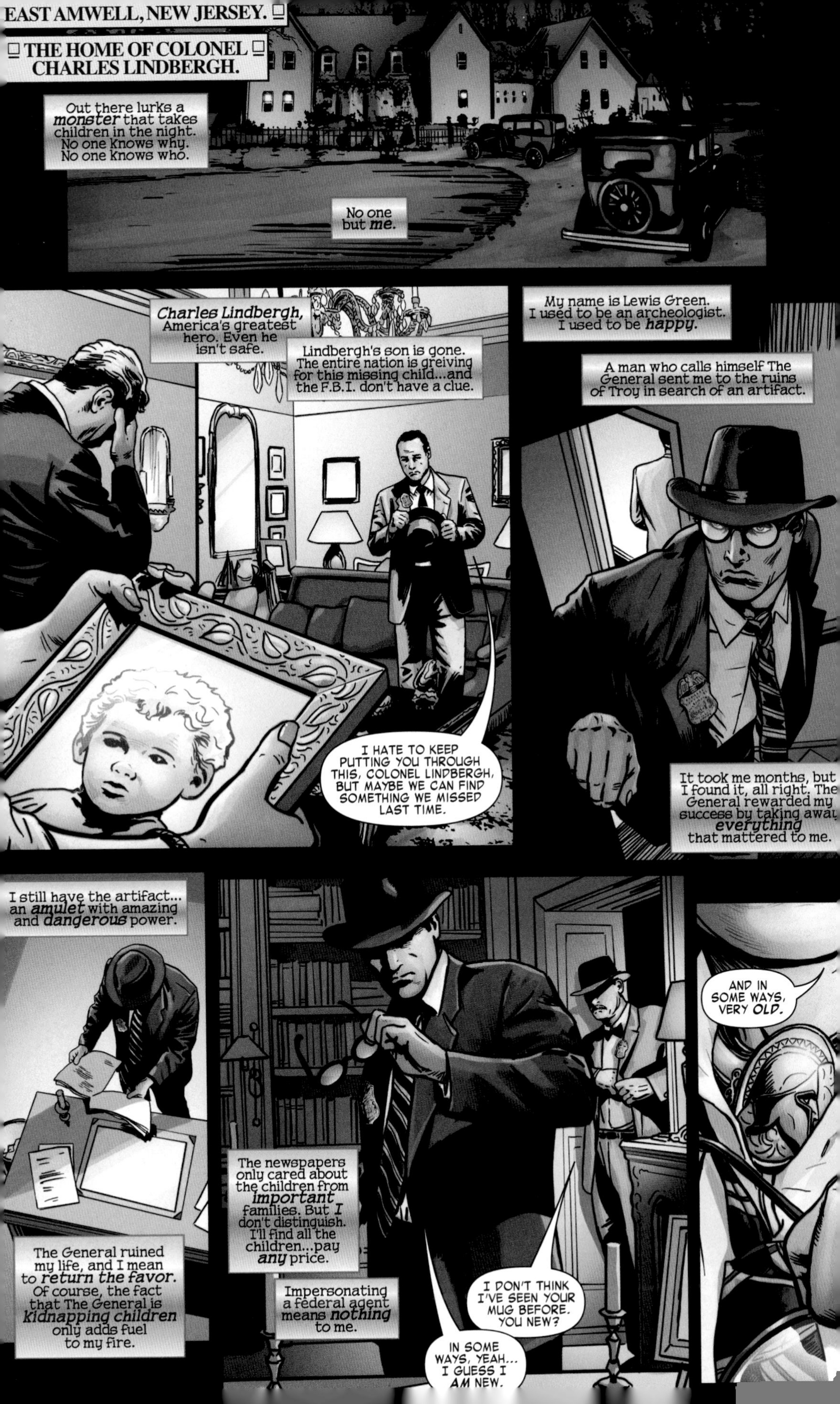

EAST AMWELL, NEW JERSEY.
THE HOME OF COLONEL CHARLES LINDBERGH.
Out there lurks a monster that takes children in the night. No one knows why. No one knows who.
No one but me.
Charles Lindbergh, America's greatest hero. Even he isn't safe.
Lindbergh's son is gone. The entire nation is greiving for this missing child...and the F.B.I. don't have a clue.
I HATE TO KEEP PUTTING YOU THROUGH THIS, COLONEL LINDBERGH, BUT MAYBE WE CAN FIND SOMETHING WE MISSED LAST TIME.
My name is Lewis Green. I used to be an archeologist. I used to be happy.
A man who calls himself The General sent me to the ruins of Troy in search of an artifact.
It took me months, but I found it, all right. The General rewarded my success by taking away everything that mattered to me.
I still have the artifact... an amulet with amazing and dangerous power.
The General ruined my life, and I mean to return the favor. Of course, the fact that The General is kidnapping children only adds fuel to my fire.
The newspapers only cared about the children from important families. But I don't distinguish. I'll find all the children...pay any price.
Impersonating a federal agent means nothing to me.
I DON'T THINK I'VE SEEN YOUR MUG BEFORE. YOU NEW?
IN SOME WAYS, YEAH... I GUESS I AM NEW.
AND IN SOME WAYS, VERY OLD.

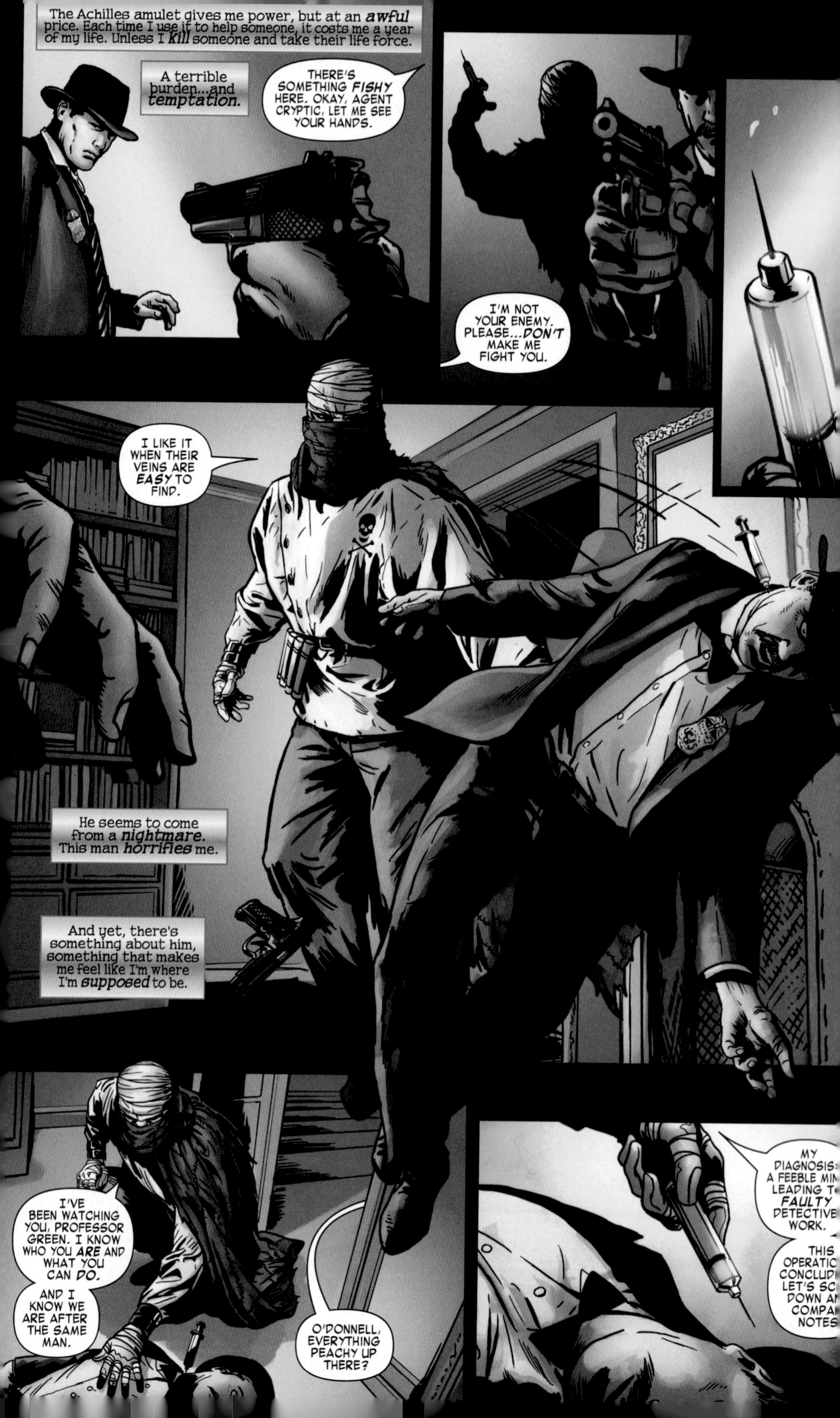
The Achilles amulet gives me power, but at an awful price. Each time I use it to help someone, it costs me a year of my life. Unless I kill someone and take their life force.
A terrible burden...and temptation.
THERE'S SOMETHING FISHY HERE. OKAY, AGENT CRYPTIC, LET ME SEE YOUR HANDS.
I'M NOT YOUR ENEMY. PLEASE...DON'T MAKE ME FIGHT YOU.
I LIKE IT WHEN THEIR VEINS ARE EASY TO FIND.
He seems to come from a nightmare. This man horrifies me.
And yet, there's something about him, something that makes me feel like I'm where I'm supposed to be.
I'VE BEEN WATCHING YOU, PROFESSOR GREEN. I KNOW WHO YOU ARE AND WHAT YOU CAN DO.
AND I KNOW WE ARE AFTER THE SAME MAN.
O'DONNELL, EVERYTHING PEACHY UP THERE?
MY DIAGNOSIS: A FEEBLE MIN LEADING T FAULTY DETECTIVE WORK.
THIS OPERATIC CONCLU LET'S SC DOWN A COMPA NOTES

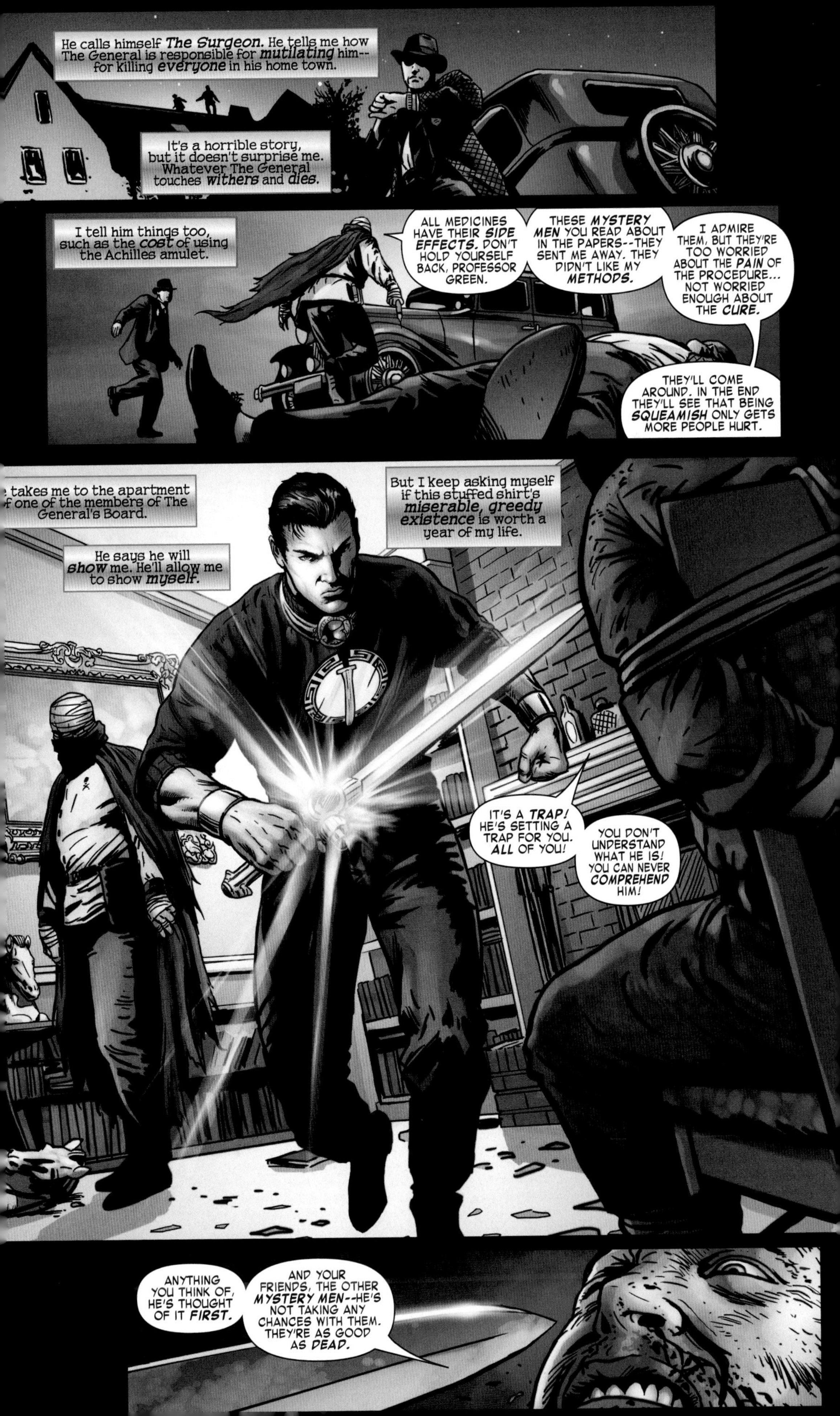
He calls himself The Surgeon. He tells me how The General is responsible for mutilating him--for killing everyone in his home town.
It's a horrible story, but it doesn't surprise me. Whatever The General touches withers and dies.
I tell him things too, such as the cost of using the Achilles amulet.
ALL MEDICINES HAVE THEIR SIDE EFFECTS. DON'T HOLD YOURSELF BACK, PROFESSOR GREEN.
THESE MYSTERY MEN YOU READ ABOUT IN THE PAPERS--THEY SENT ME AWAY. THEY DIDN'T LIKE MY METHODS.
I ADMIRE THEM, BUT THEY'RE TOO WORRIED ABOUT THE PAIN OF THE PROCEDURE... NOT WORRIED ENOUGH ABOUT THE CURE.
THEY'LL COME AROUND. IN THE END THEY'LL SEE THAT BEING SQUEAMISH ONLY GETS MORE PEOPLE HURT.
takes me to the apartment of one of the members of The General's Board.
He says he will show me. He'll allow me to show myself.
But I keep asking myself if this stuffed shirt's miserable, greedy existence is worth a year of my life.
IT'S A TRAP! HE'S SETTING A TRAP FOR YOU. ALL OF YOU!
YOU DON'T UNDERSTAND WHAT HE IS! YOU CAN NEVER COMPREHEND HIM!
ANYTHING YOU THINK OF, HE'S THOUGHT OF IT FIRST.
AND YOUR FRIENDS, THE OTHER MYSTERY MEN--HE'S NOT TAKING ANY CHANCES WITH THEM. THEY'RE AS GOOD AS DEAD.

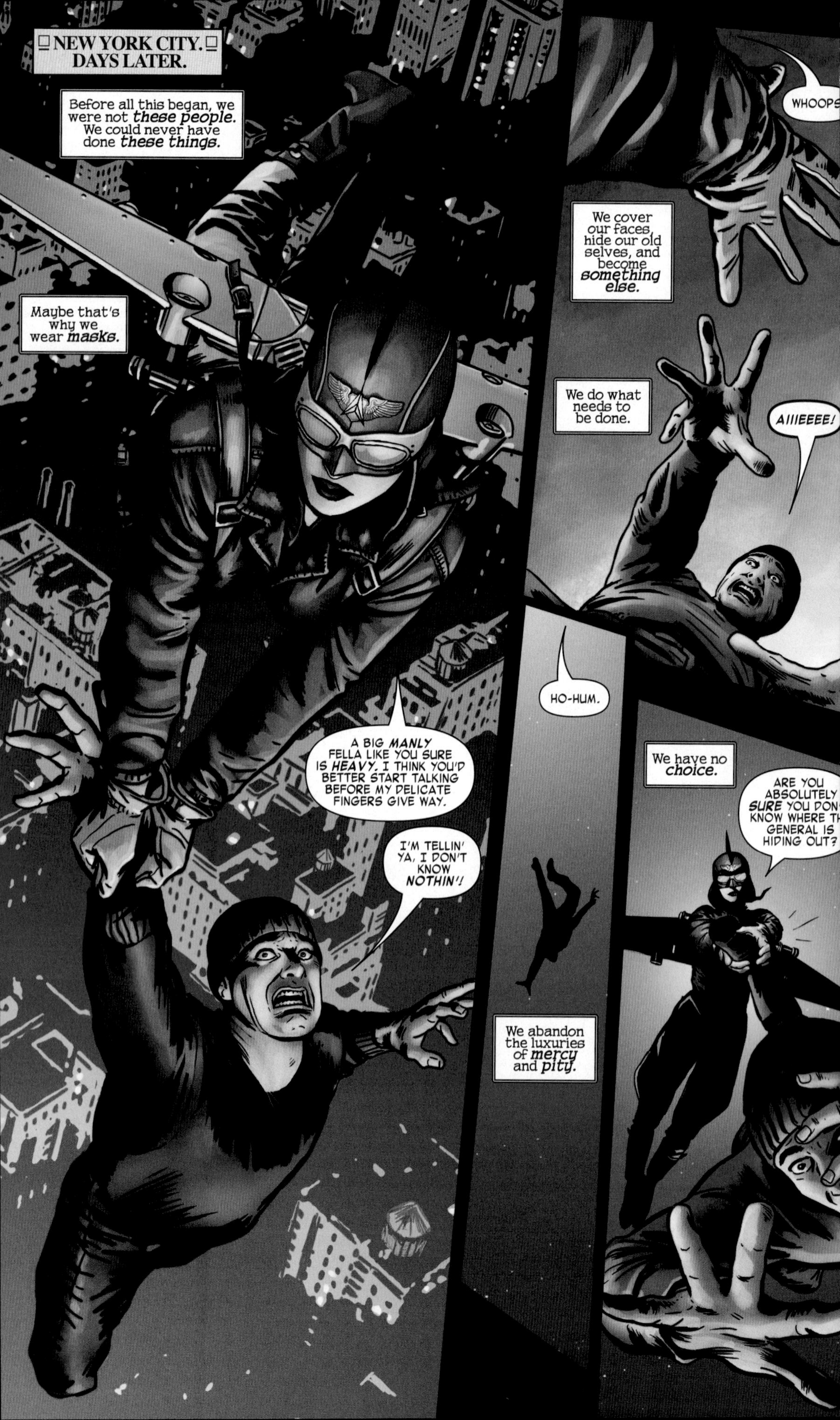

NEW YORK CITY. DAYS LATER.
Before all this began, we were not *these people.* We could never have done *these things.*
Maybe that's why we wear *masks.*
A BIG *MANLY* FELLA LIKE YOU SURE IS *HEAVY.* I THINK YOU'D BETTER START TALKING BEFORE MY DELICATE FINGERS GIVE WAY.
I'M TELLIN' YA, I DON'T KNOW *NOTHIN'!*
WHOOPS
We cover our faces, hide our old selves, and become *something else.*
We do what needs to be done.
AIIIEEEE!
HO-HUM.
We abandon the luxuries of *mercy* and *pity.*
We have no *choice.*
ARE YOU ABSOLUTELY *SURE* YOU DON'T KNOW WHERE THE GENERAL IS HIDING OUT?

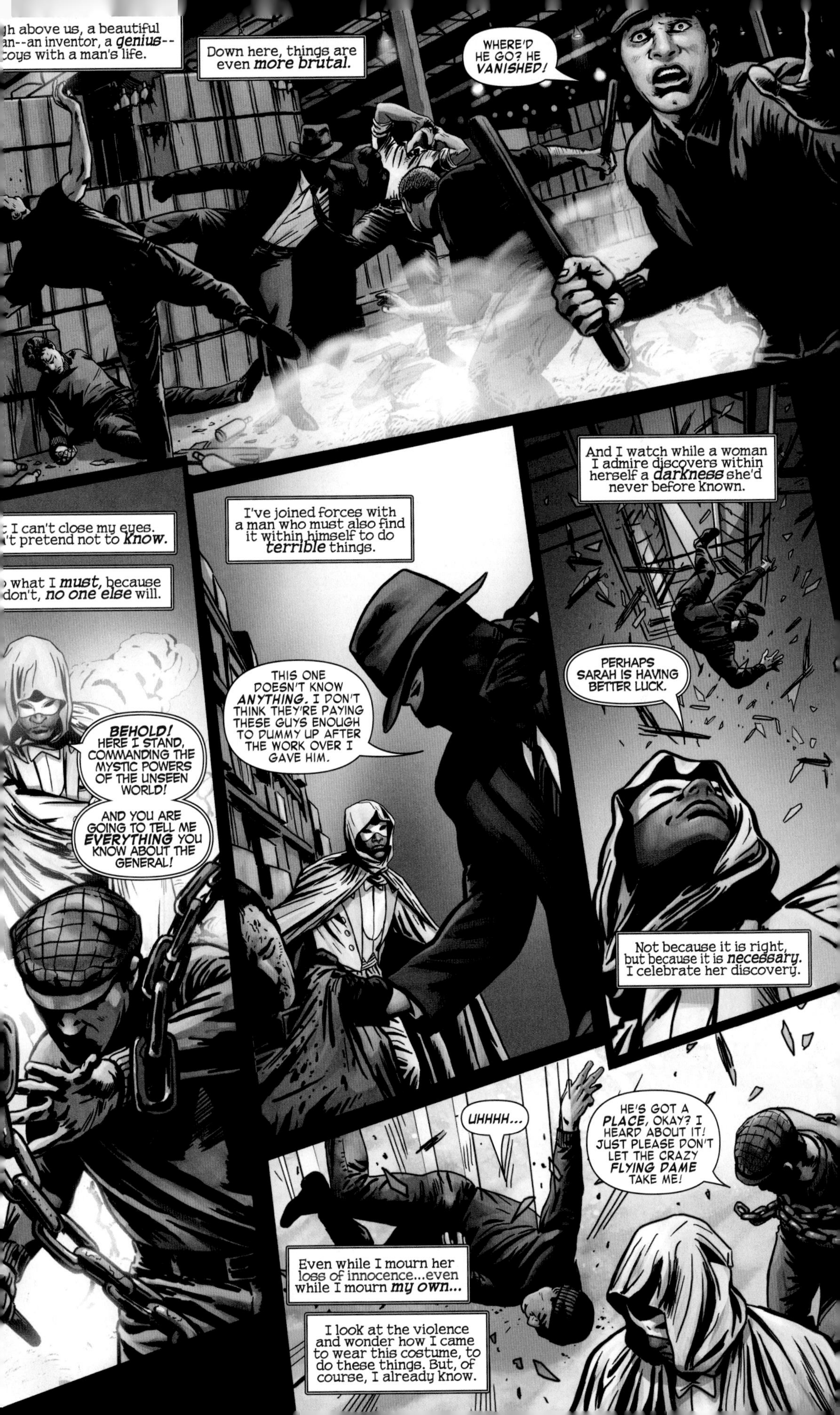

gh above us, a beautiful an--an inventor, a *genius*-- toys with a man's life.
Down here, things are even *more brutal.*
WHERE'D HE GO? HE *VANISHED!*
And I watch while a woman I admire discovers within herself a *darkness* she'd never before known.
I can't close my eyes. 't pretend not to *know.*
what I *must,* because don't, *no one else* will.
I've joined forces with a man who must also find it within himself to do *terrible* things.
BEHOLD! HERE I STAND, COMMANDING THE MYSTIC POWERS OF THE UNSEEN WORLD!
AND YOU ARE GOING TO TELL ME *EVERYTHING* YOU KNOW ABOUT THE GENERAL!
THIS ONE DOESN'T KNOW *ANYTHING.* I DON'T THINK THEY'RE PAYING THESE GUYS ENOUGH TO DUMMY UP AFTER THE WORK OVER I GAVE HIM.
PERHAPS SARAH IS HAVING BETTER LUCK.
Not because it is right, but because it is *necessary.* I celebrate her discovery.
UHHHH...
HE'S GOT A *PLACE,* OKAY? I HEARD ABOUT IT! JUST PLEASE DON'T LET THE CRAZY *FLYING DAME* TAKE ME!
Even while I mourn her loss of innocence...even while I mourn *my own...*
I look at the violence and wonder how I came to wear this costume, to do these things. But, of course, I already know.

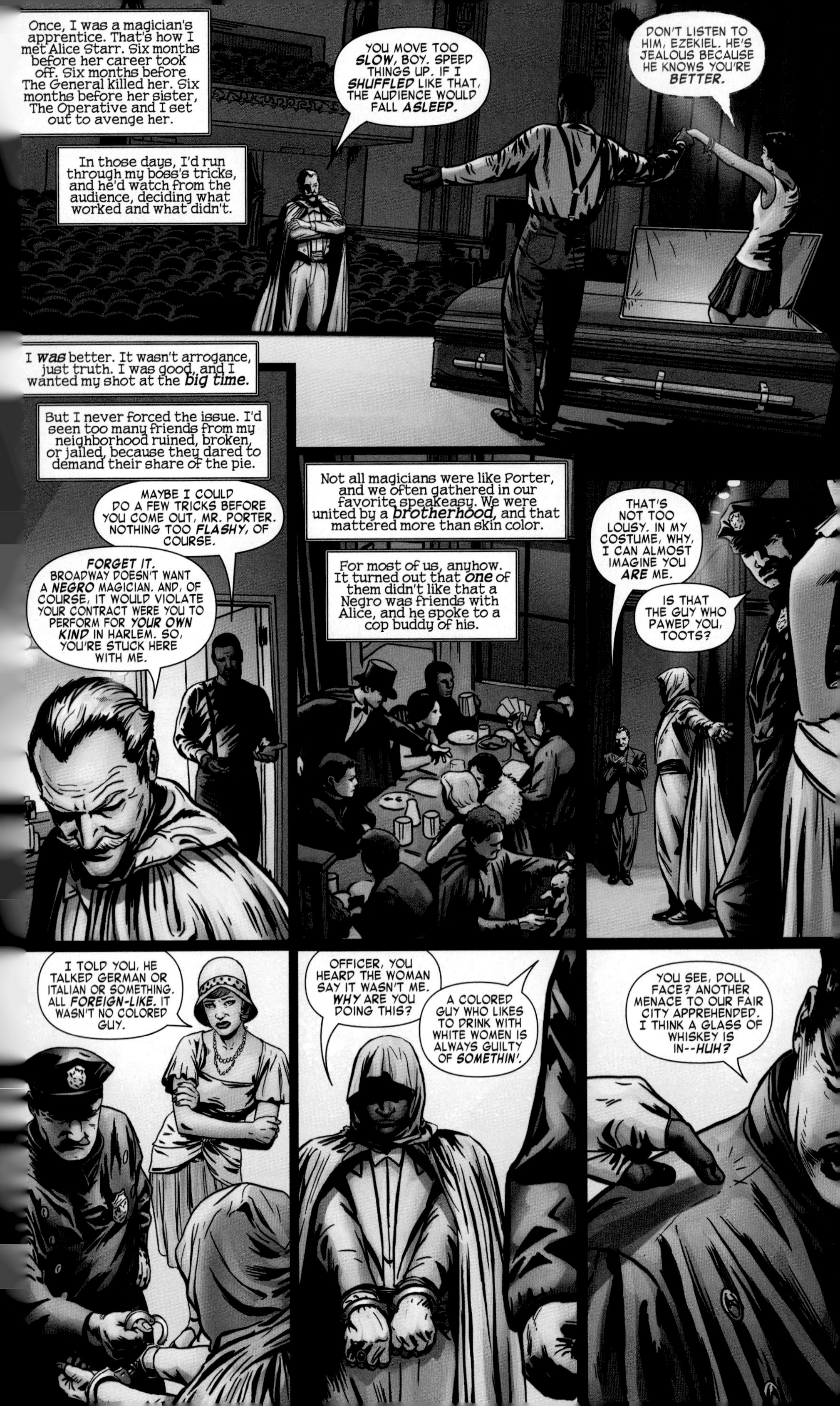

Once, I was a magician's apprentice. That's how I met Alice Starr. Six months before her career took off. Six months before The General killed her. Six months before her sister, The Operative and I set out to avenge her.
In those days, I'd run through my boss's tricks, and he'd watch from the audience, deciding what worked and what didn't.
YOU MOVE TOO SLOW, BOY. SPEED THINGS UP. IF I SHUFFLED LIKE THAT, THE AUDIENCE WOULD FALL ASLEEP.
DON'T LISTEN TO HIM, EZEKIEL. HE'S JEALOUS BECAUSE HE KNOWS YOU'RE BETTER.
I was better. It wasn't arrogance, just truth. I was good, and I wanted my shot at the big time.
But I never forced the issue. I'd seen too many friends from my neighborhood ruined, broken, or jailed, because they dared to demand their share of the pie.
MAYBE I COULD DO A FEW TRICKS BEFORE YOU COME OUT, MR. PORTER. NOTHING TOO FLASHY, OF COURSE.
FORGET IT. BROADWAY DOESN'T WANT A NEGRO MAGICIAN. AND, OF COURSE, IT WOULD VIOLATE YOUR CONTRACT WERE YOU TO PERFORM FOR YOUR OWN KIND IN HARLEM. SO, YOU'RE STUCK HERE WITH ME.
Not all magicians were like Porter, and we often gathered in our favorite speakeasy. We were united by a brotherhood, and that mattered more than skin color.
For most of us, anyhow. It turned out that one of them didn't like that a Negro was friends with Alice, and he spoke to a cop buddy of his.
THAT'S NOT TOO LOUSY. IN MY COSTUME, WHY, I CAN ALMOST IMAGINE YOU ARE ME.
IS THAT THE GUY WHO PAWED YOU, TOOTS?
I TOLD YOU, HE TALKED GERMAN OR ITALIAN OR SOMETHING. ALL FOREIGN-LIKE. IT WASN'T NO COLORED GUY.
OFFICER, YOU HEARD THE WOMAN SAY IT WASN'T ME. WHY ARE YOU DOING THIS?
A COLORED GUY WHO LIKES TO DRINK WITH WHITE WOMEN IS ALWAYS GUILTY OF SOMETHIN'.
YOU SEE, DOLL FACE? ANOTHER MENACE TO OUR FAIR CITY APPREHENDED. I THINK A GLASS OF WHISKEY IS IN--HUH?

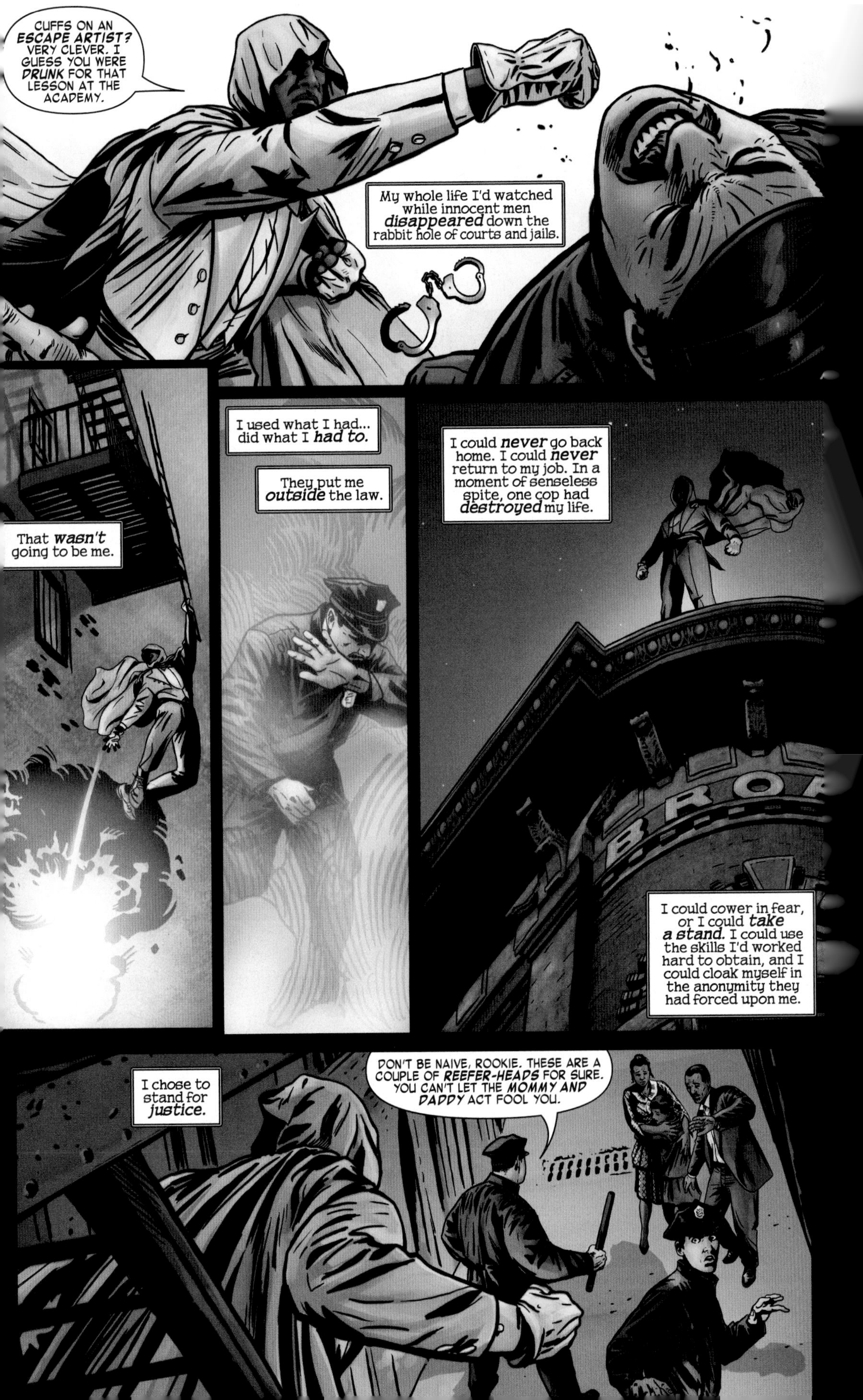

CUFFS ON AN ESCAPE ARTIST? VERY CLEVER. I GUESS YOU WERE DRUNK FOR THAT LESSON AT THE ACADEMY.
My whole life I'd watched while innocent men disappeared down the rabbit hole of courts and jails.
That wasn't going to be me.
I used what I had... did what I had to.
They put me outside the law.
I could never go back home. I could never return to my job. In a moment of senseless spite, one cop had destroyed my life.
BRO
I could cower in fear, or I could take a stand. I could use the skills I'd worked hard to obtain, and I could cloak myself in the anonymity they had forced upon me.
I chose to stand for justice.
DON'T BE NAIVE, ROOKIE. THESE ARE A COUPLE OF REEFER-HEADS FOR SURE. YOU CAN'T LET THE MOMMY AND DADDY ACT FOOL YOU.

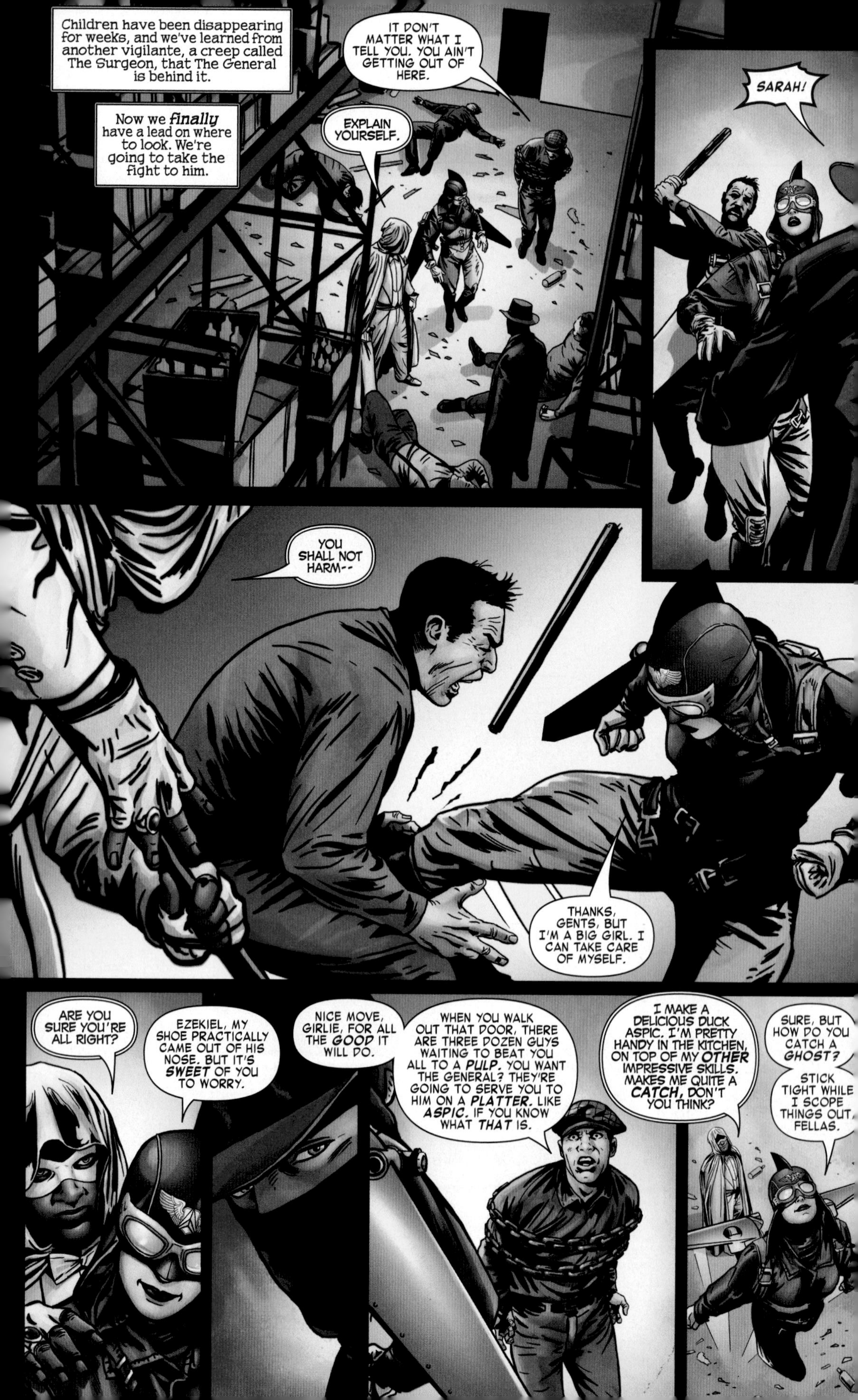
Children have been disappearing for weeks, and we've learned from another vigilante, a creep called The Surgeon, that The General is behind it.
Now we finally have a lead on where to look. We're going to take the fight to him.
IT DON'T MATTER WHAT I TELL YOU. YOU AIN'T GETTING OUT OF HERE.
EXPLAIN YOURSELF.
SARAH!
YOU SHALL NOT HARM--
THANKS, GENTS, BUT I'M A BIG GIRL. I CAN TAKE CARE OF MYSELF.
ARE YOU SURE YOU'RE ALL RIGHT?
EZEKIEL, MY SHOE PRACTICALLY CAME OUT OF HIS NOSE. BUT IT'S SWEET OF YOU TO WORRY.
NICE MOVE, GIRLIE, FOR ALL THE GOOD IT WILL DO.
WHEN YOU WALK OUT THAT DOOR, THERE ARE THREE DOZEN GUYS WAITING TO BEAT YOU ALL TO A PULP. YOU WANT THE GENERAL? THEY'RE GOING TO SERVE YOU TO HIM ON A PLATTER. LIKE ASPIC. IF YOU KNOW WHAT THAT IS.
I MAKE A DELICIOUS DUCK ASPIC. I'M PRETTY HANDY IN THE KITCHEN, ON TOP OF MY OTHER IMPRESSIVE SKILLS. MAKES ME QUITE A CATCH, DON'T YOU THINK?
SURE, BUT HOW DO YOU CATCH A GHOST?
STICK TIGHT WHILE I SCOPE THINGS OUT, FELLAS.

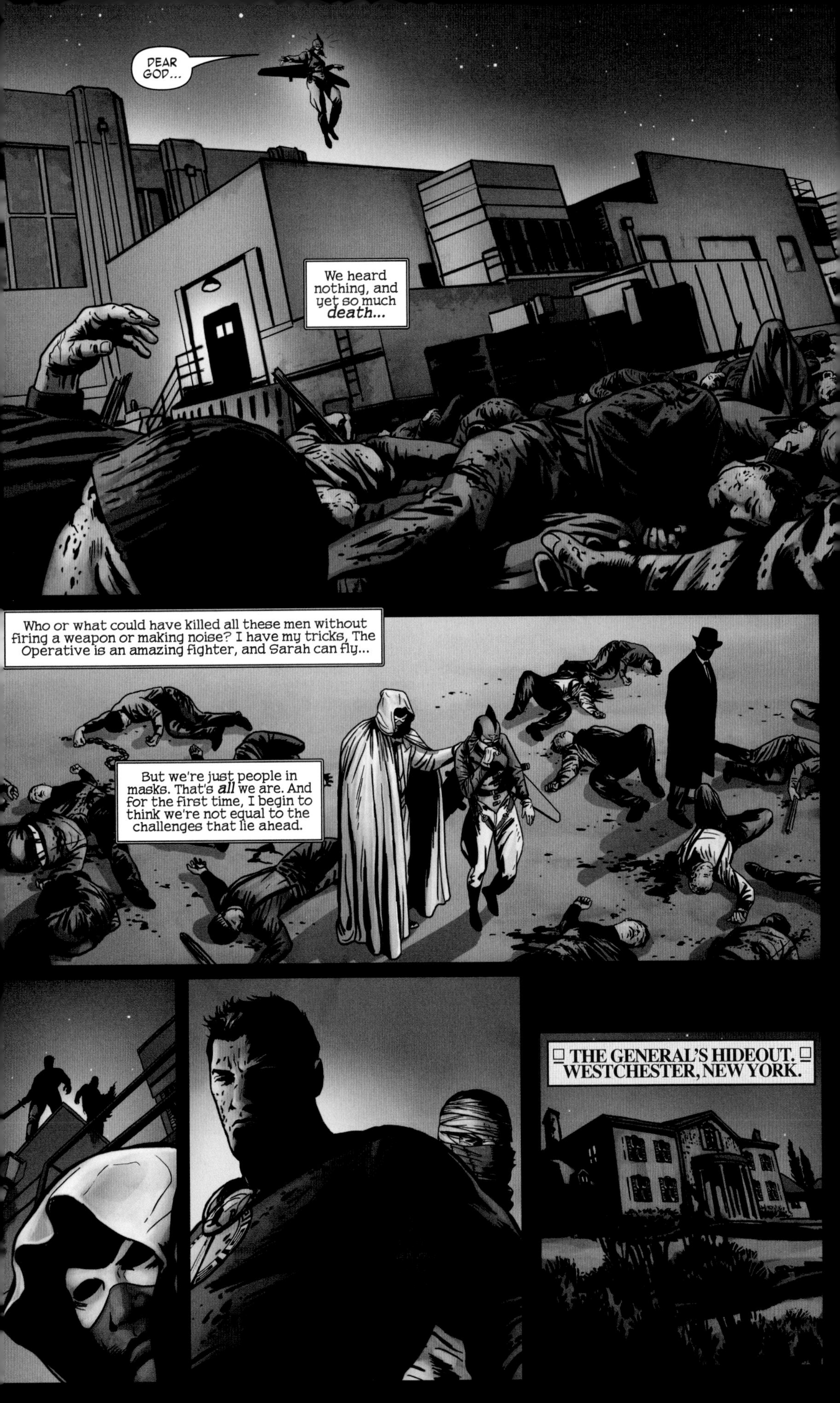
DEAR GOD...
We heard nothing, and yet so much death...
Who or what could have killed all these men without firing a weapon or making noise? I have my tricks, The Operative is an amazing fighter, and Sarah can fly...
But we're just people in masks. That's all we are. And for the first time, I begin to think we're not equal to the challenges that lie ahead.
THE GENERAL'S HIDEOUT. WESTCHESTER, NEW YORK.

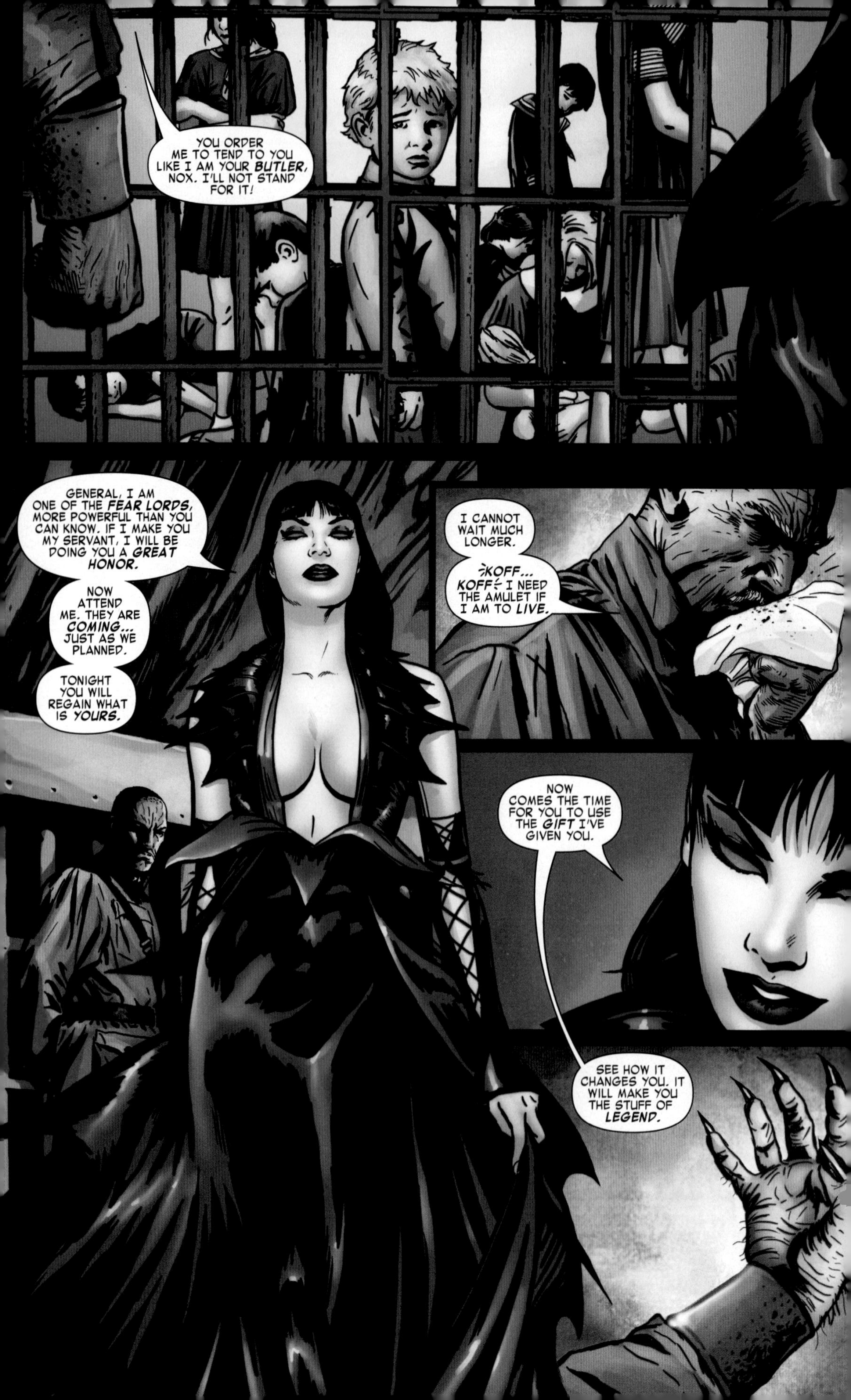
YOU ORDER ME TO TEND TO YOU LIKE I AM YOUR BUTLER, NOX. I'LL NOT STAND FOR IT!
GENERAL, I AM ONE OF THE FEAR LORDS, MORE POWERFUL THAN YOU CAN KNOW. IF I MAKE YOU MY SERVANT, I WILL BE DOING YOU A GREAT HONOR.
NOW ATTEND ME. THEY ARE COMING... JUST AS WE PLANNED.
TONIGHT YOU WILL REGAIN WHAT IS YOURS.
I CANNOT WAIT MUCH LONGER.
KOFF... KOFF I NEED THE AMULET IF I AM TO LIVE.
NOW COMES THE TIME FOR YOU TO USE THE GIFT I'VE GIVEN YOU.
SEE HOW IT CHANGES YOU. IT WILL MAKE YOU THE STUFF OF LEGEND.

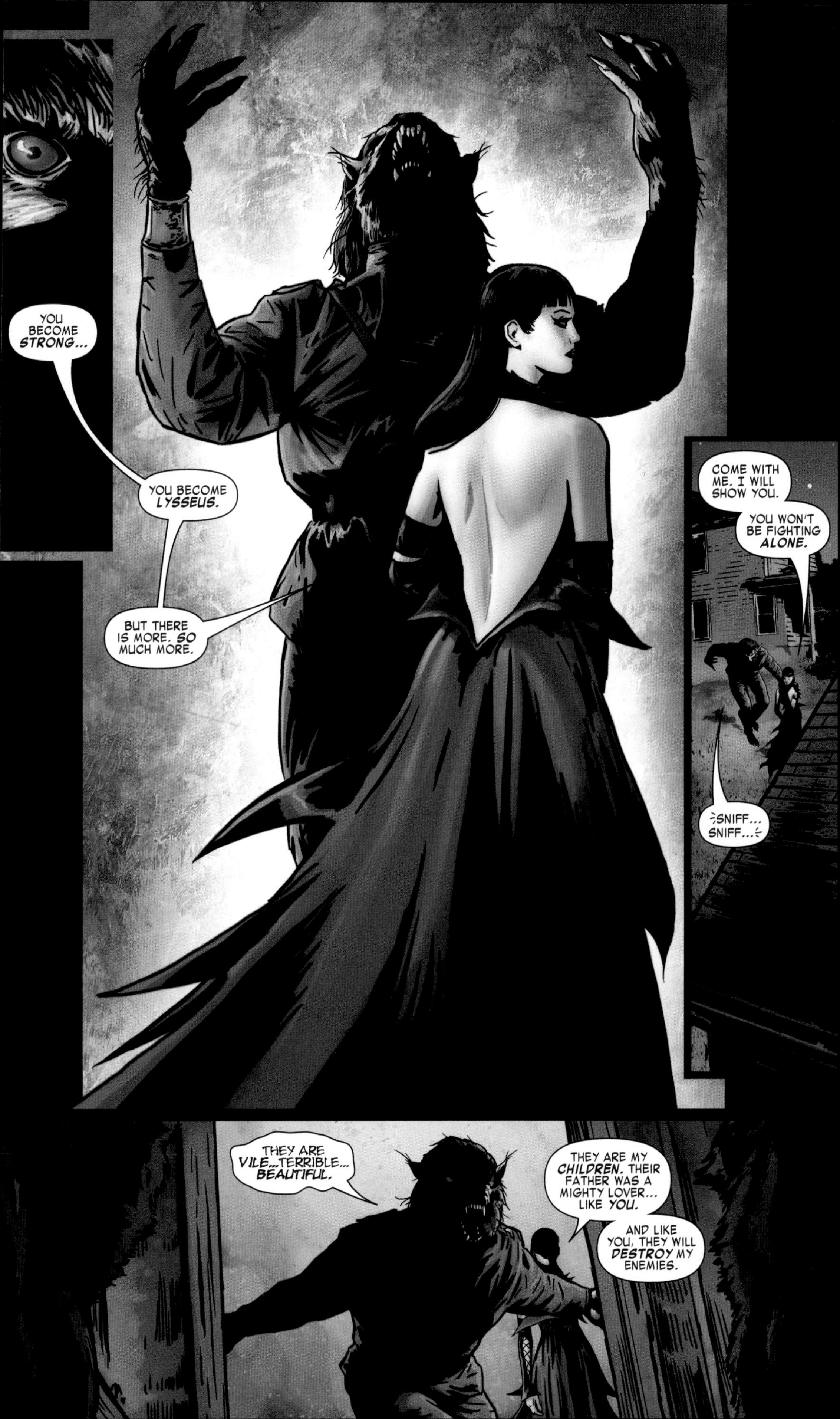

YOU BECOME STRONG...
YOU BECOME LYSSEUS.
BUT THERE IS MORE. SO MUCH MORE.
COME WITH ME. I WILL SHOW YOU.
YOU WON'T BE FIGHTING ALONE.
SNIFF... SNIFF...
THEY ARE VILE...TERRIBLE... BEAUTIFUL.
THEY ARE MY CHILDREN. THEIR FATHER WAS A MIGHTY LOVER... LIKE YOU.
AND LIKE YOU, THEY WILL DESTROY MY ENEMIES.

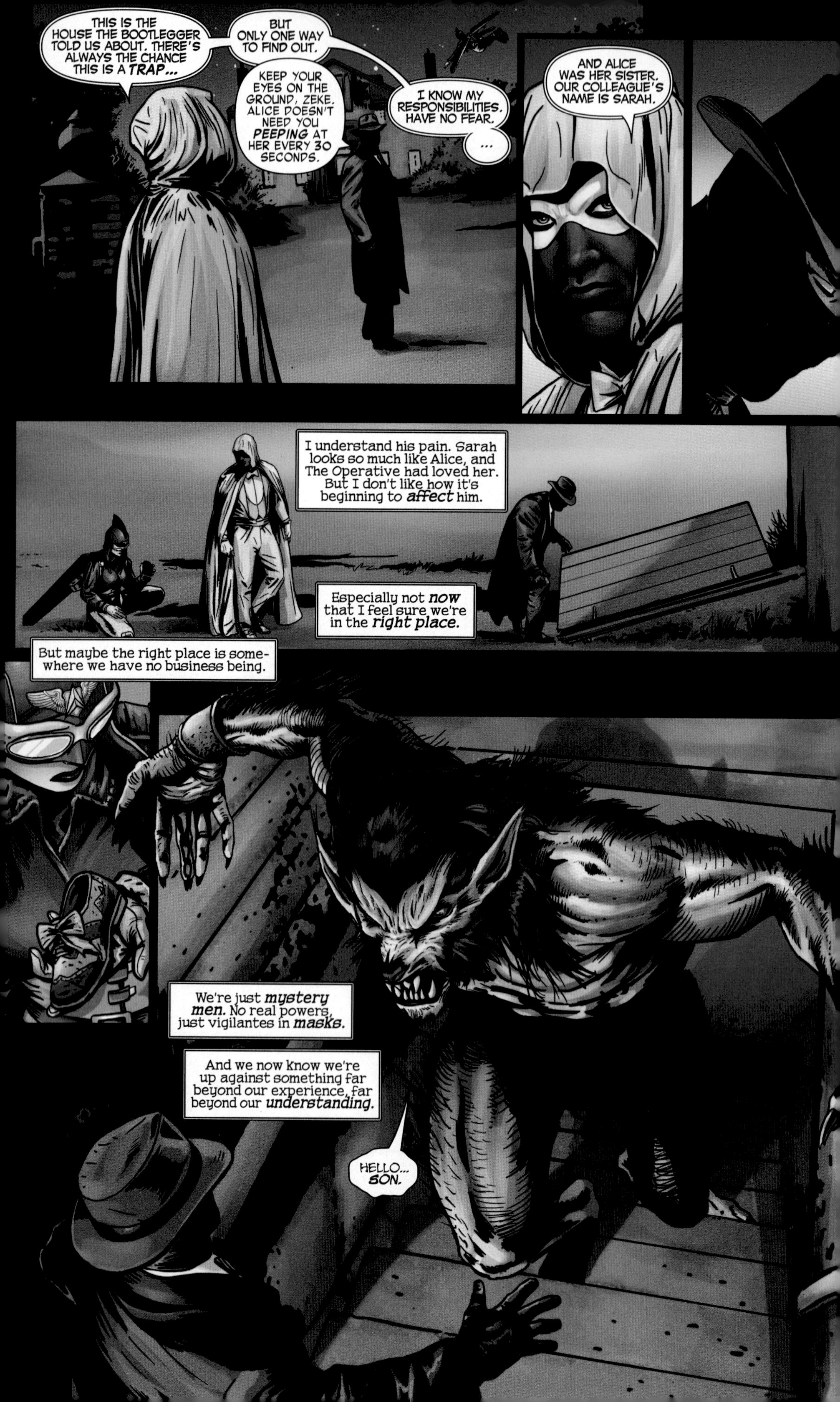
THIS IS THE HOUSE THE BOOTLEGGER TOLD US ABOUT. THERE'S ALWAYS THE CHANCE THIS IS A TRAP...
BUT ONLY ONE WAY TO FIND OUT.
KEEP YOUR EYES ON THE GROUND, ZEKE. ALICE DOESN'T NEED YOU PEEPING AT HER EVERY 30 SECONDS.
I KNOW MY RESPONSIBILITIES. HAVE NO FEAR.
...
AND ALICE WAS HER SISTER. OUR COLLEAGUE'S NAME IS SARAH.
I understand his pain. Sarah looks so much like Alice, and The Operative had loved her. But I don't like how it's beginning to affect him.
Especially not now that I feel sure we're in the right place.
But maybe the right place is somewhere we have no business being.
We're just mystery men. No real powers, just vigilantes in masks.
And we now know we're up against something far beyond our experience, far beyond our understanding.
HELLO... SON.

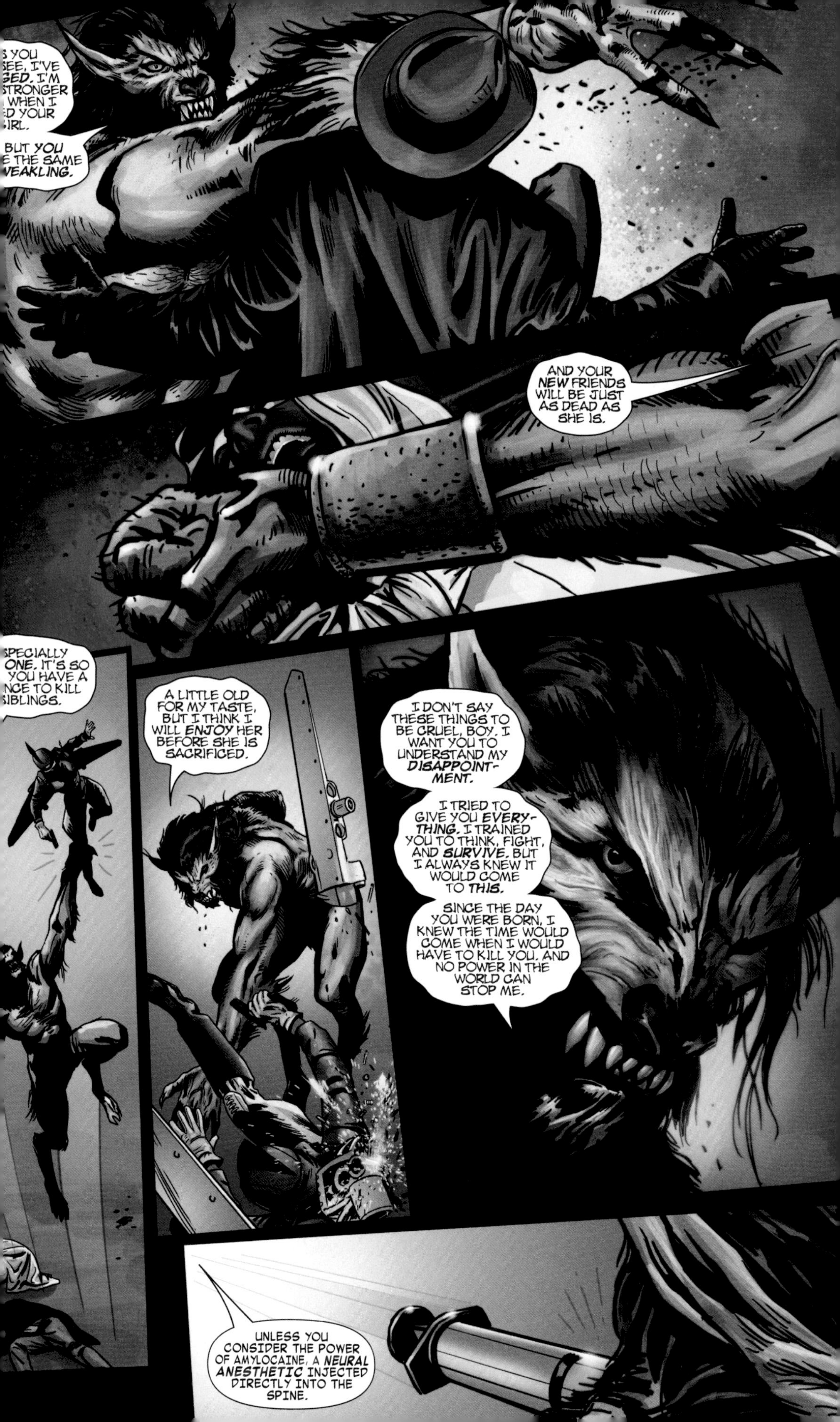
S YOU SEE, I'VE GED. I'M STRONGER WHEN I ED YOUR GIRL.
BUT YOU E THE SAME VEAKLING.
AND YOUR NEW FRIENDS WILL BE JUST AS DEAD AS SHE IS.
SPECIALLY ONE. IT'S SO YOU HAVE A NCE TO KILL SIBLINGS.
A LITTLE OLD FOR MY TASTE, BUT I THINK I WILL ENJOY HER BEFORE SHE IS SACRIFICED.
I DON'T SAY THESE THINGS TO BE CRUEL, BOY. I WANT YOU TO UNDERSTAND MY DISAPPOINT-MENT.
I TRIED TO GIVE YOU EVERY-THING. I TRAINED YOU TO THINK, FIGHT, AND SURVIVE. BUT I ALWAYS KNEW IT WOULD COME TO THIS.
SINCE THE DAY YOU WERE BORN, I KNEW THE TIME WOULD COME WHEN I WOULD HAVE TO KILL YOU. AND NO POWER IN THE WORLD CAN STOP ME.
UNLESS YOU CONSIDER THE POWER OF AMYLOCAINE, A NEURAL ANESTHETIC INJECTED DIRECTLY INTO THE SPINE.

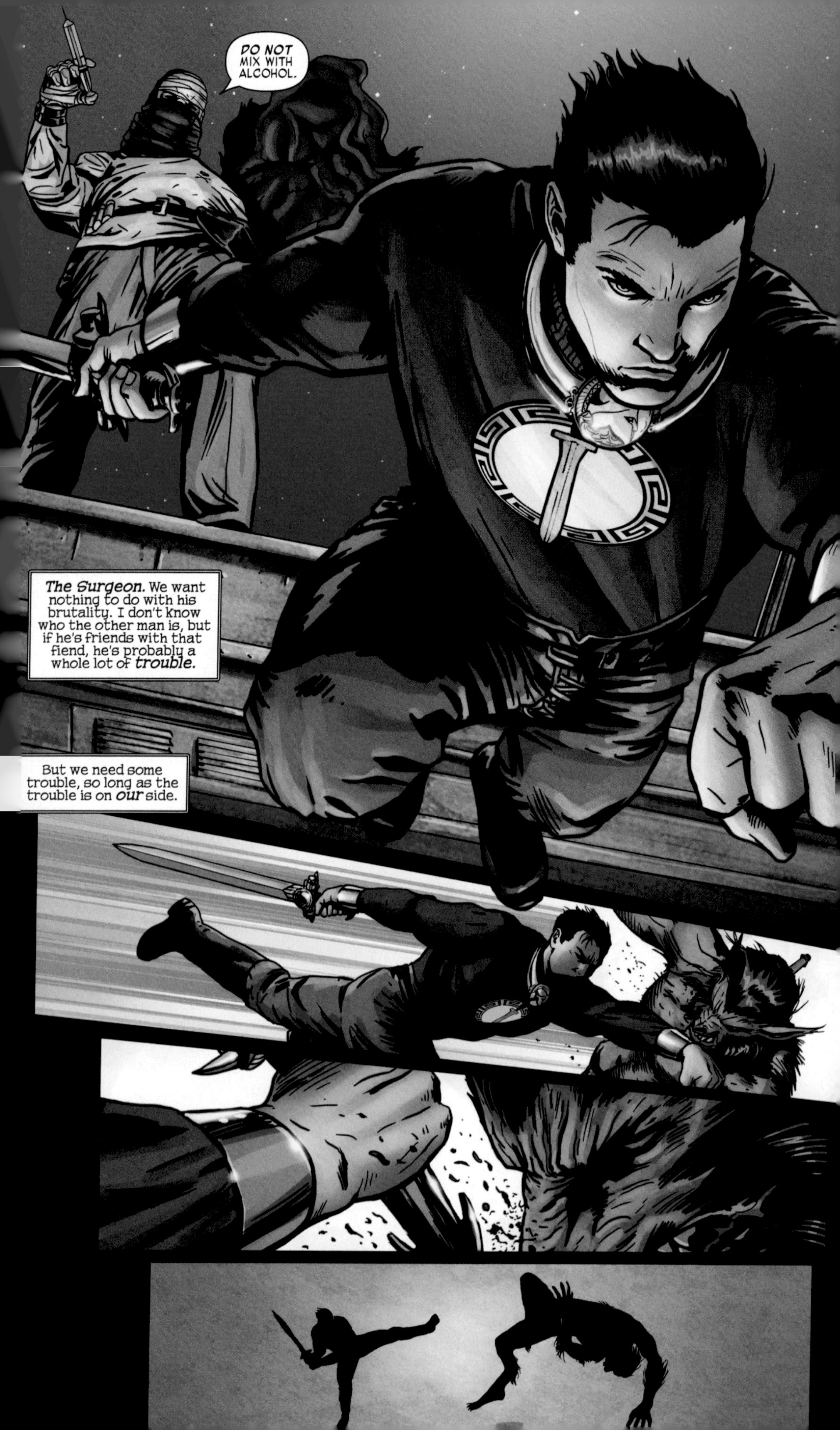
DO NOT MIX WITH ALCOHOL.
The Surgeon. We want nothing to do with his brutality. I don't know who the other man is, but if he's friends with that fiend, he's probably a whole lot of trouble.
But we need some trouble, so long as the trouble is on our side.

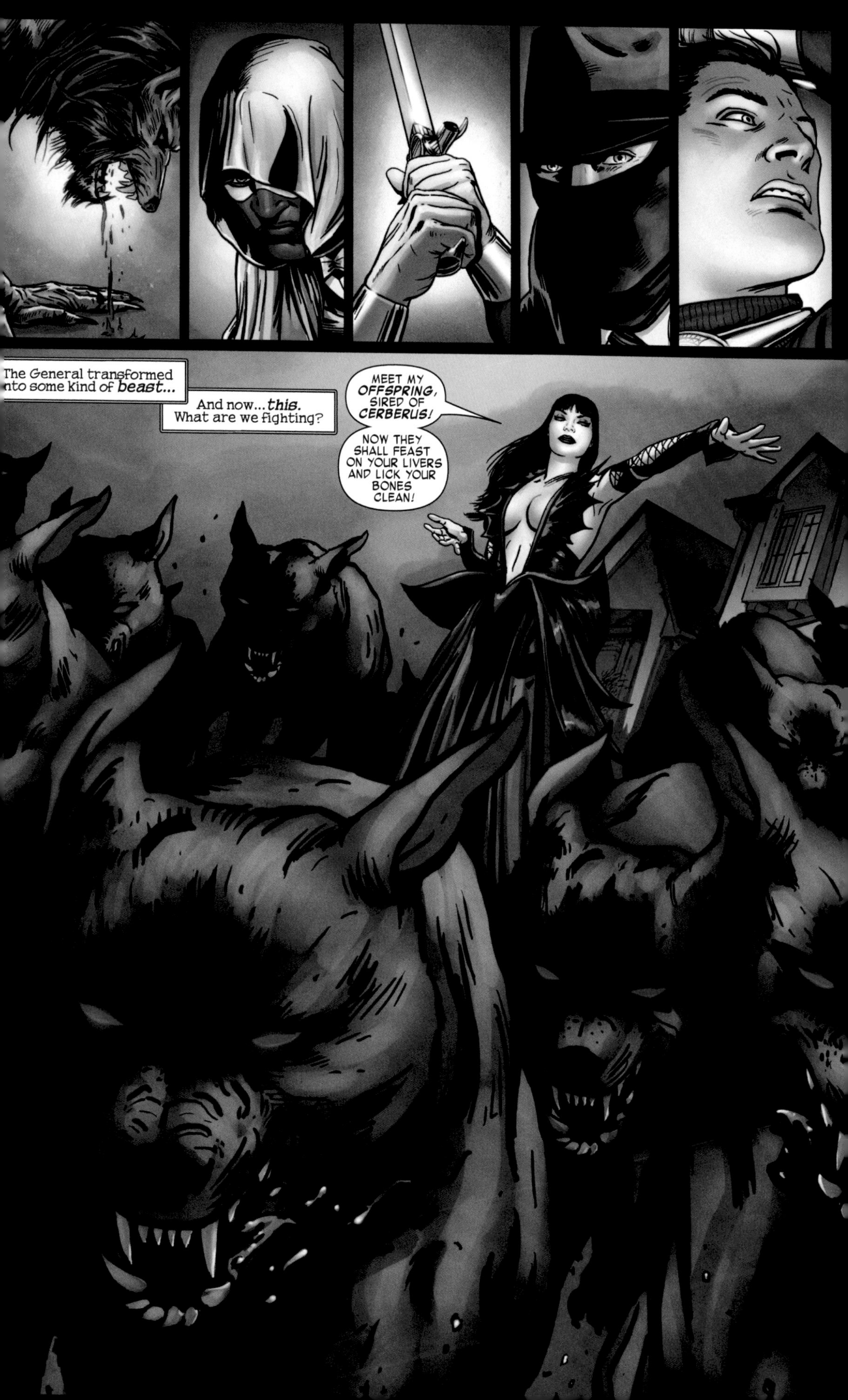
The General transformed into some kind of beast...
And now...this. What are we fighting?
MEET MY OFFSPRING, SIRED OF CERBERUS!
NOW THEY SHALL FEAST ON YOUR LIVERS AND LICK YOUR BONES CLEAN!

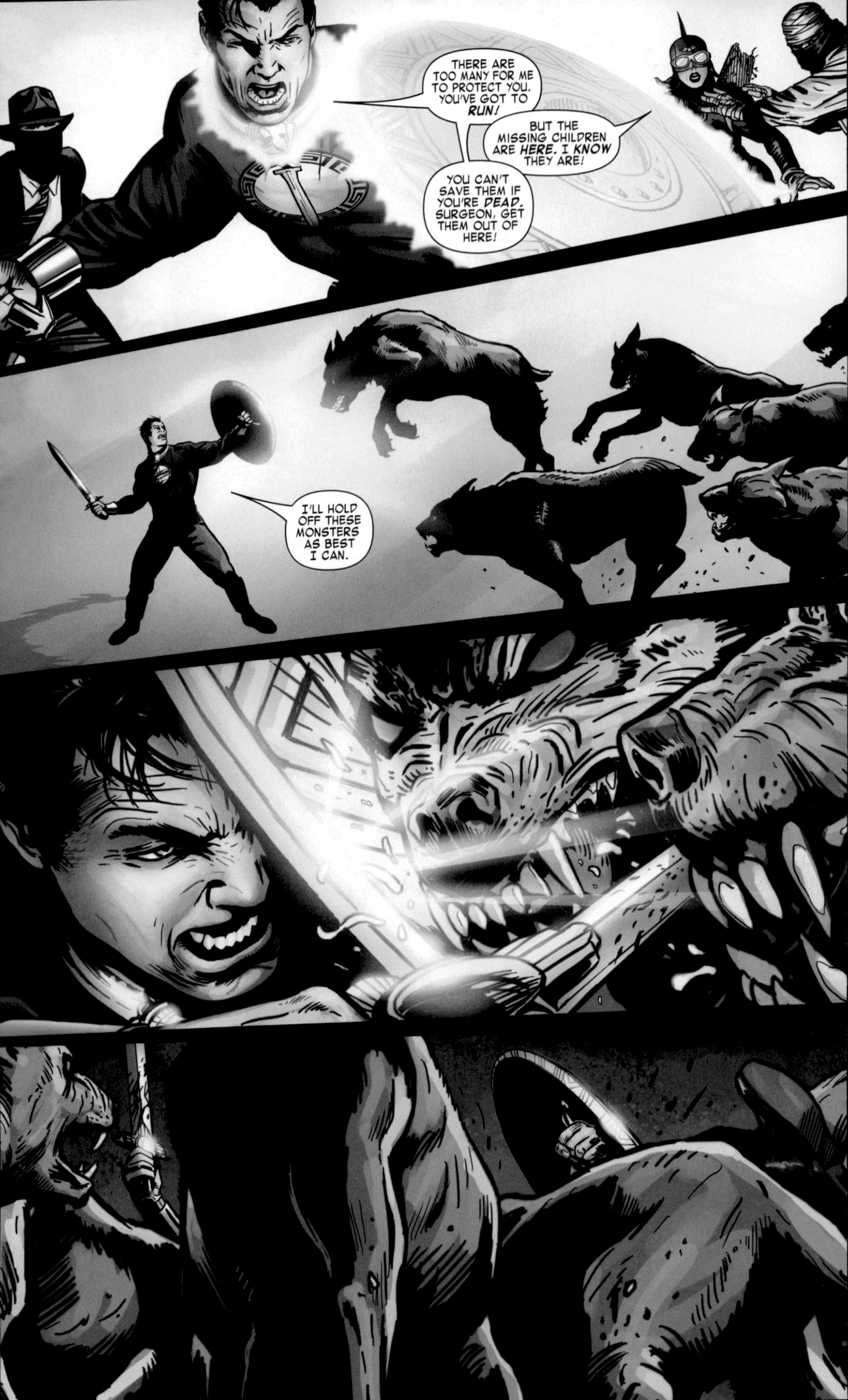
THERE ARE TOO MANY FOR ME TO PROTECT YOU. YOU'VE GOT TO RUN!
BUT THE MISSING CHILDREN ARE HERE. I KNOW THEY ARE!
YOU CAN'T SAVE THEM IF YOU'RE DEAD. SURGEON, GET THEM OUT OF HERE!
I'LL HOLD OFF THESE MONSTERS AS BEST I CAN.

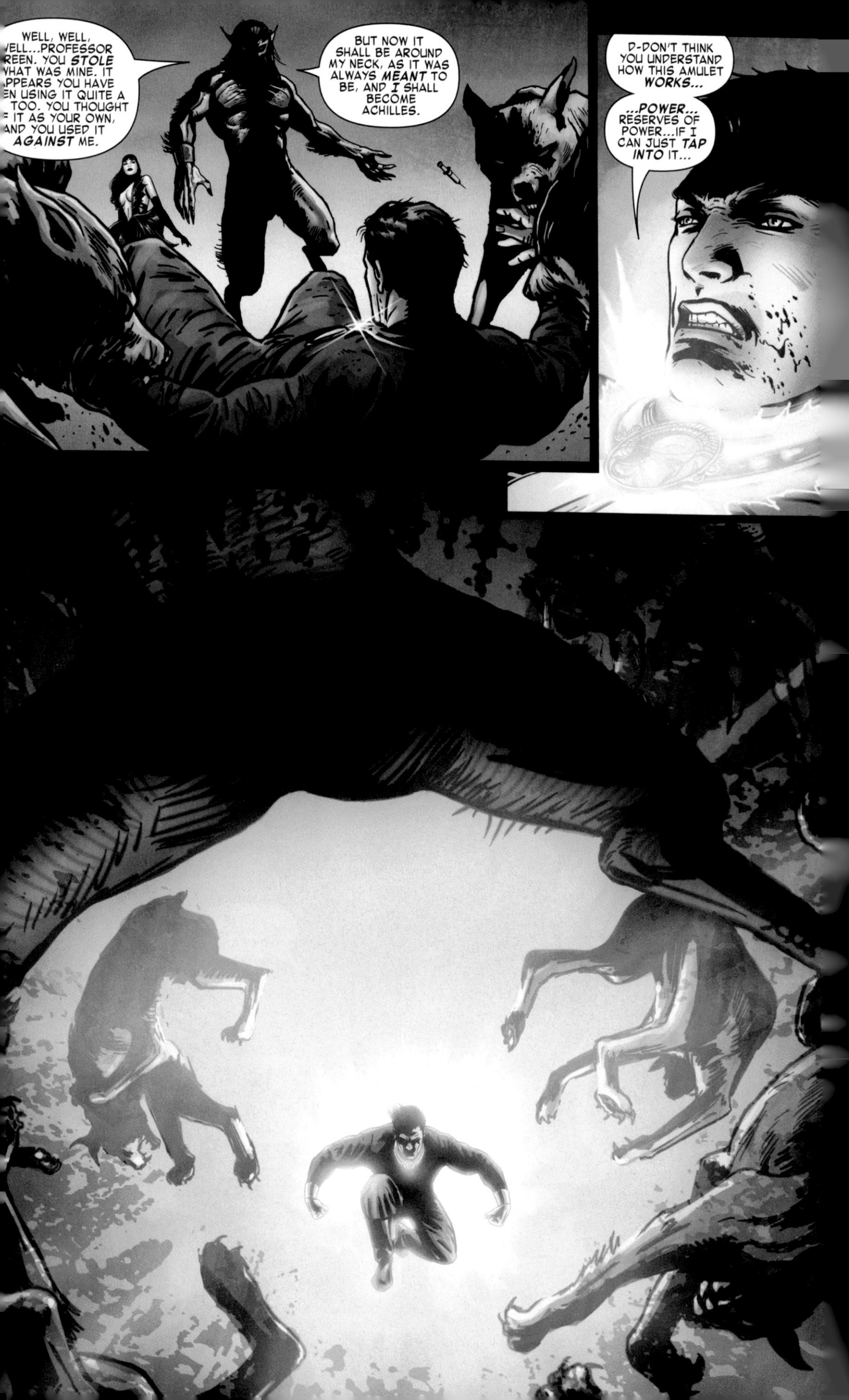

WELL, WELL, VELL...PROFESSOR REEN. YOU STOLE VHAT WAS MINE. IT PPEARS YOU HAVE EN USING IT QUITE A TOO. YOU THOUGHT F IT AS YOUR OWN, AND YOU USED IT AGAINST ME.
BUT NOW IT SHALL BE AROUND MY NECK, AS IT WAS ALWAYS MEANT TO BE, AND I SHALL BECOME ACHILLES.
D-DON'T THINK YOU UNDERSTAND HOW THIS AMULET WORKS...
...POWER... RESERVES OF POWER...IF I CAN JUST TAP INTO IT...

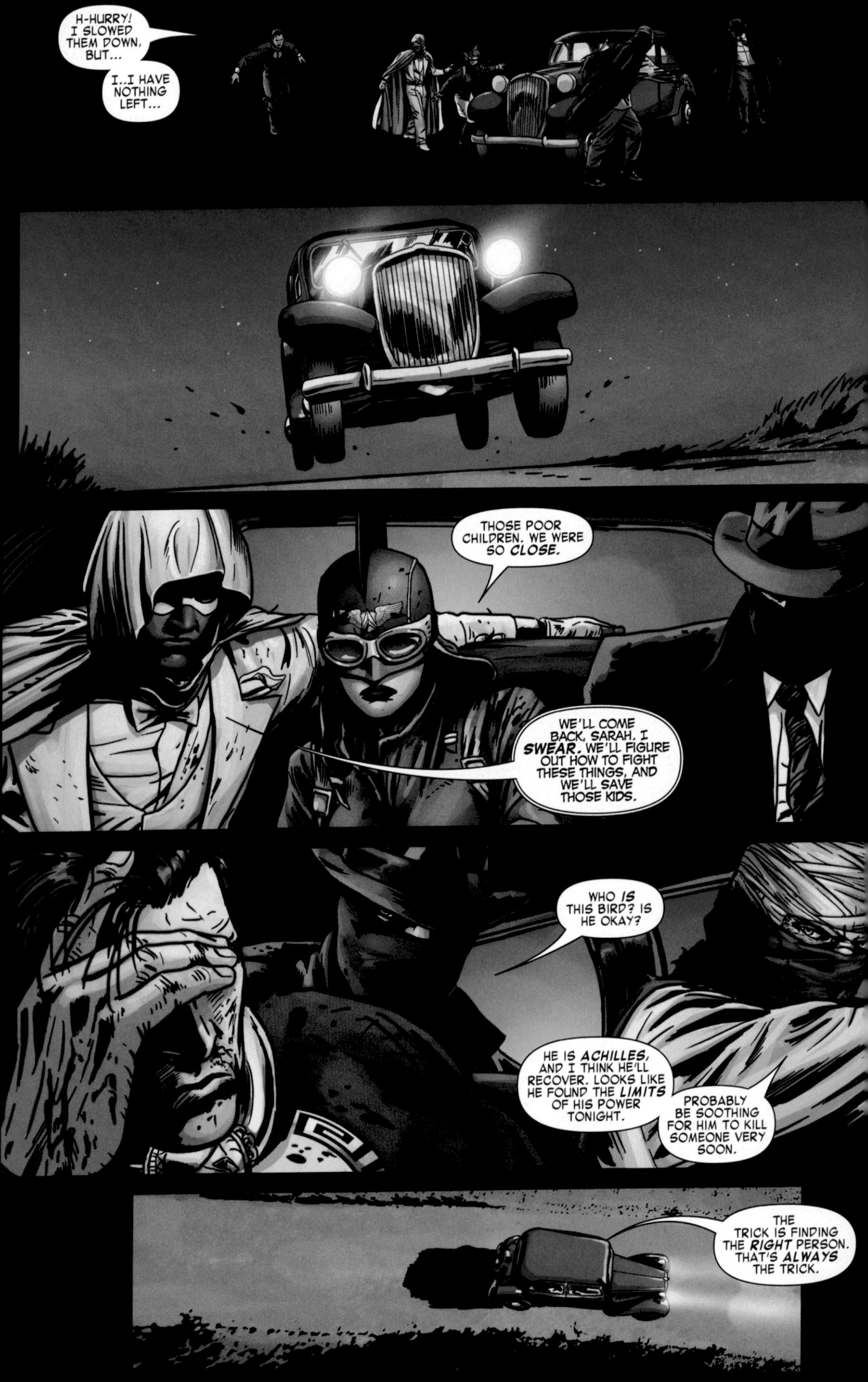
H-HURRY! I SLOWED THEM DOWN, BUT...
I..I HAVE NOTHING LEFT...
THOSE POOR CHILDREN. WE WERE SO CLOSE.
WE'LL COME BACK, SARAH. I SWEAR. WE'LL FIGURE OUT HOW TO FIGHT THESE THINGS, AND WE'LL SAVE THOSE KIDS.
WHO IS THIS BIRD? IS HE OKAY?
HE IS ACHILLES, AND I THINK HE'LL RECOVER. LOOKS LIKE HE FOUND THE LIMITS OF HIS POWER TONIGHT.
PROBABLY BE SOOTHING FOR HIM TO KILL SOMEONE VERY SOON.
THE TRICK IS FINDING THE RIGHT PERSON. THAT'S ALWAYS THE TRICK.

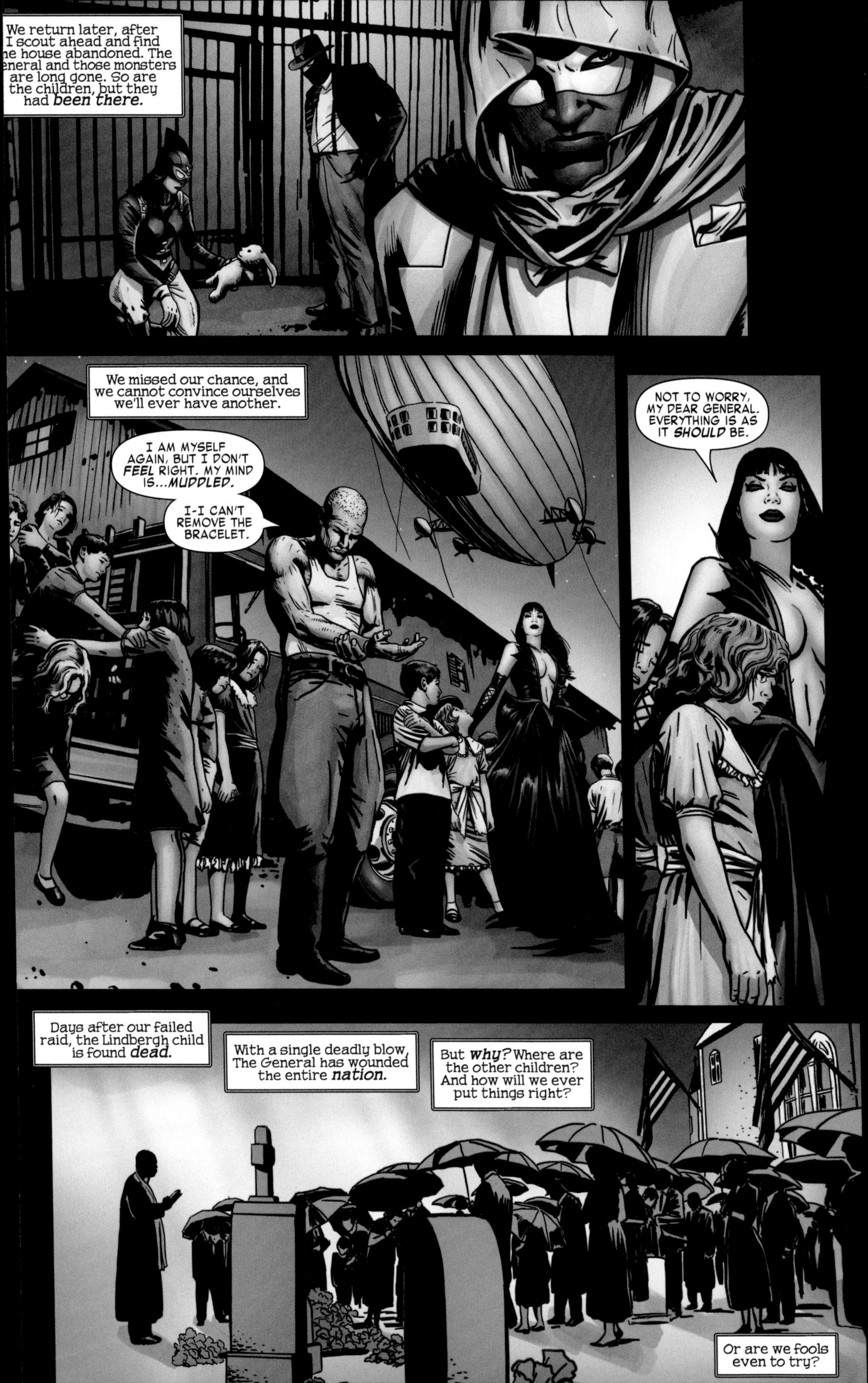

We return later, after I scout ahead and find ne house abandoned. The eneral and those monsters are long gone. So are the children, but they had been there.
We missed our chance, and we cannot convince ourselves we'll ever have another.
I AM MYSELF AGAIN, BUT I DON'T FEEL RIGHT. MY MIND IS...MUDDLED.
I-I CAN'T REMOVE THE BRACELET.
NOT TO WORRY, MY DEAR GENERAL. EVERYTHING IS AS IT SHOULD BE.
Days after our failed raid, the Lindbergh child is found dead.
With a single deadly blow, The General has wounded the entire nation.
But why? Where are the other children? And how will we ever put things right?
Or are we fools even to try?

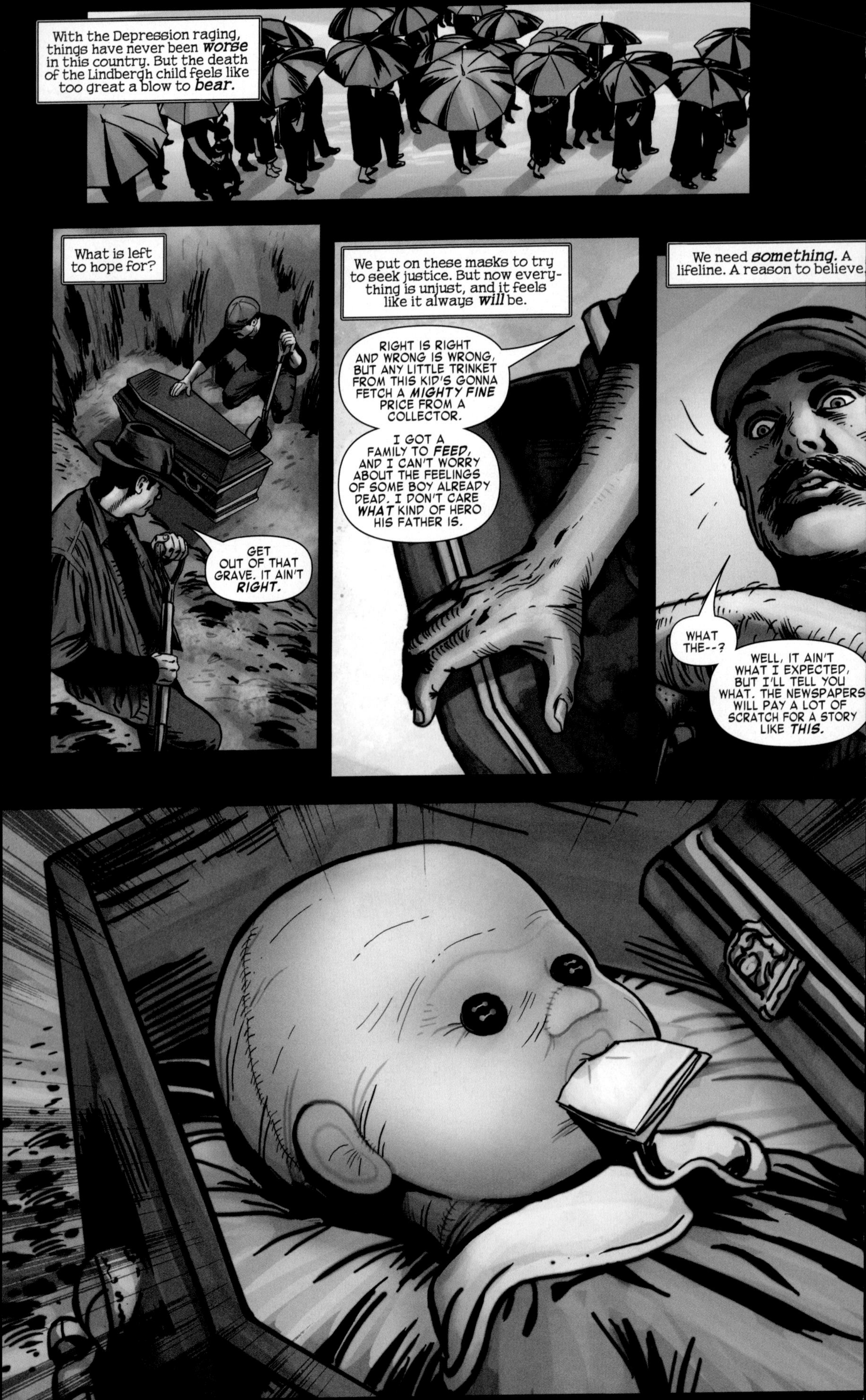

With the Depression raging, things have never been *worse* in this country. But the death of the Lindbergh child feels like too great a blow to *bear*.
What is left to hope for?
GET OUT OF THAT GRAVE. IT AIN'T *RIGHT.*
We put on these masks to try to seek justice. But now everything is unjust, and it feels like it always *will* be.
RIGHT IS RIGHT AND WRONG IS WRONG, BUT ANY LITTLE TRINKET FROM THIS KID'S GONNA FETCH A *MIGHTY FINE* PRICE FROM A COLLECTOR.
I GOT A FAMILY TO *FEED*, AND I CAN'T WORRY ABOUT THE FEELINGS OF SOME BOY ALREADY DEAD. I DON'T CARE *WHAT* KIND OF HERO HIS FATHER IS.
We need *something*. A lifeline. A reason to believe.
WHAT THE--?
WELL, IT AIN'T WHAT I EXPECTED, BUT I'LL TELL YOU WHAT. THE NEWSPAPERS WILL PAY A LOT OF SCRATCH FOR A STORY LIKE *THIS.*

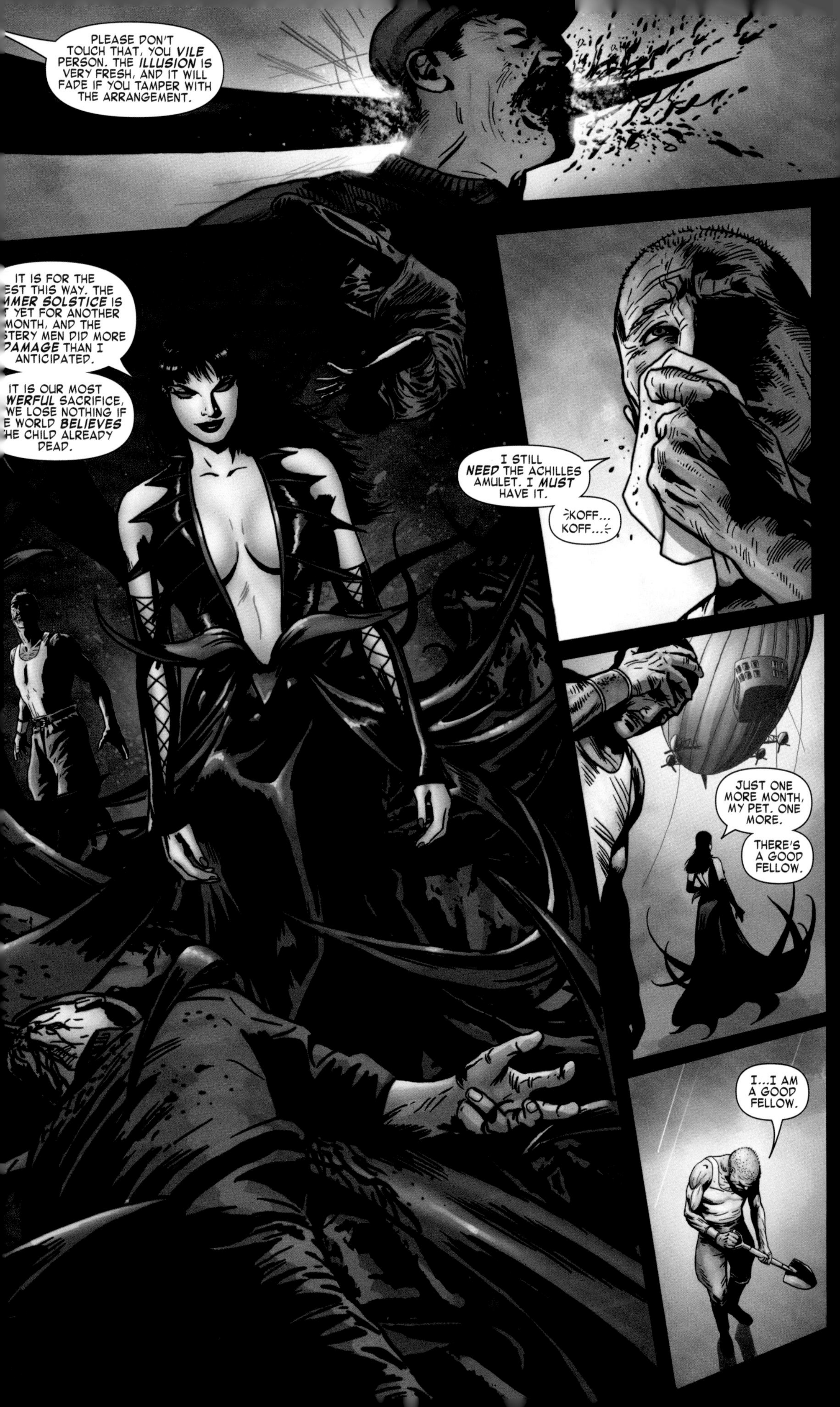
PLEASE DON'T TOUCH THAT, YOU VILE PERSON. THE ILLUSION IS VERY FRESH, AND IT WILL FADE IF YOU TAMPER WITH THE ARRANGEMENT.
IT IS FOR THE EST THIS WAY. THE MMER SOLSTICE IS YET FOR ANOTHER MONTH, AND THE STERY MEN DID MORE DAMAGE THAN I ANTICIPATED.
IT IS OUR MOST WERFUL SACRIFICE, WE LOSE NOTHING IF E WORLD BELIEVES HE CHILD ALREADY DEAD.
I STILL NEED THE ACHILLES AMULET. I MUST HAVE IT.
KOFF... KOFF...
JUST ONE MORE MONTH, MY PET. ONE MORE.
THERE'S A GOOD FELLOW.
I...I AM A GOOD FELLOW.

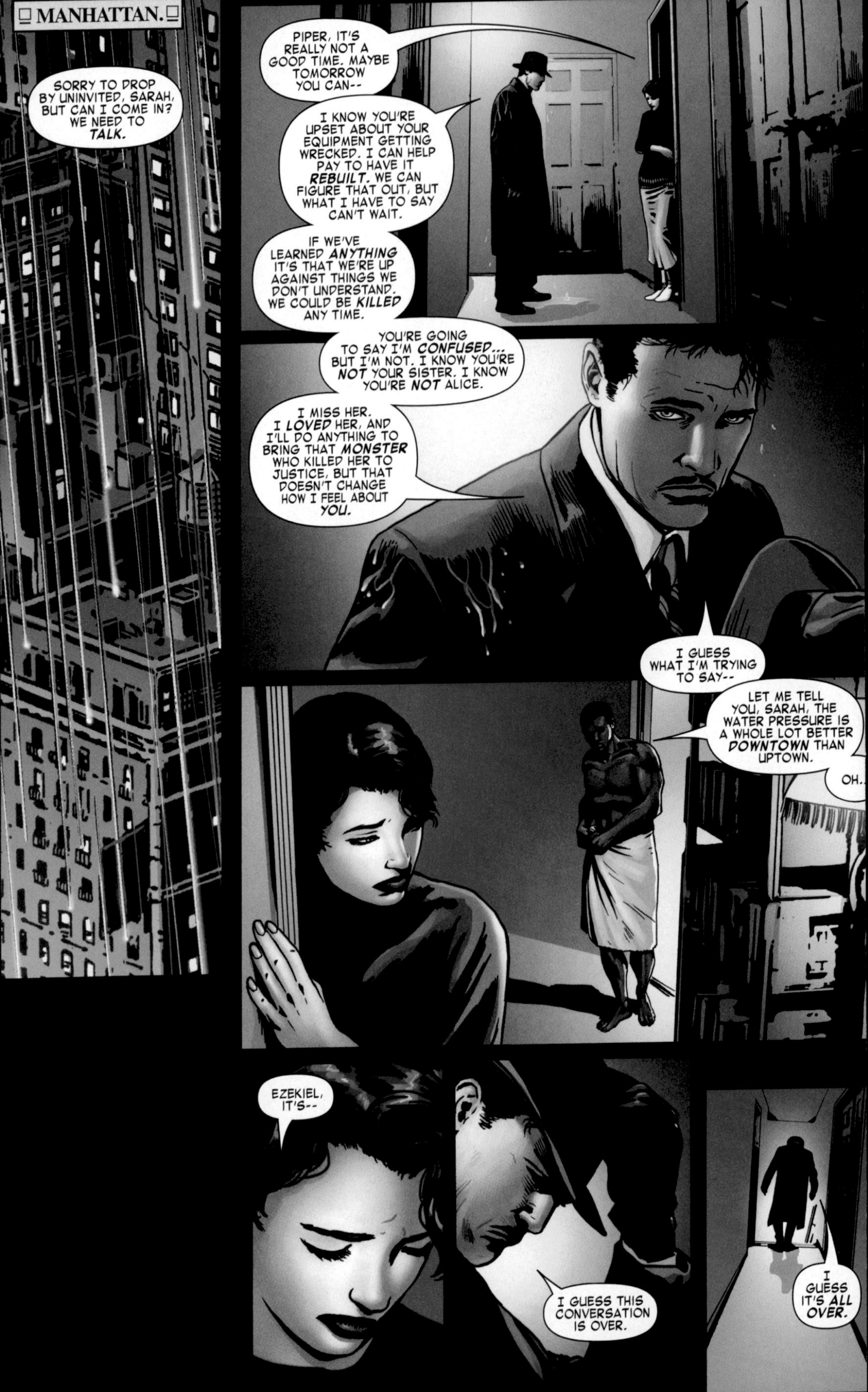
MANHATTAN.
SORRY TO DROP BY UNINVITED, SARAH, BUT CAN I COME IN? WE NEED TO TALK.
PIPER, IT'S REALLY NOT A GOOD TIME. MAYBE TOMORROW YOU CAN--
I KNOW YOU'RE UPSET ABOUT YOUR EQUIPMENT GETTING WRECKED. I CAN HELP PAY TO HAVE IT REBUILT. WE CAN FIGURE THAT OUT, BUT WHAT I HAVE TO SAY CAN'T WAIT.
IF WE'VE LEARNED ANYTHING IT'S THAT WE'RE UP AGAINST THINGS WE DON'T UNDERSTAND. WE COULD BE KILLED ANY TIME.
YOU'RE GOING TO SAY I'M CONFUSED... BUT I'M NOT. I KNOW YOU'RE NOT YOUR SISTER. I KNOW YOU'RE NOT ALICE.
I MISS HER. I LOVED HER, AND I'LL DO ANYTHING TO BRING THAT MONSTER WHO KILLED HER TO JUSTICE, BUT THAT DOESN'T CHANGE HOW I FEEL ABOUT YOU.
I GUESS WHAT I'M TRYING TO SAY--
LET ME TELL YOU, SARAH, THE WATER PRESSURE IS A WHOLE LOT BETTER DOWNTOWN THAN UPTOWN.
OH..
EZEKIEL, IT'S--
I GUESS THIS CONVERSATION IS OVER.
I GUESS IT'S ALL OVER.

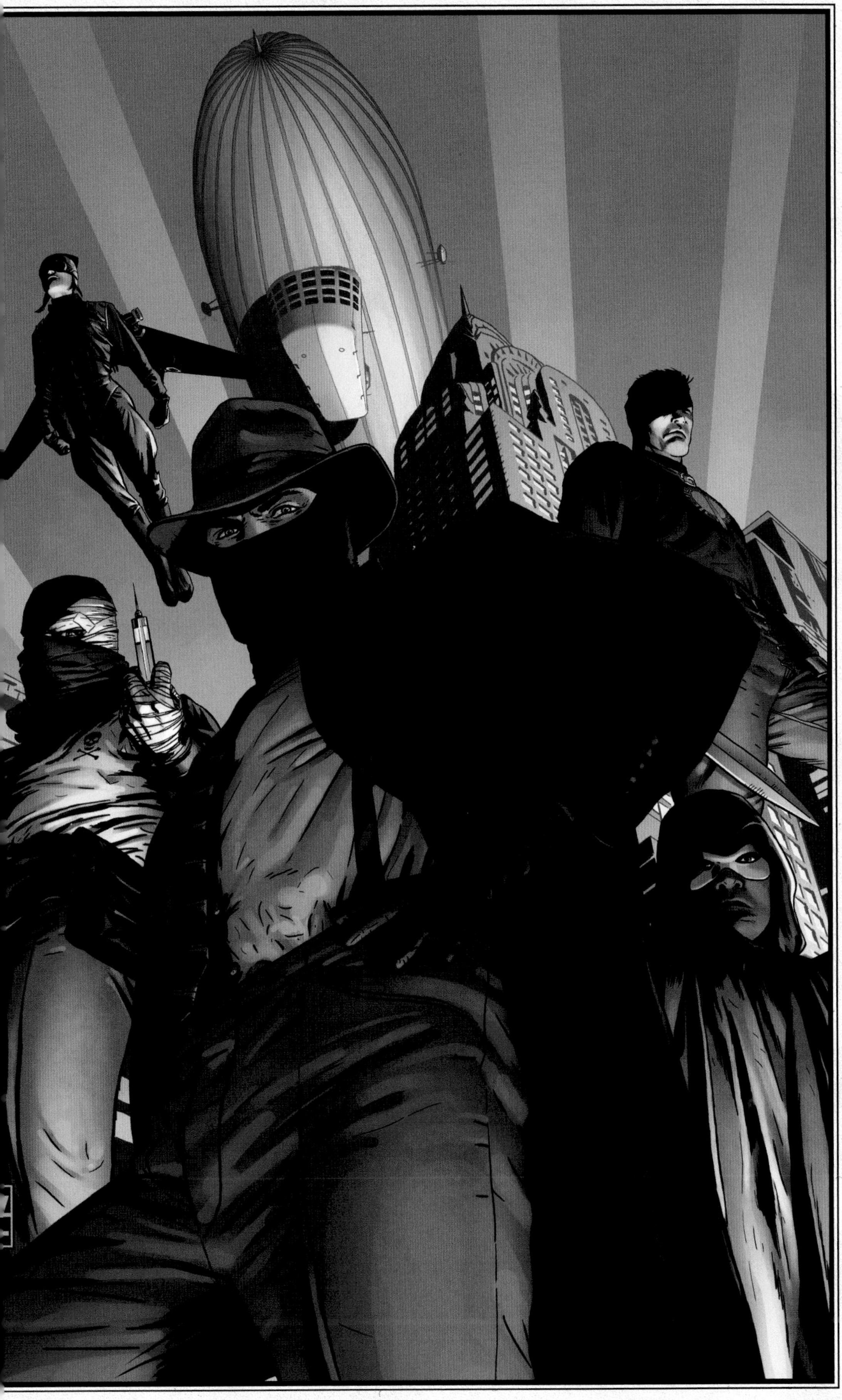

MYSTERY MEN #5

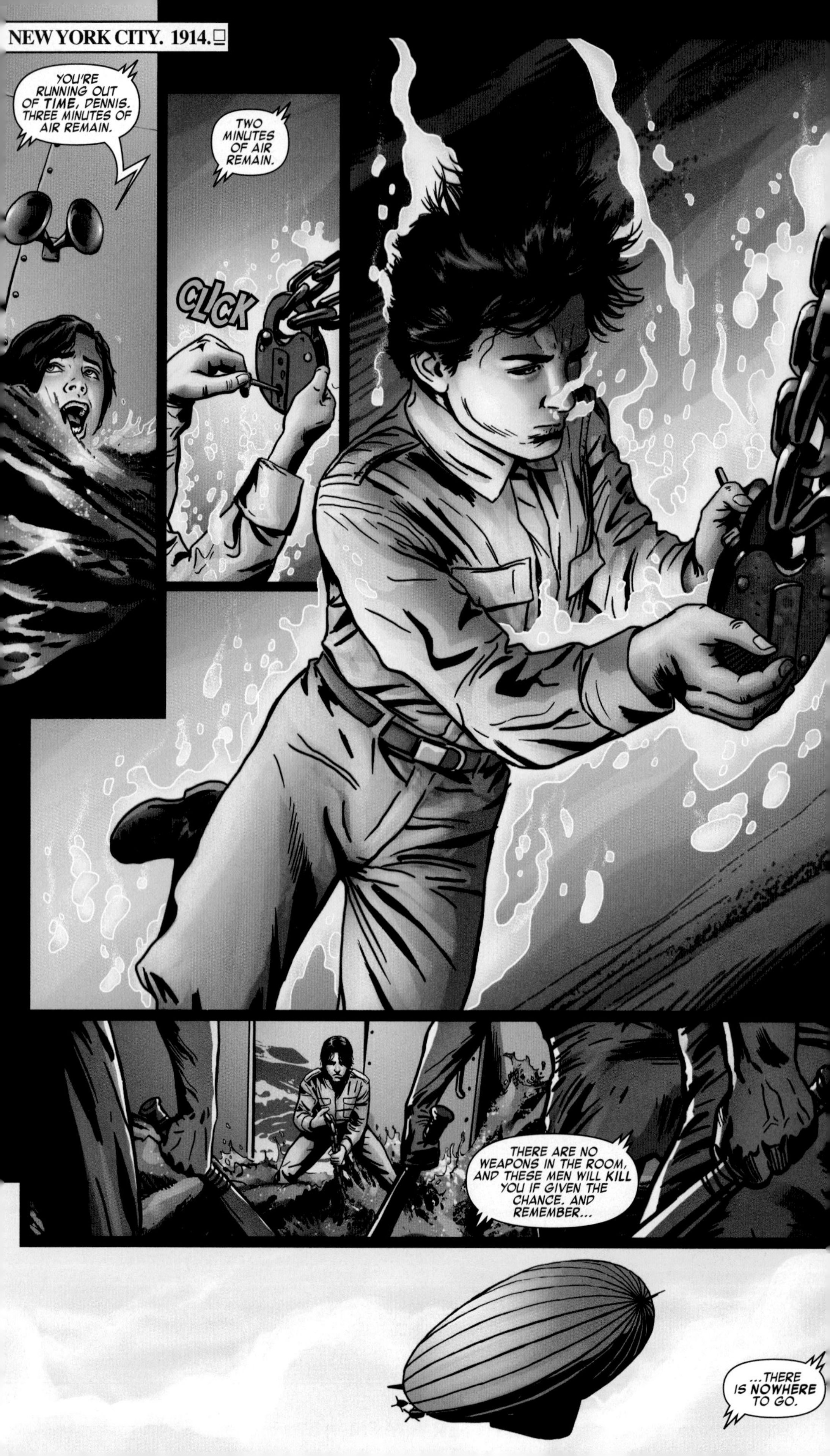
NEW YORK CITY. 1914.
YOU'RE RUNNING OUT OF TIME, DENNIS. THREE MINUTES OF AIR REMAIN.
TWO MINUTES OF AIR REMAIN.
CLICK
THERE ARE NO WEAPONS IN THE ROOM, AND THESE MEN WILL KILL YOU IF GIVEN THE CHANCE. AND REMEMBER...
...THERE IS NOWHERE TO GO.

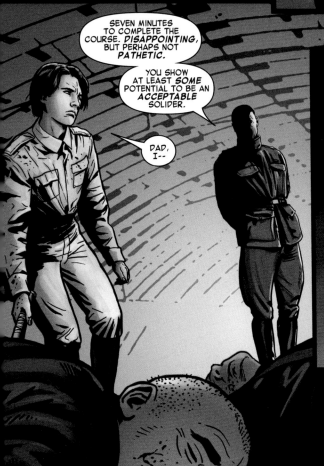

SEVEN MINUTES TO COMPLETE THE COURSE. *DISAPPOINTING*, BUT PERHAPS NOT *PATHETIC*.

YOU SHOW AT LEAST *SOME* POTENTIAL TO BE AN *ACCEPTABLE* SOLIDER.

DAD, I--

MAJOR!

MAJOR...I DON'T *WANT* TO BE A SOLDIER.

YOU DO NOT *CHOOSE* WHAT YOU WANT, SON.

DESTINY CHOOSES FOR YOU.

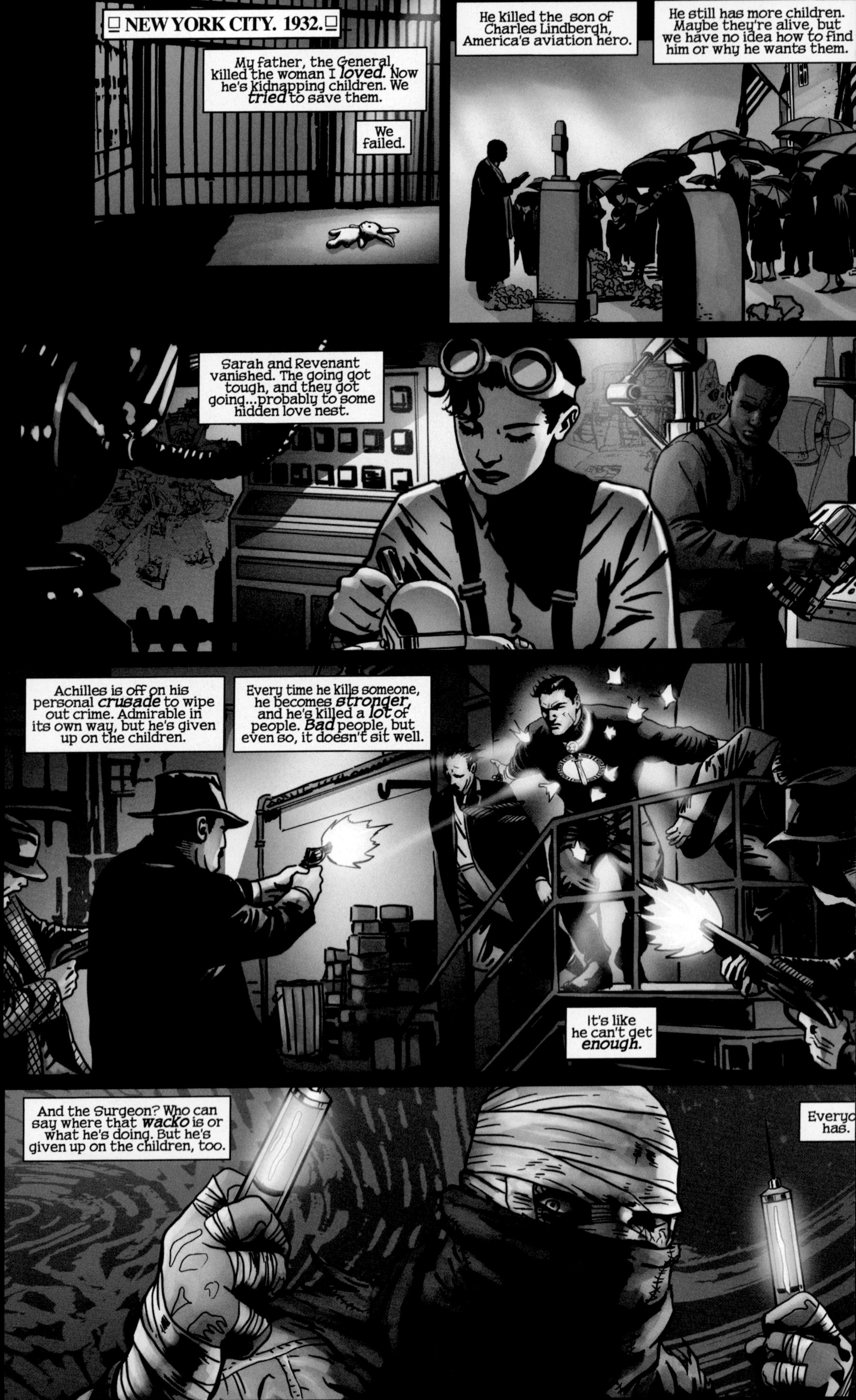
NEW YORK CITY. 1932.
My father, the General, killed the woman I loved. Now he's kidnapping children. We tried to save them.
We failed.
He killed the son of Charles Lindbergh, America's aviation hero.
He still has more children. Maybe they're alive, but we have no idea how to find him or why he wants them.
Sarah and Revenant vanished. The going got tough, and they got going...probably to some hidden love nest.
Achilles is off on his personal crusade to wipe out crime. Admirable in its own way, but he's given up on the children.
Every time he kills someone, he becomes stronger, and he's killed a lot of people. Bad people, but even so, it doesn't sit well.
It's like he can't get enough.
And the Surgeon? Who can say where that wacko is or what he's doing. But he's given up on the children, too.

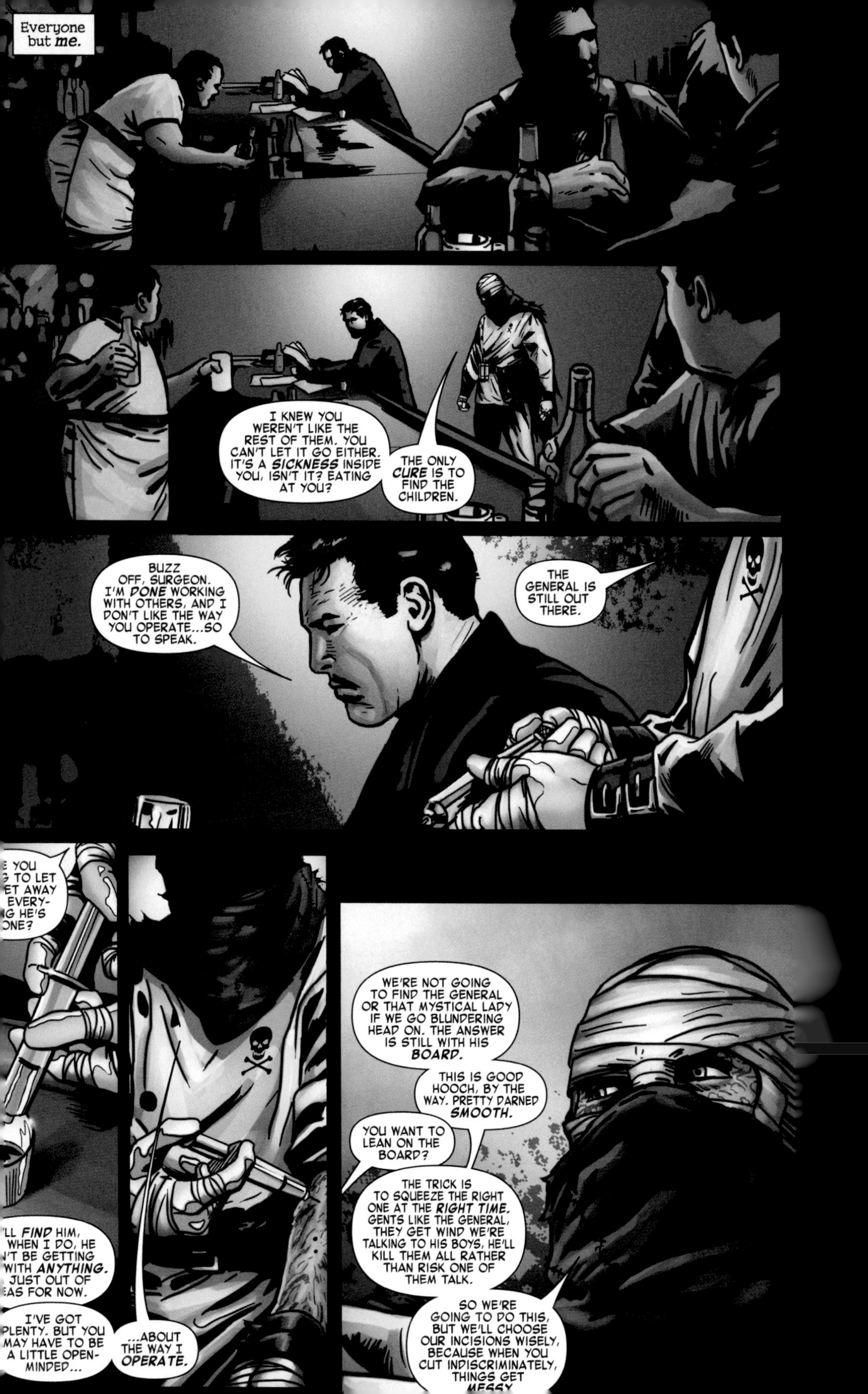
Everyone but *me.*
I KNEW YOU WEREN'T LIKE THE REST OF THEM. YOU CAN'T LET IT GO EITHER. IT'S A *SICKNESS* INSIDE YOU, ISN'T IT? EATING AT YOU?
THE ONLY *CURE* IS TO FIND THE CHILDREN.
BUZZ OFF, SURGEON. I'M *DONE* WORKING WITH OTHERS, AND I DON'T LIKE THE WAY YOU OPERATE...SO TO SPEAK.
THE GENERAL IS STILL OUT THERE.
'LL *FIND* HIM, WHEN I DO, HE N'T BE GETTING WITH *ANYTHING.* JUST OUT OF EAS FOR NOW.
I'VE GOT PLENTY. BUT YOU MAY HAVE TO BE A LITTLE OPEN-MINDED...
...ABOUT THE WAY I *OPERATE.*
WE'RE NOT GOING TO FIND THE GENERAL OR THAT MYSTICAL LADY IF WE GO BLUNDERING HEAD ON. THE ANSWER IS STILL WITH HIS *BOARD.*
THIS IS GOOD HOOCH, BY THE WAY. PRETTY DARNED *SMOOTH.*
YOU WANT TO LEAN ON THE BOARD?
THE TRICK IS TO SQUEEZE THE RIGHT ONE AT THE *RIGHT TIME.* GENTS LIKE THE GENERAL, THEY GET WIND WE'RE TALKING TO HIS BOYS, HE'LL KILL THEM ALL RATHER THAN RISK ONE OF THEM TALK.
SO WE'RE GOING TO DO THIS, BUT WE'LL CHOOSE OUR INCISIONS WISELY, BECAUSE WHEN YOU CUT INDISCRIMINATELY, THINGS GET

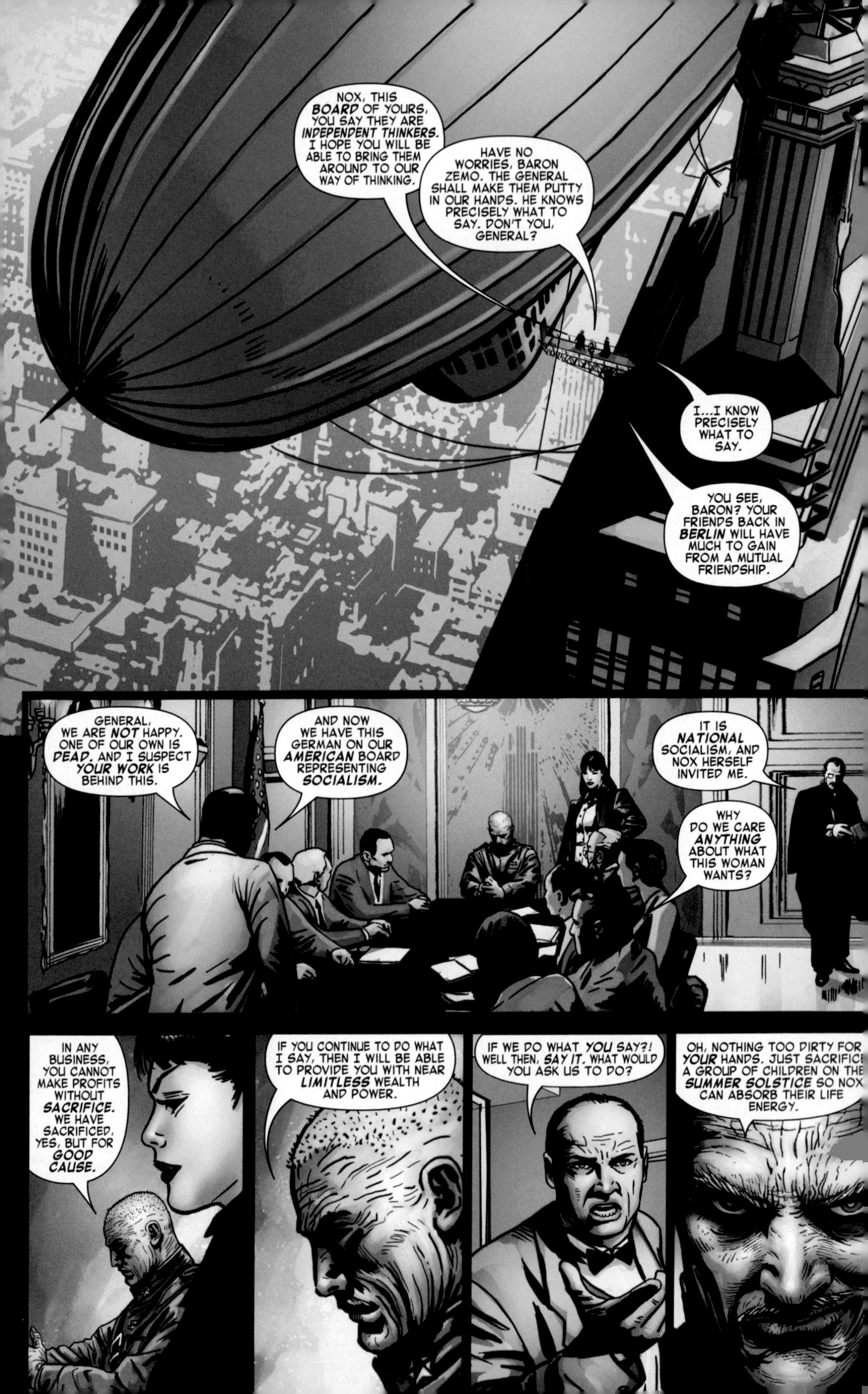
NOX, THIS BOARD OF YOURS, YOU SAY THEY ARE INDEPENDENT THINKERS. I HOPE YOU WILL BE ABLE TO BRING THEM AROUND TO OUR WAY OF THINKING.
HAVE NO WORRIES, BARON ZEMO. THE GENERAL SHALL MAKE THEM PUTTY IN OUR HANDS. HE KNOWS PRECISELY WHAT TO SAY. DON'T YOU, GENERAL?
I...I KNOW PRECISELY WHAT TO SAY.
YOU SEE, BARON? YOUR FRIENDS BACK IN BERLIN WILL HAVE MUCH TO GAIN FROM A MUTUAL FRIENDSHIP.
GENERAL, WE ARE NOT HAPPY. ONE OF OUR OWN IS DEAD. AND I SUSPECT YOUR WORK IS BEHIND THIS.
AND NOW WE HAVE THIS GERMAN ON OUR AMERICAN BOARD REPRESENTING SOCIALISM.
IT IS NATIONAL SOCIALISM, AND NOX HERSELF INVITED ME.
WHY DO WE CARE ANYTHING ABOUT WHAT THIS WOMAN WANTS?
IN ANY BUSINESS, YOU CANNOT MAKE PROFITS WITHOUT SACRIFICE. WE HAVE SACRIFICED, YES, BUT FOR GOOD CAUSE.
IF YOU CONTINUE TO DO WHAT I SAY, THEN I WILL BE ABLE TO PROVIDE YOU WITH NEAR LIMITLESS WEALTH AND POWER.
IF WE DO WHAT YOU SAY?! WELL THEN, SAY IT. WHAT WOULD YOU ASK US TO DO?
OH, NOTHING TOO DIRTY FOR YOUR HANDS. JUST SACRIFICE A GROUP OF CHILDREN ON THE SUMMER SOLSTICE SO NOX CAN ABSORB THEIR LIFE ENERGY.

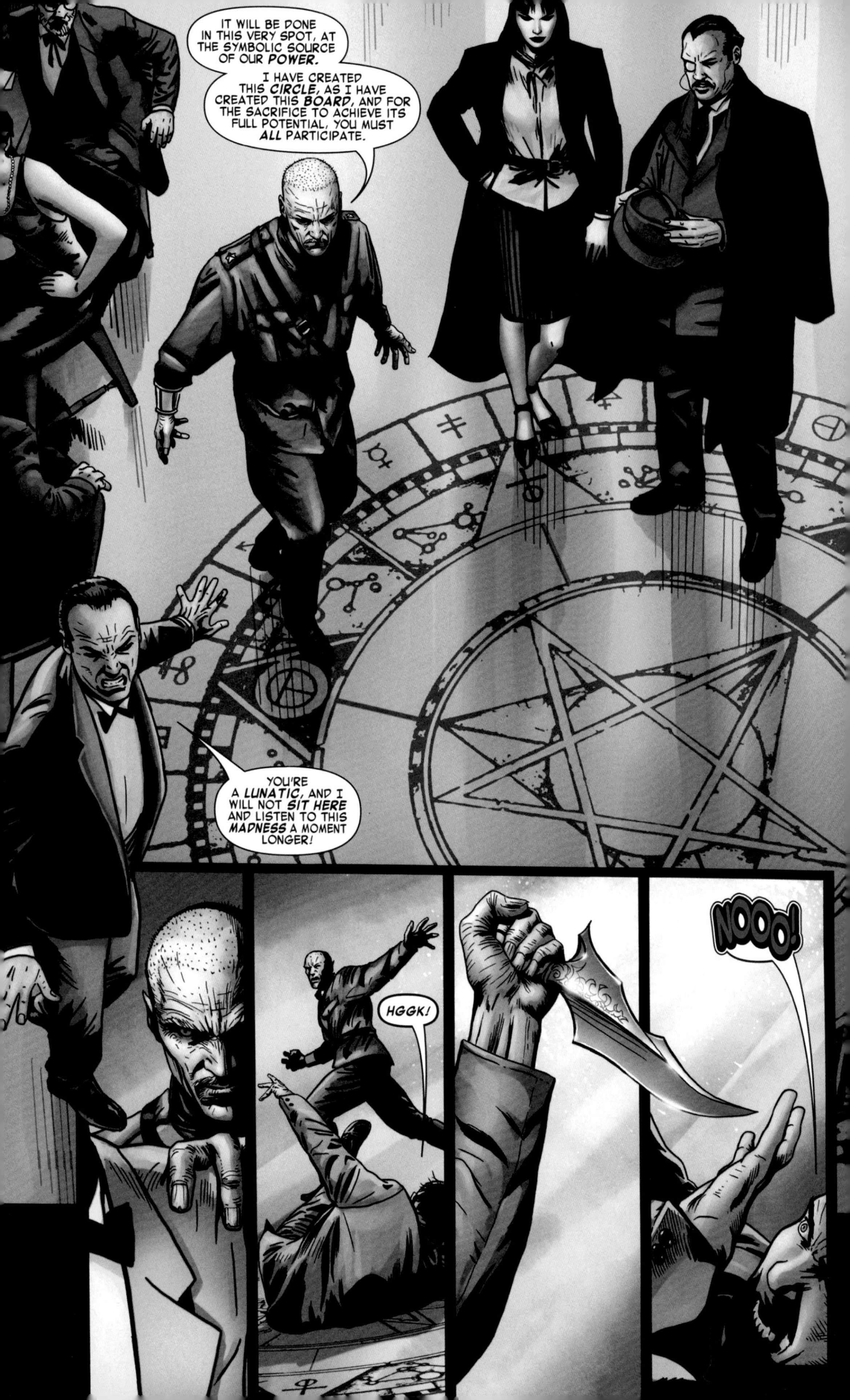
IT WILL BE DONE IN THIS VERY SPOT, AT THE SYMBOLIC SOURCE OF OUR POWER.
I HAVE CREATED THIS CIRCLE, AS I HAVE CREATED THIS BOARD, AND FOR THE SACRIFICE TO ACHIEVE ITS FULL POTENTIAL, YOU MUST ALL PARTICIPATE.
YOU'RE A LUNATIC, AND I WILL NOT SIT HERE AND LISTEN TO THIS MADNESS A MOMENT LONGER!
HGGK!
NOOO!

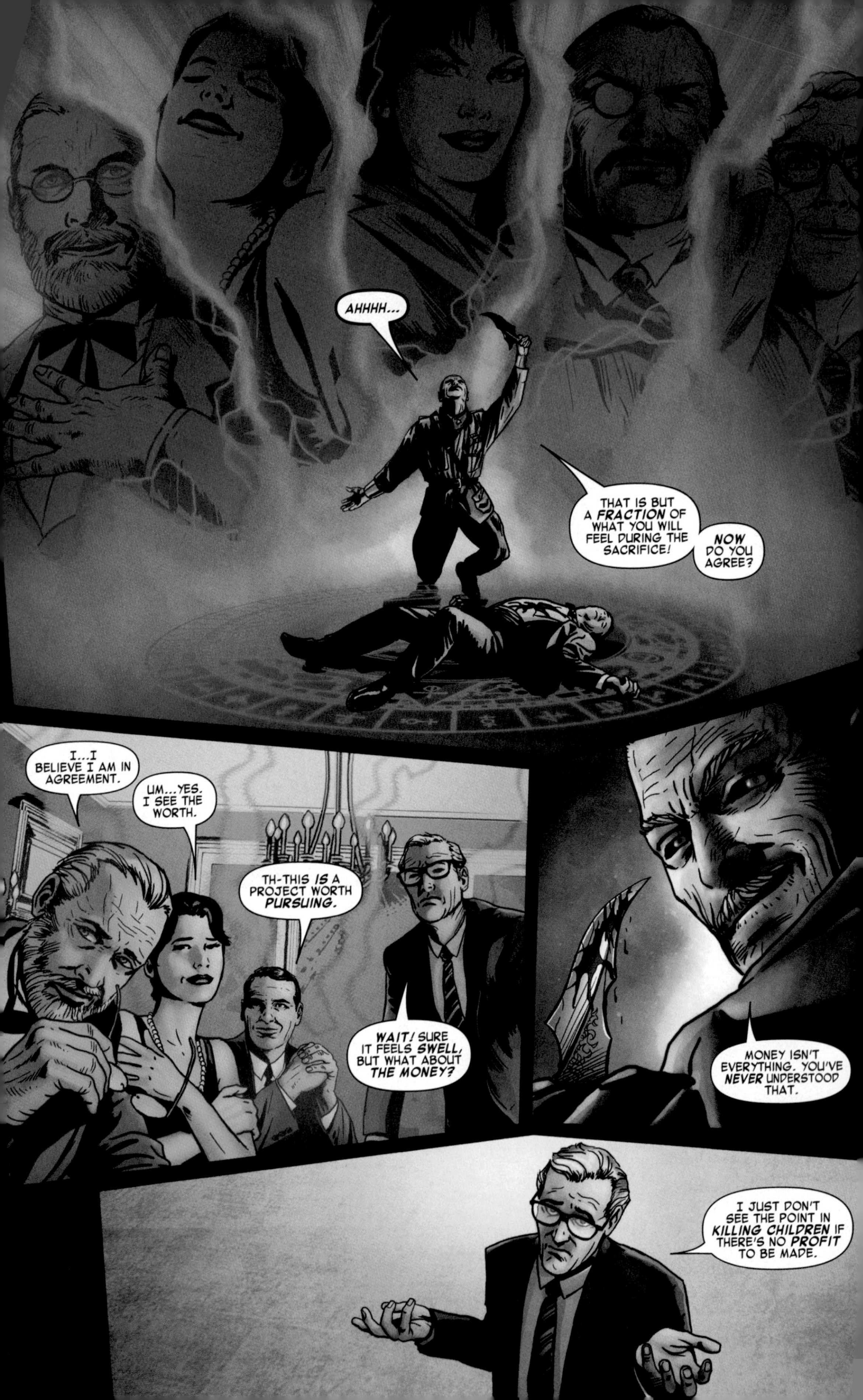
AHHHH...
THAT IS BUT A FRACTION OF WHAT YOU WILL FEEL DURING THE SACRIFICE!
NOW DO YOU AGREE?
I...I BELIEVE I AM IN AGREEMENT.
UM...YES. I SEE THE WORTH.
TH-THIS IS A PROJECT WORTH PURSUING.
WAIT! SURE IT FEELS SWELL, BUT WHAT ABOUT THE MONEY?
MONEY ISN'T EVERYTHING. YOU'VE NEVER UNDERSTOOD THAT.
I JUST DON'T SEE THE POINT IN KILLING CHILDREN IF THERE'S NO PROFIT TO BE MADE.

YOU READY, DOC?

TIME FOR A HOUSE CALL.

LOOK, I DON'T WANT ANY PART OF THIS. IT'S *CRAZY*. THEY'RE GOING TO SACRIFICE *CHILDREN*--EVEN THE *LINDBERGH* BOY!

THE POOR KID IS ALREADY DEAD.

HE'S *NOT*. DON'T YOU GET IT? THE COUNTRY LOVES LINDBERGH, AND THAT MAKES HIS SON THE MOST POWERFUL SACRIFICE OF ALL. AT LEAST THAT'S WHAT THEY *THINK*.

I KNOW WE'VE DONE SOME *LOUSY* THINGS ON THE BOARD-- UNION SUPPRESSION, DRUG SALES, WHITE SLAVERY--AND I'M REALLY *SORRY* ABOUT ALL THAT.

BUT YOU *CAN'T* ACT ON THIS. IF THEY FIND OUT I TOLD YOU, THEY'LL *KILL* ME.

NO NEED TO WORRY. SOON, THEY WON'T EVEN BE ABLE TO *RECOGNIZE* YOU.

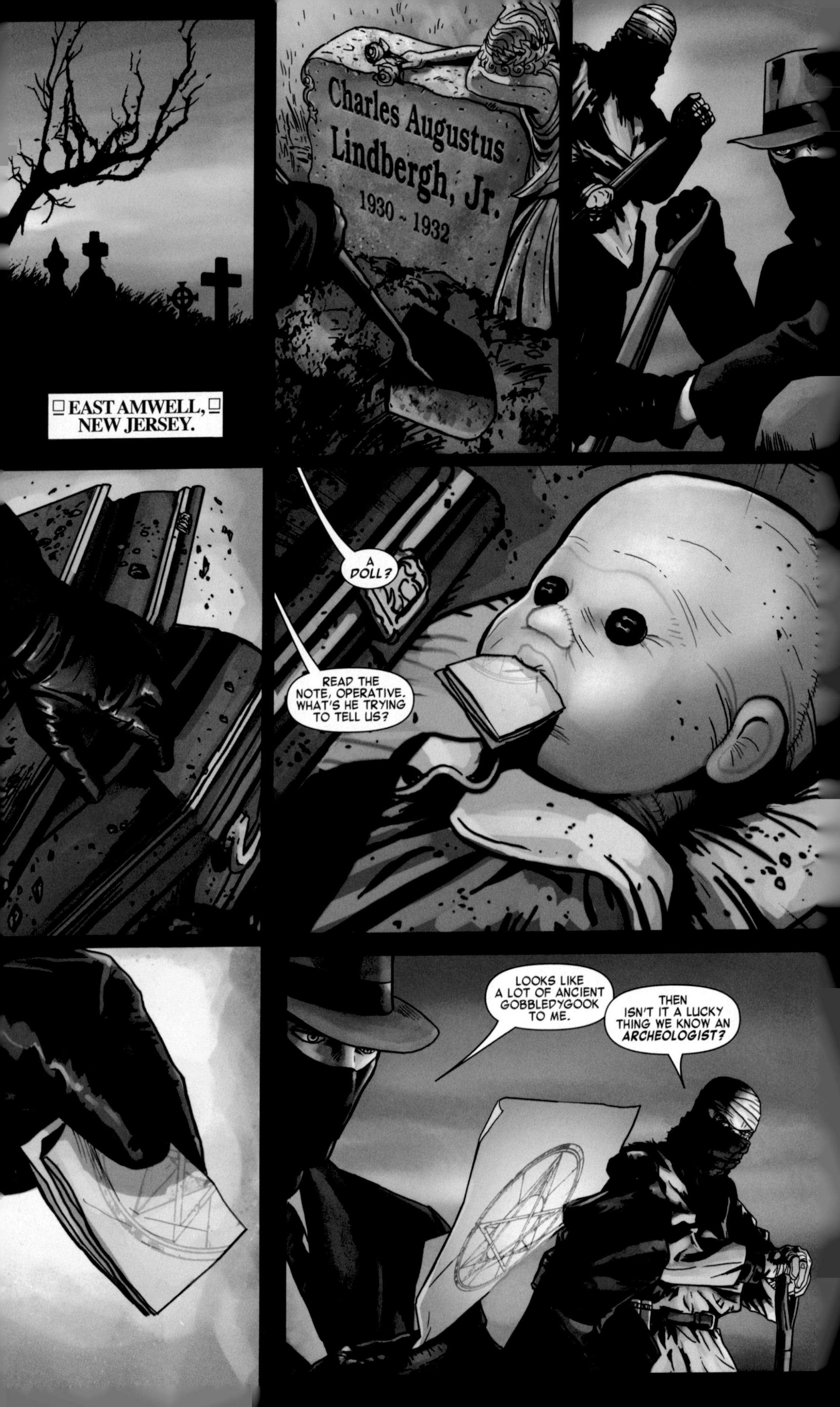

EAST AMWELL, NEW JERSEY.
Charles Augustus Lindbergh, Jr. 1930 ~ 1932
A DOLL?
READ THE NOTE, OPERATIVE. WHAT'S HE TRYING TO TELL US?
LOOKS LIKE A LOT OF ANCIENT GOBBLEDYGOOK TO ME.
THEN ISN'T IT A LUCKY THING WE KNOW AN ARCHEOLOGIST?

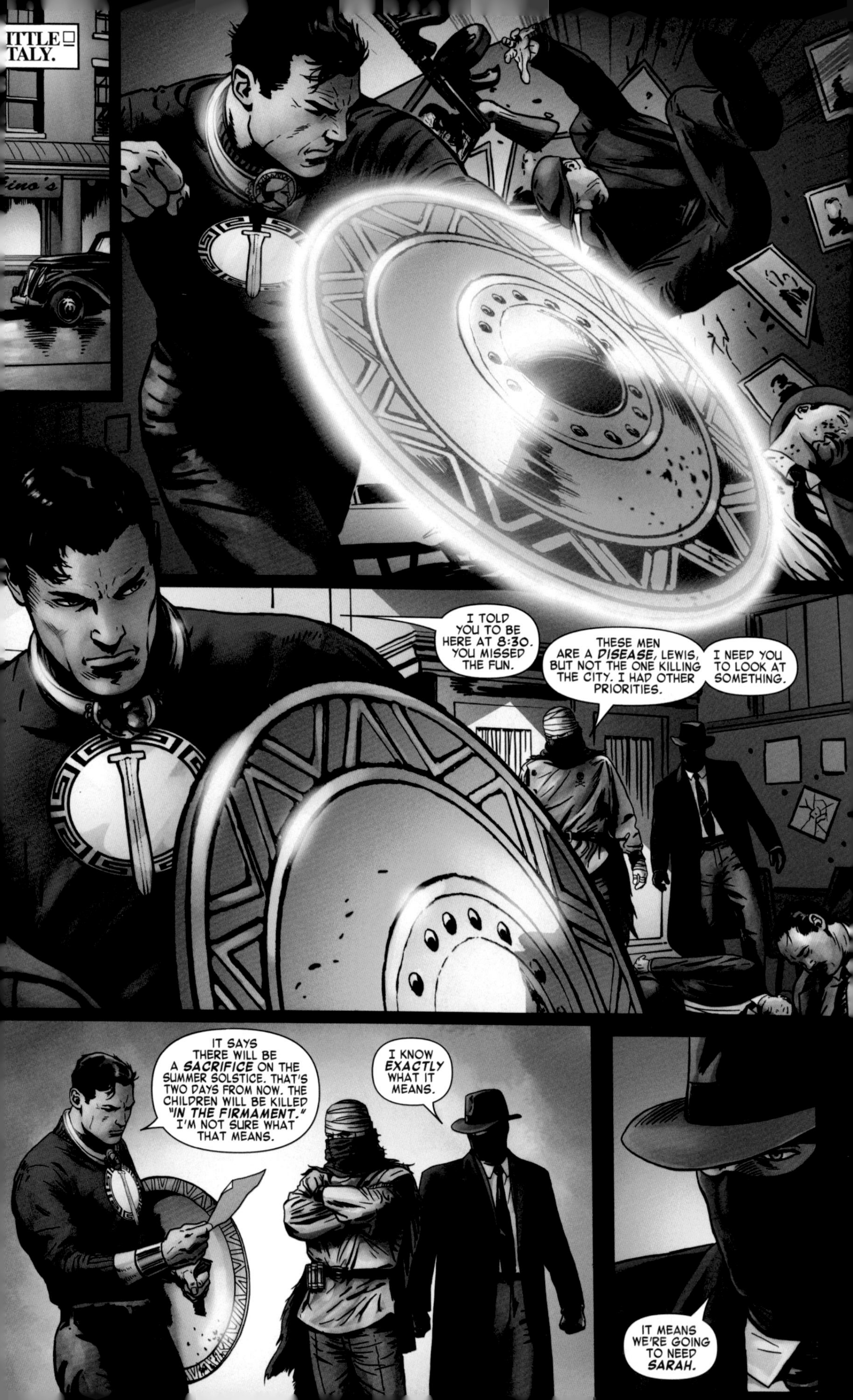

ITTLE TALY.
I TOLD YOU TO BE HERE AT 8:30. YOU MISSED THE FUN.
THESE MEN ARE A DISEASE, LEWIS, BUT NOT THE ONE KILLING THE CITY. I HAD OTHER PRIORITIES.
I NEED YOU TO LOOK AT SOMETHING.
IT SAYS THERE WILL BE A SACRIFICE ON THE SUMMER SOLSTICE. THAT'S TWO DAYS FROM NOW. THE CHILDREN WILL BE KILLED "IN THE FIRMAMENT." I'M NOT SURE WHAT THAT MEANS.
I KNOW EXACTLY WHAT IT MEANS.
IT MEANS WE'RE GOING TO NEED SARAH.

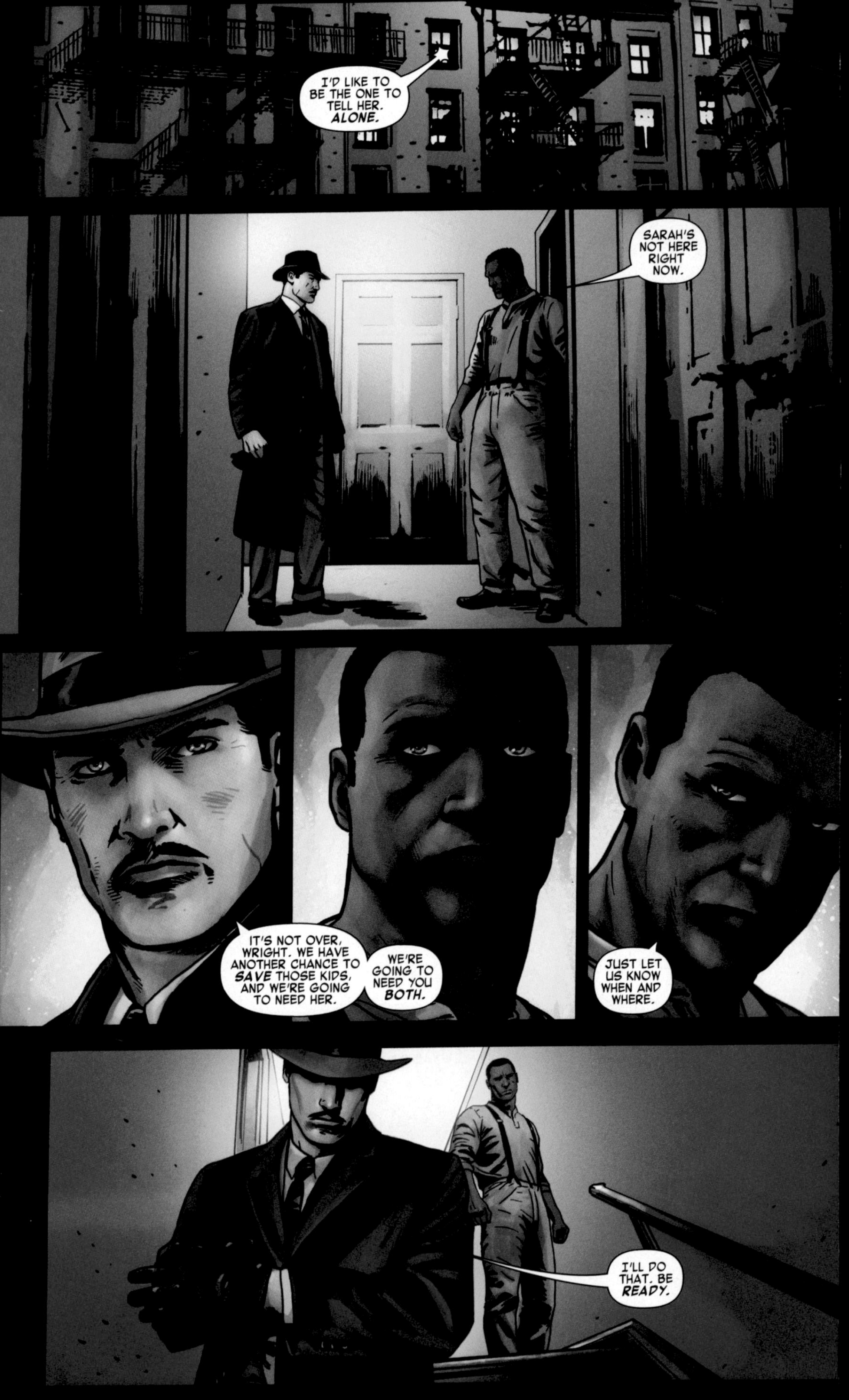
I'D LIKE TO BE THE ONE TO TELL HER. ALONE.
SARAH'S NOT HERE RIGHT NOW.
IT'S NOT OVER, WRIGHT. WE HAVE ANOTHER CHANCE TO SAVE THOSE KIDS, AND WE'RE GOING TO NEED HER.
WE'RE GOING TO NEED YOU BOTH.
JUST LET US KNOW WHEN AND WHERE.
I'LL DO THAT. BE READY.

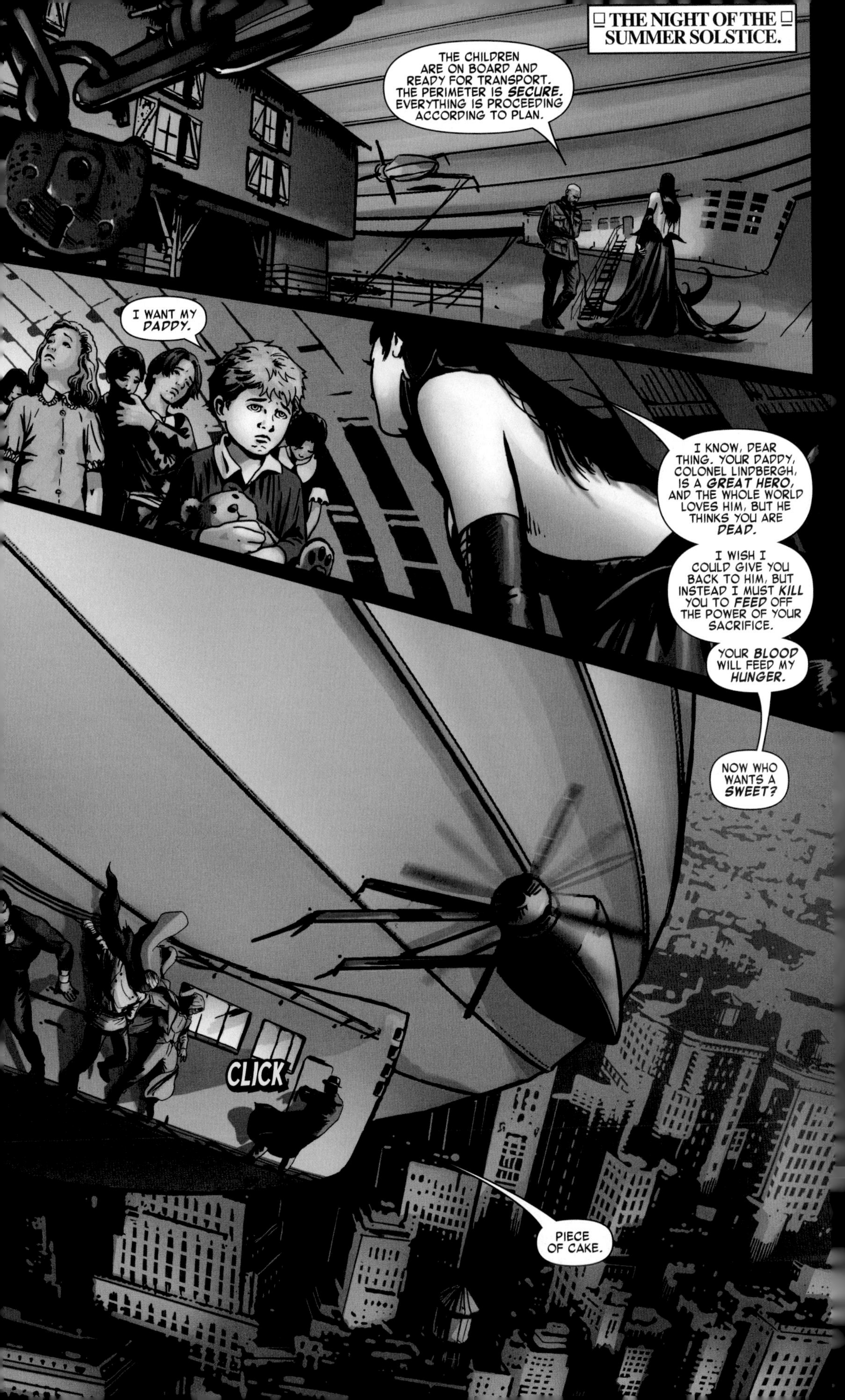
THE NIGHT OF THE SUMMER SOLSTICE.
THE CHILDREN ARE ON BOARD AND READY FOR TRANSPORT. THE PERIMETER IS SECURE. EVERYTHING IS PROCEEDING ACCORDING TO PLAN.
I WANT MY DADDY.
I KNOW, DEAR THING. YOUR DADDY, COLONEL LINDBERGH, IS A GREAT HERO, AND THE WHOLE WORLD LOVES HIM, BUT HE THINKS YOU ARE DEAD.
I WISH I COULD GIVE YOU BACK TO HIM, BUT INSTEAD I MUST KILL YOU TO FEED OFF THE POWER OF YOUR SACRIFICE.
YOUR BLOOD WILL FEED MY HUNGER.
NOW WHO WANTS A SWEET?
CLICK
PIECE OF CAKE.

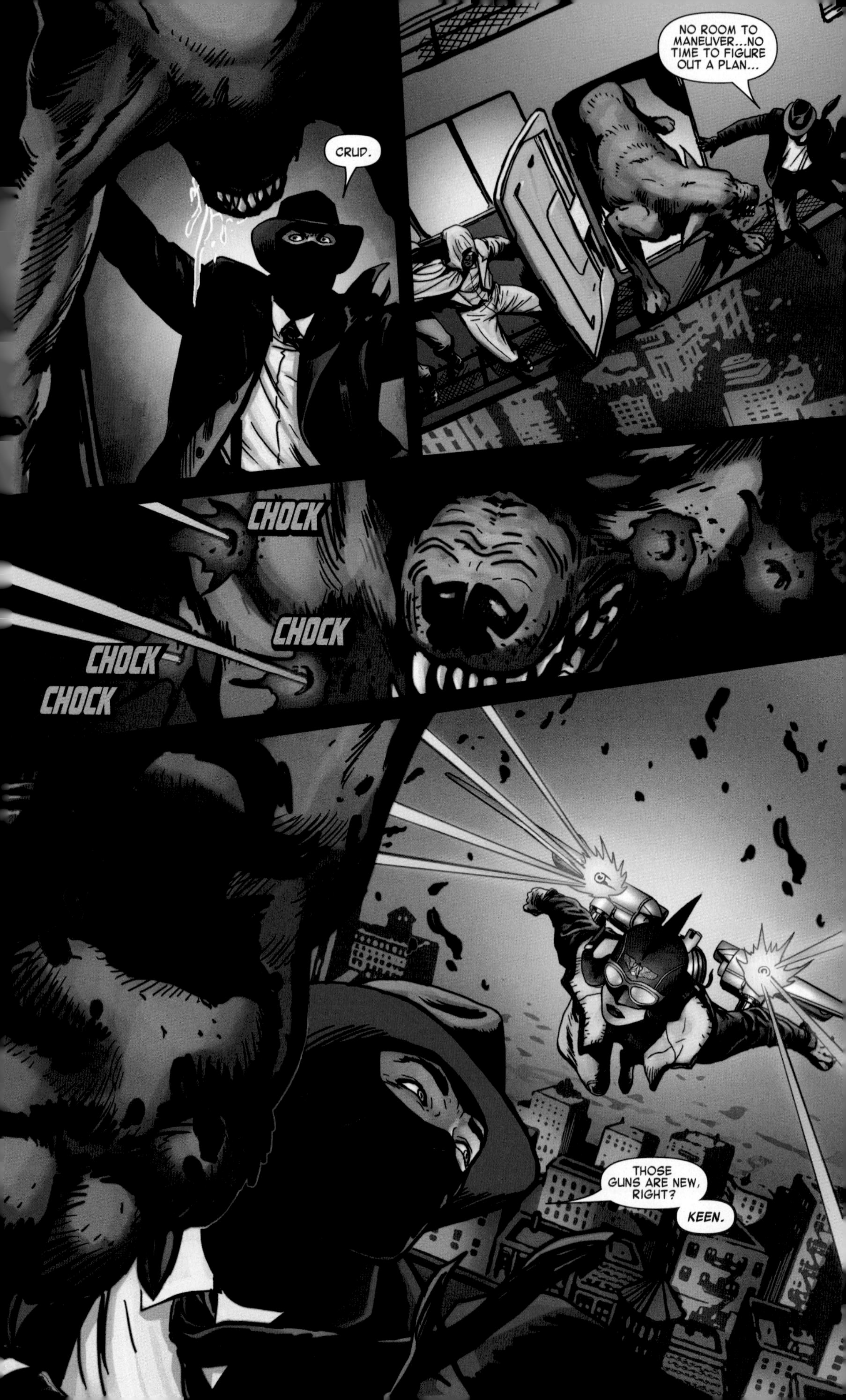
CRUD.
NO ROOM TO MANEUVER...NO TIME TO FIGURE OUT A PLAN...
CHOCK
CHOCK
CHOCK
CHOCK
THOSE GUNS ARE NEW, RIGHT?
KEEN.

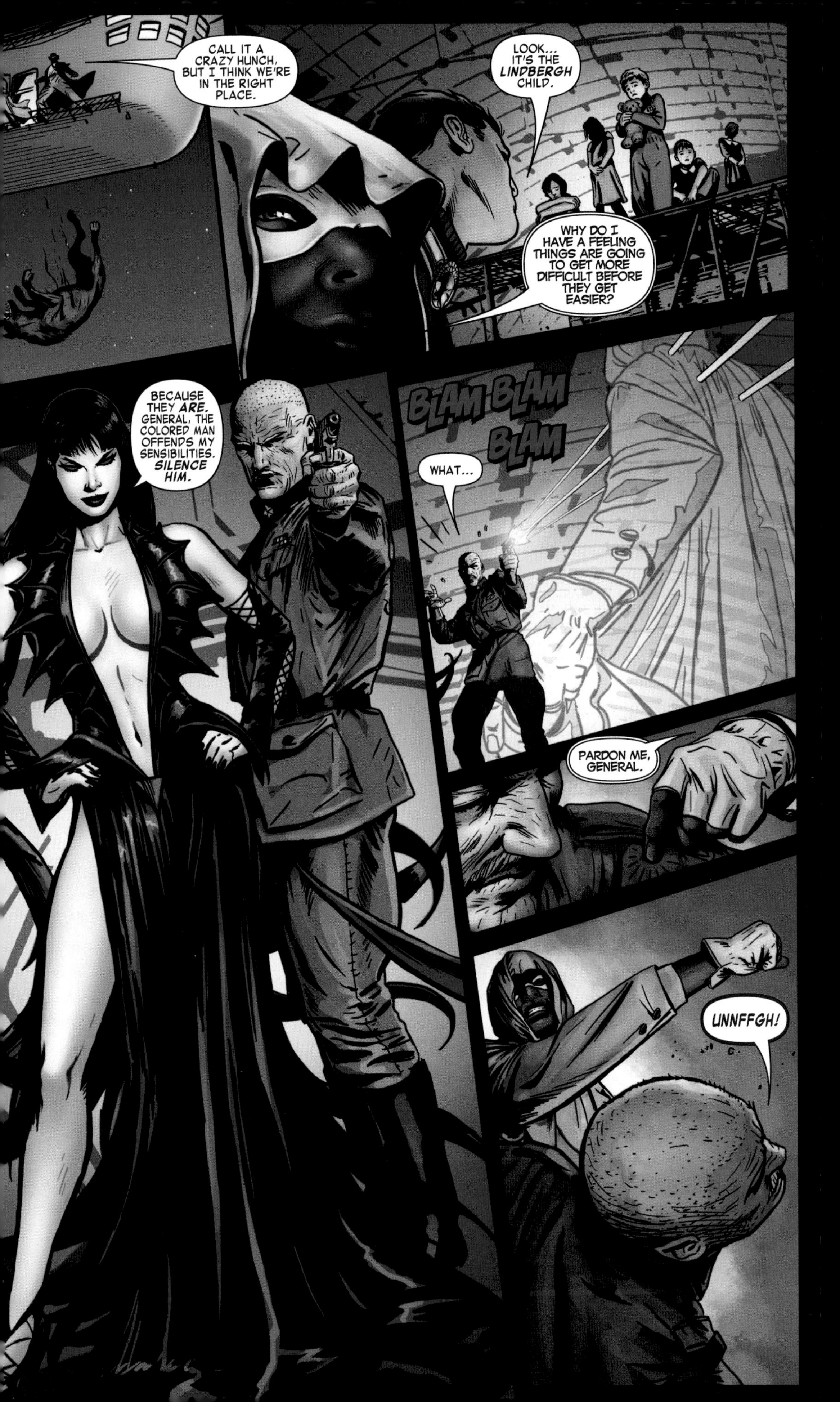

CALL IT A CRAZY HUNCH, BUT I THINK WE'RE IN THE RIGHT PLACE.
LOOK... IT'S THE LINDBERGH CHILD.
WHY DO I HAVE A FEELING THINGS ARE GOING TO GET MORE DIFFICULT BEFORE THEY GET EASIER?
BECAUSE THEY ARE. GENERAL, THE COLORED MAN OFFENDS MY SENSIBILITIES. SILENCE HIM.
BLAM BLAM BLAM
WHAT...
PARDON ME, GENERAL.
UNNFFGH!

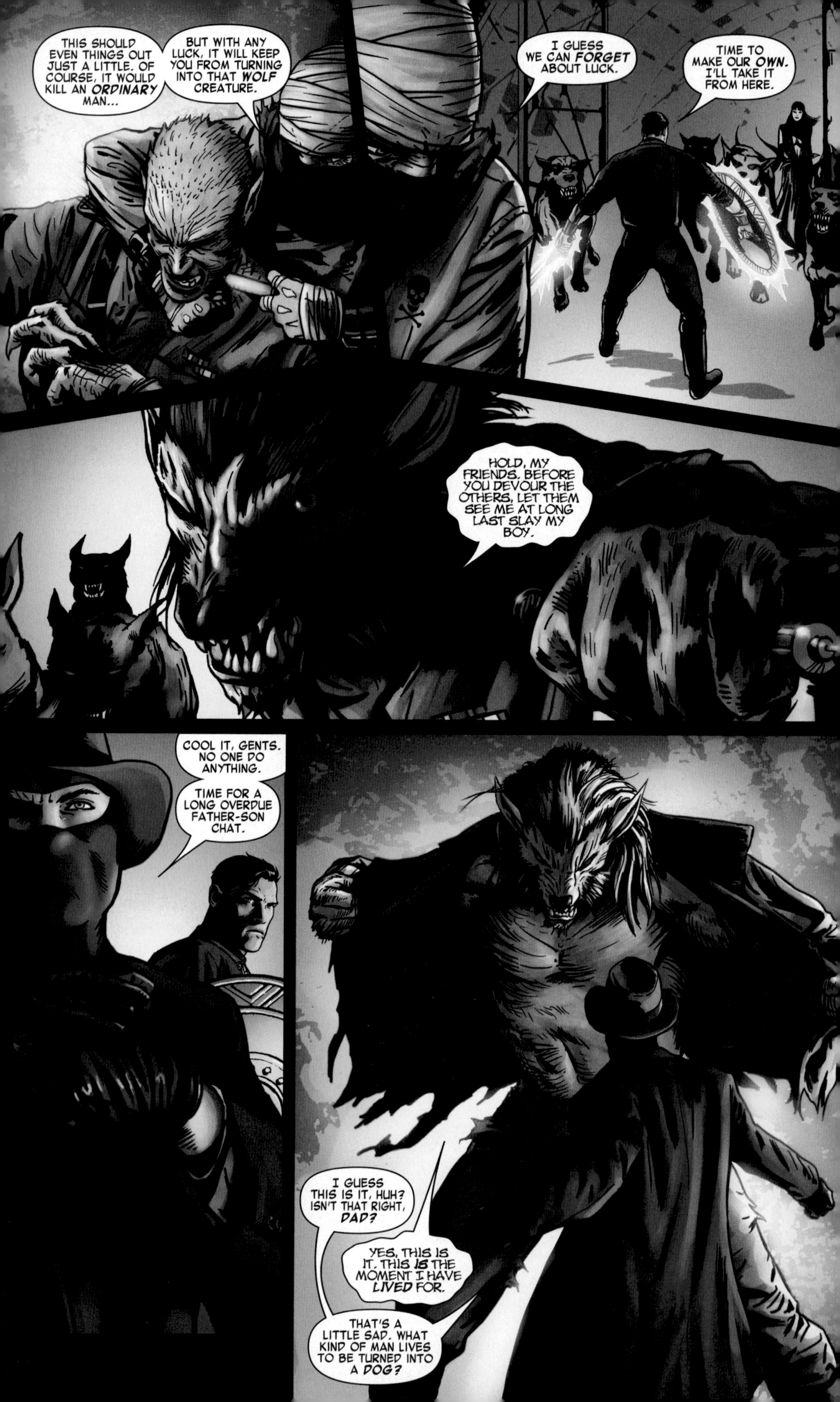
THIS SHOULD EVEN THINGS OUT JUST A LITTLE. OF COURSE, IT WOULD KILL AN ORDINARY MAN...
BUT WITH ANY LUCK, IT WILL KEEP YOU FROM TURNING INTO THAT WOLF CREATURE.
I GUESS WE CAN FORGET ABOUT LUCK.
TIME TO MAKE OUR OWN. I'LL TAKE IT FROM HERE.
HOLD, MY FRIENDS. BEFORE YOU DEVOUR THE OTHERS, LET THEM SEE ME AT LONG LAST SLAY MY BOY.
COOL IT, GENTS. NO ONE DO ANYTHING.
TIME FOR A LONG OVERDUE FATHER-SON CHAT.
I GUESS THIS IS IT, HUH? ISN'T THAT RIGHT, DAD?
YES, THIS IS IT. THIS IS THE MOMENT I HAVE LIVED FOR.
THAT'S A LITTLE SAD. WHAT KIND OF MAN LIVES TO BE TURNED INTO A DOG?

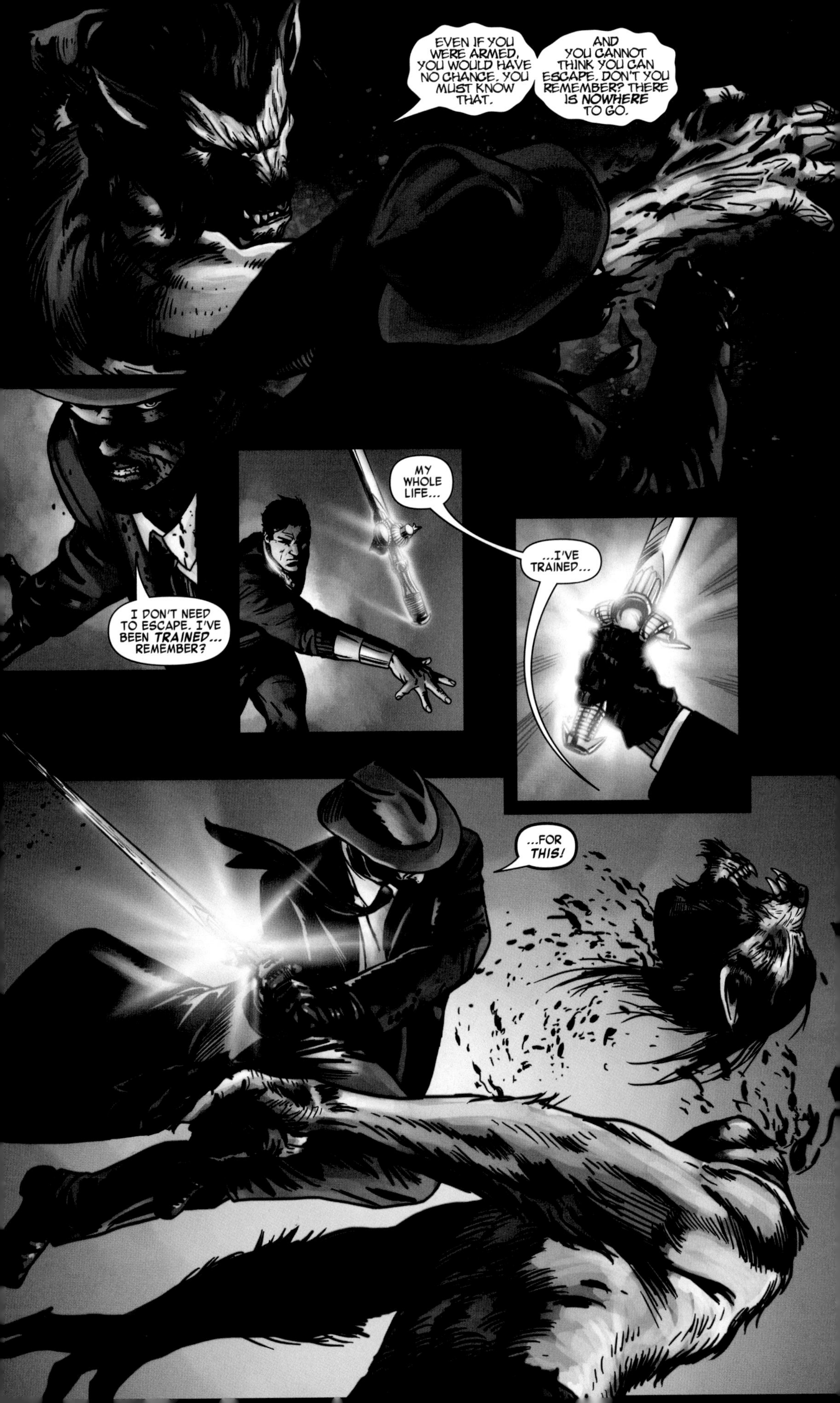
EVEN IF YOU WERE ARMED, YOU WOULD HAVE NO CHANCE. YOU MUST KNOW THAT.
AND YOU CANNOT THINK YOU CAN ESCAPE. DON'T YOU REMEMBER? THERE IS NOWHERE TO GO.
I DON'T NEED TO ESCAPE. I'VE BEEN TRAINED... REMEMBER?
MY WHOLE LIFE...
...I'VE TRAINED...
...FOR THIS!

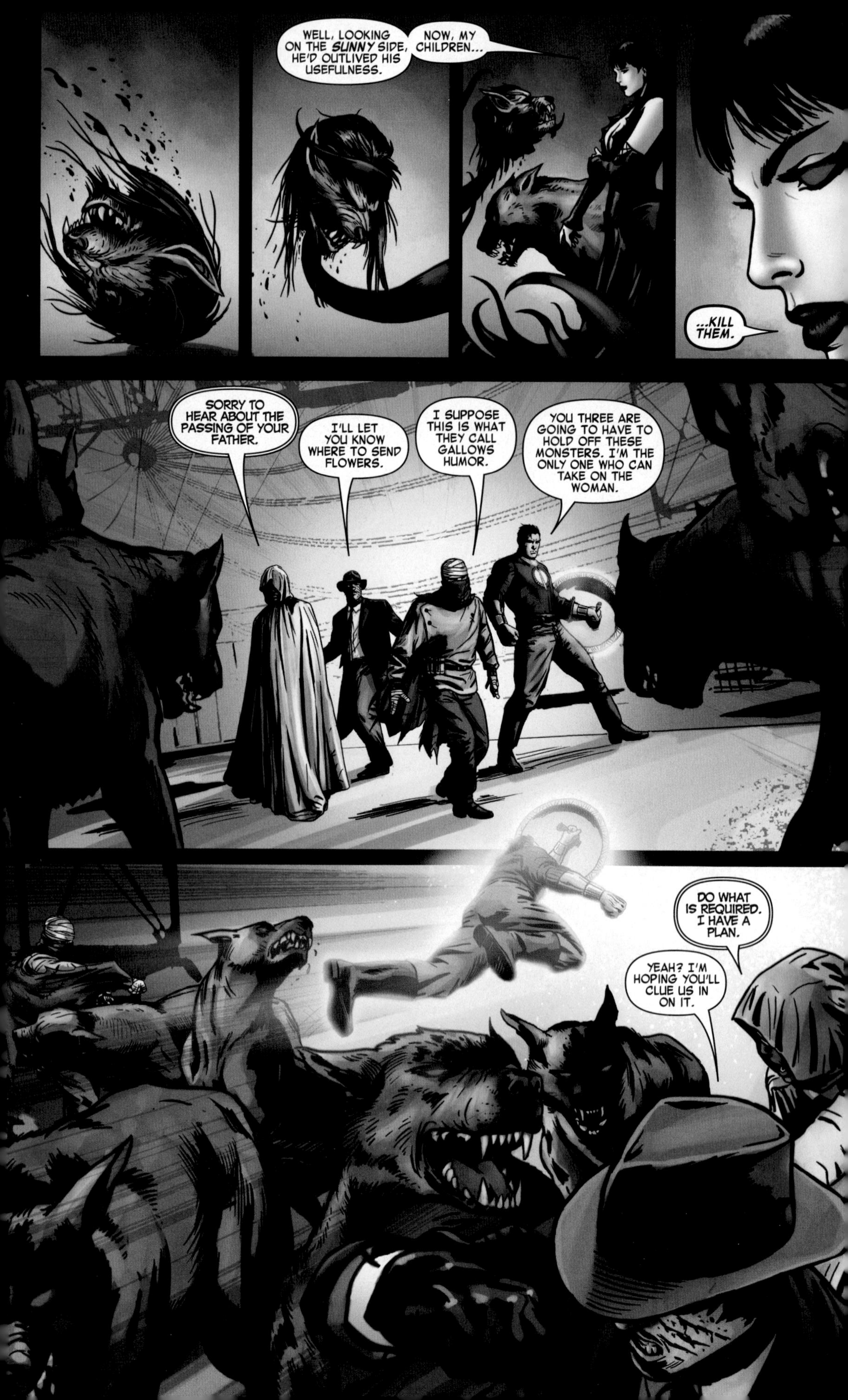
WELL, LOOKING ON THE SUNNY SIDE, HE'D OUTLIVED HIS USEFULNESS.
NOW, MY CHILDREN...
...KILL THEM.
SORRY TO HEAR ABOUT THE PASSING OF YOUR FATHER.
I'LL LET YOU KNOW WHERE TO SEND FLOWERS.
I SUPPOSE THIS IS WHAT THEY CALL GALLOWS HUMOR.
YOU THREE ARE GOING TO HAVE TO HOLD OFF THESE MONSTERS. I'M THE ONLY ONE WHO CAN TAKE ON THE WOMAN.
DO WHAT IS REQUIRED. I HAVE A PLAN.
YEAH? I'M HOPING YOU'LL CLUE US IN ON IT.

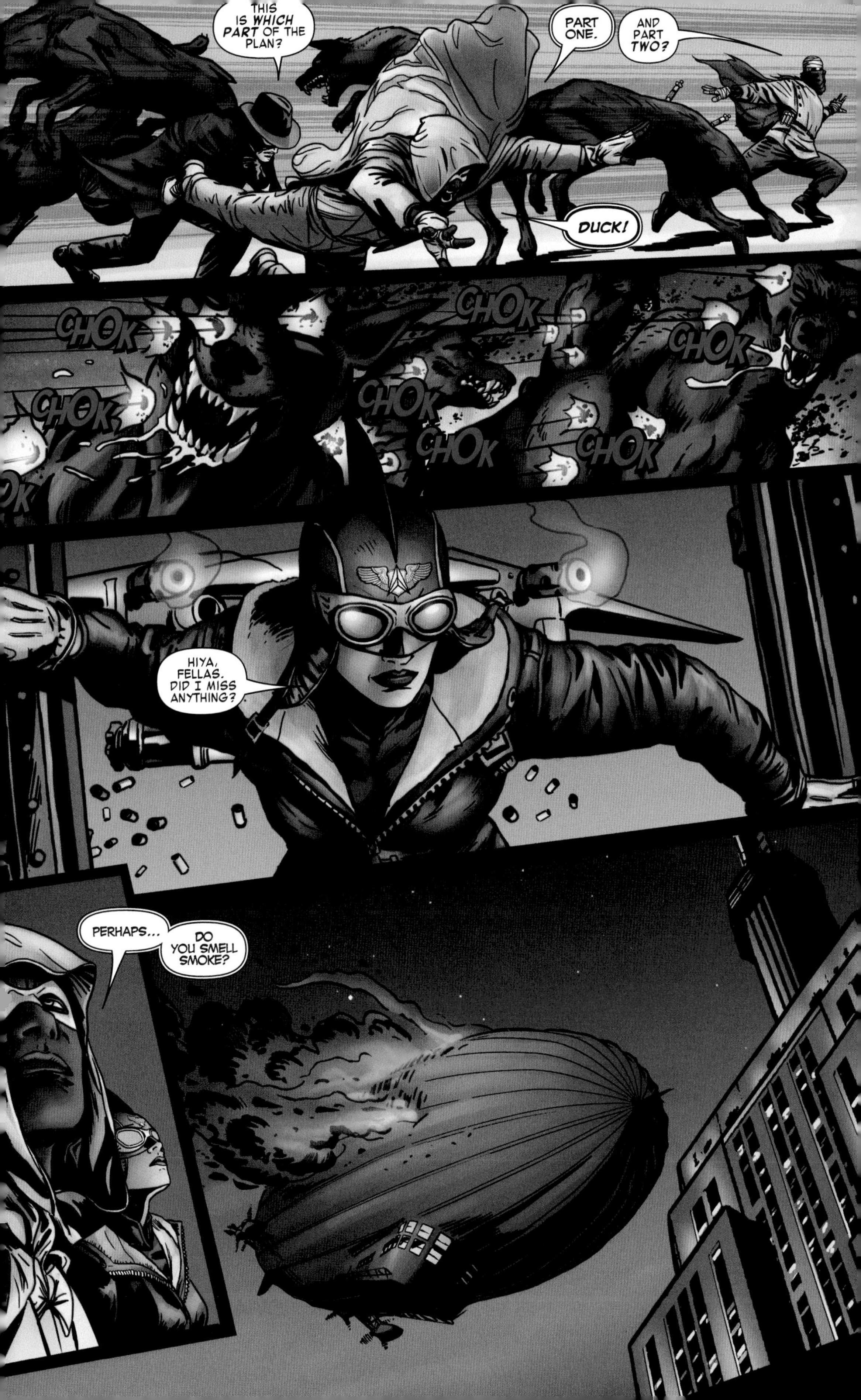
THIS IS WHICH PART OF THE PLAN?
PART ONE.
AND PART TWO?
DUCK!
CHOK
CHOK
CHOK
CHOK
CHOK
CHOK
CHOK
HIYA, FELLAS. DID I MISS ANYTHING?
PERHAPS...
DO YOU SMELL SMOKE?

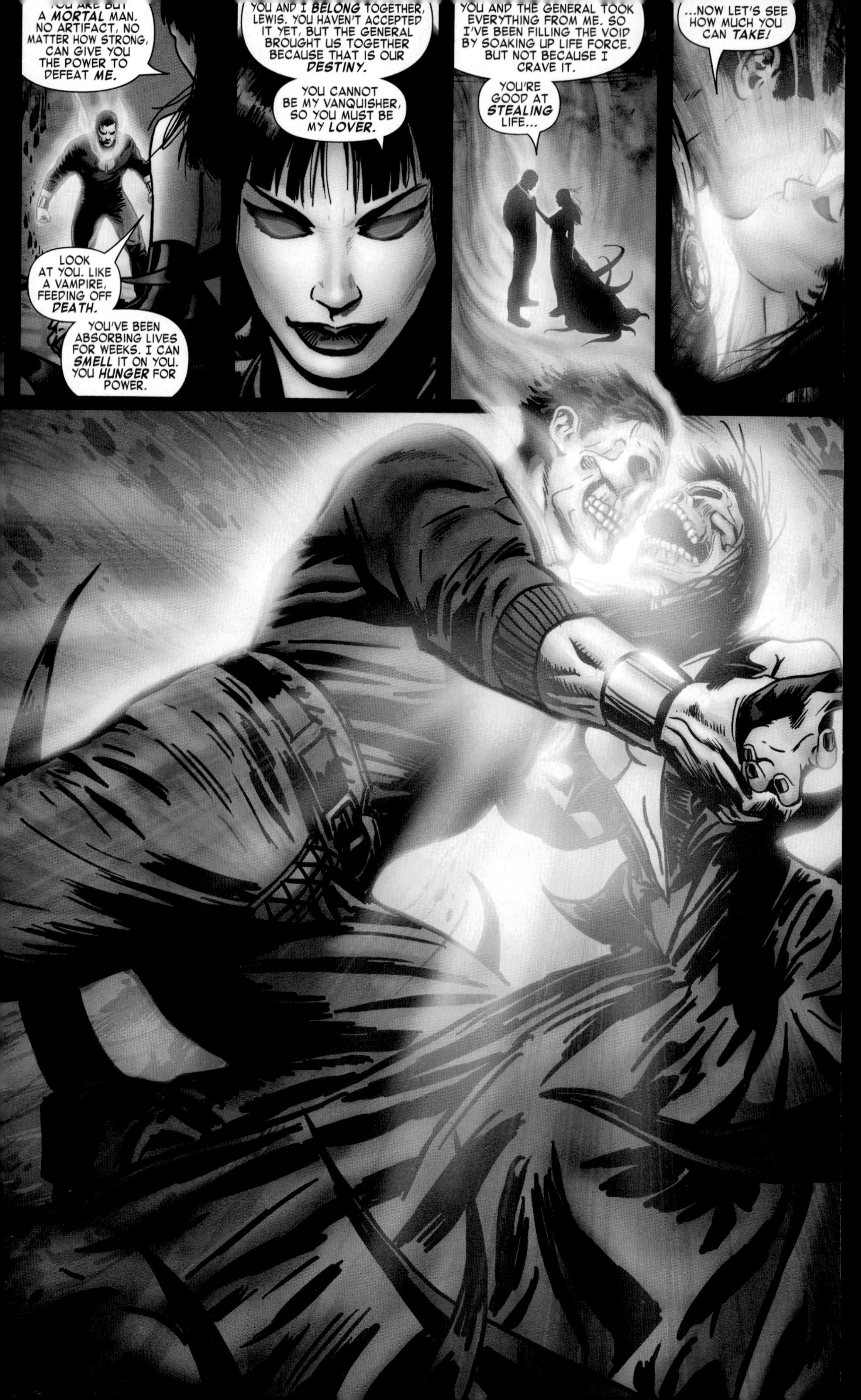

A MORTAL MAN. NO ARTIFACT, NO MATTER HOW STRONG, CAN GIVE YOU THE POWER TO DEFEAT ME.
LOOK AT YOU. LIKE A VAMPIRE, FEEDING OFF DEATH.
YOU'VE BEEN ABSORBING LIVES FOR WEEKS. I CAN SMELL IT ON YOU. YOU HUNGER FOR POWER.
YOU AND I BELONG TOGETHER, LEWIS. YOU HAVEN'T ACCEPTED IT YET, BUT THE GENERAL BROUGHT US TOGETHER BECAUSE THAT IS OUR DESTINY.
YOU CANNOT BE MY VANQUISHER, SO YOU MUST BE MY LOVER.
YOU AND THE GENERAL TOOK EVERYTHING FROM ME. SO I'VE BEEN FILLING THE VOID BY SOAKING UP LIFE FORCE. BUT NOT BECAUSE I CRAVE IT.
YOU'RE GOOD AT STEALING LIFE...
...NOW LET'S SEE HOW MUCH YOU CAN TAKE!

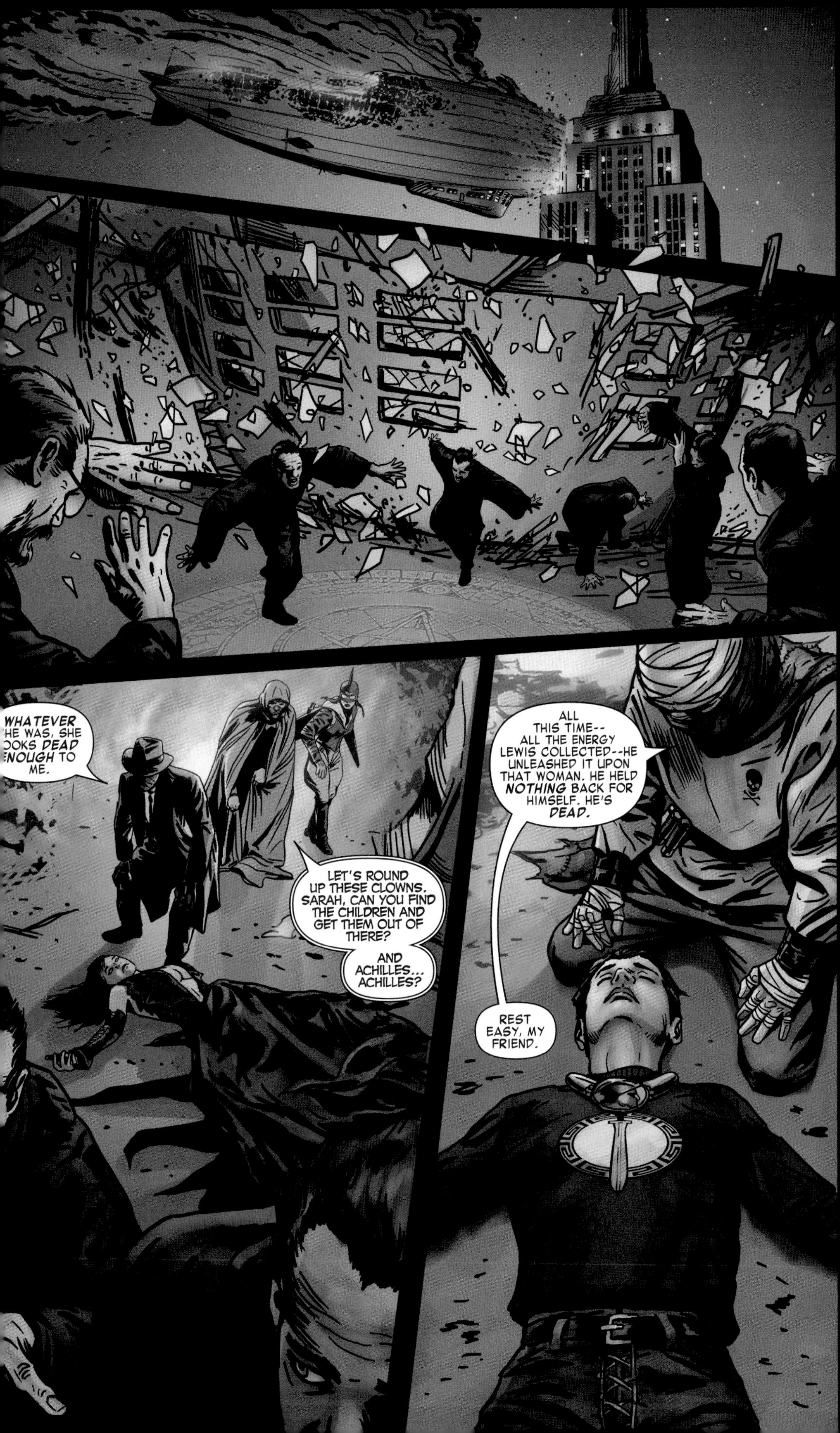
WHATEVER HE WAS, SHE LOOKS DEAD ENOUGH TO ME.
LET'S ROUND UP THESE CLOWNS. SARAH, CAN YOU FIND THE CHILDREN AND GET THEM OUT OF THERE?
AND ACHILLES... ACHILLES?
ALL THIS TIME-- ALL THE ENERGY LEWIS COLLECTED--HE UNLEASHED IT UPON THAT WOMAN. HE HELD NOTHING BACK FOR HIMSELF. HE'S DEAD.
REST EASY, MY FRIEND.

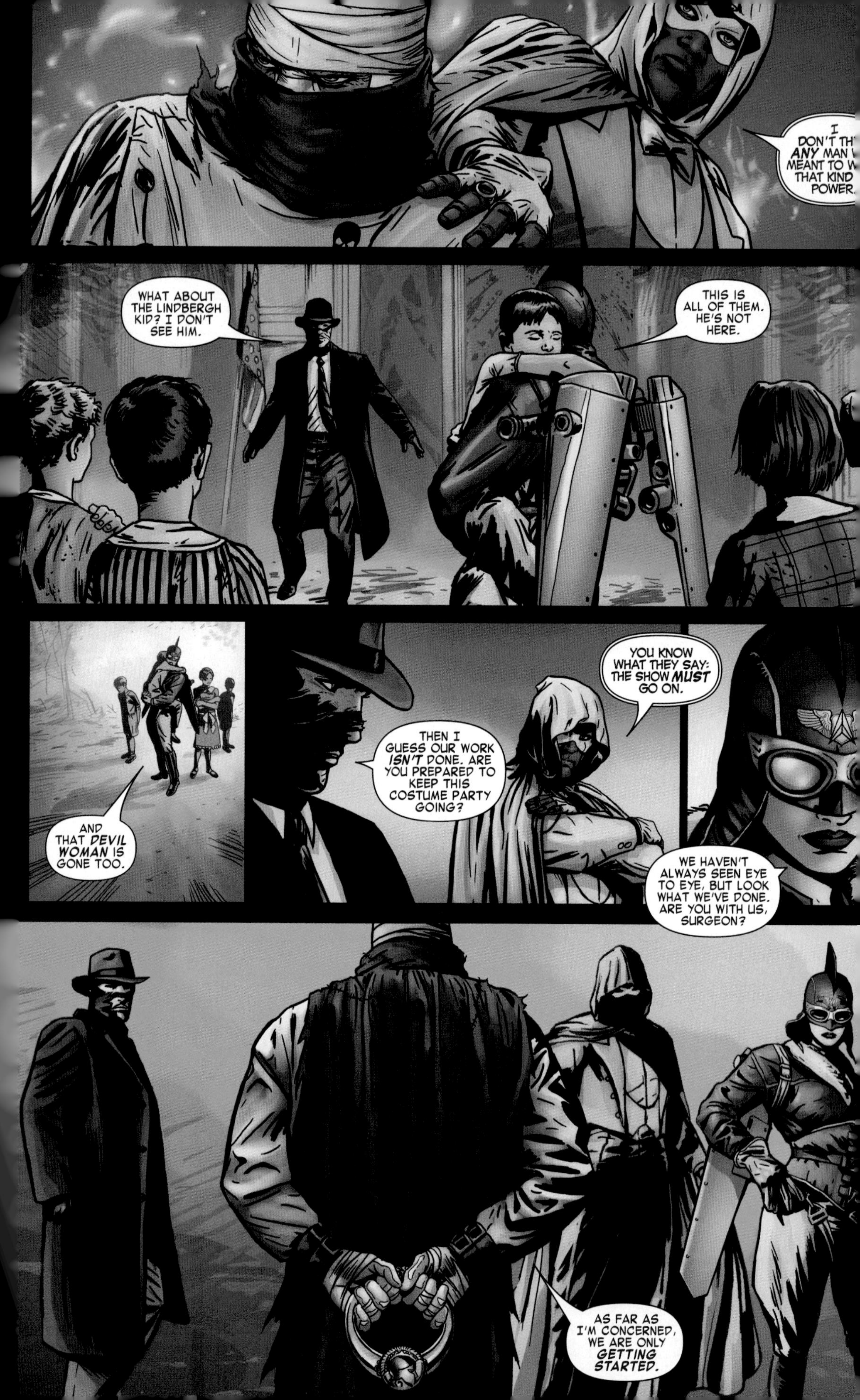
I DON'T TH ANY MAN MEANT TO W THAT KIND POWER.
WHAT ABOUT THE LINDBERGH KID? I DON'T SEE HIM.
THIS IS ALL OF THEM. HE'S NOT HERE.
AND THAT DEVIL WOMAN IS GONE TOO.
THEN I GUESS OUR WORK ISN'T DONE. ARE YOU PREPARED TO KEEP THIS COSTUME PARTY GOING?
YOU KNOW WHAT THEY SAY: THE SHOW MUST GO ON.
WE HAVEN'T ALWAYS SEEN EYE TO EYE, BUT LOOK WHAT WE'VE DONE. ARE YOU WITH US, SURGEON?
AS FAR AS I'M CONCERNED, WE ARE ONLY GETTING STARTED.

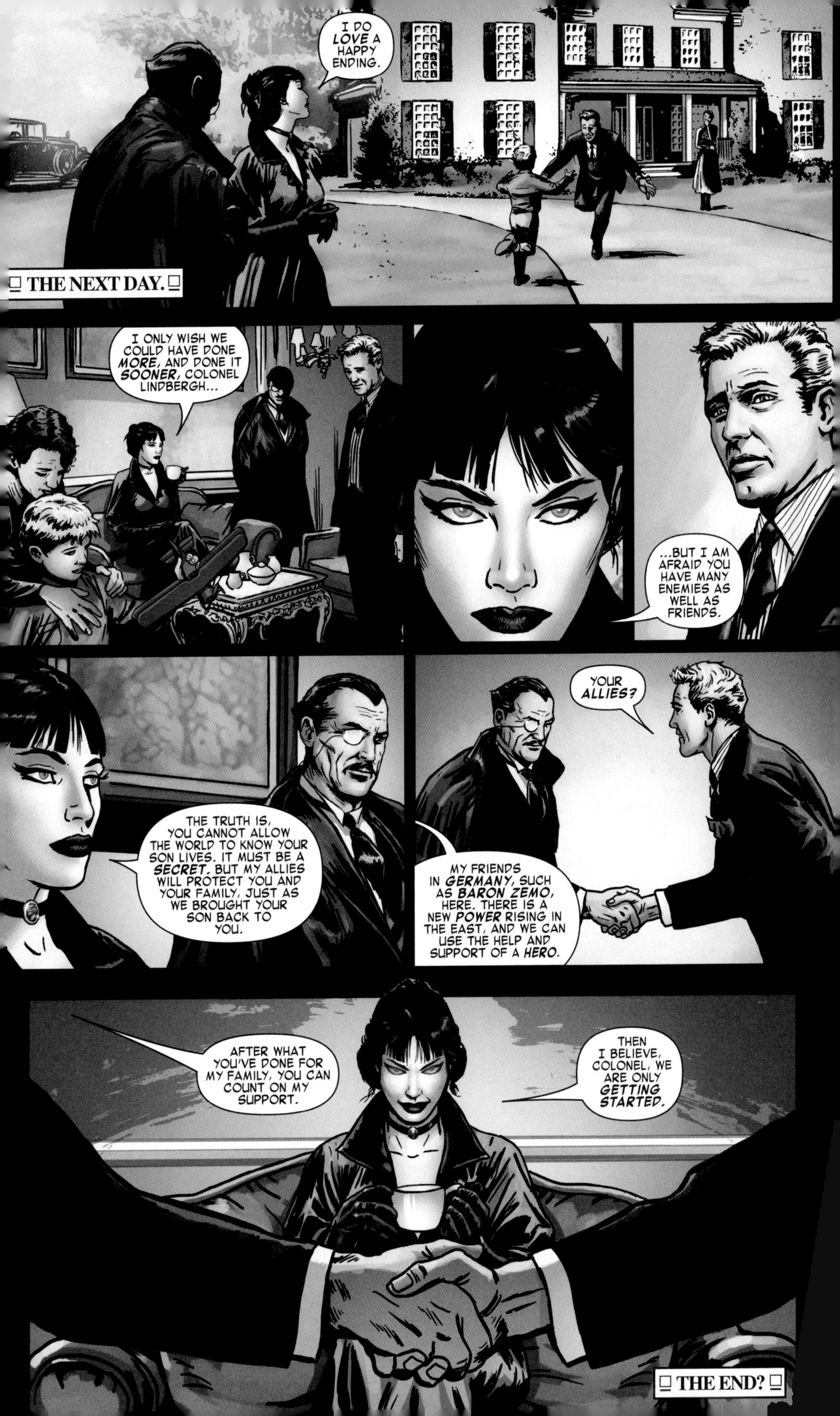
I DO LOVE A HAPPY ENDING.
THE NEXT DAY.
I ONLY WISH WE COULD HAVE DONE MORE, AND DONE IT SOONER, COLONEL LINDBERGH...
...BUT I AM AFRAID YOU HAVE MANY ENEMIES AS WELL AS FRIENDS.
THE TRUTH IS, YOU CANNOT ALLOW THE WORLD TO KNOW YOUR SON LIVES. IT MUST BE A SECRET. BUT MY ALLIES WILL PROTECT YOU AND YOUR FAMILY, JUST AS WE BROUGHT YOUR SON BACK TO YOU.
YOUR ALLIES?
MY FRIENDS IN GERMANY, SUCH AS BARON ZEMO, HERE. THERE IS A NEW POWER RISING IN THE EAST, AND WE CAN USE THE HELP AND SUPPORT OF A HERO.
AFTER WHAT YOU'VE DONE FOR MY FAMILY, YOU CAN COUNT ON MY SUPPORT.
THEN I BELIEVE, COLONEL, WE ARE ONLY GETTING STARTED.
THE END?

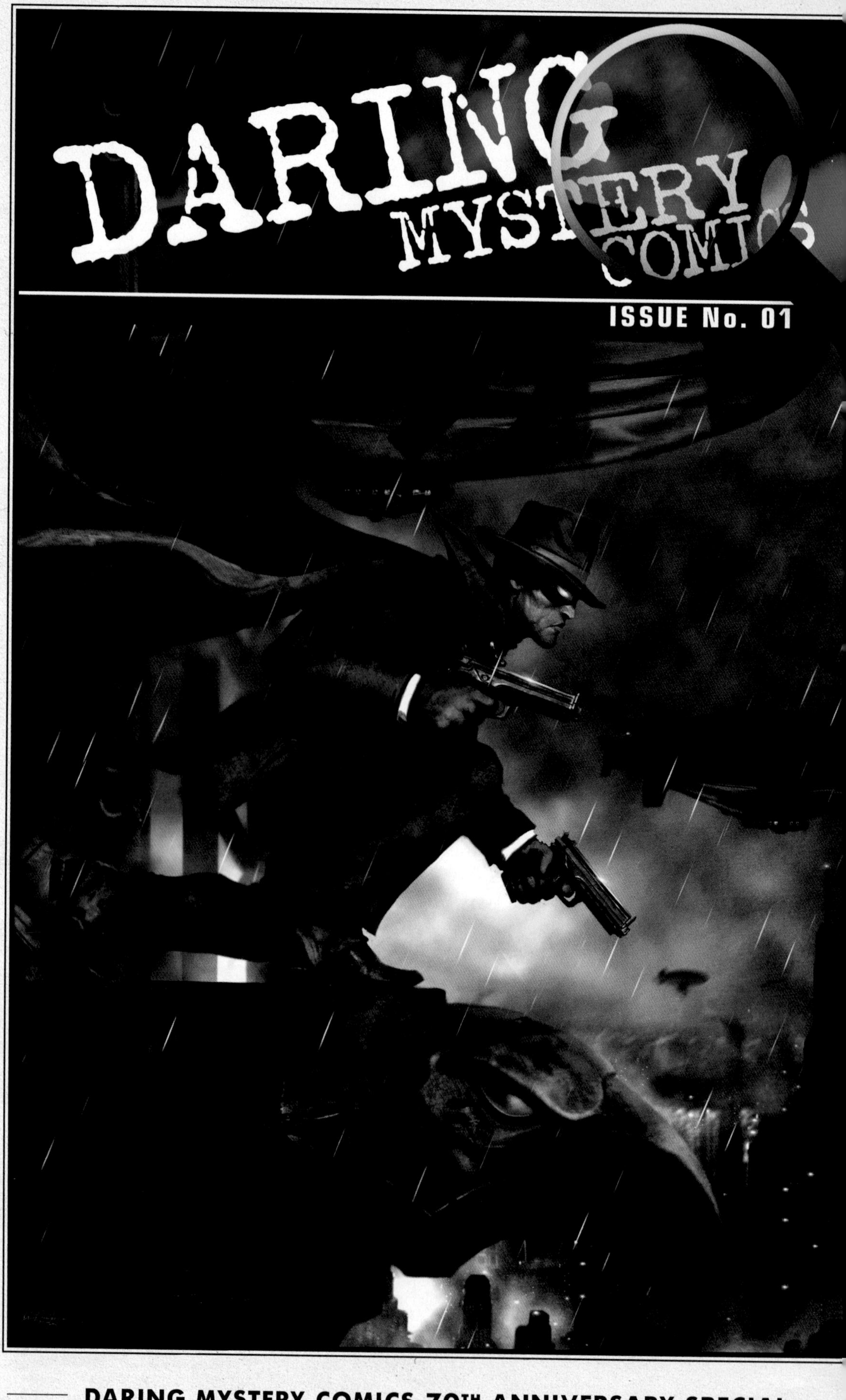
DARING MYSTERY COMICS
ISSUE No. 01

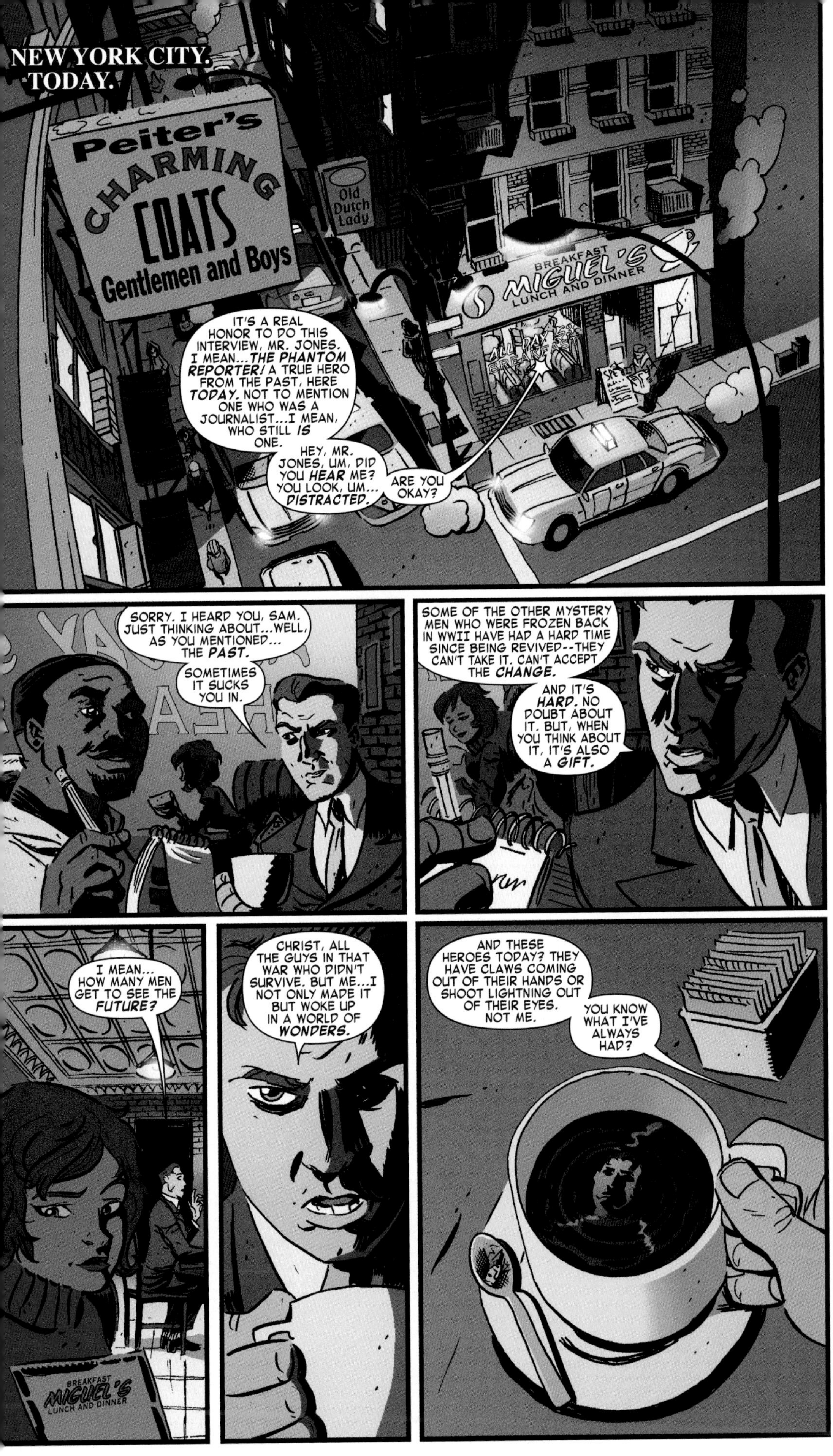
NEW YORK CITY. TODAY.
Peiter's CHARMING COATS Gentlemen and Boys
Old Dutch Lady
BREAKFAST MIGUEL'S LUNCH AND DINNER
IT'S A REAL HONOR TO DO THIS INTERVIEW, MR. JONES. I MEAN...THE PHANTOM REPORTER! A TRUE HERO FROM THE PAST, HERE TODAY. NOT TO MENTION ONE WHO WAS A JOURNALIST...I MEAN, WHO STILL IS ONE.
HEY, MR. JONES, UM, DID YOU HEAR ME? YOU LOOK, UM... DISTRACTED.
ARE YOU OKAY?
SORRY. I HEARD YOU, SAM. JUST THINKING ABOUT...WELL, AS YOU MENTIONED... THE PAST.
SOMETIMES IT SUCKS YOU IN.
SOME OF THE OTHER MYSTERY MEN WHO WERE FROZEN BACK IN WWII HAVE HAD A HARD TIME SINCE BEING REVIVED--THEY CAN'T TAKE IT. CAN'T ACCEPT THE CHANGE.
AND IT'S HARD. NO DOUBT ABOUT IT. BUT, WHEN YOU THINK ABOUT IT, IT'S ALSO A GIFT.
I MEAN... HOW MANY MEN GET TO SEE THE FUTURE?
CHRIST, ALL THE GUYS IN THAT WAR WHO DIDN'T SURVIVE. BUT ME...I NOT ONLY MADE IT BUT WOKE UP IN A WORLD OF WONDERS.
AND THESE HEROES TODAY? THEY HAVE CLAWS COMING OUT OF THEIR HANDS OR SHOOT LIGHTNING OUT OF THEIR EYES. NOT ME.
YOU KNOW WHAT I'VE ALWAYS HAD?
BREAKFAST MIGUEL'S LUNCH AND DINNER

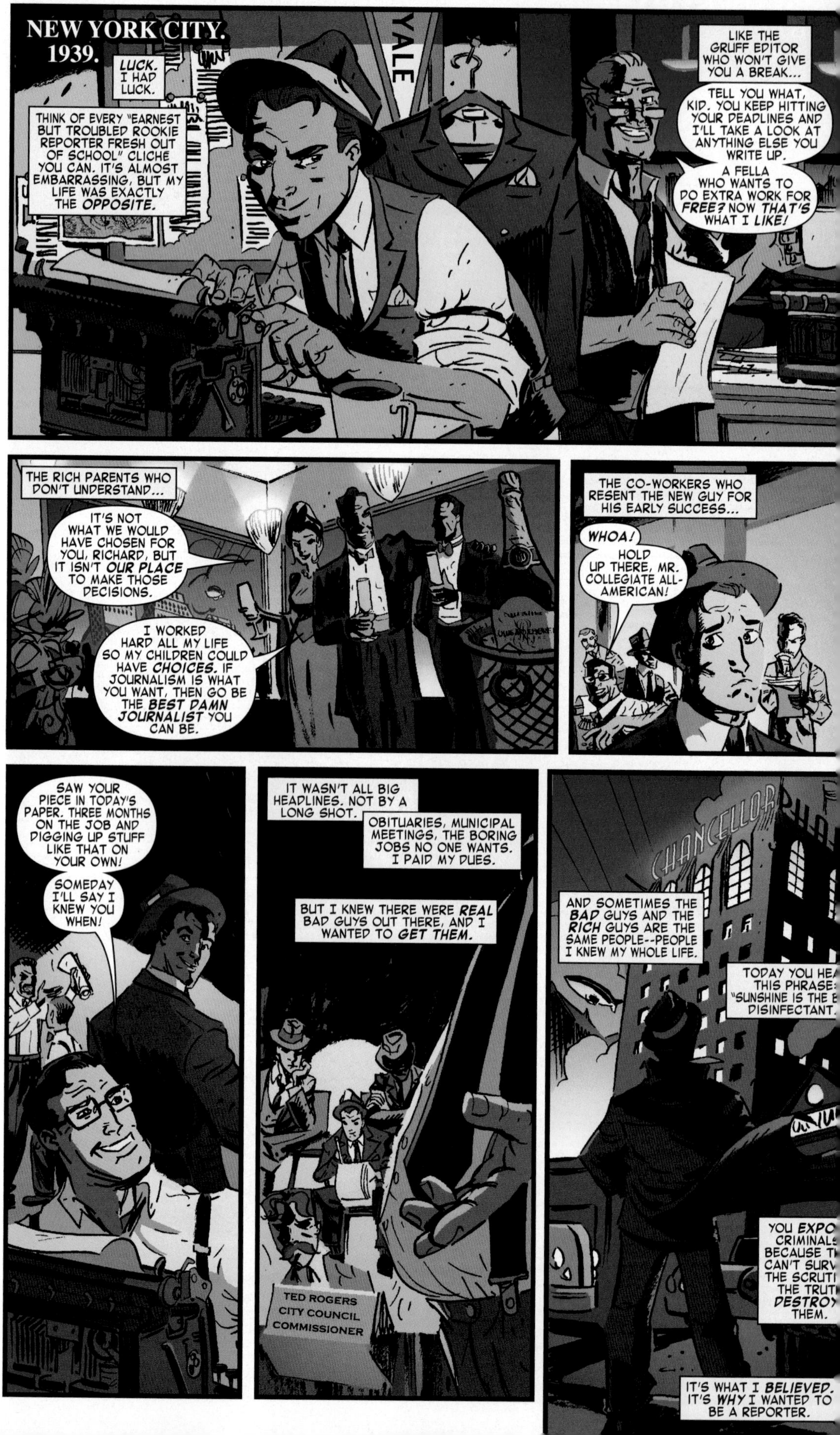

NEW YORK CITY. 1939.
LUCK. I HAD LUCK.
THINK OF EVERY "EARNEST BUT TROUBLED ROOKIE REPORTER FRESH OUT OF SCHOOL" CLICHE YOU CAN. IT'S ALMOST EMBARRASSING, BUT MY LIFE WAS EXACTLY THE OPPOSITE.
YALE
LIKE THE GRUFF EDITOR WHO WON'T GIVE YOU A BREAK...
TELL YOU WHAT, KID. YOU KEEP HITTING YOUR DEADLINES AND I'LL TAKE A LOOK AT ANYTHING ELSE YOU WRITE UP.
A FELLA WHO WANTS TO DO EXTRA WORK FOR FREE? NOW THAT'S WHAT I LIKE!
THE RICH PARENTS WHO DON'T UNDERSTAND...
IT'S NOT WHAT WE WOULD HAVE CHOSEN FOR YOU, RICHARD, BUT IT ISN'T OUR PLACE TO MAKE THOSE DECISIONS.
I WORKED HARD ALL MY LIFE SO MY CHILDREN COULD HAVE CHOICES. IF JOURNALISM IS WHAT YOU WANT, THEN GO BE THE BEST DAMN JOURNALIST YOU CAN BE.
THE CO-WORKERS WHO RESENT THE NEW GUY FOR HIS EARLY SUCCESS...
WHOA!
HOLD UP THERE, MR. COLLEGIATE ALL-AMERICAN!
SAW YOUR PIECE IN TODAY'S PAPER. THREE MONTHS ON THE JOB AND DIGGING UP STUFF LIKE THAT ON YOUR OWN!
SOMEDAY I'LL SAY I KNEW YOU WHEN!
IT WASN'T ALL BIG HEADLINES. NOT BY A LONG SHOT.
OBITUARIES, MUNICIPAL MEETINGS, THE BORING JOBS NO ONE WANTS. I PAID MY DUES.
BUT I KNEW THERE WERE REAL BAD GUYS OUT THERE, AND I WANTED TO GET THEM.
TED ROGERS
CITY COUNCIL
COMMISSIONER
CHANCELLOR
AND SOMETIMES THE BAD GUYS AND THE RICH GUYS ARE THE SAME PEOPLE--PEOPLE I KNEW MY WHOLE LIFE.
TODAY YOU HEA
THIS PHRASE:
"SUNSHINE IS THE
DISINFECTANT.
YOU EXPO
CRIMINAL
BECAUSE T
CAN'T SURV
THE SCRUTI
THE TRUT
DESTROY
THEM.
IT'S WHAT I BELIEVED. IT'S WHY I WANTED TO BE A REPORTER.

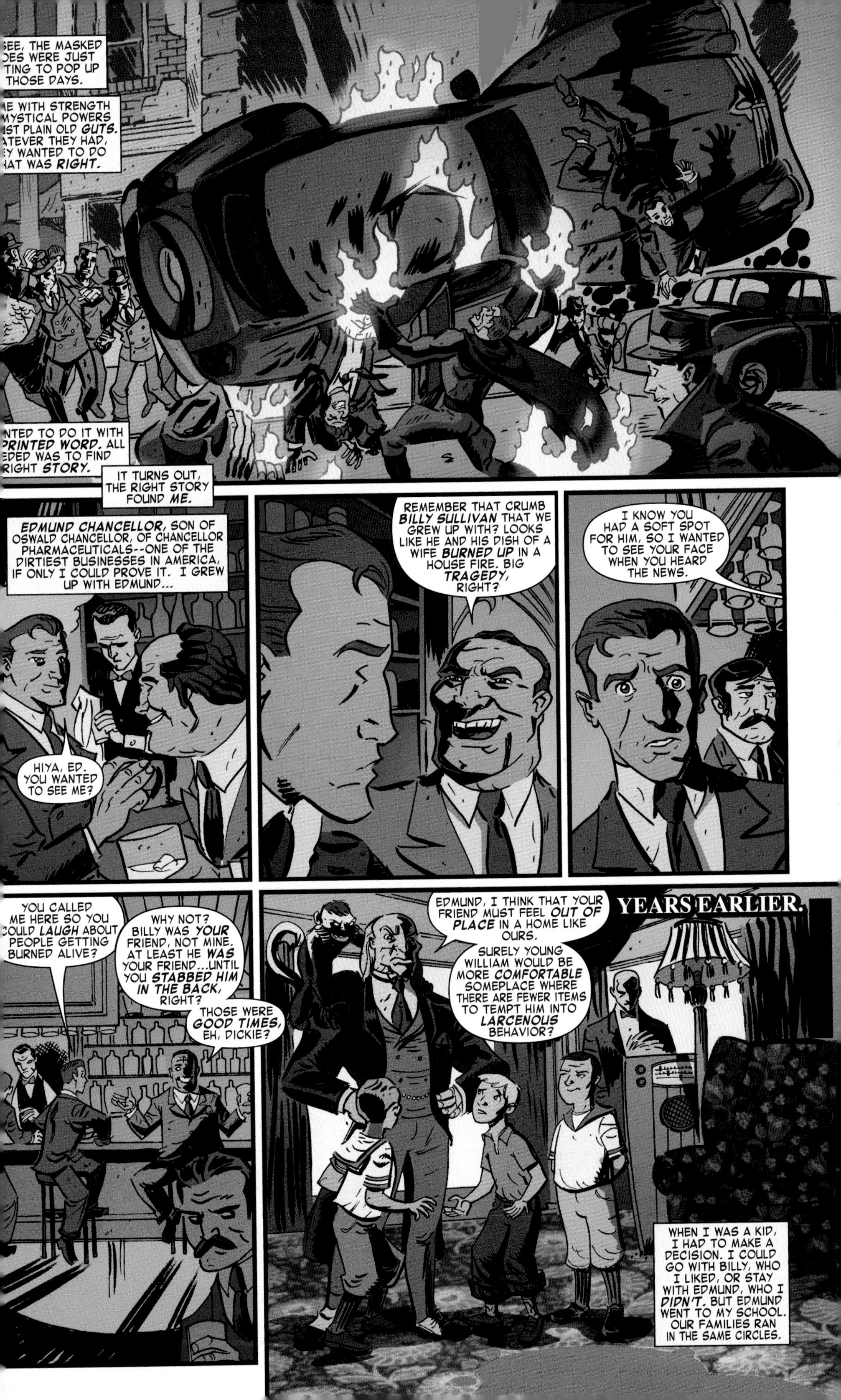

SEE, THE MASKED
DES WERE JUST
TING TO POP UP
THOSE DAYS.
E WITH STRENGTH
MYSTICAL POWERS
ST PLAIN OLD GUTS.
ATEVER THEY HAD,
Y WANTED TO DO
AT WAS RIGHT.
NTED TO DO IT WITH
PRINTED WORD. ALL
EDED WAS TO FIND
RIGHT STORY.
IT TURNS OUT, THE RIGHT STORY FOUND ME.
EDMUND CHANCELLOR, SON OF OSWALD CHANCELLOR, OF CHANCELLOR PHARMACEUTICALS--ONE OF THE DIRTIEST BUSINESSES IN AMERICA, IF ONLY I COULD PROVE IT. I GREW UP WITH EDMUND...
HIYA, ED. YOU WANTED TO SEE ME?
REMEMBER THAT CRUMB BILLY SULLIVAN THAT WE GREW UP WITH? LOOKS LIKE HE AND HIS DISH OF A WIFE BURNED UP IN A HOUSE FIRE. BIG TRAGEDY, RIGHT?
I KNOW YOU HAD A SOFT SPOT FOR HIM, SO I WANTED TO SEE YOUR FACE WHEN YOU HEARD THE NEWS.
YOU CALLED ME HERE SO YOU COULD LAUGH ABOUT PEOPLE GETTING BURNED ALIVE?
WHY NOT? BILLY WAS YOUR FRIEND, NOT MINE. AT LEAST HE WAS YOUR FRIEND...UNTIL YOU STABBED HIM IN THE BACK, RIGHT?
THOSE WERE GOOD TIMES, EH, DICKIE?
YEARS EARLIER.
EDMUND, I THINK THAT YOUR FRIEND MUST FEEL OUT OF PLACE IN A HOME LIKE OURS.
SURELY YOUNG WILLIAM WOULD BE MORE COMFORTABLE SOMEPLACE WHERE THERE ARE FEWER ITEMS TO TEMPT HIM INTO LARCENOUS BEHAVIOR?
WHEN I WAS A KID, I HAD TO MAKE A DECISION. I COULD GO WITH BILLY, WHO I LIKED, OR STAY WITH EDMUND, WHO I DIDN'T. BUT EDMUND WENT TO MY SCHOOL. OUR FAMILIES RAN IN THE SAME CIRCLES.

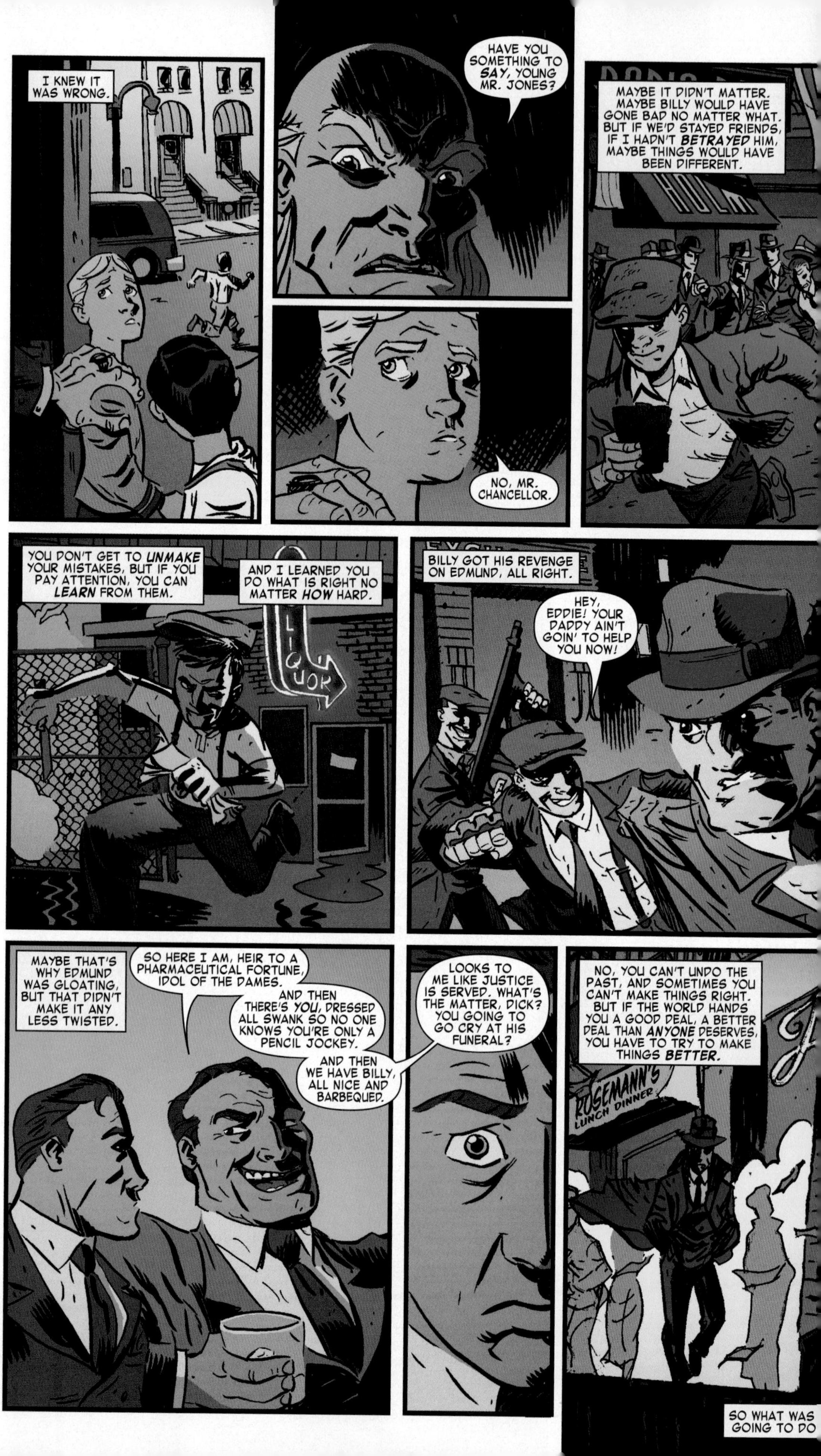
I KNEW IT WAS WRONG.
HAVE YOU SOMETHING TO *SAY*, YOUNG MR. JONES?
NO, MR. CHANCELLOR.
MAYBE IT DIDN'T MATTER. MAYBE BILLY WOULD HAVE GONE BAD NO MATTER WHAT. BUT IF WE'D STAYED FRIENDS, IF I HADN'T *BETRAYED* HIM, MAYBE THINGS WOULD HAVE BEEN DIFFERENT.
YOU DON'T GET TO *UNMAKE* YOUR MISTAKES, BUT IF YOU PAY ATTENTION, YOU CAN *LEARN* FROM THEM.
AND I LEARNED YOU DO WHAT IS RIGHT NO MATTER *HOW* HARD.
LIQUOR
BILLY GOT HIS REVENGE ON EDMUND, ALL RIGHT.
HEY, EDDIE! YOUR DADDY AIN'T GOIN' TO HELP YOU NOW!
MAYBE THAT'S WHY EDMUND WAS GLOATING, BUT THAT DIDN'T MAKE IT ANY LESS TWISTED.
SO HERE I AM, HEIR TO A PHARMACEUTICAL FORTUNE, IDOL OF THE DAMES.
AND THEN THERE'S *YOU*, DRESSED ALL SWANK SO NO ONE KNOWS YOU'RE ONLY A PENCIL JOCKEY.
AND THEN WE HAVE BILLY, ALL NICE AND BARBEQUED.
LOOKS TO ME LIKE JUSTICE IS SERVED. WHAT'S THE MATTER, DICK? YOU GOING TO GO CRY AT HIS FUNERAL?
NO, YOU CAN'T UNDO THE PAST, AND SOMETIMES YOU CAN'T MAKE THINGS RIGHT. BUT IF THE WORLD HANDS YOU A GOOD DEAL, A BETTER DEAL THAN *ANYONE* DESERVES, YOU HAVE TO TRY TO MAKE THINGS *BETTER*.
ROSEMANN'S LUNCH DINNER
SO WHAT WAS GOING TO DO

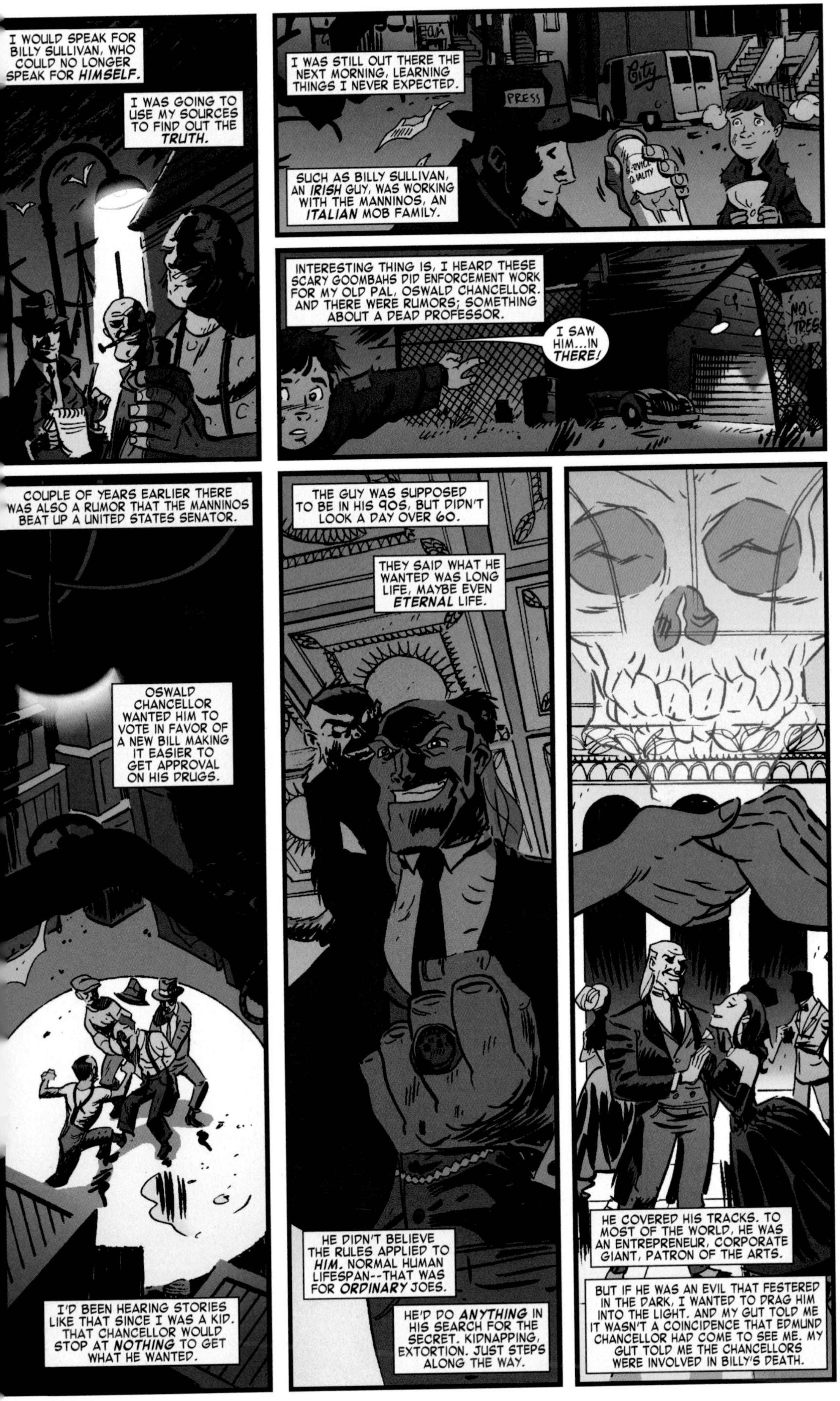
I WOULD SPEAK FOR BILLY SULLIVAN, WHO COULD NO LONGER SPEAK FOR HIMSELF.
I WAS GOING TO USE MY SOURCES TO FIND OUT THE TRUTH.
I WAS STILL OUT THERE THE NEXT MORNING, LEARNING THINGS I NEVER EXPECTED.
PRESS
City
SUCH AS BILLY SULLIVAN, AN IRISH GUY, WAS WORKING WITH THE MANNINOS, AN ITALIAN MOB FAMILY.
INTERESTING THING IS, I HEARD THESE SCARY GOOMBAHS DID ENFORCEMENT WORK FOR MY OLD PAL, OSWALD CHANCELLOR. AND THERE WERE RUMORS; SOMETHING ABOUT A DEAD PROFESSOR.
I SAW HIM...IN THERE!
COUPLE OF YEARS EARLIER THERE WAS ALSO A RUMOR THAT THE MANNINOS BEAT UP A UNITED STATES SENATOR.
OSWALD CHANCELLOR WANTED HIM TO VOTE IN FAVOR OF A NEW BILL MAKING IT EASIER TO GET APPROVAL ON HIS DRUGS.
I'D BEEN HEARING STORIES LIKE THAT SINCE I WAS A KID. THAT CHANCELLOR WOULD STOP AT NOTHING TO GET WHAT HE WANTED.
THE GUY WAS SUPPOSED TO BE IN HIS 90S, BUT DIDN'T LOOK A DAY OVER 60.
THEY SAID WHAT HE WANTED WAS LONG LIFE, MAYBE EVEN ETERNAL LIFE.
HE DIDN'T BELIEVE THE RULES APPLIED TO HIM. NORMAL HUMAN LIFESPAN--THAT WAS FOR ORDINARY JOES.
HE'D DO ANYTHING IN HIS SEARCH FOR THE SECRET. KIDNAPPING, EXTORTION. JUST STEPS ALONG THE WAY.
HE COVERED HIS TRACKS. TO MOST OF THE WORLD, HE WAS AN ENTREPRENEUR, CORPORATE GIANT, PATRON OF THE ARTS.
BUT IF HE WAS AN EVIL THAT FESTERED IN THE DARK, I WANTED TO DRAG HIM INTO THE LIGHT. AND MY GUT TOLD ME IT WASN'T A COINCIDENCE THAT EDMUND CHANCELLOR HAD COME TO SEE ME. MY GUT TOLD ME THE CHANCELLORS WERE INVOLVED IN BILLY'S DEATH.

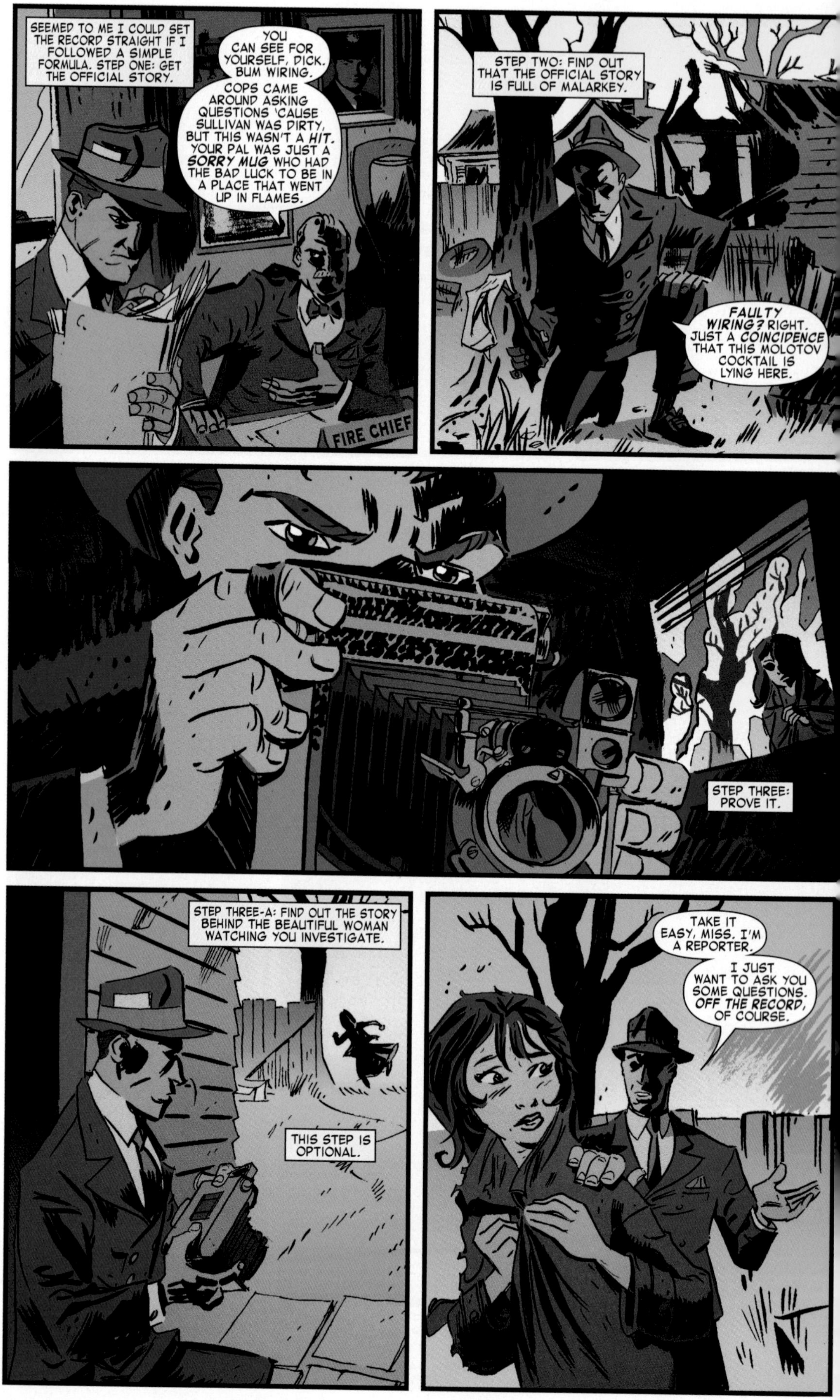
SEEMED TO ME I COULD SET THE RECORD STRAIGHT IF I FOLLOWED A SIMPLE FORMULA. STEP ONE: GET THE OFFICIAL STORY.
YOU CAN SEE FOR YOURSELF, DICK. BUM WIRING.
COPS CAME AROUND ASKING QUESTIONS 'CAUSE SULLIVAN WAS DIRTY, BUT THIS WASN'T A HIT. YOUR PAL WAS JUST A SORRY MUG WHO HAD THE BAD LUCK TO BE IN A PLACE THAT WENT UP IN FLAMES.
FIRE CHIEF
STEP TWO: FIND OUT THAT THE OFFICIAL STORY IS FULL OF MALARKEY.
FAULTY WIRING? RIGHT. JUST A COINCIDENCE THAT THIS MOLOTOV COCKTAIL IS LYING HERE.
STEP THREE: PROVE IT.
STEP THREE-A: FIND OUT THE STORY BEHIND THE BEAUTIFUL WOMAN WATCHING YOU INVESTIGATE.
THIS STEP IS OPTIONAL.
TAKE IT EASY, MISS. I'M A REPORTER.
I JUST WANT TO ASK YOU SOME QUESTIONS. OFF THE RECORD, OF COURSE.

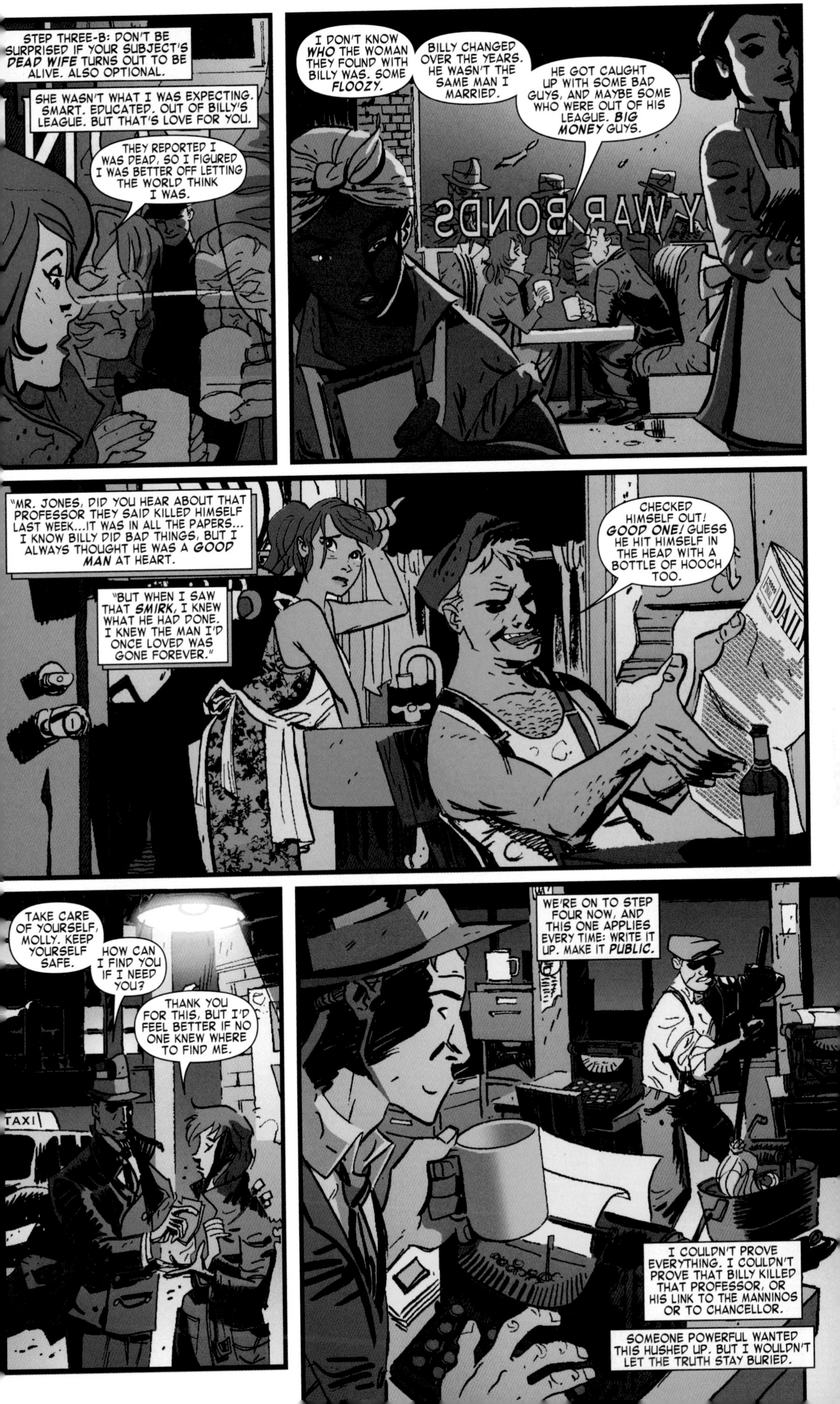

STEP THREE-B: DON'T BE SURPRISED IF YOUR SUBJECT'S DEAD WIFE TURNS OUT TO BE ALIVE. ALSO OPTIONAL.
SHE WASN'T WHAT I WAS EXPECTING. SMART. EDUCATED. OUT OF BILLY'S LEAGUE. BUT THAT'S LOVE FOR YOU.
THEY REPORTED I WAS DEAD, SO I FIGURED I WAS BETTER OFF LETTING THE WORLD THINK I WAS.
I DON'T KNOW WHO THE WOMAN THEY FOUND WITH BILLY WAS. SOME FLOOZY.
BILLY CHANGED OVER THE YEARS. HE WASN'T THE SAME MAN I MARRIED.
HE GOT CAUGHT UP WITH SOME BAD GUYS, AND MAYBE SOME WHO WERE OUT OF HIS LEAGUE. BIG MONEY GUYS.
Y WAR BONDS
"MR. JONES, DID YOU HEAR ABOUT THAT PROFESSOR THEY SAID KILLED HIMSELF LAST WEEK...IT WAS IN ALL THE PAPERS... I KNOW BILLY DID BAD THINGS, BUT I ALWAYS THOUGHT HE WAS A GOOD MAN AT HEART.
"BUT WHEN I SAW THAT SMIRK, I KNEW WHAT HE HAD DONE. I KNEW THE MAN I'D ONCE LOVED WAS GONE FOREVER."
CHECKED HIMSELF OUT! GOOD ONE! GUESS HE HIT HIMSELF IN THE HEAD WITH A BOTTLE OF HOOCH TOO.
DAIL
TAKE CARE OF YOURSELF, MOLLY. KEEP YOURSELF SAFE.
HOW CAN I FIND YOU IF I NEED YOU?
THANK YOU FOR THIS, BUT I'D FEEL BETTER IF NO ONE KNEW WHERE TO FIND ME.
TAXI
WE'RE ON TO STEP FOUR NOW, AND THIS ONE APPLIES EVERY TIME: WRITE IT UP. MAKE IT PUBLIC.
I COULDN'T PROVE EVERYTHING. I COULDN'T PROVE THAT BILLY KILLED THAT PROFESSOR, OR HIS LINK TO THE MANNINOS OR TO CHANCELLOR.
SOMEONE POWERFUL WANTED THIS HUSHED UP. BUT I WOULDN'T LET THE TRUTH STAY BURIED.

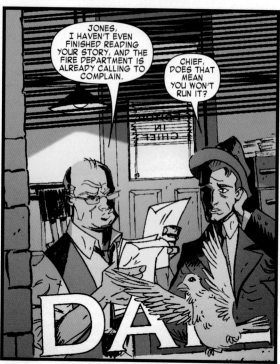

JONES, I HAVEN'T EVEN FINISHED READING YOUR STORY, AND THE FIRE DEPARTMENT IS ALREADY CALLING TO COMPLAIN.

CHIEF, DOES THAT MEAN YOU WON'T RUN IT?

THIS IS A *NEWSPAPER*, KID. WE'RE NOT DOING OUR JOB IF THERE *AREN'T* BIG SHOTS MAD AT US.

IF THIS CHECKS OU I'LL RUN IT *PAGE ONE!*

THE NEXT DAY OUR RIVAL PAPER HAD THE COVER-UP IN FULL SWING.

RECKLESS REPORTER MAKES BASELESS ACCUSATION

Trust CHANCELLOR PHARMACEUTICALS *Quality you can trust.*

SUDDENLY, INSTEAD OF THE TRUTH, THERE WAS *OUR* STORY AND *THEIR* STORY. THE ORDINARY JOE COULDN'T KNOW *WHO* TO BELIEVE.

DON'T SWEAT IT, DICK. OUR COMPETITION IS IN CHANCELLOR'S POCKET, SO OF COURSE THEY'RE GOING TO COME AFTER *YOU.* THE BIG BOYS PLAY *HARD.*

BUT LOOK AT THIS. THEY *RE-BURNED* BILLY'S HOUSE. BLAMED IT ON HOBOS. NOW I CAN'T PROVE ANYTHING.

WHAT, YOU THINK THERE'S NO OTHER LINK BETWEEN THIS CRIME AND THE PEOPLE WHO COMMITTED IT?

YOU *BOXED* IN COLLEGE, RIGHT? WELL, IT'S TIME TO *FIGHT.* I'M PUTTING YOU ON THIS FULL TIME. NOW *GET OUT THERE* AND DIG ME UP SOME *DIRT!*

I MADE A FEW CALLS, ASKED A FEW QUESTIONS. THESE LED ME UPTOWN TO AN UNDER-GROUND GAMBLING CLUB.

EXIT

NOTHING LIKE BOOZE AND MONEY--WINNING OR LOSING--TO LOOSEN TONGUES.

HEY, I SEEN THAT FIRE CHIEF IN THIS JOINT, BUT HE HAD A HARD TIME PAYING UP, AND HE GOT THE *BOOT.*

NOW I SEE HIM AT OLSON'S. NASTY CLIP JOINT, RUN BY THE *MANNINOS.* I HEAR HE'S IN SO DEEP HE AIN'T *NEVER* COMING OUT.

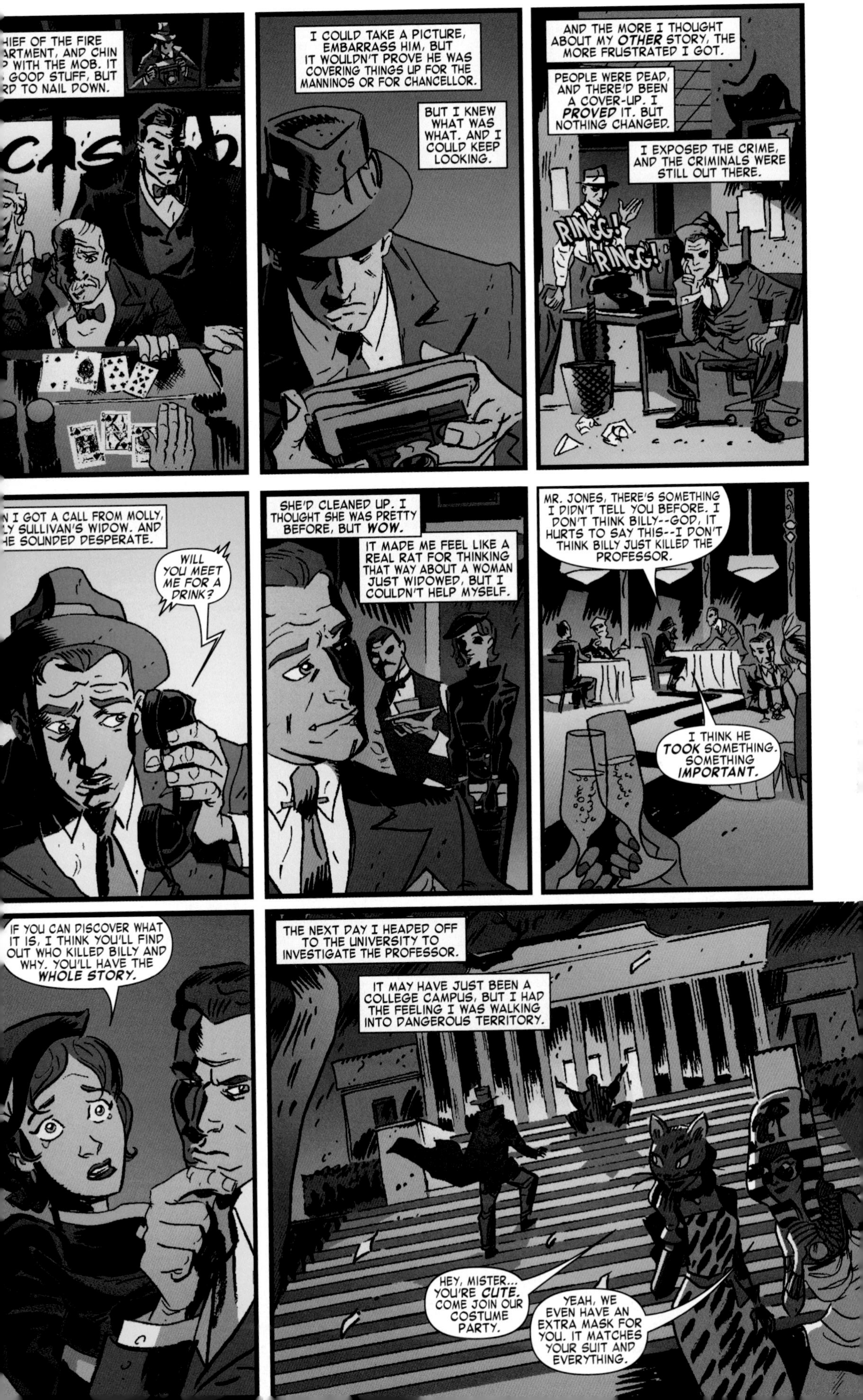
HIEF OF THE FIRE
ARTMENT, AND CHIN
P WITH THE MOB. IT
GOOD STUFF, BUT
RD TO NAIL DOWN.
I COULD TAKE A PICTURE, EMBARRASS HIM, BUT IT WOULDN'T PROVE HE WAS COVERING THINGS UP FOR THE MANNINOS OR FOR CHANCELLOR.
BUT I KNEW WHAT WAS WHAT. AND I COULD KEEP LOOKING.
AND THE MORE I THOUGHT ABOUT MY OTHER STORY, THE MORE FRUSTRATED I GOT.
PEOPLE WERE DEAD, AND THERE'D BEEN A COVER-UP. I PROVED IT. BUT NOTHING CHANGED.
I EXPOSED THE CRIME, AND THE CRIMINALS WERE STILL OUT THERE.
RINGG! RINGG!
N I GOT A CALL FROM MOLLY,
LY SULLIVAN'S WIDOW. AND
HE SOUNDED DESPERATE.
WILL YOU MEET ME FOR A DRINK?
SHE'D CLEANED UP. I THOUGHT SHE WAS PRETTY BEFORE, BUT WOW.
IT MADE ME FEEL LIKE A REAL RAT FOR THINKING THAT WAY ABOUT A WOMAN JUST WIDOWED, BUT I COULDN'T HELP MYSELF.
MR. JONES, THERE'S SOMETHING I DIDN'T TELL YOU BEFORE. I DON'T THINK BILLY--GOD, IT HURTS TO SAY THIS--I DON'T THINK BILLY JUST KILLED THE PROFESSOR.
I THINK HE TOOK SOMETHING. SOMETHING IMPORTANT.
IF YOU CAN DISCOVER WHAT IT IS, I THINK YOU'LL FIND OUT WHO KILLED BILLY AND WHY. YOU'LL HAVE THE WHOLE STORY.
THE NEXT DAY I HEADED OFF TO THE UNIVERSITY TO INVESTIGATE THE PROFESSOR.
IT MAY HAVE JUST BEEN A COLLEGE CAMPUS, BUT I HAD THE FEELING I WAS WALKING INTO DANGEROUS TERRITORY.
HEY, MISTER... YOU'RE CUTE. COME JOIN OUR COSTUME PARTY.
YEAH, WE EVEN HAVE AN EXTRA MASK FOR YOU. IT MATCHES YOUR SUIT AND EVERYTHING.

I WASN'T ABOUT TO PUT ON A MASK, BUT IT MADE ME *THINK*.

MAYBE IT WASN'T SUCH A GOOD IDEA TO USE MY REAL NAME.

I WASN'T AFRAID TO BECOME A TARGET, BUT I HAD TO GET THAT STORY PRINTED FIRST.

THE HISTORY DEPARTMENT SECRETARY WASN'T HAPPY TO TALK, BUT SHE STILL GAVE ME THE FILE ON THE PROFESSOR.

YOU'LL SEE FOR YOURSELF. HE WROTE THREE BOOKS ON THE HISTORY OF ALCHEMY.

NOT CRACKPOT STUFF, BUT, YOU KNOW...RESEARCH ON THE PEOPLE WHO BELIEVED IN IT.

NOT THAT *I* READ THE BOOKS. TOO *DRY* FOR ME.

CALL IT A REPORTER'S INTUITION, BUT THERE WAS SOMETHING I DIDN'T LIKE ABOUT HER.

YOU TOLD ME TO CALL IF ANYONE CAME BY.

YEAH, WELL THERE WAS A NOSY GUY JUST IN HERE. SAID HE WAS A *REPORTER*, BUT CONVENIENTLY FORGOT TO GIVE ME HIS NAME.

HE JUST LEFT NOW--TALL GUY, GOOD LOOKING. HE'S GOT PURPLE LINING IN HIS SUIT AND ON HIS HAT.

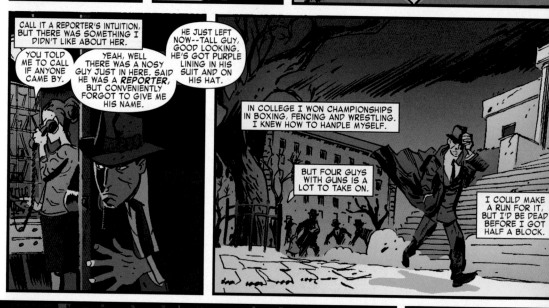

IN COLLEGE I WON CHAMPIONSHIPS IN BOXING, FENCING AND WRESTLING. I KNEW HOW TO HANDLE MYSELF.

BUT FOUR GUYS WITH GUNS IS A LOT TO TAKE ON.

I COULD MAKE A RUN FOR IT, BUT I'D BE DEAD BEFORE I GOT HALF A BLOCK.

I NEEDED AN EDGE, AND MAYBE THE MASK THOSE PARTY GIRLS GAVE ME WAS THE ANSWER.

THOSE COSTUMED HEROES COVER THEIR FACES TO KEEP THEIR NAMES A SECRET, BUT I THOUGHT MAYBE IT WAS FOR *OTHER* REASONS TOO.

MAYBE FIGHTING A MAN IN A MASK IS DISTRACTING... *FRIGHTENING* EVEN.

MAYBE THE MASK WAS THE ONLY CHANCE I HAD TO GET OUT OF THERE ALIVE.

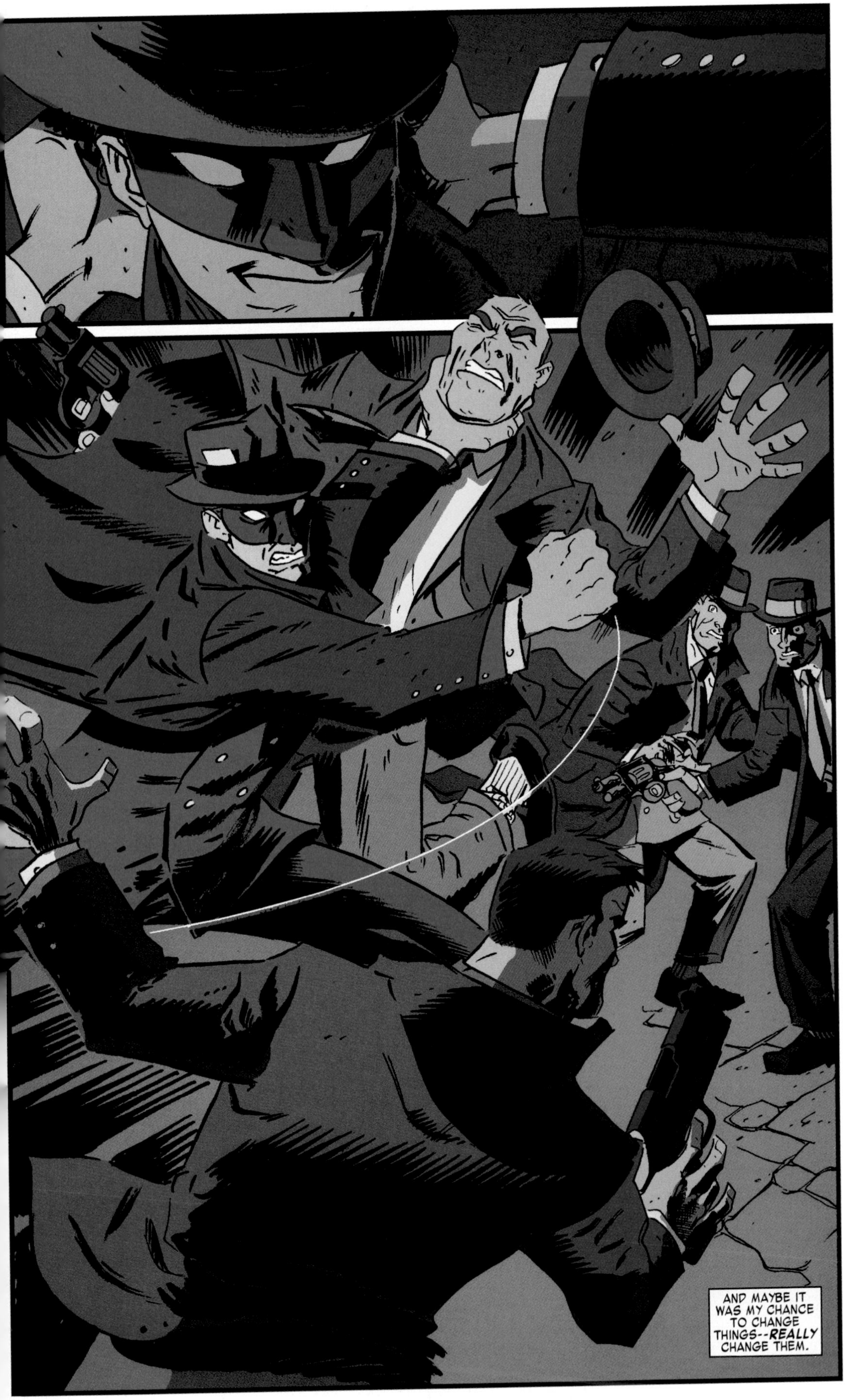
AND MAYBE IT WAS MY CHANCE TO CHANGE THINGS--*REALLY* CHANGE THEM.

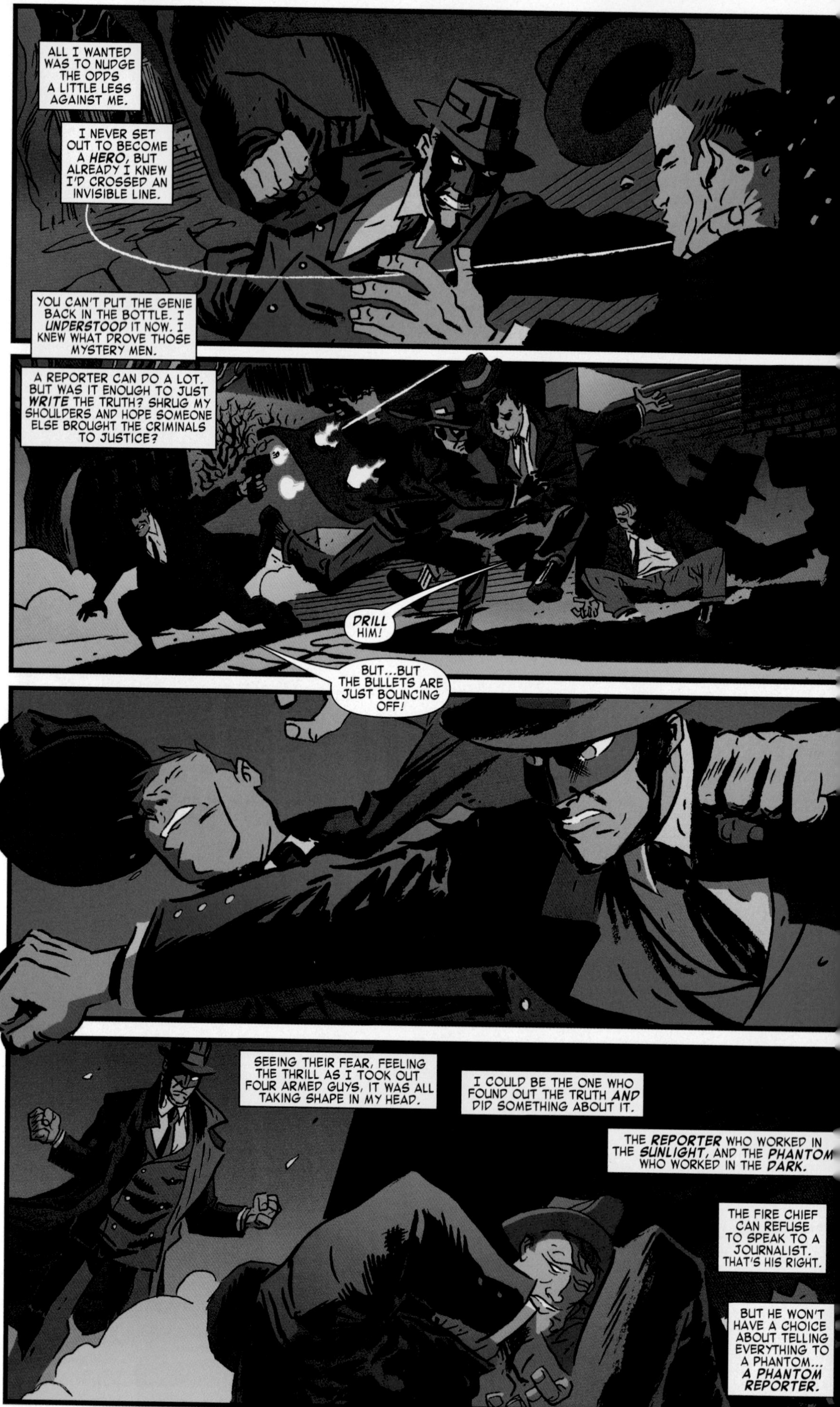

ALL I WANTED WAS TO NUDGE THE ODDS A LITTLE LESS AGAINST ME.
I NEVER SET OUT TO BECOME A HERO, BUT ALREADY I KNEW I'D CROSSED AN INVISIBLE LINE.
YOU CAN'T PUT THE GENIE BACK IN THE BOTTLE. I UNDERSTOOD IT NOW. I KNEW WHAT DROVE THOSE MYSTERY MEN.
A REPORTER CAN DO A LOT. BUT WAS IT ENOUGH TO JUST WRITE THE TRUTH? SHRUG MY SHOULDERS AND HOPE SOMEONE ELSE BROUGHT THE CRIMINALS TO JUSTICE?
DRILL HIM!
BUT...BUT THE BULLETS ARE JUST BOUNCING OFF!
SEEING THEIR FEAR, FEELING THE THRILL AS I TOOK OUT FOUR ARMED GUYS, IT WAS ALL TAKING SHAPE IN MY HEAD.
I COULD BE THE ONE WHO FOUND OUT THE TRUTH AND DID SOMETHING ABOUT IT.
THE REPORTER WHO WORKED IN THE SUNLIGHT, AND THE PHANTOM WHO WORKED IN THE DARK.
THE FIRE CHIEF CAN REFUSE TO SPEAK TO A JOURNALIST. THAT'S HIS RIGHT.
BUT HE WON'T HAVE A CHOICE ABOUT TELLING EVERYTHING TO A PHANTOM... A PHANTOM REPORTER.

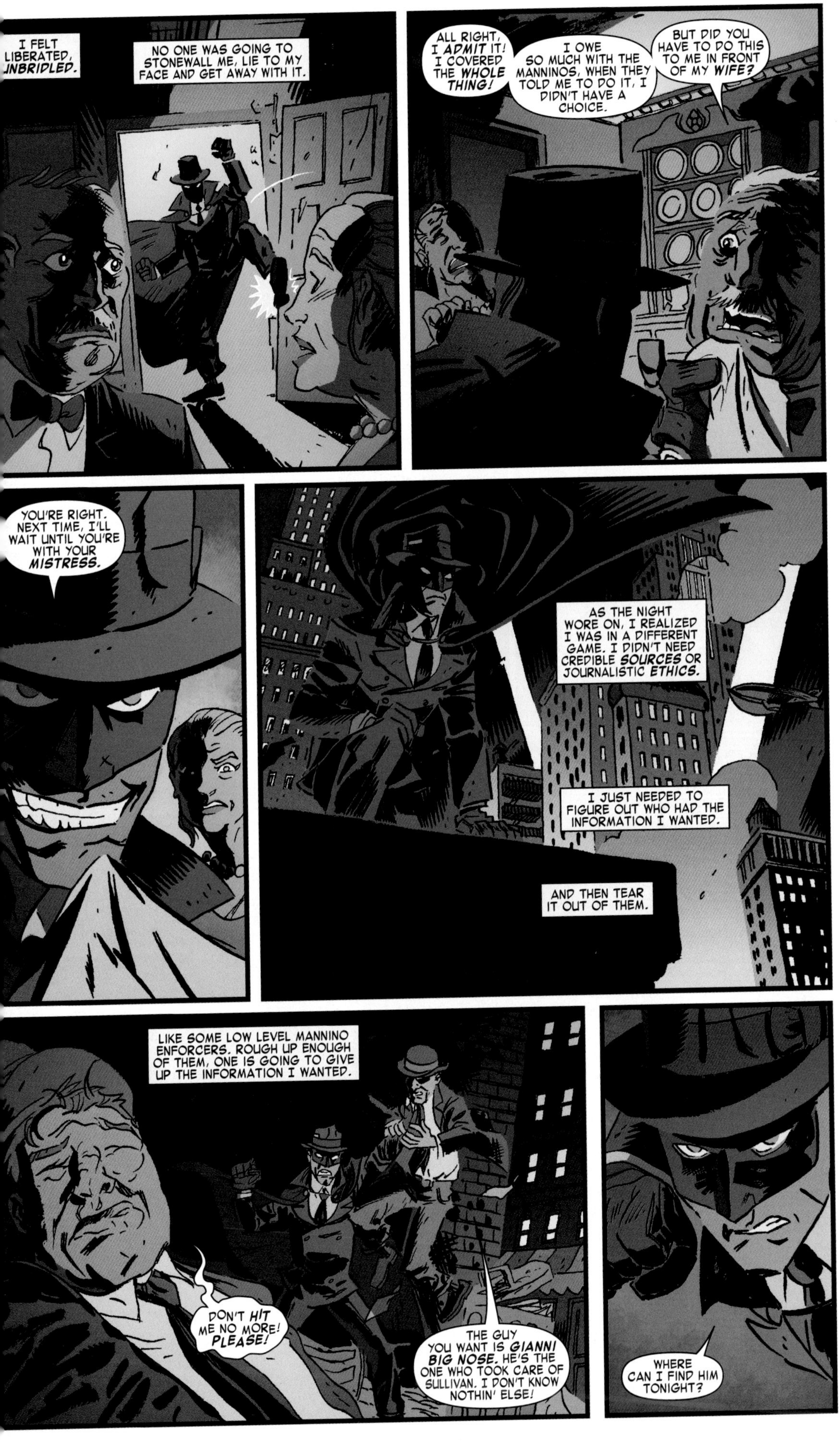
I FELT LIBERATED, UNBRIDLED.
NO ONE WAS GOING TO STONEWALL ME, LIE TO MY FACE AND GET AWAY WITH IT.
ALL RIGHT, I ADMIT IT! I COVERED THE WHOLE THING!
I OWE SO MUCH WITH THE MANNINOS, WHEN THEY TOLD ME TO DO IT, I DIDN'T HAVE A CHOICE.
BUT DID YOU HAVE TO DO THIS TO ME IN FRONT OF MY WIFE?
YOU'RE RIGHT. NEXT TIME, I'LL WAIT UNTIL YOU'RE WITH YOUR MISTRESS.
AS THE NIGHT WORE ON, I REALIZED I WAS IN A DIFFERENT GAME. I DIDN'T NEED CREDIBLE SOURCES OR JOURNALISTIC ETHICS.
I JUST NEEDED TO FIGURE OUT WHO HAD THE INFORMATION I WANTED.
AND THEN TEAR IT OUT OF THEM.
LIKE SOME LOW LEVEL MANNINO ENFORCERS. ROUGH UP ENOUGH OF THEM, ONE IS GOING TO GIVE UP THE INFORMATION I WANTED.
DON'T HIT ME NO MORE! PLEASE!
THE GUY YOU WANT IS GIANNI BIG NOSE. HE'S THE ONE WHO TOOK CARE OF SULLIVAN. I DON'T KNOW NOTHIN' ELSE!
WHERE CAN I FIND HIM TONIGHT?

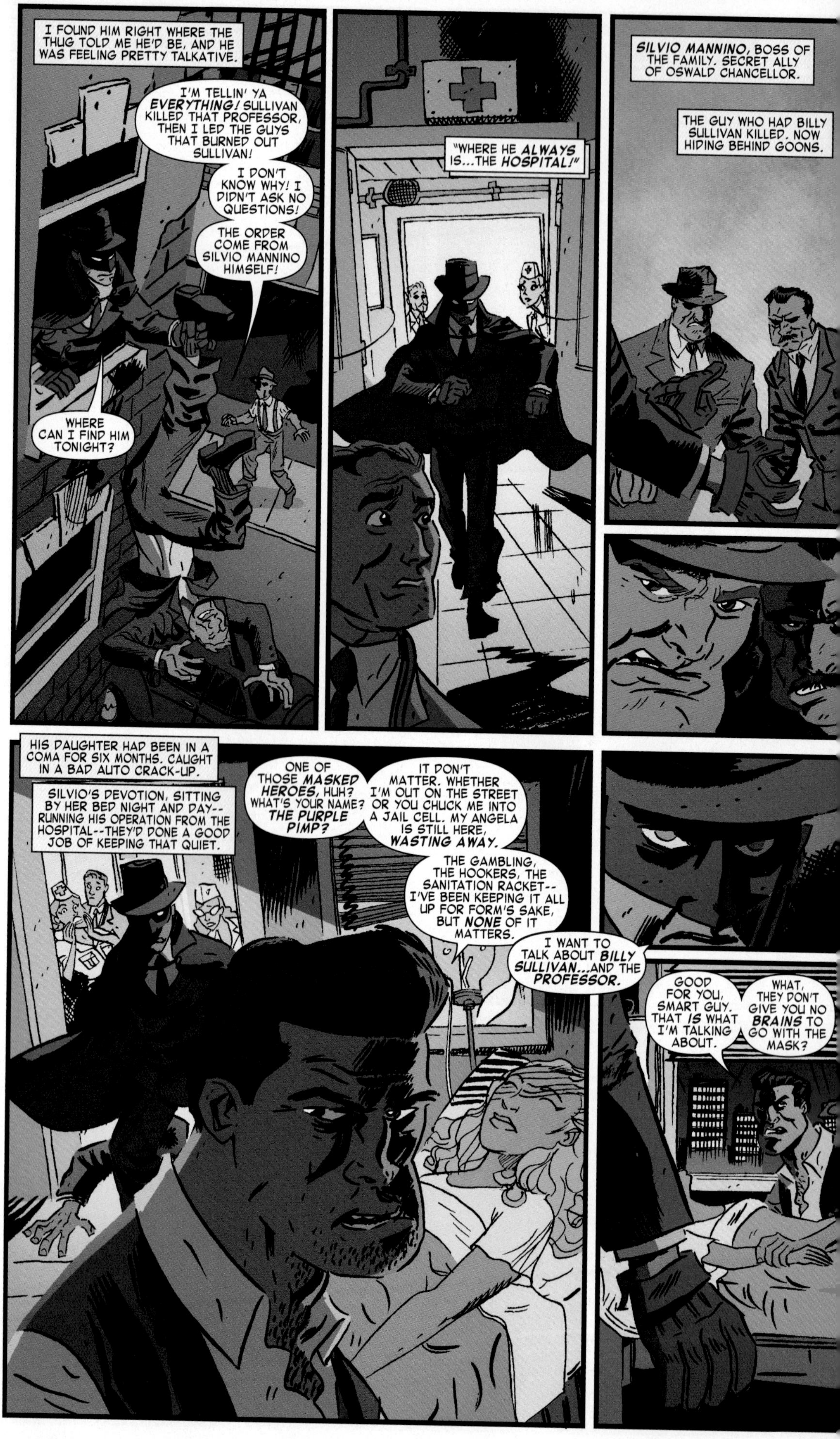
I FOUND HIM RIGHT WHERE THE THUG TOLD ME HE'D BE, AND HE WAS FEELING PRETTY TALKATIVE.
I'M TELLIN' YA EVERYTHING! SULLIVAN KILLED THAT PROFESSOR, THEN I LED THE GUYS THAT BURNED OUT SULLIVAN!
I DON'T KNOW WHY! I DIDN'T ASK NO QUESTIONS!
THE ORDER COME FROM SILVIO MANNINO HIMSELF!
WHERE CAN I FIND HIM TONIGHT?
"WHERE HE ALWAYS IS...THE HOSPITAL!"
SILVIO MANNINO, BOSS OF THE FAMILY. SECRET ALLY OF OSWALD CHANCELLOR.
THE GUY WHO HAD BILLY SULLIVAN KILLED. NOW HIDING BEHIND GOONS.
HIS DAUGHTER HAD BEEN IN A COMA FOR SIX MONTHS. CAUGHT IN A BAD AUTO CRACK-UP.
SILVIO'S DEVOTION, SITTING BY HER BED NIGHT AND DAY-- RUNNING HIS OPERATION FROM THE HOSPITAL--THEY'D DONE A GOOD JOB OF KEEPING THAT QUIET.
ONE OF THOSE MASKED HEROES, HUH? WHAT'S YOUR NAME? THE PURPLE PIMP?
IT DON'T MATTER. WHETHER I'M OUT ON THE STREET OR YOU CHUCK ME INTO A JAIL CELL. MY ANGELA IS STILL HERE, WASTING AWAY.
THE GAMBLING, THE HOOKERS, THE SANITATION RACKET-- I'VE BEEN KEEPING IT ALL UP FOR FORM'S SAKE, BUT NONE OF IT MATTERS.
I WANT TO TALK ABOUT BILLY SULLIVAN...AND THE PROFESSOR.
GOOD FOR YOU, SMART GUY. THAT IS WHAT I'M TALKING ABOUT.
WHAT, THEY DON'T GIVE YOU NO BRAINS TO GO WITH THE MASK?

EN, HERO, THE PROFESSOR WORKED
R CHANCELLOR, AND CHANCELLOR
ND I HAVE AN *UNDERSTANDING.*

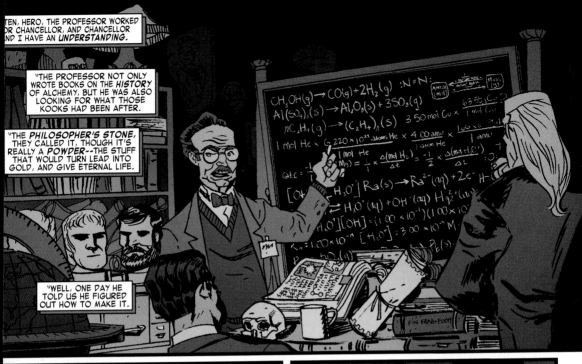

"THE PROFESSOR NOT ONLY WROTE BOOKS ON THE *HISTORY* OF ALCHEMY, BUT HE WAS ALSO LOOKING FOR WHAT THOSE KOOKS HAD BEEN AFTER."

"THE *PHILOSOPHER'S STONE,* THEY CALLED IT, THOUGH IT'S REALLY A *POWDER*--THE STUFF THAT WOULD TURN LEAD INTO GOLD, AND GIVE ETERNAL LIFE."

"WELL, ONE DAY HE TOLD US HE FIGURED OUT HOW TO MAKE IT."

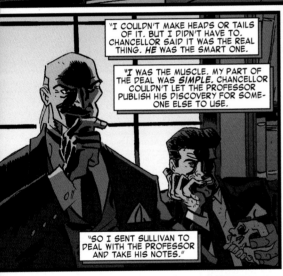

"I COULDN'T MAKE HEADS OR TAILS OF IT. BUT I DIDN'T HAVE TO. CHANCELLOR SAID IT WAS THE REAL THING. *HE* WAS THE SMART ONE.

"*I* WAS THE MUSCLE. MY PART OF THE DEAL WAS *SIMPLE.* CHANCELLOR COULDN'T LET THE PROFESSOR PUBLISH HIS DISCOVERY FOR SOME-ONE ELSE TO USE."

"SO I SENT SULLIVAN TO DEAL WITH THE PROFESSOR AND TAKE HIS NOTES."

"WHY SULLIVAN? WHY NOT ONE OF YOUR OWN GUYS, SILVIO?"

"HEY, IF YOU CAN'T FIGURE THAT OUT FOR YOURSELF, IT'S TIME TO GIVE UP THE GOOD GUY BUSINESS."

"YOU WANTED SOMEONE YOU WOULDN'T MIND *ELIMINATING* IF HE DISCOVERED TOO MUCH."

"*BINGO.* IT'S A GAME OF MOVES, HERO. YOU HAVE TO THINK *FIVE* STEPS AHEAD, OR YOU'RE *DEAD MEAT.*"

I KNOW WHAT YOU GOT HERE, BIG NOSE, AND I KNOW IT'S WORTH A LOT MORE THAN YOUR BOSS IS PAYING ME.

SO, I TURN EVERYTHING OVER TO CHANCELLOR BECAUSE HE'S GOING TO USE THIS FORMULA TO HELP MY DAUGHTER.

ONLY NOW HE'S HEMMING AND HAWING. HE'S NOT GIVING THE FORMULA UP UNTIL HE TURNS MY FAMILY INTO HIS OWN PRIVATE SECURITY FORCE.

THE DOCS SAY ANGELA COULD LAST FOR *YEARS* IN THE COMA, SO CHANCELLOR KNOWS HE CAN STRING ME ALONG. I CAN'T TAKE HIM OUT, CAN I? NOT WHILE HE'S GOT *THIS* OVER ME.

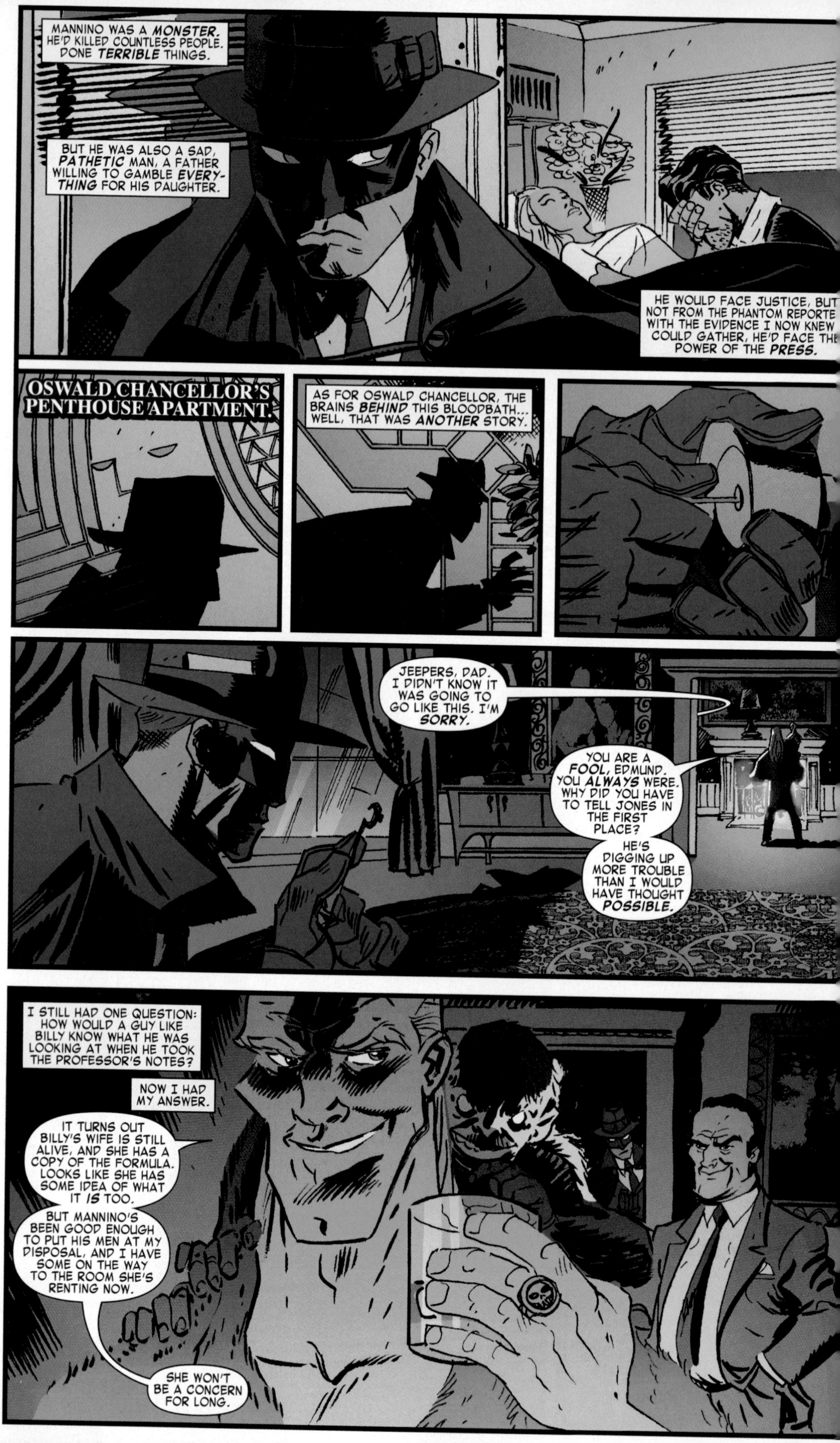
MANNINO WAS A MONSTER. HE'D KILLED COUNTLESS PEOPLE. DONE TERRIBLE THINGS.
BUT HE WAS ALSO A SAD, PATHETIC MAN, A FATHER WILLING TO GAMBLE EVERY-THING FOR HIS DAUGHTER.
HE WOULD FACE JUSTICE, BUT NOT FROM THE PHANTOM REPORTE WITH THE EVIDENCE I NOW KNEW COULD GATHER, HE'D FACE THE POWER OF THE PRESS.
OSWALD CHANCELLOR'S PENTHOUSE APARTMENT.
AS FOR OSWALD CHANCELLOR, THE BRAINS BEHIND THIS BLOODBATH... WELL, THAT WAS ANOTHER STORY.
JEEPERS, DAD. I DIDN'T KNOW IT WAS GOING TO GO LIKE THIS. I'M SORRY.
YOU ARE A FOOL, EDMUND. YOU ALWAYS WERE. WHY DID YOU HAVE TO TELL JONES IN THE FIRST PLACE?
HE'S DIGGING UP MORE TROUBLE THAN I WOULD HAVE THOUGHT POSSIBLE.
I STILL HAD ONE QUESTION: HOW WOULD A GUY LIKE BILLY KNOW WHAT HE WAS LOOKING AT WHEN HE TOOK THE PROFESSOR'S NOTES?
NOW I HAD MY ANSWER.
IT TURNS OUT BILLY'S WIFE IS STILL ALIVE, AND SHE HAS A COPY OF THE FORMULA. LOOKS LIKE SHE HAS SOME IDEA OF WHAT IT IS TOO.
BUT MANNINO'S BEEN GOOD ENOUGH TO PUT HIS MEN AT MY DISPOSAL, AND I HAVE SOME ON THE WAY TO THE ROOM SHE'S RENTING NOW.
SHE WON'T BE A CONCERN FOR LONG.

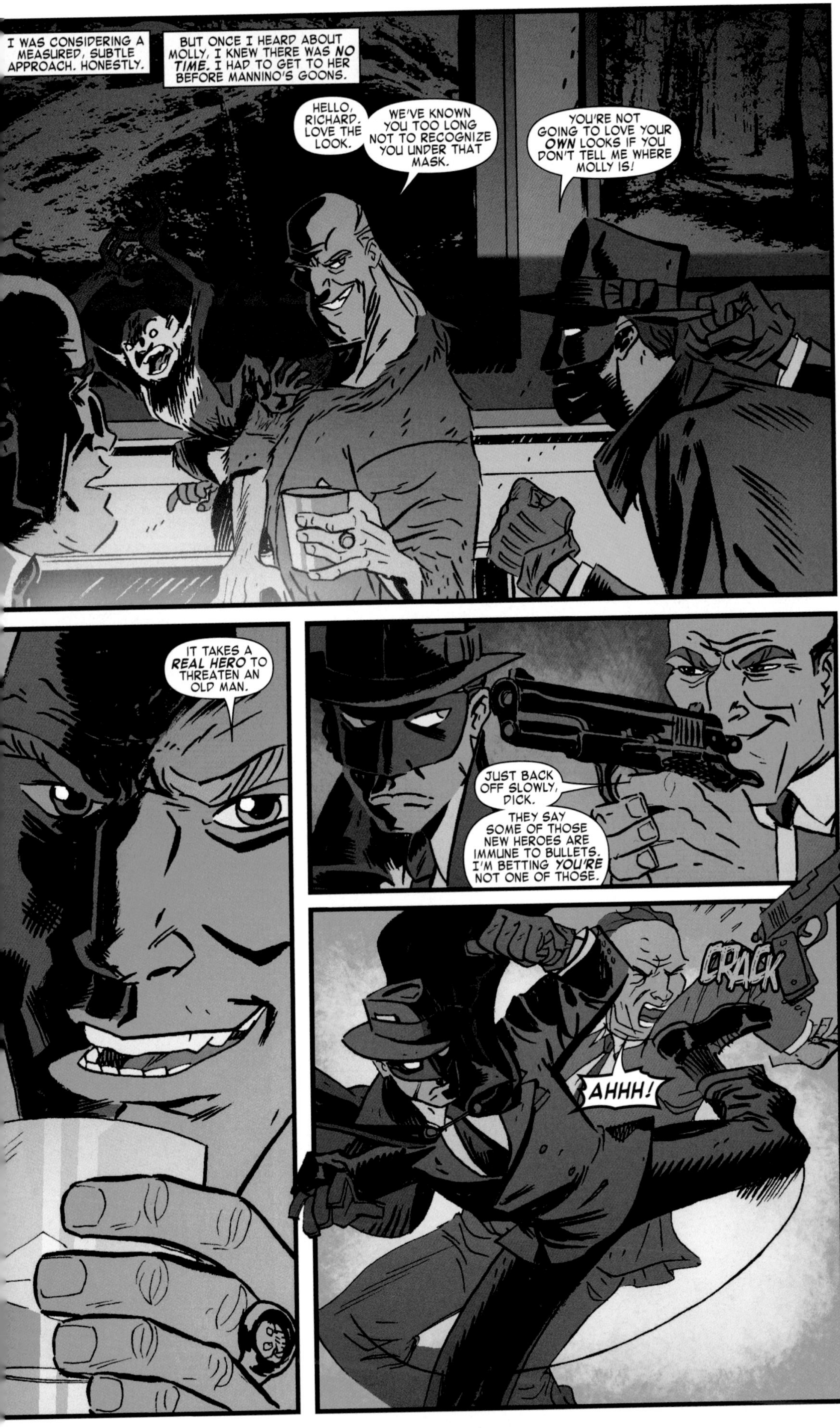
I WAS CONSIDERING A MEASURED, SUBTLE APPROACH. HONESTLY.
BUT ONCE I HEARD ABOUT MOLLY, I KNEW THERE WAS NO TIME. I HAD TO GET TO HER BEFORE MANNINO'S GOONS.
HELLO, RICHARD. LOVE THE LOOK.
WE'VE KNOWN YOU TOO LONG NOT TO RECOGNIZE YOU UNDER THAT MASK.
YOU'RE NOT GOING TO LOVE YOUR OWN LOOKS IF YOU DON'T TELL ME WHERE MOLLY IS!
IT TAKES A REAL HERO TO THREATEN AN OLD MAN.
JUST BACK OFF SLOWLY, DICK.
THEY SAY SOME OF THOSE NEW HEROES ARE IMMUNE TO BULLETS. I'M BETTING YOU'RE NOT ONE OF THOSE.
CRACK
AHHH!

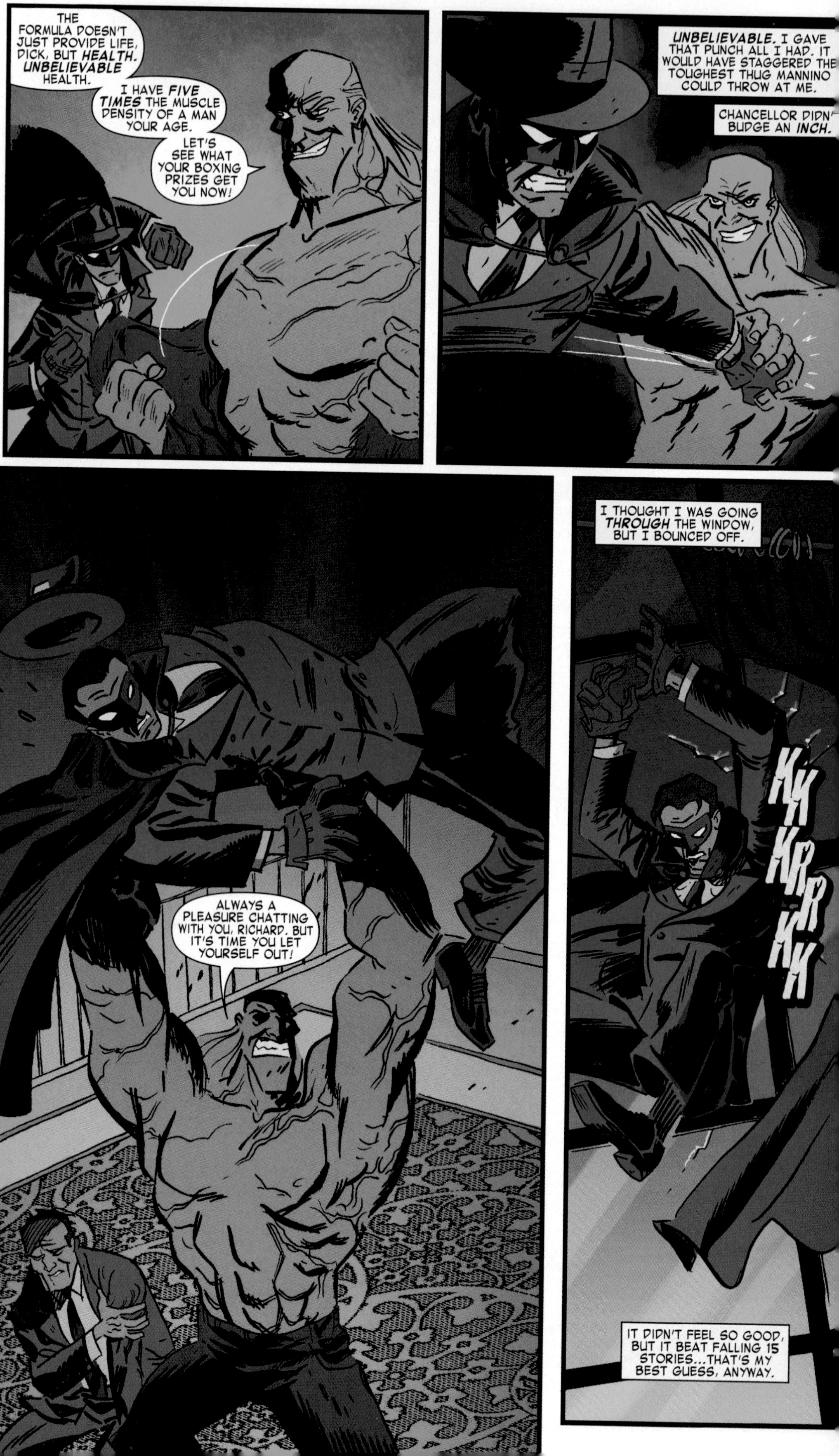
THE FORMULA DOESN'T JUST PROVIDE LIFE, DICK, BUT HEALTH. UNBELIEVABLE HEALTH.
I HAVE FIVE TIMES THE MUSCLE DENSITY OF A MAN YOUR AGE.
LET'S SEE WHAT YOUR BOXING PRIZES GET YOU NOW!
UNBELIEVABLE. I GAVE THAT PUNCH ALL I HAD. IT WOULD HAVE STAGGERED THE TOUGHEST THUG MANNINO COULD THROW AT ME.
CHANCELLOR DIDN'T BUDGE AN INCH.
ALWAYS A PLEASURE CHATTING WITH YOU, RICHARD. BUT IT'S TIME YOU LET YOURSELF OUT!
I THOUGHT I WAS GOING THROUGH THE WINDOW, BUT I BOUNCED OFF.
KKKRRRKKK
IT DIDN'T FEEL SO GOOD, BUT IT BEAT FALLING 15 STORIES...THAT'S MY BEST GUESS, ANYWAY.

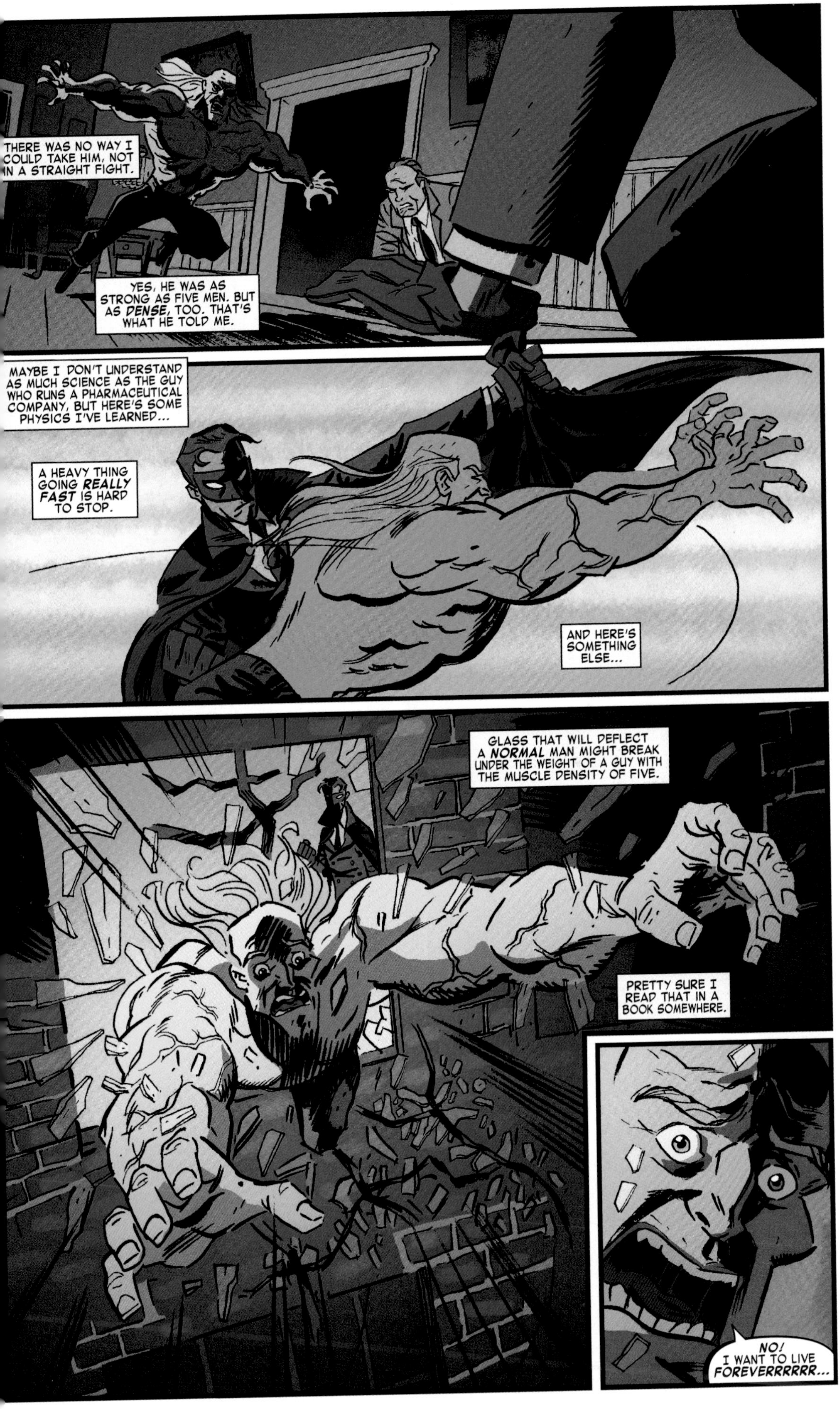

THERE WAS NO WAY I COULD TAKE HIM, NOT IN A STRAIGHT FIGHT.
YES, HE WAS AS STRONG AS FIVE MEN. BUT AS *DENSE*, TOO. THAT'S WHAT HE TOLD ME.
MAYBE I DON'T UNDERSTAND AS MUCH SCIENCE AS THE GUY WHO RUNS A PHARMACEUTICAL COMPANY, BUT HERE'S SOME PHYSICS I'VE LEARNED...
A HEAVY THING GOING *REALLY FAST* IS HARD TO STOP.
AND HERE'S SOMETHING ELSE...
GLASS THAT WILL DEFLECT A *NORMAL* MAN MIGHT BREAK UNDER THE WEIGHT OF A GUY WITH THE MUSCLE DENSITY OF FIVE.
PRETTY SURE I READ THAT IN A BOOK SOMEWHERE.
NO! I WANT TO LIVE *FOREVERRRRRR...*

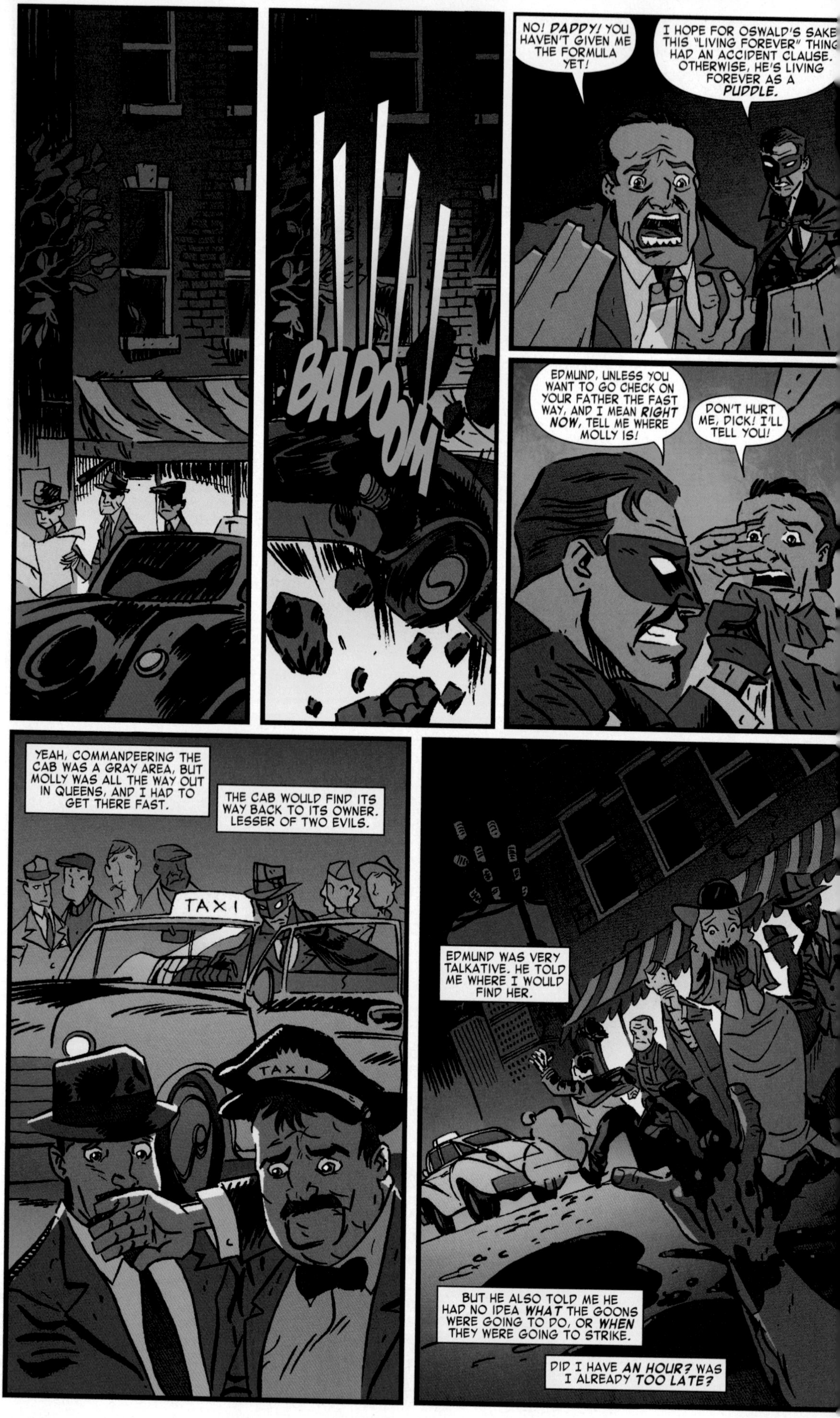

BADOOM
NO! DADDY! YOU HAVEN'T GIVEN ME THE FORMULA YET!
I HOPE FOR OSWALD'S SAKE THIS "LIVING FOREVER" THING HAD AN ACCIDENT CLAUSE. OTHERWISE, HE'S LIVING FOREVER AS A PUDDLE.
EDMUND, UNLESS YOU WANT TO GO CHECK ON YOUR FATHER THE FAST WAY, AND I MEAN RIGHT NOW, TELL ME WHERE MOLLY IS!
DON'T HURT ME, DICK! I'LL TELL YOU!
YEAH, COMMANDEERING THE CAB WAS A GRAY AREA, BUT MOLLY WAS ALL THE WAY OUT IN QUEENS, AND I HAD TO GET THERE FAST.
THE CAB WOULD FIND ITS WAY BACK TO ITS OWNER. LESSER OF TWO EVILS.
TAXI
TAXI
EDMUND WAS VERY TALKATIVE. HE TOLD ME WHERE I WOULD FIND HER.
BUT HE ALSO TOLD ME HE HAD NO IDEA WHAT THE GOONS WERE GOING TO DO, OR WHEN THEY WERE GOING TO STRIKE.
DID I HAVE AN HOUR? WAS I ALREADY TOO LATE?

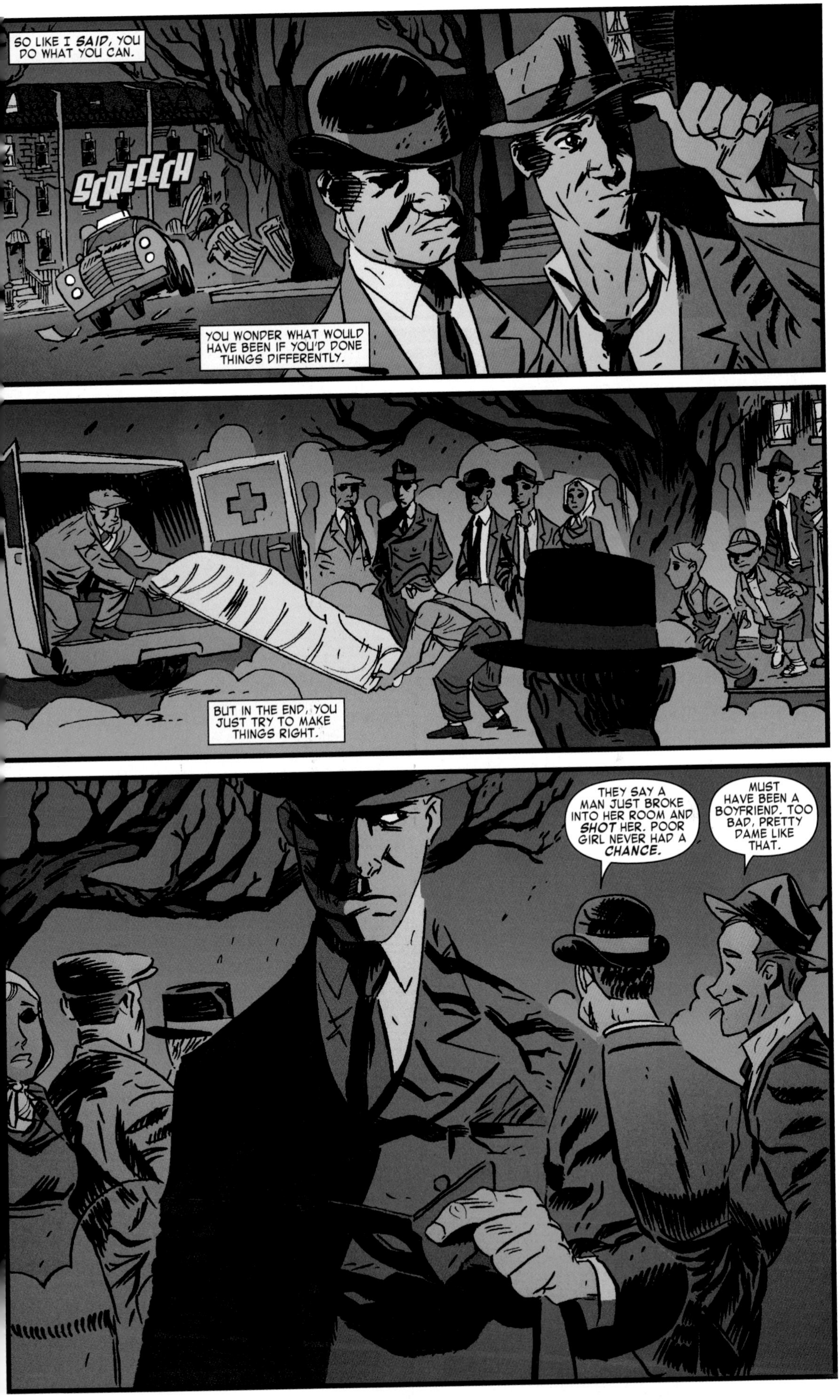
SO LIKE I SAID, YOU DO WHAT YOU CAN.
SCREEEECH
YOU WONDER WHAT WOULD HAVE BEEN IF YOU'D DONE THINGS DIFFERENTLY.
BUT IN THE END, YOU JUST TRY TO MAKE THINGS RIGHT.
THEY SAY A MAN JUST BROKE INTO HER ROOM AND SHOT HER. POOR GIRL NEVER HAD A CHANCE.
MUST HAVE BEEN A BOYFRIEND. TOO BAD, PRETTY DAME LIKE THAT.

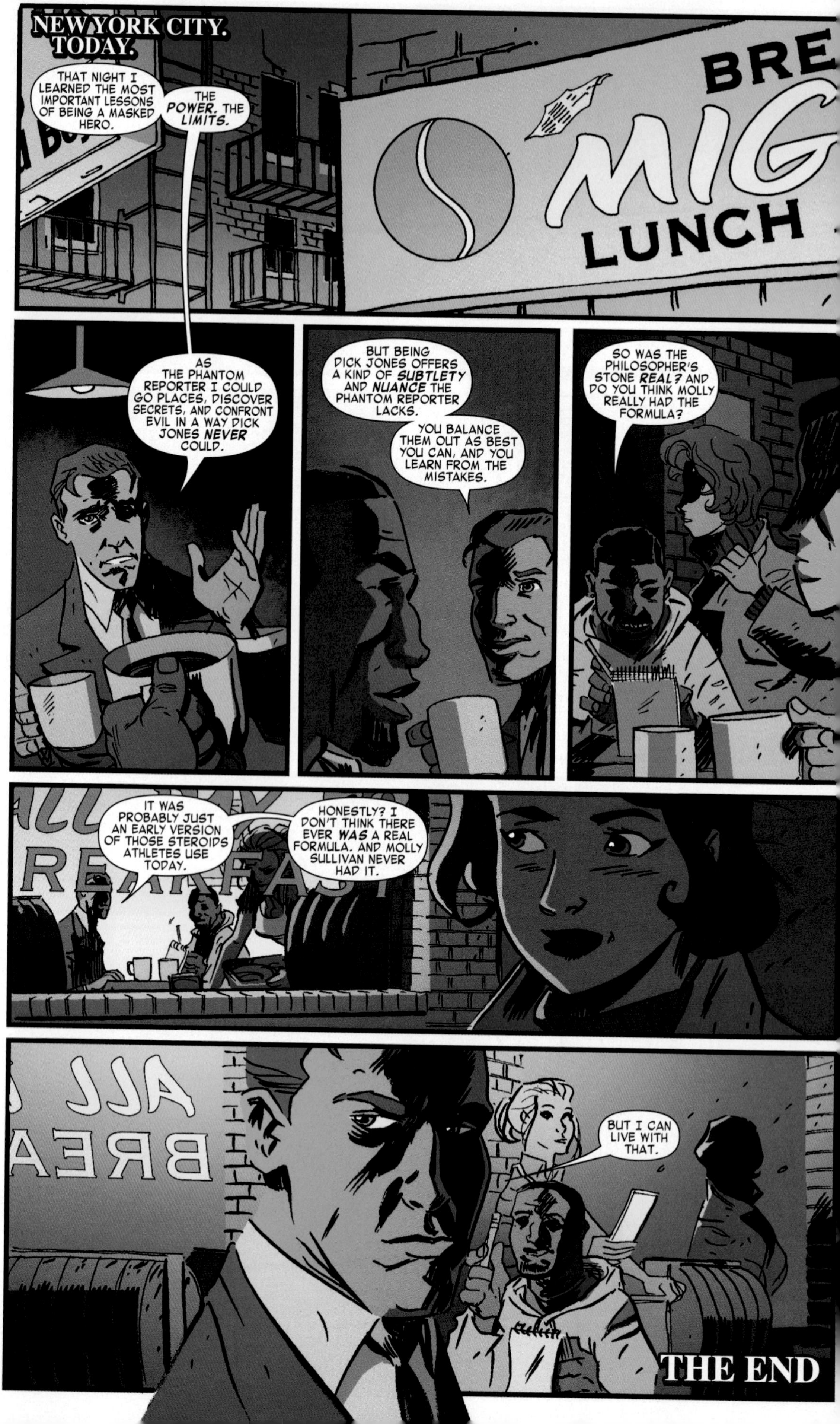
NEW YORK CITY. TODAY.
THAT NIGHT I LEARNED THE MOST IMPORTANT LESSONS OF BEING A MASKED HERO.
THE POWER. THE LIMITS.
BRE
MIG
LUNCH
AS THE PHANTOM REPORTER I COULD GO PLACES, DISCOVER SECRETS, AND CONFRONT EVIL IN A WAY DICK JONES NEVER COULD.
BUT BEING DICK JONES OFFERS A KIND OF SUBTLETY AND NUANCE THE PHANTOM REPORTER LACKS.
YOU BALANCE THEM OUT AS BEST YOU CAN, AND YOU LEARN FROM THE MISTAKES.
SO WAS THE PHILOSOPHER'S STONE REAL? AND DO YOU THINK MOLLY REALLY HAD THE FORMULA?
IT WAS PROBABLY JUST AN EARLY VERSION OF THOSE STEROIDS ATHLETES USE TODAY.
HONESTLY? I DON'T THINK THERE EVER WAS A REAL FORMULA. AND MOLLY SULLIVAN NEVER HAD IT.
BUT I CAN LIVE WITH THAT.
THE END

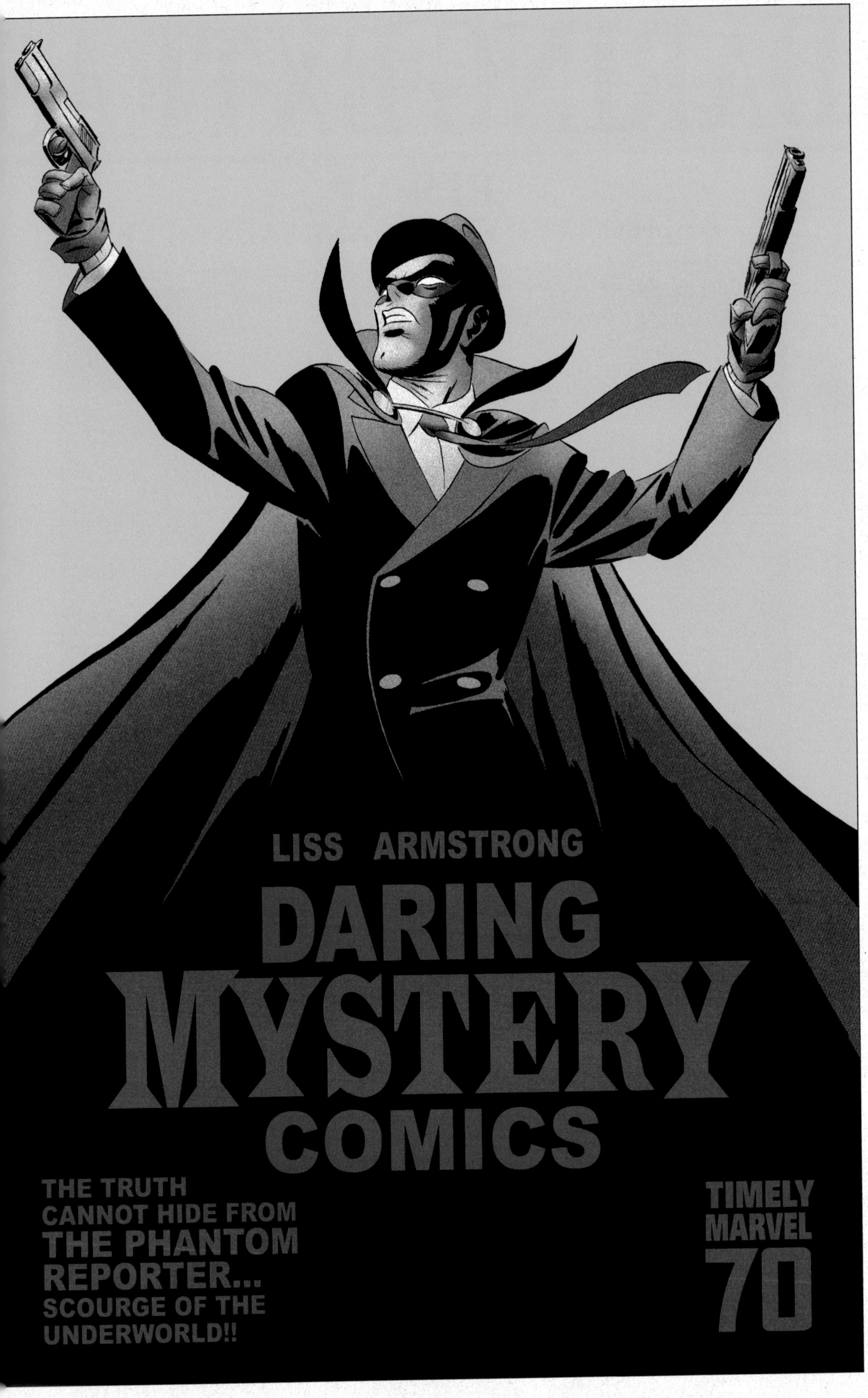
LISS ARMSTRONG
DARING MYSTERY COMICS
THE TRUTH CANNOT HIDE FROM THE PHANTOM REPORTER... SCOURGE OF THE UNDERWORLD!!
TIMELY MARVEL 70

DARING MYSTERY COMICS 70TH ANNIVERSARY SPECIAL VARIANT BY MARCOS MARTIN

DARING EXTRAS

PIN-UP
BY JASON ARMSTRONG AND VAL STAPLES

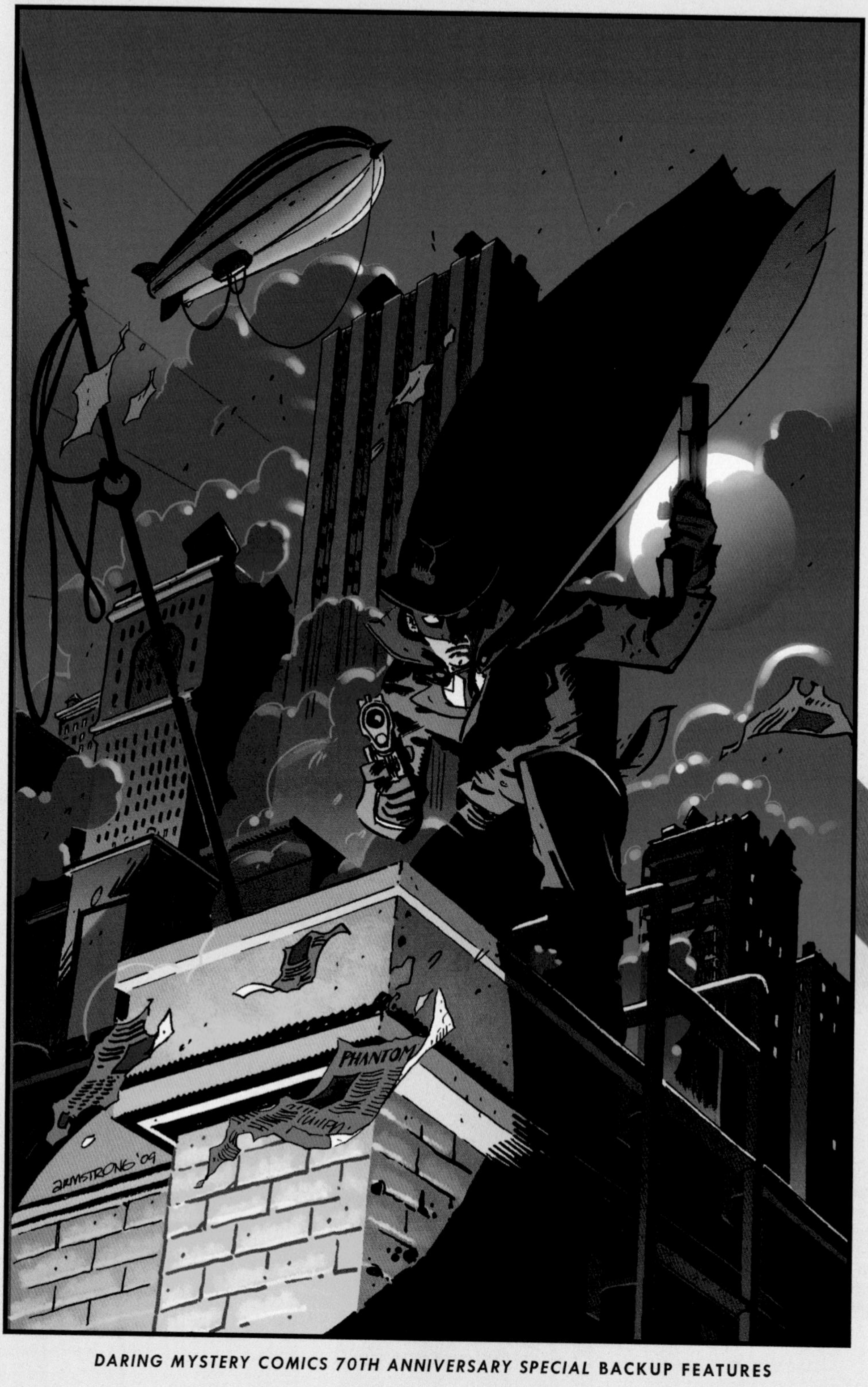

PHANTOM
ARMSTRONG '09

DARING EXTRAS

IN-UP SKETCHES BY JASON ARMSTRONG

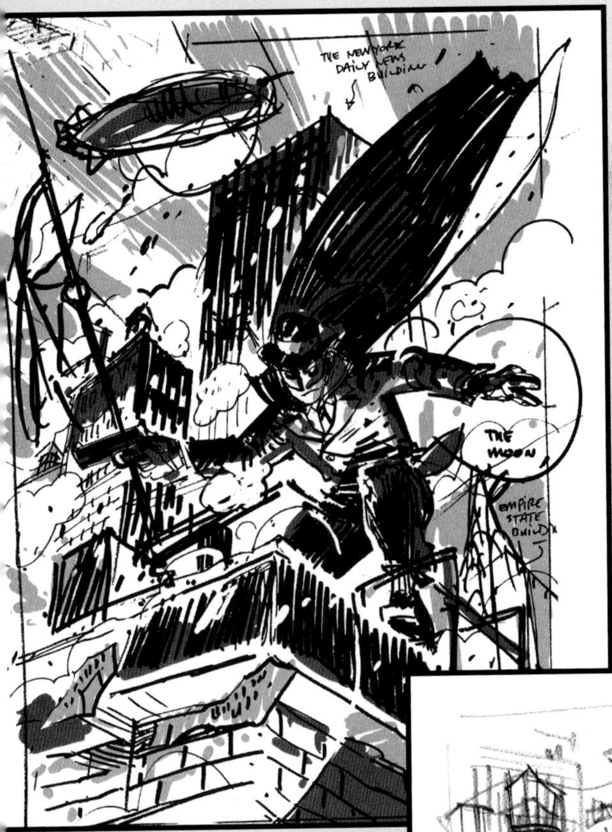
THE NEW YORK DAILY NEWS BUILDIN
THE MOON
EMPIRE STATE BUILDI

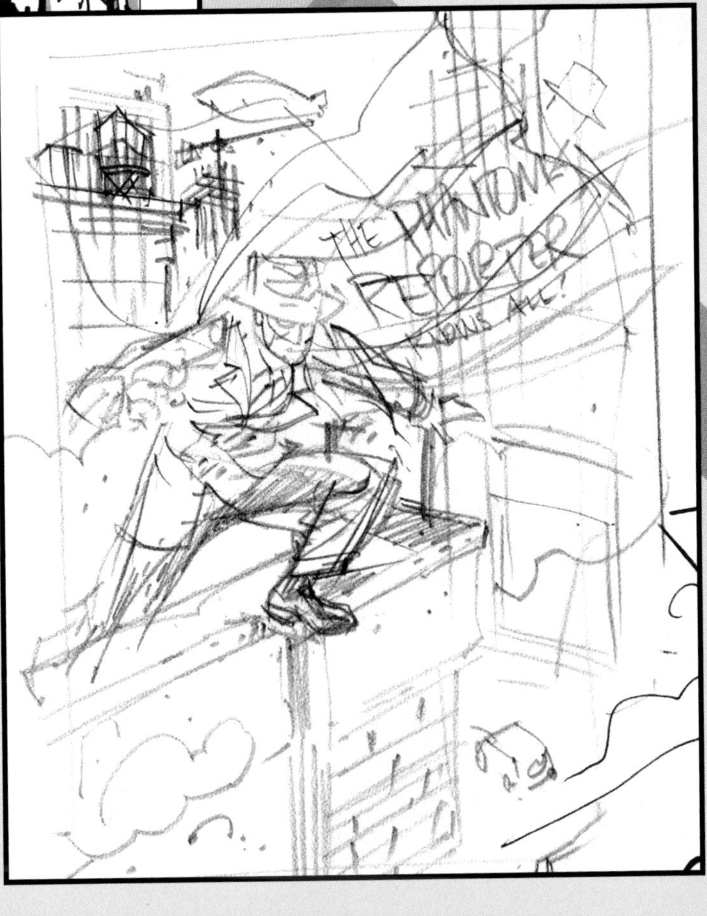
THE PHANTOM REPORTER
KNOWS ALL!

DARING EXTRAS

CHARACTER STUDIES

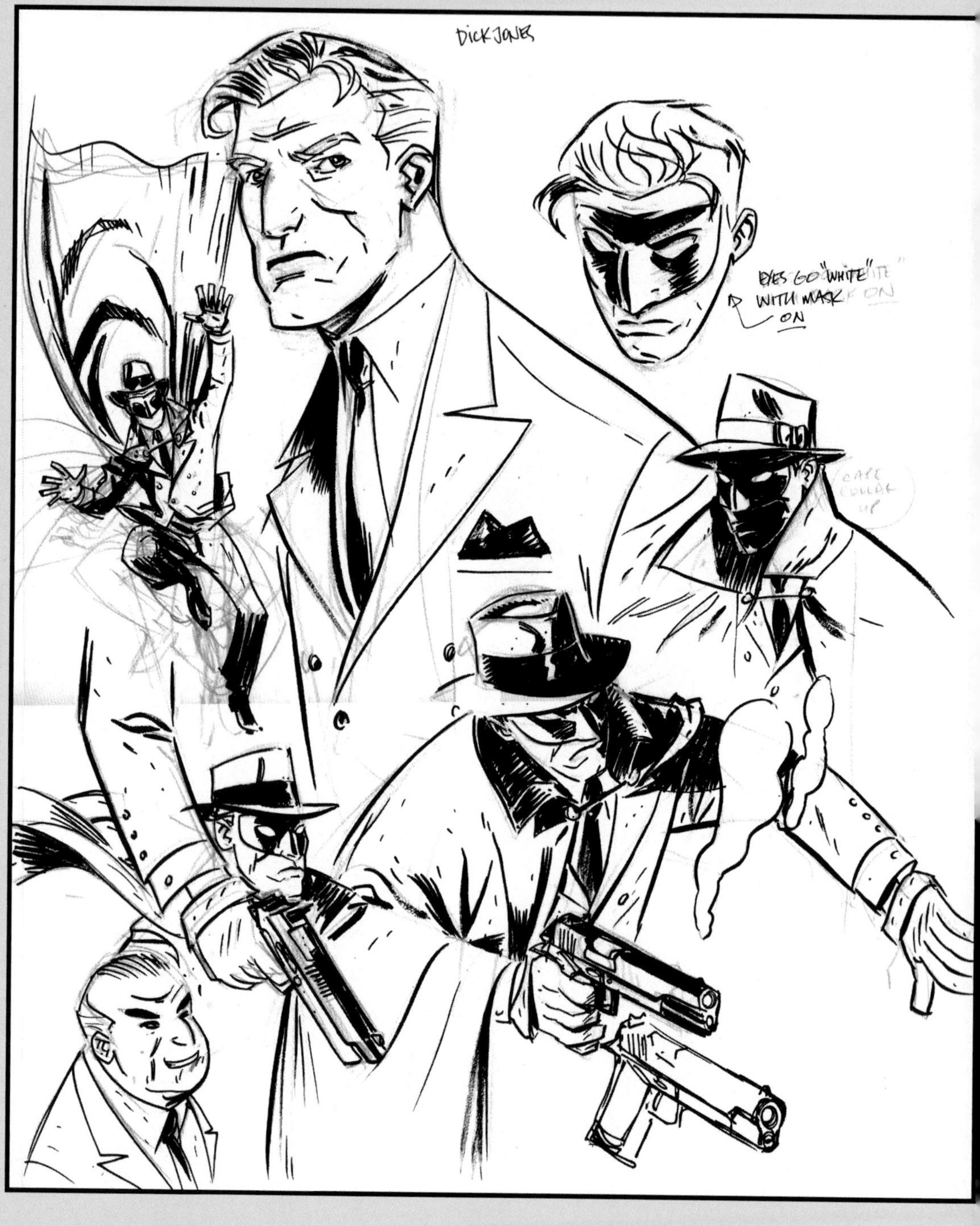
DICK JONES
EYES GO "WHITE" WITH MASK ON
CAPE COLLAR UP

DARING EXTRAS

BY JASON ARMSTRONG

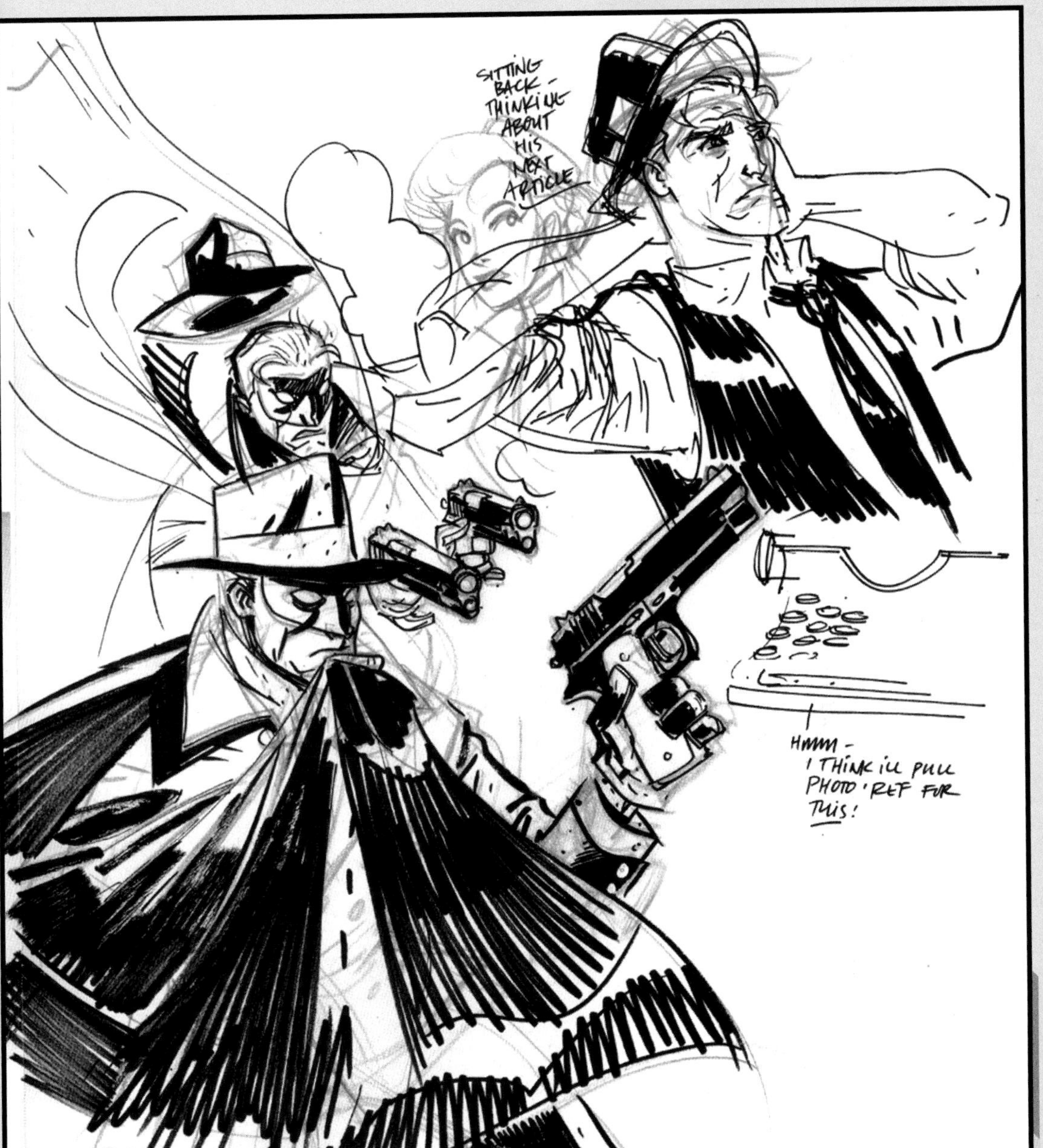

SITTING BACK - THINKING ABOUT HIS NEXT ARTICLE
HMMM - I THINK ILL PULL PHOTO 'REF FOR THIS!

DARING EXTRAS

LAYOUTS BY JASON ARMSTRONG

Dick puts on the mask for the 1st time!

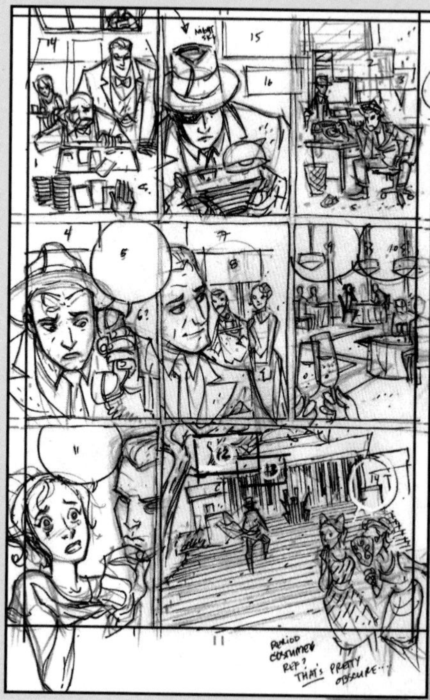
PERIOD COSTUMED REP? THAT'S PRETTY OBSCURE...

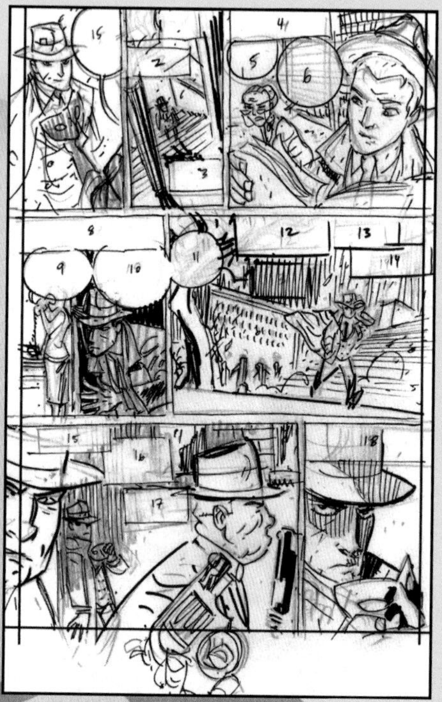

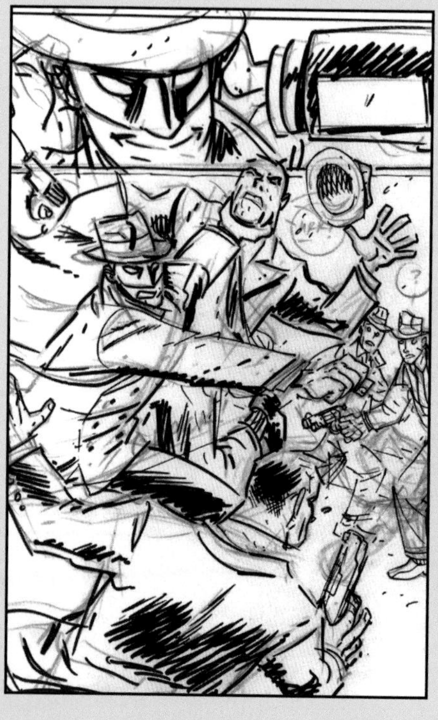

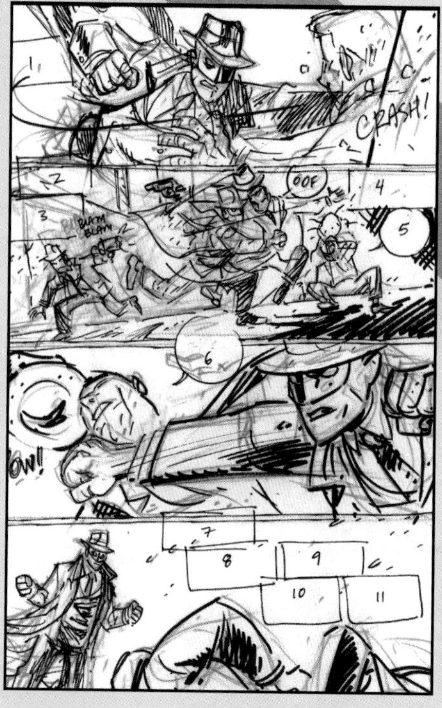
CRASH!
OOF
OW!

DARING EXTRAS

PENCILED PAGES BY JASON ARMSTRONG

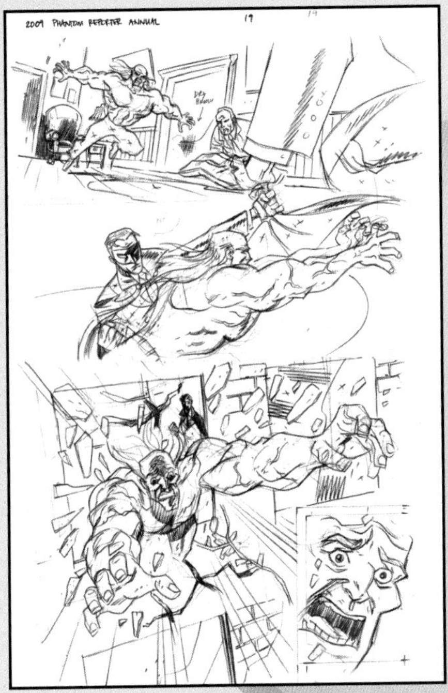
2009 PHANTOM REPORTER ANNUAL
19

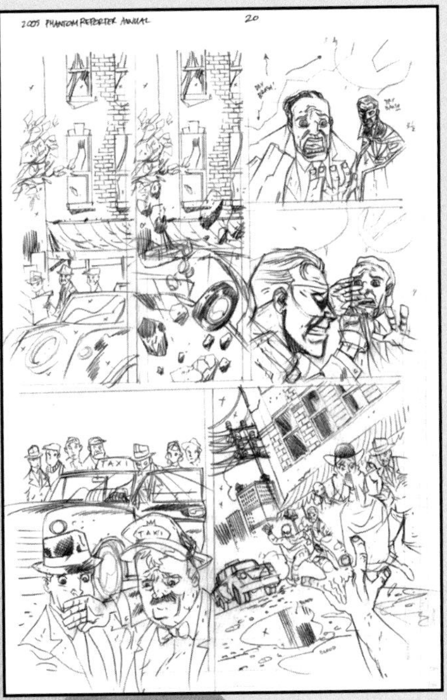
2009 PHANTOM REPORTER ANNUAL
20
TAXI

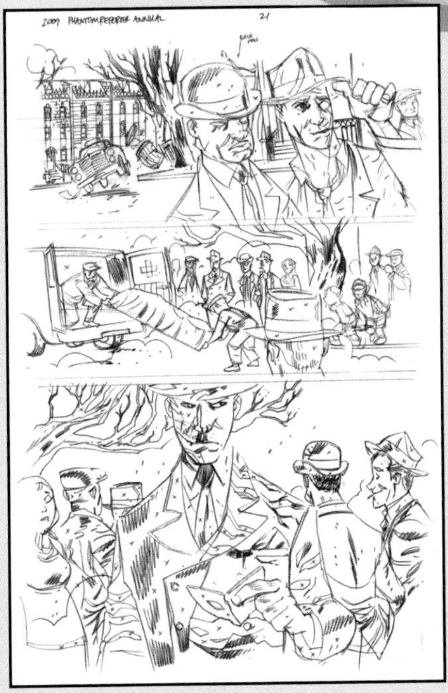
2009 PHANTOM REPORTER ANNUAL
21

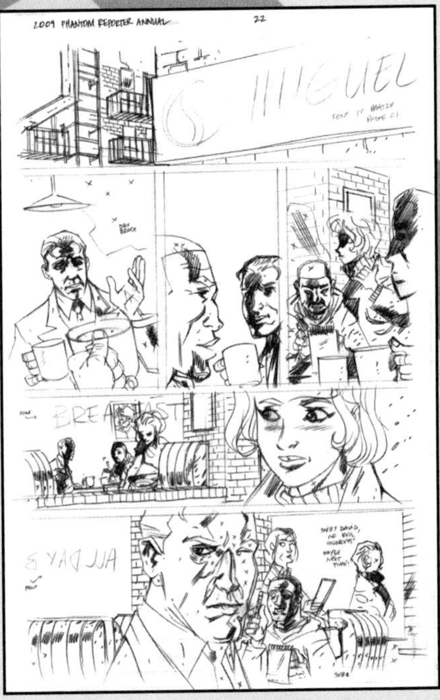
2009 PHANTOM REPORTER ANNUAL
22

DAVID LISS: WRITING THE REPORTER

What you hold in your hands is my first effort at writing graphic fiction. I'll consider it a success if you have some small fraction of the fun reading it that I had writing it.

For the last ten years I've been writing research-intensive historical novels, but the characters who inhabit them have always been at least a little influenced by my lifelong love of super heroes. In fact, Bill Rosemann, the tireless editor of this book, first contacted me because he saw an affinity between one of my protagonists and Marvel stalwart, Luke Cage. But liking comics and writing them are two different things, and putting this script together has been consistently challenging and exciting.

I don't think I could have found a better character to break me in than The Phantom Reporter. The limited background of the Golden Age hero gave me a relatively free hand to reshape him into a modern figure, and it also gave me a chance to do an origin story – and I love origin stories. The original Phantom Reporter is a sketchy character at best – almost silly in his pure, relentless id. At the same time, for all his broadly painted strokes, he contains the core elements of what is so satisfying about the masked vigilante: a rigid sense of right and wrong, and the power to enforce it. The challenge for me was to work backwards, to create a real, three-dimensional character who would do that

most unlikely of things – put on a ma[sk] and risk his life to fight villains – and ha[ve] it all ring true. I hope it does.

The creative process of writing comi[cs] certainly rings true for me. I'm now in t[he] planning stages of my second (curren[tly] top secret) project with Marvel, and I'[m] working on a proposal for an original sup[er] hero series I hope to convince someo[ne] to take a chance on. The bottom line [is] I'm hooked, and I plan to keep on writi[ng] comics as long as someone is willing [to] publish them.

David Liss is the author six novels, most recently The Devil's Compa[ny]. He has five previous best-selling novels: A Conspiracy of Paper, winner [of] the 2000 Edgar Award for Best First Novel, The Coffee Trader, A Sp[ec-] tacle of Corruption, The Ethical Assassin and The Whiskey Rebels. Fo[ur] of these novels, and one of his short stories, are currently in developm[ent] as film projects. He lives in San Antonio with his wife and children, a[nd] can be reached via his web page: davidliss.com, which features his e[nd-] lessly fascinating and edifying blog.

DATE	INVESTIGATOR	CASE FILE
JUNE 08	DAVID LISS	MM 001

I was still very new to writing comics when editor Bill Rosemann asked me if I was interested in writing a miniseries about pulp-era characters set in Marvel continuity. Looking back, I'm glad I was new because if I'd understood what a rare and important opportunity this was, I might have been too intimidated to accept. Creating all-new characters that evoked the pulp aesthetic but also felt like real Marvel heroes, and creating a new chapter in the history of the Marvel U. How cool is that?

Over the course of a few weeks, Bill and I hashed out what kinds of characters we wanted for this book. I thought we had some good ideas, but good ideas aren't enough, and a comic book has to look good. Bill proposed a lot of names as he searched for the right artist, and I would have been thrilled to work with any of them, but when he mentioned Patch Zircher, I knew he was the person I wanted on this title. If you are reading this, then you are holding the book in your hands, and so you know why. Mystery Men is, without doubt, one of the best looking comics out there. Period.

Any story set in the New York of the early 1930s should evoke some of the real issues of the period. The '30s were about more than speakeasies, dirigibles and awesome hats, and so we threw in issues of race and gender inequity, poverty and greed, unfair labor practices, and many other gritty realities of the Depression. We also wanted the book to be set firmly in the Marvel U., so keep your eyes peeled for some familiar names and faces.

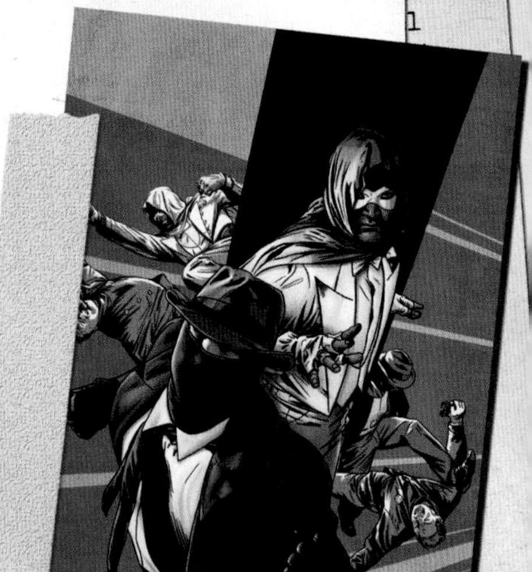

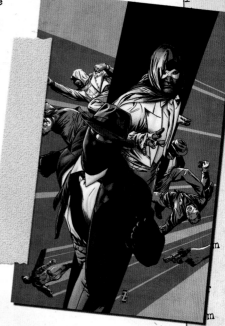

It was never anything but a blast to work on a project wedding time-honored archetypes, modern sensibilities, awesome art, and a new chapter in Marvel history. Some things went absolutely according to plan, and some evolved organically during the creative process, but the end result is something I feel lucky to have worked on. I hope you enjoy reading it as much as we enjoyed creating it.

***MYSTERY MEN #1* AFTERWORD BY DAVID LISS**

DATE	INVESTIGATOR	CASE FILE
JUNE 22	Patch Zircher	MM 002

A lot of the attraction of working on MYSTERY MEN comes from the cast of characters that David Liss has created for the book, a group that satisfies any artist's yearning to draw pulp heroes. With The Operative we have a character that's probably the most representative of all the pulps, the detective (his name is even inspired by Dashiell Hammett's Continental Op). This is the character with clothes that most bring to mind classic noir movies; fedora, suit, black leather shoes. But our Operative is also a jewel thief and cat burglar--and a masked man. Working out a mask that avoids the well-known look of The Spirit and Green Hornet but still functions with a hat, I simply inverted the cut of the mask, leaving the area around the eyes open and the rest of the face concealed. I liked it immediately. In the stories themselves, we added a long dark coat and trimmed him down a few pounds to enhance the style and mood and to match Dennis Piper's suaveness out of costume.

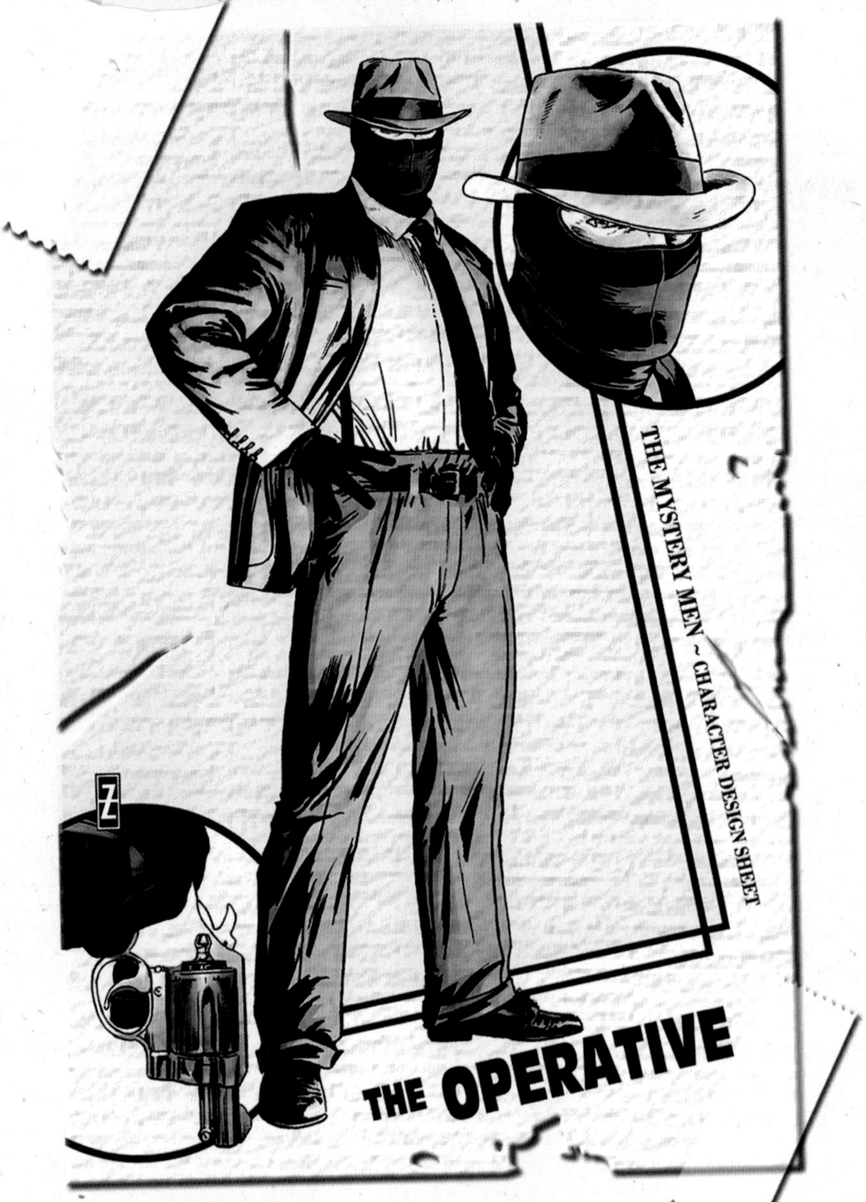
THE MYSTERY MEN ~ CHARACTER DESIGN SHEET
THE OPERATIVE

MYSTERY MEN CHARACTER DESIGNS BY PATCH ZIRCHER

DATE
JUNE 22

INVESTIGATOR
Patch Zircher

CASE FILE
MM 002

THE MYSTERY MEN ~ CHARACTER DESIGN SHEET

THE REVENANT

The Revenant's name is derived from English folklore as a kind of ghost or spirit and, initially, he was going to have a ragged, spectral appearance. But as designs for the other Mystery Men emerged it became apparent a ragged look would interfere with the atmosphere we wanted to have surrounding The Surgeon. Instead we found ghostly qualities in his all-white costume and in his manner and abilities, such as his sudden appearances and disappearances, the roiling smoke that appears around him, his hooded cloak, fingerless gloves, and so forth. Ezekiel Wright's costume, as you'll see in upcoming issues, also has roots in the glamour and theatrics of Broadway of the '20s and '30s--his tuxedo, dress shoes, and showy ring are designed to reflect that. So by concentrating on giving The Revenant a separate, individual identity, and by keeping in mind his origin, he developed a look that I now can't imagine him not having.

DATE	INVESTIGATOR	CASE FILE
JULY 13	Patch Zircher	MM 003

The Surgeon's horrifying origin and modus operandi (getting what he wants out of the bad guys with scalpels and syringes) places him on the edge of being a hero, on the edge of sanity for that matter. We wanted a look that represented that: the scarred tissue around his eyes, the bandages, the ragged and stitched cloak, and gurney restraints for wristbands. The white doctor's coat adds a weird chill to his look as well. For a color scheme, blood red seemed exactly right for the cloak. And just what's in those glowing green syringes? Don't ask.

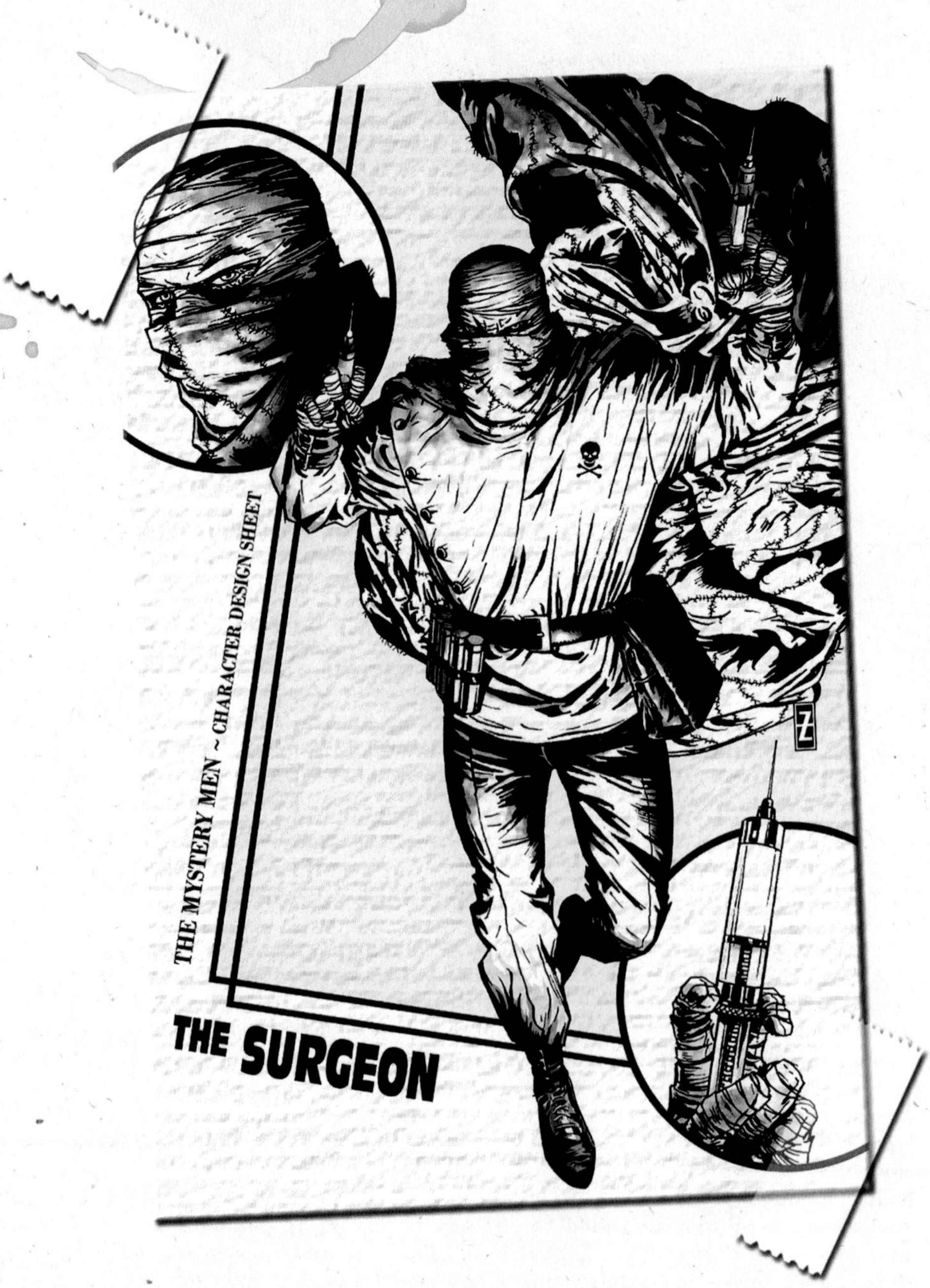
THE MYSTERY MEN ~ CHARACTER DESIGN SHEET
THE SURGEON

DATE JULY 13	INVESTIGATOR Patch Zircher	CASE FILE MM 002

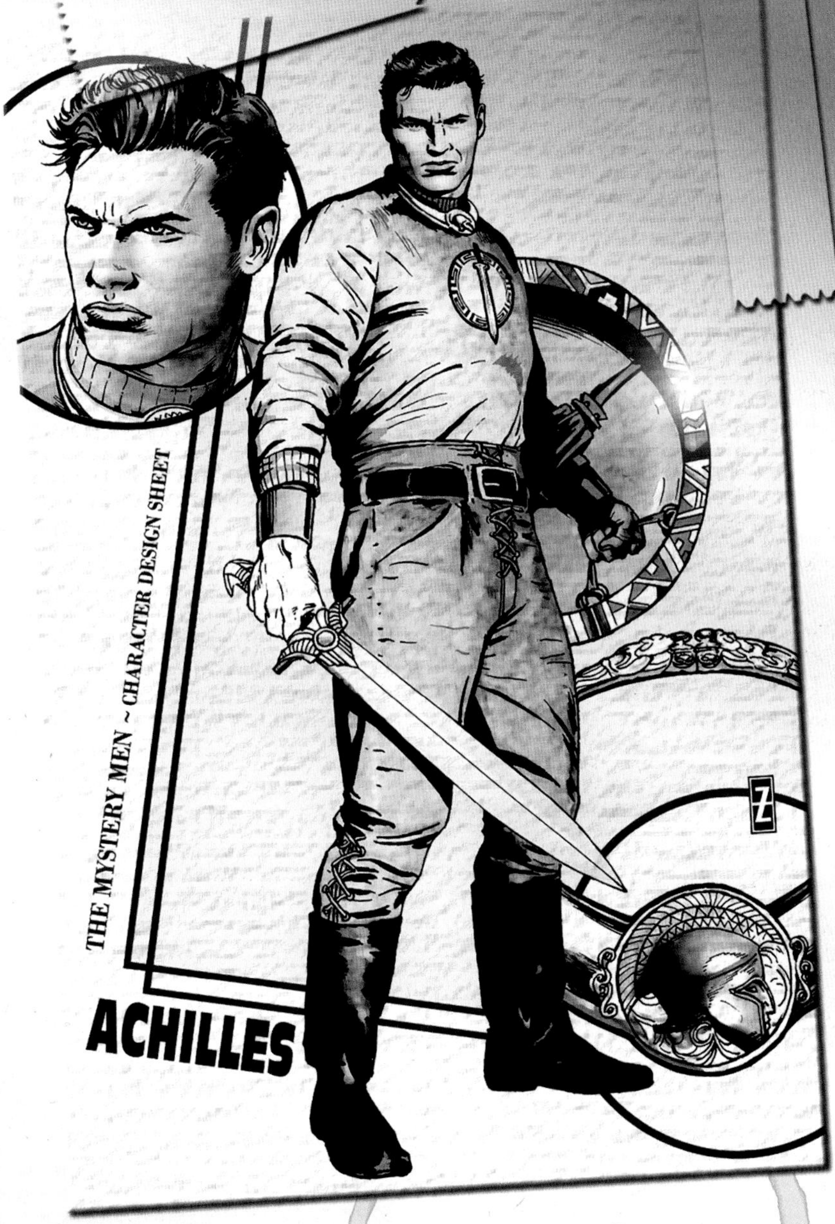
THE MYSTERY MEN ~ CHARACTER DESIGN SHEET
ACHILLES

Achilles underwent a lot of change in development. Initially a mild-mannered young Professor who transforms into a classic Greek warrior, he was to have a Greek helmet, spear, chest plate, and so forth. The spear and helmet never really took and the first designs were appropriate but didn't feel 'pulp.' So we re-imagined his transformation. Armed with a sword and shield, Achilles' armor was replaced with a bold shirt and logo and footballer's trousers. His hairstyle now more Buster Crabbe than historical hero. All in all, a costume influenced by the young, meek Professor's love of history but also the wish-fulfillment of the mighty pulps. He undergoes a transformation into not just a warrior but an adventurer as well.

DATE	INVESTIGATOR	CASE FILE
AUGUST 24	Patch Zircher	MM 004

Aviatrix, more than any of the character designs, was a collaborative effort between writer, editors, and artist. Because she is a female aviator, I looked to old photos of women pilots through history. They were actually quite the rage in the '20s and '30s and, like Amelia Earhart, several of them made the headlines. Aviatrix began with a jet pack which was later given wings to help differentiate her from the late Dave Steven's popular and much-loved hero, the Rocketeer. Former Editor-in-Chief (and current CCO) Joe Quesada even stepped in, suggesting a fin on her headgear.

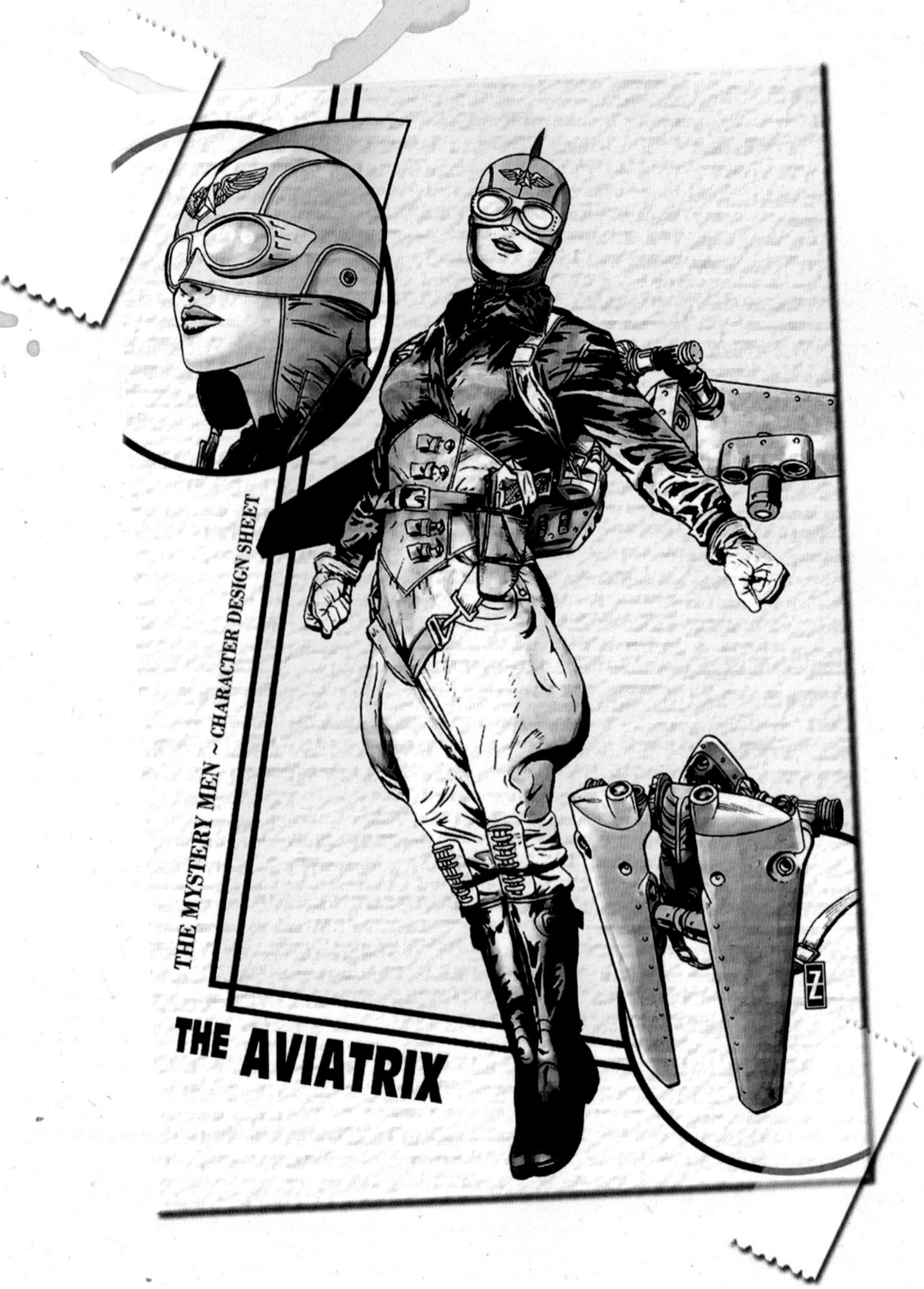
THE MYSTERY MEN ~ CHARACTER DESIGN SHEET
THE AVIATRIX

THE MYSTERY MAKER DESIGN SHEET

NOX

Nox is a powerful character of mythic origin who has actual ties to Marvel's past in the pages of Dr. Strange. While she retained the color scheme of those earlier appearances, most everything else about her was changed to make her increasingly sinister and vampish. She flaunts social convention with her sensuous, sexy attire and, frankly, I can imagine her not bothering with clothes at all. However...her dresses are modified exaggerations of some of the dresses I found in old fashion books of the '30s and '40s.

DATE	INVESTIGATOR	CASE FILE
SEPTEMBER 14	LISS/ZIRCHER/ROSEMANN	MM 005

All creative projects end up different than they were originally conceived, and that's far more true of collaborative efforts like comic books than solo efforts like novels. When I started working on *Mystery Men*, it was my first multi-issue project for Marvel, and while I had a good sense of where I wanted it to go, the final product was far more realized and vivid and exciting to work on than I could have imagined. Thanks to invaluable and insightful editorial guidance from Bill Rosemann and Tom Brevoort, Dave Sharpe's period-perfect lettering, Andy Troy's dynamic and evocative coloring and, of course, Patch Zircher's brilliant art, *Mystery Men* became a living, breathing creation that I'm intensely proud to have been part of.

It is always exciting to create something new, but I think there is a special pleasure that comes from creating something new in a world already well-established. Working our characters into the murky pre-WWII years of Marvel's history gave us a chance both to give context to a future and explain a past. I know I especially loved the opportunity to inject modern Marvel sensibilities into older pulp archetypes. Here's to the opportunity to return to the scene of the crime.

David Liss

What can I say about working on this project... working with David, Bill, and Andy? They're all consummate professionals, talented individuals, and a pleasure to work with. Pulp stories have always held a huge attraction for me -- from catching black-and-white Flash Gordon serials on Saturday mornings to discovering James Bama's cover art on Doc Savage paperbacks to watching the great, classic noir movies. Making these stories -- well-- this is about *Mystery Men*, so I'll put it out there like an old song from the era: "Heaven, I was in heaven and my heart beat so that I could hardly speak."

Patch Zircher

While every project holds its own unique surprises and memories, *Mystery Men* was a true dream. A special thanks to Joe Quesada and Dan Buckley for their faith, and to Tom Brevoort, who provided key insights and a steady hand throughout the entire process. Most of all thanks to David, Patch, Andy and Dave for creating magic... and to all of you for joining us on this dark and wonderful ride.

Bill Rosemann

***MYSTERY MEN* #5 AFTERWORD**

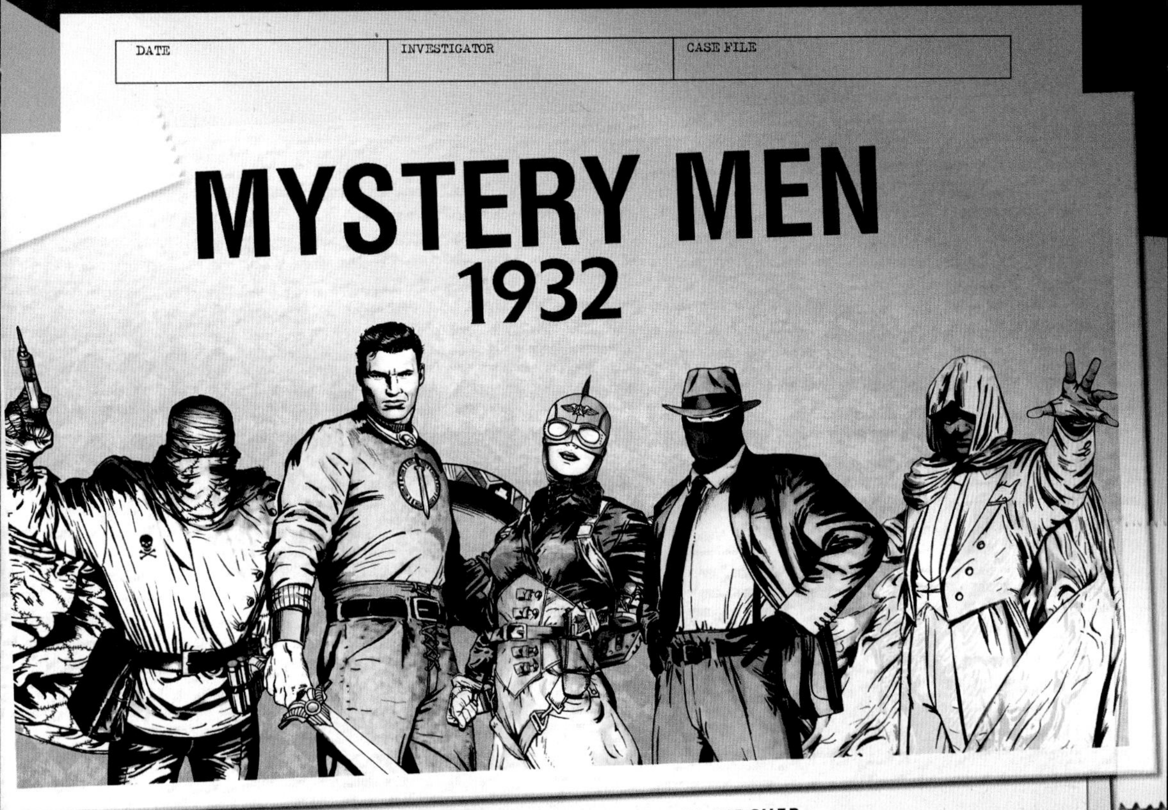
DATE
INVESTIGATOR
CASE FILE
MYSTERY MEN
1932

MYSTERY MEN TEAM SKETCH BY PATCH ZIRCHER

NOX

REAL NAME: Possibly Nyx
ALIASES: Night, Lady Nox; impersonated Aphrodite
IDENTITY: No dual identity
OCCUPATION: Goddess of the night
CITIZENSHIP: Unrevealed
PLACE OF BIRTH: Unrevealed
KNOWN RELATIVES: Deimos, Phobos (sons, deceased), Ophion, Eurynome (parents), several unidentified gods and goddesses (spawn)
GROUP AFFILIATION: Fear Lords
EDUCATION: Unrevealed
FIRST APPEARANCE: Dr. Strange: Sorcerer Supreme #31 (1991)

HISTORY: Nox (Greek for night) is one of the seven known Fear Lords, mysterious other-dimensional beings who thrive on the purest forms of fear. While the other Fear Lords require fear for sustenance, Nox uses fear as an aesthetic pleasure, and inspires fear in others via complex schemes. The daughter of Greek Titans Ophion and Eurynome, Nox spawned numerous gods and goddess that became associated with negative aspects of life. Many years ago, Nox posed as the goddess Aphrodite and conceived two sons after an encounter with the war god Ares, naming them Phobos and Deimos (Greek for "fear" and "terror"); both sons would later perish in battle with Thor and Hercules. In recent years, she secretly influenced the Microverse scientist Psycho-Man in developing his fear-enhancing device and manipulated the demon Thog in using Nightmare Boxes to cause universal madness. Nox joined the other Fear Lords (except Straw Man) in a plot to drive humanity to the brink of madness. Nox attacked mystics Dr. Strange, Clea and Rintrah, drawing upon the world's fear to resurrect Phobos and Deimos. Nox prepared to kill Clea and Rintrah, but the heroes regrouped and slew her sons. Furious, Nox called upon various magical sources to enfold and slay the heroes in night's shadow, but Strange bathed her in the Eye of Agamotto's mystical light, weakening her. Nox fled to avoid capture.

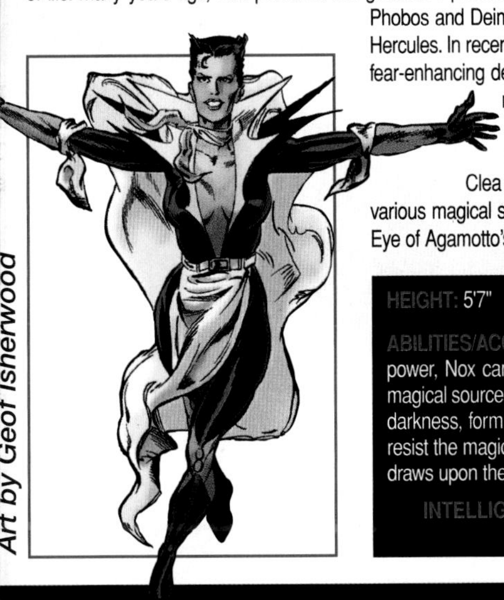

Art by Geof Isherwood

HEIGHT: 5'7" **WEIGHT:** 270 lbs. **EYES:** Black **HAIR:** Black

ABILITIES/ACCESSORIES: An apparently immortal and extradimensional sorceress of immense power, Nox can monitor other dimensions and mentally influence others by drawing upon various magical sources and entities. She can disguise her shape, travel across dimensions, cast a pervasive darkness, form the deadly Sword of Night to slay souls, create the ensnaring Tendrils of Night, and resist the magic of others. Though Nox is vulnerable to light sources, her power increases when she draws upon the fears of others.

INTELLIGENCE: 6 **STRENGTH:** 3 **SPEED:** 3/7 (Nox is a teleporter) **DURABILITY:** 6 **ENERGY PROJECTION:** 3 **FIGHTING SKILLS:** 4

NOX PROFILE FROM *OFFICIAL HANDBOOK OF THE MARVEL UNIVERSE A-Z VOL. 8 HC.*
TEXT BY CHAD ANDERSON & JACOB ROUGEMONT

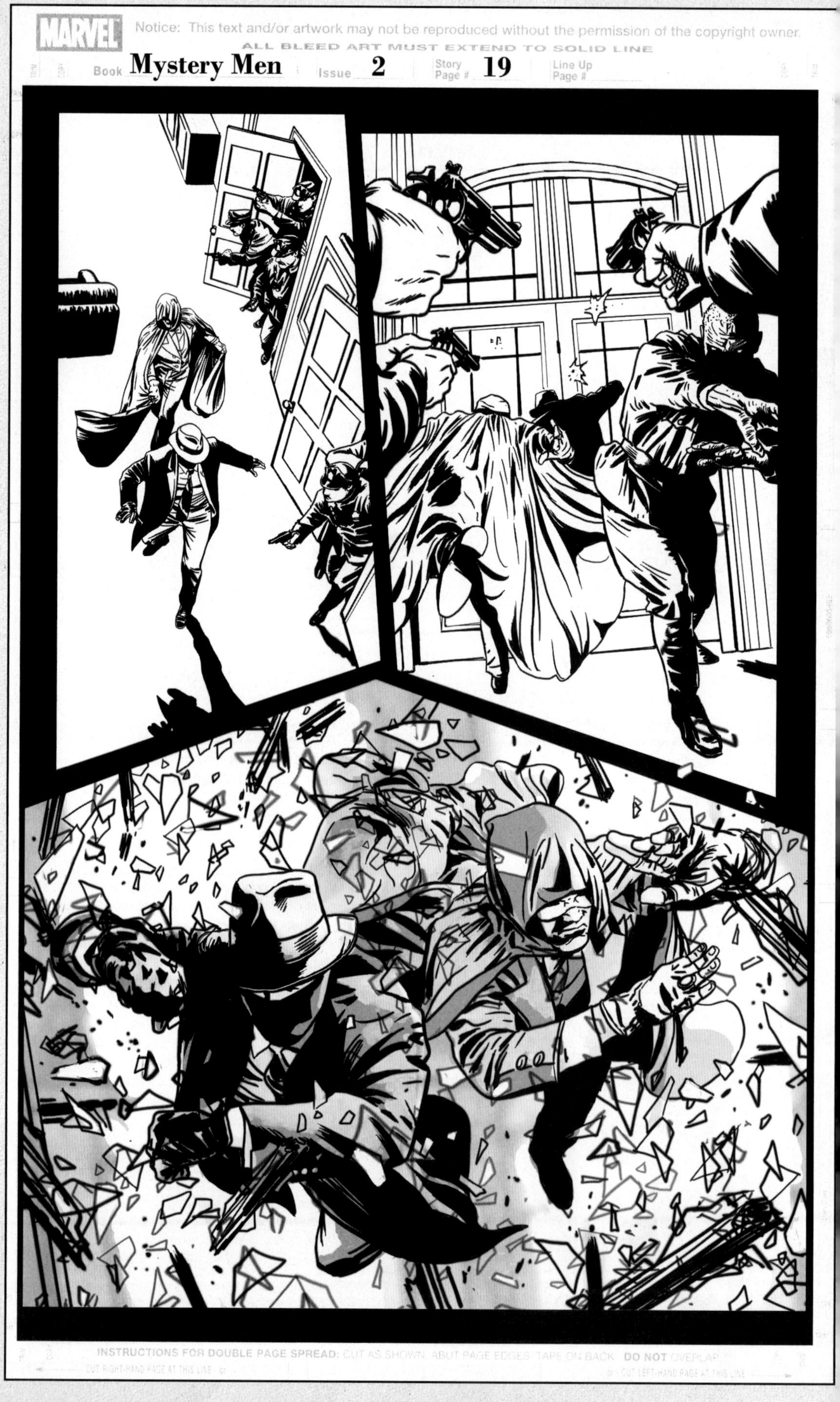
Notice: This text and/or artwork may not be reproduced without the permission of the copyright owner.
ALL BLEED ART MUST EXTEND TO SOLID LINE
Book Mystery Men
Issue 2
Story Page # 19
Line Up Page #
INSTRUCTIONS FOR DOUBLE PAGE SPREAD: CUT AS SHOWN. ABUT PAGE EDGES. TAPE ON BACK. DO NOT OVERLAP.
CUT RIGHT-HAND PAGE AT THIS LINE
CUT LEFT-HAND PAGE AT THIS LINE

***MYSTERY MEN* #2, PAGE 19 ART BY PATCH ZIRCHER**

MYSTERY MEN #3, PAGE 9 ART BY PATCH ZIRCHER

MYSTERY MEN #3, PAGE 21 ART BY PATCH ZIRCHER